LICENSURE TESTING: PURPOSES, PROCEDURES, AND PRACTICES

Buros-Nebraska Series
on
Measurement & Testing

Series Editor

JAMES C. IMPARA

Managing Editor

LINDA L. MURPHY

**Buros Institute of Mental Measurements
and
Department of Educational Psychology
University of Nebraska-Lincoln**

LICENSURE TESTING: PURPOSES, PROCEDURES, AND PRACTICES

Edited by

JAMES C. IMPARA
University of Nebraska-Lincoln

BUROS INSTITUTE OF MENTAL MEASUREMENTS
University of Nebraska-Lincoln

Buros Institute of Mental Measurements
135 Bancroft Hall
University of Nebraska-Lincoln
Lincoln, NE 68588-0348

The paper used in this publication meets the minimum requirements of American
National Standard for Information Sciences—Permanence of Paper for Printed Library
Materials, ANSI Z39.48-1984.

ISBN 0-910674-39-6

Printed in the United States of America

Contents

Dedication

The impetus for this book and for my involvement in it are due principally to the efforts of three people: Jimmie Fortune, Howard Stoker, and Barbara Plake. Jimmie edited (and contributed to) an earlier book devoted to licensure testing (Fortune, J. C., & Associates, 1985, *Understanding Testing in Occupational Licensing*, Jossey Bass: San Francisco.). Shortly after that book was published he told me that he felt some important topics had not been included and that another book was needed. He encouraged me on several occasions to edit a new book that picked up where his left off and expand it to include some additional topics. I discussed Jimmie's suggestions with my friend and mentor, Howard Stoker and he, too, encouraged me to put the book-editing process in motion. He offered to be a contributor even though he was in the process of retiring (for the third time!). Finally, I moved to the University of Nebraska-Lincoln and to the Buros Institute of Mental Measurements where I began to work with Barbara Plake and the wonderful people here. When I mentioned the possibility of editing a book on licensure testing, she encouraged me and was instrumental in finally pushing me over the edge. Jimmie, Howard, and Barbara all made excellent recommendations of possible chapter authors and each agreed to be a contributor. Without their support and encouragement this book would not have happened. If you find this book to be helpful, they deserve much of the credit. If this book is not what you thought it should be, then the blame is mine because I made the final decisions about content and structure.

James C. Impara
July, 1995

Preface

This book represents a unique effort for the Buros Institute of Mental Measurements and the Buros-Nebraska Series on Measurement and Testing. All of the previous books in this series have been associated with a symposium sponsored by the Buros Institute of Mental Measurements and the University of Nebraska. This book is "free standing" in that it is an independent effort intended to fulfill a perceived need for a book, but without preceding the book with a symposium. There are few books devoted solely to the topic of licensure testing, but each state and the federal government is involved in this form of testing. Licensure testing is far too important to be undertaken casually, because it is big business and it has implications and consequences for thousands of people annually. Every author in this book is involved in some way with licensure testing. Some authors work for professional organizations that are responsible for development of licensure tests. Other authors work for companies that contract with licensure boards to develop licensure tests. The rest serve as consultants to one or more licensure boards to assist in the development and maintenance of licensure testing programs.

The intent of this book is to provide licensure board members with practical information that will help them to understand and carry out their measurement related responsibilities. Many licensure boards employ consultants to assist in developing or selecting measures to use in making the licensure decision. They employ such consultants for a number of reasons (e.g., because they do not have large numbers of employees who are trained in test development, because the occupations they are charged with regulating may have only small numbers of applicants, or because they have little funding and must issue licenses based on results of tests developed by national professional organizations). The reason for employing outside consultants is not really material, the board is the legally responsible agent and the board must make decisions about the test. This book is intended to help board members make such decisions.

This book is also intended to aid measurement consultants by providing them with specific information written in the context of licensure testing. This book provides some technical guidance useful in the development of licensure tests. Most chapters contain some technical content (especially the chapters in Part Two); however, there was an attempt to make most of the content readable by board members while providing measurement consultants with guidelines and references that will assist them in their consulting role.

All the authors in this book tried to walk a fine line between writing for board members and for measurement experts alike. I hope we have achieved that end.

The book is divided into three parts: Part One addresses the purposes for licensure and it includes discussion of legal and policy issues in licensure. The contents of the three chapters in Part One represent essential knowledge for licensure board members. These three chapters constitute the basis for licensure testing and are entirely non-technical. Part Two provides the details of setting up and operating a licensure testing program. This part represents the bulk of the book and it consists of the rationale for the various steps involved in developing a licensure test and those activities necessary for operating an ongoing licensure testing program. It provides the licensure board member with an understanding of why certain activities must be undertaken (such as a job analysis and conducting an analysis of differential item functioning for different candidate populations) and it contains information helpful in making decisions about such issues as which testing strategies and which methods of setting the cut score are most appropriate under different conditions . The basis for doing many of the technical tasks is also explained in ways a board member can understand. The measurement consultant will also appreciate this part of the book. It provides the details and rationale for undertaking many of the technical steps used in developing and maintaining a licensure testing program. It does not always go into the level of detail necessary for the measurement expert, but when that level of detail is missing the reference list should provide citations to aid the expert. In Part Three some futuristic looks at the practice of licensure testing are taken.

Part One begins with Kara Schmidt's chapter in which she defines licensure, with its emphasis on protecting the public, and differentiates it from certification and registration. She characterizes the history of the licensure process and gives examples of different legislative approaches to licensure. Schmidt reminds us that licensure is a responsibility of state government, except for those few occupations licensed by the federal government (e.g., merchant marine officers, pilots, and nuclear power plant operators).

William Mehrens describes the legal bases for licensure testing. He describes several sets of guidelines for testing that are recommended by various professional organizations. In this discussion he characterizes the relevant guidelines that are intended to drive the development of licensure examinations and he differentiates between licensure testing and employment testing. Mehrens cites case law to describe various requirements in licensure and he provides illustrations of board responsibilities as described by the courts. His examples come from a variety of occupations, but most are from education where much confusion occurs in the certification (or licensure) of teachers.

Chapter 3, by Rosenfeld, Tannenbaum, and Wesley, discusses in detail three issues of extreme importance: making necessary accommodations required by the Americans with Disabilities Act (ADA); testing repeaters (those who fail the licensure test the first time), and coaching for licensure examinations. Their insightful comments and analyses of various research activities provide much useful information about the implications of these issues on the licensure testing process.

Part Two begins with a concise overview of the licensure testing process. In this overview, I attempt to provide an advanced organizer for the remainder of the book. The overview does not summarize each chapter; instead it attempts to provide the overarching framework for developing and administering a licensure testing program that is detailed in each of the subsequent chapters.

Chapter 4, by Joan and Lenora Knapp, details the rationale and processes by which a practice analysis is undertaken. Practice analysis (often called job analysis) is a critical step in the licensure testing process. The entire test is constructed on the basis of this analysis.

Because the practice analysis represents the basis for establishing the content of the test, the next two chapters describe different types of testing strategies. In chapter 5, LaDuca, Downing, and Henzel focus mainly on multiple-choice and other selected response items. They describe the relevance of the practice analysis to item content and they provide several illustrations of the method used in many medical contexts to develop items that represent the practice analysis for the licensure examination for physicians. They also describe several different types of selected response items and discuss conditions when the different item types are most useful. In chapter 6 Fortune and Cromack provide detailed illustrations for developing clinical examinations. Their examples are drawn from several licensure testing settings. Their approach reflects how boards can reduce many complex tasks into items that can be reliably scored and provide valid interpretations.

The psychometric properties of reliability and validity of the scores, and of the decisions made from the licensure examination scores are critical elements. Stoker and Impara's chapter on basic psychometric issues follows the development of test items. This chapter defines reliability and validity, and it describes techniques for conducting reliability and validity studies. In addition to defining the terms and describing how to estimate these properties of the test scores, we provide information to help in selecting appropriate methods for estimating reliability and validity.

In chapter 8, Bergstrom and Gershon provide a comprehensive discussion of the advantages of developing a computerized item bank. The computer software requirements are described as are the kinds of information that should be contained in the typical item bank. Using the item bank to undertake test construction is also described.

A major concern for all tests, and particularly tests used to make critical decisions about people, is the fairness of the items for the examinee population. Plake provides descriptions of how to assess if the items function differently for different groups of examinees. In her chapter she defines the concept of differential item functioning (DIF)—the assessment of whether examinee performance is biased based on such factors as gender or race. She also outlines several methods for detecting differential item functioning.

Chapter 10 redirects the focus from item development, item characteristics, and item banking to issues associated with the overall test. Once tests are developed it is necessary to determine the performance standard (the cut score) that will be used to make the distinction between those who are licensed and those who are not licensed. Mills describes several ways to set the cut score and he discusses the advantages of the various methods as they apply to a typical licensure examination. He also discusses several recently developed methods for setting cut scores for complex performance tests (e.g., portfolios). Mills then details several procedures one might use to conduct a cut-score study and how "adjustments" in the cut score might be undertaken if they are deemed appropriate.

Another issue associated with fairness to examinees is ensuring that the licensure decision is a function of the candidate's level of knowledge, skills, and abilities and is not dependent on the particular version of the test that was taken. Shea and Norcini discuss both traditional and contemporary methods of equating different forms of tests. They also describe a variety of software that can be used to perform the test equating process.

Section Three summarizes current practices and indicates how these practices might influence emerging trends in licensure testing. Vale's discussion of computers in licensure testing describes several uses of the computer, including his perspective that computer adaptive testing in licensure testing is not highly efficacious.

Chapter 14 looks across the various components of the process of licensure testing and projects how these components might change over the next few years. Nettles recognizes the importance of stability in the process of licensure testing and, while predicting some important changes, implies that change may occur slowly in licensure testing.

Licensure testing is different from much other testing that occurs in the United States. Few other testing activities carry the burden that licensure testing does. Persons' careers depend on the results of licensure tests. This is not the case in most instances of educational testing, nor is it the case in many instances of certification or employment testing. For these reasons licensure boards have particularly difficult jobs. One of the dilemmas they face is to make certain that the public is protected by setting high performance standards for licensure, while at the same time making certain that licensure candidates are protected by setting high standards for the psychometric quality of the tests used to make licensure decisions. I hope this book helps board members and psychometric consultants make licensure tests be of the highest psychometric quality.

James C. Impara
July, 1995

Section One

Purposes and Policy Issues

WHAT IS LICENSURE?

Kara Schmitt

Bureau of Occup & Prof Reg

When most individuals hear the terms *license* and *licensure*, their first reaction is that these are easily understood and relatively simple words. Everyone knows what these terms mean. Or do they?

What is licensure? It is a multi-faceted, complex governmental system of regulation with the stated purpose being public protection. According to Webster's dictionary (Guralnik, 1976), a *license* is defined as "a formal permission to do something: esp., authorization by law to do some specified thing (*license* to marry, practice medicine, hunt, etc.)." The term *Licensure* is then defined to mean "the act or practice of granting licenses, as to practice a profession." Unfortunately, the dictionary definitions encompass a myriad of activities for which the terms *license* or *licensure* may be applicable and only serve to further complicate what is meant by these related terms.

Licensure confers upon a licensee the legal authority to practice an occupation or profession[1]. In 1952, The Council of State Governments defined licensing as:

> the granting by some competent authority of a right or permission to carry on a business or do an act which would otherwise be illegal. The essential elements

Recognition and appreciation is given to Lise Smith-Peters, CLEAR, for her assistance in compiling the 1993 regulatory data. Thanks also goes to Bruce Douglas and Eric Werner (CO Dept. of Regulatory Agencies); Robert Nebiker (VA Dept. of Health Professions); and Rae Ramsdell (MI Dept. of Commerce - BOPR) for their review and critique of the material.

[1]Licensure is one of the forms of regulatory control states have over individuals wishing to practice certain occupations or professions. The term "regulation" will be used throughout this chapter to include all forms of states' authority to control practice. Note that although licensure is the responsibility of individual states, there are a few professions that require federal licensure (e.g., airplane pilots, certain railroaders, nuclear power plant operators, and certain classes of merchant seamen).

of licensing involve the *stipulation of circumstances* under which permission to perform an otherwise prohibited activity may be granted—largely a legislative function; and the actual granting of the permission in specific cases—generally an administrative responsibility. (p. 5)

Later, Shimberg and Roederer (1994) rephrased the above definition of professional licensure.

> Licensing is a process by which an agency of government grants permission to an individual to engage in a given occupation upon finding that the applicant has attained the minimal degree of competency required to ensure that the public health, safety, and welfare will be reasonably well protected. (p. 1)

Occupational and professional licensure is an activity reserved to each state by the federal constitution; the exercising of a state's inherent police power. Licensure is designed to protect citizens from mental, physical, or economic harm that could be caused by practitioners who may not be sufficiently competent to enter the profession.

Whether licensure is viewed as a privilege or a right, it is to be granted only to individuals who demonstrate to the satisfaction of a state that they possess, at the time of *initial* licensure, the requisite minimal level of knowledge, skills, and abilities determined necessary to practice competently. Malcolm Parsons (1952) emphasized that *permission* is the essential element of licensure and that such permission "may be granted or denied, renewed or refused to be renewed, withdrawn temporarily through suspension, or withdrawn altogether through revocation" (p. 4). A license is not unconditionally granted to an individual, but usually for only a finite period of time and can be removed or limited by a state for a number of reasons.

Paradoxically, although freedom is a cornerstone of the Constitution of the United States, licensure imposes considerable restrictions upon an individual's freedom to pursue certain career choices. Once a profession has been legislatively mandated to be licensed, it is illegal for an individual to practice that profession or use a specific title without first obtaining the necessary license. Additionally, in order to obtain a license, an individual must have been successful at meeting a variety of requirements.

Even with the expanded definitions of licensure, it is still a complex and often misunderstood term. The Hindoo fable, as told by John Saxe (1949), entitled *The Blind Men and The Elephant* provides an allegorical framework for appreciating the complexity associated with licensing.

Once there were six blind men who went to "see" an elephant so that through touch they might satisfy themselves as to what an elephant was. Each man touched a different part of the elephant and accordingly determined that an elephant was like six different items with which they were familiar. The first touched the side and proclaimed the elephant to be like a wall. The second felt the tusk and decided it was similar to a spear. The third took hold of the trunk and said that the elephant was like a snake. The fourth reached out and touched the knee and declared the elephant to be like a tree. The fifth found the ear and as the ear moved, the blind man decided it was like a fan. Finally, the sixth man seized upon the swinging tail and thought the elephant was like a rope. The fable ends with the following lines:

And so these men of Indostan
Disputed loud and long,
Each in his own opinion
Exceeding stiff and strong,
Though each was partly in the right
And all were in the wrong! (p. 123)

The moral of this fable is that confrontations and wars are often started because the parties "rail on in utter ignorance of what each other mean, *And prate about an Elephant not one of them has seen!*" (Saxe, 1949, p. 123). Until the various factions are familiar with and understand the opposing views of all parties, battles and confusion will continue with little hope of resolution.

Although many individuals have encountered the "beast" called licensure, their perception of it is blinded by their personal involvement with it. In many instances, the various perceptions and encounters with licensure create a situation in which "each [is] partly in the right and all [are] in the wrong." Furthermore, although debates about licensure may not lead to a full scale war, there are certainly a number of battles being fought over licensure in terms of what it entails, the scope of regulated activity, who should be licensed, and how it should be organized.

For members of a profession seeking initial licensure legislation, it may be viewed as a political game that must be won. For the candidate who hopes to practice a licensed profession, it may be viewed as an overwhelming hurdle that must be jumped. For the regulator, it is like walking a tightrope trying to balance the interests of the profession along those of the state/public. For the investigator, it is similar to a game of poker in which both skill and luck are necessary in order to obtain sufficient proof of wrongdoing. Board members who are also licensees may view it as a tug of war in which they are pulled between the mandates of their appointed public position and the desires of their professional association.

Regardless of the various perceptions, if members of each of these groups were asked to define licensure, the responses would undoubtedly be fairly similar and incorporate the following phrase—*protection of the public.* Even if everyone were to use the same phrase, the individual perceptions of licensure create continuous conflicts as to what is *really* meant by the term. In essence, licensure involves politics, economic considerations for the public and profession, cost analyses in terms of the benefits derived versus the costs involved, conflict resolution, police power, discipline, competency assurance, mediation, and above all, an attempt to protect the public.

There is a built–in premise that a license is necessary to promote proficiency and maintain standards in a profession. In and of itself, licensure cannot guarantee the public's protection nor the competency of the licensee. It merely indicates that an individual has met the *initial* requirements of education, experience, minimal competence as measured by an examination, or a combination of the three. Continued competence, not just continuing education, is rarely required to be demonstrated and a licensee's ethics and morals are generally evaluated only when the potential for disciplinary action is being considered. Granted, a number of professions require an individual to possess "good moral character" at the time of licensure, yet the meaning of this term is often nebulous. With the exception of a criminal conviction, good moral character is rarely used as grounds for the denial of a license.

The public relies upon the credentials of an individual to evaluate whether a practitioner is competent. And yet, is this an accurate method by which to judge someone who will have a direct physical, emotional, or financial impact on one's life? Carl Rogers (1973), past president of the American Psychological Association, would claim that reliance upon a license to judge a professional should be used only if additional information about that person's competence is available. Although Dr. Roger's comments reference certification, the same sentiment could apply to licensure.

> If you had a good friend badly in need of therapeutic help and I gave you the name of a therapist who was a Diplomate in Clinical Psychology, with no other information, would you send your friend to him? Of course not. You would want to know what he is like as a person and as a therapist, recognizing that there are many with diplomas on their walls who are not fit to do therapy, lead a group, or help a marriage. So, certification is *not* equivalent to competence. (Rogers, 1973, p. 382)

As Dr. Rogers points out, there is more involved in ensuring public protection than simply hanging a license on a wall.

Historical Perspective

How did licensure evolve? The first attempt to regulate any professions may have been the tariff imposed on medical practitioners in the year 2000 B.C. (Gross, 1984; Hogan, 1979; and Young, 1987). The Babylonian Code of Hammurabi stipulated both surgeon's fees and penalties for what is now considered malpractice. According to historical writings, one such penalty was the severing of a surgeon's hand when an operation resulted in a patient's death. The restrictions on women practicing certain professions dates back to 300 B.C. when the laws of Greece specifically barred women from medical practice.

In the 13th century, the king of Sicily established the foundation for current licensing laws by implementing standards to control the medical profession. Prior to becoming recognized as a medical doctor, an individual had to have completed 3 years of philosophy, 5 years of medicine, and 1 year of practical experience, and must have passed an examination prepared by a medical facility. Practicing without a license was prohibited. The law also established fee schedules, mandated that free service be available to indigents, established ethical codes with strong penalties, and made it unlawful for a physician to own an apothecary.

During the later 13th through middle 15th centuries, various professional Guilds were established throughout Europe. Although the initial Guilds had fairly lax requirements, eventually they became quite restrictive in their membership by means of imposing stringent requirements, similar to today's licensure requirements. Guilds required compulsory membership; high entrance fees with approval of other members before a new member could be admitted; a period of apprenticeship (up to 7 years in some instances); a limitation on the number of apprentices that a member might have; and the establishment of minimum prices for services and a maximum wage for workers. The Guilds started to disappear during the 15th century because a more laissez–faire system became dominant plus there was an increase in the economic market and general accumulation of wealth.

The first actual licensing law, comparable to those of today, involved medical doctors and was enacted in England in 1511. Three classes within the medical field were licensed—physicians, surgeons, and apothecaries. Battle lines were drawn with the physicians feeling they were the superior group and attempting to reduce the size of the other two professions. The Apothecaries Act of 1815 gave the Society of Apothecaries the right to examine and establish standards for those wishing to become apothecaries. It also established penalties for individuals who practiced medicine illegally. Unfortunately, the enforcement powers of this act were not very extensive and regulatory efforts were quite weak.

Finally, the Medical Act of 1858 merged the three professions and led to the enforcement of uniform standards in the examinations. It also provided for the creation of a list of licensees and only those on the list could sue for medical fees or hold public office. The law did not, however, forbid the practice of medicine by lay persons.

The earliest licensing laws (medical profession) in the United States were enacted by Virginia in 1639, Massachusetts in 1649, and New York in 1665. The Virginia law was created as a result of numerous complaints about the fees charged by the medical profession. The Massachusetts law was intended to regulate activities of:

> "Chirurgeons, Midwives, Physitians or others [who were] imployed at any time about the bodye of men, women or children, for preservation of life, or health." No such persons were to practice "without the advice and consent of such as are skillful in the same Art (if such may be had) or at least some of the wisest and gravest then present". If these rules were not obeyed, violators were subject to "such severe punishment as the nature of the fact may deserve." (Shryock, 1967, p. 1)

Although the above language may give the appearance that the regulation was intended to protect the public from harm, the prevailing reason for medical licensing may have actually been unrelated to a concern for competency. During the early days of regulation, the colonial laws and court actions were generally more concerned with fees than with the quality of service provided.

Virtually no further legislation regulating the medical profession, or any other profession, occurred until the mid–1700s at which time a number of other states instituted legislation to regulate medical doctors as well as lawyers. During the next 100 years (until the mid–1800s), many states enacted regulatory legislation and then eliminated the legislation due to conflicts between whether graduation from a "chartered" school was sufficient for licensure or whether additional requirements were necessary.

By 1850, the practice of medicine in the United States was available to almost anyone who desired to perform the tasks associated with medicine. Only New Jersey and the District of Columbia had a law in 1850 that even resembled regulation of the medical profession. One reason for deregulation was that the education of medical practitioners was perceived to be so much greater than it had been when the laws were first established. Also, the medical facilities were effective in convincing the legislators that training standards were being met. The same was true for the legal profession. In fact, nearly two–thirds of the states had abolished all regulation of lawyers by 1840 and many states were even contemplating the abolishment of the legal profession in its entirety.

The attitude of state legislators concerning the necessity for regulation changed again in the late 1800s. State medical societies were becoming increasingly distressed with the lack of standards and the poor quality of many emerging proprietary schools. In an attempt to force change, the individual state societies formed the American Medical Association, which was finally able to make an impact on the need for regulation. Texas was the first state to pass a law establishing a state examining board. Following the Texas action in 1873, states began re–instituting medical licensing boards and enacting regulatory legislation. By the end of the 19th century, 37 states regulated the medical profession. New Hampshire was the last state (1915) to license the profession (The Council of State Governments, 1952, p. 80).

Present Status of Licensure

During the first half of the 20th century, licensing laws were primarily limited to those professions having a direct relationship to public health and safety. The basic premise was that most consumers of services provided by health care practitioners could not judge adequately the quality of the care provided. Following the enactment of regulation for a few professions on the basis of this premise, the need for "public protection" quickly became a convenient, but effective, argument for every group seeking regulation.

Milton Friedman (1961) references a study indicating that "occupational licensure is by now very widespread....and by 1952, more than 80 separate occupations ... had been licensed by state law" (p. 139). He must be aghast at how widespread occupational licensure is now. In 1968, the median number of professions licensed by states was 37, ranging from 25 in Washington to a high of 57 in Michigan (The Council of State Governments, 1968, p.1). A 1986 report by the American Association of Retired Persons estimated that there were at least 800 professions licensed. According to a 1990 publication, states collectively regulated over 1,000 professions, yet fewer than 60 professions were regulated by all or most states (Brinegar, 1990).

It is probably impossible to know exactly how many professions are actually regulated because of the various ways in which the data are collected and analyzed. Regardless of whether the above figures are completely accurate, it is clear that an "overwhelming" number of professions are regulated by states.

For approximately 60 professions (i.e., Medicine, Nursing, Engineering, and Architects) comparable licensing requirements exist in all states, the District of Columbia, and many of the U.S. territories. For most professions, however, the regulation of occupations and professions varies among the states. Some of the more unusual professions regulated in at least one state include: Babcock testers, bankruptcy salespersons, wire rope inspectors, lime vendors, mussel fishers, pheas-ant club operators, safe mechanics, apprentice scalers, resident and non–resident sea moss rakers, tree injectors, weather modifiers, livestock weighers, lightning rod installers, hemp growers, endless chain agents, and egg brokers (Brinegar, 1990). What individuals in these occupations actually do and why regulation is needed may not always be comprehensible.

In the immediate past, the emphasis was on licensure, licensure, and more licensure without the appearance of much regard for whether the laws were necessary to protect the public from harm or quackery. Any profession that could get the support of a senator or representative had an excellent chance of obtaining licensure status. In fact, licensing legislation may have been based not so much on logic, but rather on who introduced the bill, who the lobbyist was, and how much financial backing was available.

In the 1950s an ill–conceived licensure bill was introduced into the California legislature. The proposed legislation required licensure for anyone, including children, who mowed lawns for money. The penalty for noncompliance would have been a fine up to $500 and imprisonment for up to 6 months. Fortunately, this bill failed to win support by the legislature as it definitely would not have been in the public's best interest. Such legislative foresight has not always been apparent as evidenced by the previous noninclusive list of questionable regulation.

One reason for the increase in regulation during the 1970s and 1980s may have been the growth of allied health professions. These professions alone did not, however, account for the rapid rise in professional and occupational regulation during the last 40 years.

During a series of four regional workshops conducted in 1975[2], the following comments were made by some of the legislators who attended. Based on their comments, these legislators were cognizant that requests for licensure are not always based on public protection. Similar views may not have been held by other legislators as the proliferation of licensing laws continued for the next 15 years.

> We have been besieged, as have most legislative bodies, by requests from groups for additional licensure. All kinds of groups are coming to us requesting that they be given the right to license....obviously the only way the legislation could proceed [is] if there was some public interest at stake.

> Another big problem is this proliferation that we are running into. Everybody wants to be licensed or certified. Don't kid yourself—they want it because it is a status thing, and we're fighting them as hard as we can.

> New licensing—those who would like to be licensed—shocks me. When I came into this arena I could not believe that everyone in the country felt they needed a license. The stack of licensing bills I have is so high you wouldn't believe. I

---

[2]Ben Shimberg, a leading authority in regulation, coordinated these four regional workshops. The purposes for these conferences were to (a) determine problems and issues related to regulation; (b) ascertain the interest of state officials to participate in cooperative projects aimed at resolving these problems; and (c) develop strategies which would help bring about needed regulatory change. Nearly 100 individuals from 30 states attended these meetings. Various comments expressed by the participants are included in this chapter.

personally do not see the need for it. I don't think it means better service to the people of our state.

Nobody has defined which things should be licensed and which shouldn't. Where do you draw the line? Which are valid public purposes and which are simply for the aggrandizement of a particular group? (Shimberg, 1976, pp. 11–12)

The enactment of new licensing laws appears to have slowed during the last few years even though the number of licensure bills continues to flourish. In some states, the decline in the number of newly licensed professions may, unfortunately, be based more on budgetary reasons than on the legislators' thorough understanding of when licensing laws should or should not be enacted.

The stated purpose for licensure is public protection and yet licensure laws have rarely been enacted as a result of the public's outcry that they were being harmed. It is not the public demanding the enactment of these laws, but rather the professions themselves who spend thousands of dollars on lobbyists to ensure that "their" bill is passed. According to Linda McCready, "a good lobbyist can do more for the interest of a profession than years of national conventions can" (1982, p. 74).

Legislative decisions regarding licensure are generally made with little or no input from the public. On the other hand, members of a profession seeking licensure are always well represented. "Of course, they are more aware than others of how much they exploit the customer and so perhaps they can lay claim to expert knowledge" (Friedman, 1962, p. 140). The legislative process may, at best, only coincidentally serve the interests of the public. According to Milton Friedman (1962),

The declaration by a large number of different state legislatures that barbers must be approved by a committee of other barbers is hardly persuasive evidence that there is in fact a public interest in having such legislation. Surely the explanation is different; it is that a produce group tends to be more concentrated politically than a consumer group. (p. 143)

The principal argument offered by professions seeking licensure is that the public is incapable of determining or judging whether a practitioner is competent. This argument may be appropriate in some instances, but not in all cases. Shimberg (1991) states that "virtually all licensing laws have been passed at the behest of the occupational group to get certain benefits for their members, and, [only] incidentally, to help the public" (p. 1). In addition to the main argument offered in their attempt to secure licensure status, there are a number of other reasons why professions actually seek regulation. Members of professional associations believe that licensure will:

1. Lead to enhanced economic benefits;
2. Provide practitioners with increased status;
3. Protect the reputation of the profession;
4. Provide a symbol of respectability;
5. Demonstrate that the profession is well established;
6. Define the professional field more clearly;

7. Provide for the payment of services by third–party payers; and
8. Control the number and geographic distribution of practitioners.

Although there is nothing inherently wrong with the first seven licensure *outcomes*, they should not serve as the principal reasons for seeking or being granted licensure status. Controlling the number and geographic distribution of practitioners, however, should never be the purpose for or the intended result of licensure.

Critics claim that licensure serves only the interests of a specific group by enhancing their status and limiting competition which improves their economic position. Unreasonable restrictions on job entry and mobility impact negatively upon the availability, quality, and cost of services.

In the past, anticompetitive regulations were viewed by legislators and the public as being "essential to ensure high professional morality and performance" (Blair & Rubin, 1980, p. vii). As exemplified by the following statement, this view is no longer being accepted by the public: "A gullible public was taken in by the propaganda about protecting consumers from cheats and incompetents. Now consumers are beginning to see that they are being forced to pay a very high price for protection of dubious value" (Shimberg, 1976, p. 46).

Sunrise

In an effort to better ensure that new regulation of additional occupations and professions is for the benefit of the public rather than solely for the profession, a number of states have implemented Sunrise legislation. Sunrise is a legislative process applying specific criteria to evaluate the appropriateness of the requested new regulatory legislation.

Typically, professional groups or associations draft legislation providing for the regulation of the profession and then attempt to convince the legislature of its necessity. Under the Sunrise process, the legislature, a legislatively enacted body, and/or a designated administrative body review the applications for regulation to determine whether licensure, or another form of regulation, should be granted. Restricting the number of new licensed professions is viewed by the proponents of Sunrise to be more effective than trying to eliminate those already in existence.

The first Sunrise legislation was enacted by Minnesota in 1973 and dealt exclusively with the regulation of allied health personnel. Since that time, 17 states have implemented formal Sunrise reviews of proposed regulation. States that have formal Sunrise legislation are indicated in Table 1. Many other states, particularly those with central agencies responsible for overseeing the administrative components of regulation, have instituted similar reviews of proposed legislation even though there is no mandate to perform this task.

Shimberg and Roederer (1994) have suggested that all legislators, particularly those who do not have a formal Sunrise process, consider carefully the answers obtained from asking the following questions of occupations or professions who wish licensure status:

1. What is the problem?
2. Why should the occupational group be regulated?
3. What efforts have been made to address the problems?

Table 1. Sunrise and Sunset Legislation By State[1]

STATE	SUNRISE LEGISLATION	SUNSET LEGISLATION
Alabama	No	Yes
Alaska	No	Yes
Arizona	No	Yes
Arkansas	No	Yes
California	Yes	No
Colorado	Yes	Yes
Connecticut	No	Yes
Delaware	No	Yes
Florida	Yes	No[2]
Georgia	Yes	No[2]
Hawaii	Yes	Yes
Idaho	No	No
Illinois	Yes	Yes
Indiana	No	No
Iowa	No	No
Kansas	Yes	Yes
Kentucky	No	No
Louisiana	No	Yes
Maine	Yes	Yes
Maryland	No	Yes
Massachusetts	No	No
Michigan	No	No
Minnesota	Yes	No
Mississippi	No	No
Missouri	No	No
Montana	Yes	No
Nebraska	Yes	No
Nevada	No	No
New Hampshire	No	No
New Jersey	No	No
New Mexico	Yes	Yes
New York	No	No
North Carolina	No	No
North Dakota	No	No
Ohio	No	No
Oklahoma	No	Yes
Oregon	No	No
Pennsylvania	No	No
Rhode Island	No	No
South Carolina	Yes	Yes
South Dakota	No	No

(continued....)

Table 1 (continued)

STATE	SUNRISE LEGISLATION	SUNSET LEGISLATION
Tennessee	Yes	Yes
Texas	No	Yes
Utah	No	Yes
Vermont	Yes	Yes
Virginia	Yes	No
Washington	Yes	Yes
West Virginia	No	Yes
Wisconsin	No	No
Wyoming	No	No
Washington, DC	No	No
TOTALS	17	22

[1]Information was obtained through an informal telephone survey conducted by CLEAR in October, 1993.

[2]Sunset Legislation was repealed in 1993

4. Have alternatives to licensure been considered?
5. Will the public benefit from regulation of the occupation?
6. Will regulation be harmful to the public?
7. How will the regulatory activity be administered?
8. Who is sponsoring the regulatory program?
9. Why is regulation being sought? (pp. 25–33)

In addition to these questions, legislators should also make certain that each of the following conditions exists before regulation is enacted.

1. Clear evidence demonstrates a significant danger to the public's health, safety or welfare by the unregulated practice.
2. A scope of practice can be clearly defined and includes acts, tasks and functions related to demonstrable skills and the acquisition of a substantive body of knowledge.
3. Professional practice is done independently with little or no supervision by presently licensed individuals or agencies.
4. The cost of regulation will be reasonable and the resultant impact of regulation on the cost and availability of services will be minimal compared to the protection afforded the public.
5. Expanded availability and/or a lower cost of service will occur and are in the public's best interest.
6. Assistance is required for the public to differentiate between qualified and unqualified practitioners or the public is unable to differentiate among professional titles where similar services are provided.
7. Unnecessary barriers to entry will not be created.

8. The efficient use of auxiliary or paraprofessional personnel will not be adversely affected.

9. Evidence exists that the public cannot be protected effectively through other means.

If most of these conditions do not apply to a profession seeking licensure, the proposed regulatory bill should be defeated or less restrictive regulation enacted. Sunrise, or any type of preregulation legislative review, will lose its effectiveness if a careful analysis of these, and other, issues is not performed.

Sunset

In an attempt to overcome unnecessary, outdated, or inefficient regulation, a number of states have instituted Sunset legislation. Sunset is the formal legislative review of regulation that currently exists as opposed to the review of proposed legislation. William O. Douglas, Chairman of the Securities and Exchange Commission under Franklin D. Roosevelt, is credited with the idea for a Sunset–type approach to legislative oversight. His proposal was that federal agencies should be abolished after 10 years (Kearney, 1990).

Colorado was the first state to adopt a Sunset Law in 1976. Two comments from participants at the 1975 workshops directly relate to the tasks performed by Sunset Review:

... establish a review process so that "deregulation" or program modification would take place when the need for regulation ceased to exist or when the program was not fulfilling its public purpose in an acceptable manner. (Shimberg, 1976, p. 11)

The objectives of regulation [should] be stated as precisely as possible at the time each regulatory law is enacted. The extent to which these goals were met would constitute the major basis for deciding whether or not the regulatory law should be continued. (Shimberg, 1976, p. 16)

Sunset was promoted as a way to eliminate unnecessary agencies, curtail the proliferation of rules and regulations, and force greater accountability. The process has been used to evaluate not only licensing boards and functions, but all agencies of the executive branch within a state. Sunset requires legislators to evaluate the existing laws, rules, and operations of agencies and determine whether they are in the public's interest and should be continued, modified, or eliminated. Sunset legislation also mandates that an agency and its regulatory activities cease to exist on a specified date unless the legislature takes affirmative action to continue the existence of the agency (regulation) by enactment or replacement with a new statute.

In general, Sunset reviews focus on the following questions:

*   Is the regulation needed to protect the public interest?
*   If it is needed, is the current regulation effective?
*   If it is not effective, can it be improved?
*   Is the current regulation unnecessarily restrictive and, if so, how could it be revised? (Douglas, 1988)

Based on the answers to these questions, agencies and the regulation of certain professions may be eliminated or revisions made to the corresponding laws and rules. Administrative procedures may also be revised based on a Sunset review. In some instances, a professional board itself may be discontinued, but the regulation is continued under a different administrative structure. In rare instances, professions might be combined so that future decisions are made by a joint board composed of members from the various professions. Regardless of the outcome, the Sunset process provides an impetus for reform and requires legislators to focus on problems and issues that face the public, a profession, and the agency overseeing the profession.

Sunset is intended to promote and provide for an open, apolitical structure in which reform and improvements can be made to the regulatory operations. Unfortunately, this has not always occurred as evidenced by events that took place in two states—Colorado in 1981 and Texas in 1993.

Starting in 1978, the State Board of Registration for Professional Engineers and the Colorado Department of Regulatory Agencies, the central agency responsible for administration of this and other boards, became embittered in numerous confrontations centering on personnel matters and policy issues. At one point, the Board sued the Department Director and later drafted legislation that would have eliminated the entire Department. As might be anticipated, there was a lot of mutual suspicion and resentment as well as a lot of political maneuvering when the Sunset Review for Engineers was initiated in 1981.

> The Colorado Engineering Council ... worked extensively on sunset and appointed a standing committee that drafted its own bill, obtained its own sponsors and basically shut the Department out of the process. We were not invited to the meetings, our requests to participate were refused and so on. The profession clearly decided that they were going to do it their own [way] using their political influence in the legislature and not deal with the Department, which still had the responsibility under Colorado law for framing recommendations to the legislature and performing the actual review and report on the need for regulation.

> It became apparent that a bill was going to be introduced, which the Department had never even seen or had access to, and we felt that this would result in a complete end run around the sunset process, setting a dangerous precedent for the future of sunset. (Douglas, 1988, p. 7)

In an effort to counteract the secret bill being drafted on behalf of the engineers, two employees of the Department drafted their own secret bill, recruited a senator to sponsor the bill, and convinced the attorney doing the legislative drafting of the engineers' bill to set it aside and provide a quick 2–day turn–around on the Department's bill. The second bill was calendared for a hearing during the first week that the senate reconvened, much to the amazement of the engineers. Battle lines were quickly drawn and confusion reigned. The engineers were forced to testify against the Department's bill even though it would have continued the regulation of the profession. The Department's bill was finally postponed, without a vote, once the lobbyists figured out the strategy behind it.

Eventually, the two organizations were able to reach a compromise during this confrontational initial Sunset review. When the State Board of Registration for Professional Engineers was reviewed again in 1988, the two organizations worked in a cooperative and supportive atmosphere. According to Mr. Douglas, the lesson learned during the initial review was that "both sides should try to put themselves in the other's shoes, should learn to live with each other and respect our differences" (Douglas, 1988, p. 10).

Confrontations have not been restricted to the early days of Sunset review. Two similar conflicts occurred during the 1991–1993 Sunset review process in Texas.

Sunset review in Texas is conducted by a Sunset Advisory Commission composed of eight legislators and two public members. Between 1991 and 1993, the Commission was responsible for reviewing 30 agencies, including 20 licensing boards. During the most recent review, the legislature nearly passed a measure to wipe out the commission itself because of disagreements over some of the recommendations. According to an editorial in the *Houston Post*,

> The major argument legislative leaders have used in advocating the commission's demise is that the sunset process has allowed special– interest lobbyists to gain too much influence. But that is not the fault of the commission. The blame belongs to the Legislature, which rejects too many commission recommendations and too often does the bidding of lobbyists. (Paxton, April/May 1993, p. 4)

Eventually a compromise was reached with the creation of a panel to study thoroughly the responsibilities and authority of the commission. A report is to be presented to the Texas legislature in 1995.

In another instance, conflict among the profession, legislature, and the Sunset Advisory Commission caused the dentists and dental hygienists to lose their licensing board on August 31, 1994 because the legislature adjourned without reauthorizing the board. The scheduled Sunset (expiration) date for the board was four months before the legislature would reconvene unless a special session was held. The governor, upset with the actions of the Dental Association, ensured that a special session to handle this issue was *not* held. The Texas Dental Association had actively lobbied the legislature to vote against the reauthorization bill because they did not like some of the recommendations. These included a recommendation that the governor appoint the chairperson of the dental board; the Dental Association wanted the chairperson to be appointed by the dental board itself or require the governor to appoint a dentist rather than a public member.

The other area of conflict evolved around the governor being granted the authority to appoint three persons of a six–member internal board to oversee dental hygienists. Under the previous structure, there were eight members on the internal board and all were appointed by the dental examiners. No action could occur regarding this recommendation, or the previous one, until the boardwas reauthorized (Paxton, April/May, 1993).

Finally, after a lawsuit was brought against the Dental Board and the State of Texas, the legislature reauthorized the Board of Dental Examiners on February 6, 1995, with an effective date of March 1, 1995. The legislative action occurred just three days prior to the deadline imposed by the State District Judge. Had the legislature failed to reconstitute the Board, the Judge would have ruled the Dental Practice Act as being unconstitutional and the licenses of all Texas dentists and dentla hygientists would have been invalid.

Ironically, in spite of the various confrontations, including the one between the commission and legislature, 19 significant across–the–board recommendations were approved by the legislature for the 30 agencies reviewed. An additional 10 general recommendations were approved for 20 agencies with licensing functions and a multitude of specific changes were implemented for each of the individual licensing boards. Even with the contentiousness surrounding the Sunset review, 1993 was one of the most reform–filled years for Texas licensure.

When Sunset was first introduced, the concept was heralded as a major step forward in revising, revamping, and improving the regulatory process. Between the years of 1976 and 1982, all 50 state legislatures as well as Congress considered the adoption of Sunset laws. By the end of 1981, 36 states had adopted Sunset. Since then, there has been no new Sunset legislation and as of 1993 only 22 states had retained Sunset legislation. Two states, Florida and Georgia, repealed their legislation in 1993. (Refer back to Table 1 for a list of states with formal Sunset reviews)

North Carolina was the first state to repeal Sunset (1981). Since then, Arkansas, Mississippi, Nebraska, New Hampshire, and Wyoming have also re-pealed their Sunset laws; Illinois, Montana, Nevada, Rhode Island, South Dakota, and Connecticut have allowed Sunset to become inactive. With the exception of Illinois, most of the dropout states have "part–time legislatures with low levels of professionalism, low salaries, low staffing levels and below average spending on the legislative institution" (Kearney, 1990, p. 55). A number of states, including California, Michigan, New Jersey, Ohio, and Wisconsin, have included Sunset clauses in selected programs although they have never adopted broad Sunset legislation.

Why the change from eager acceptance to disenchantment? One of the reasons is that wide–spread elimination of licensing boards or other agencies did not occur as anticipated when Sunset was first introduced. Although there have been many reforms and improvements, as evidenced by Texas' most recent review, professions with strong lobbying and financial backing have managed to escape elimination or major modification that could have resulted from the reviews. The most frequently cited problems with Sunset are:

> (1) failure to reduce the size of government; (2) high temporal and monetary costs of the process for legislators and staff; (3) lack of meaningful citizen participating and the disproportionate influence of agencies and their lobbyists; and (4) lack of adequate evaluation criteria to apply to agencies under review. (Kearney, 1990, p. 51)

Regardless of the problems associated with Sunset, when implemented prop-erly, significant benefits have been achieved. Sunset has resulted in (a) an improvement in agency structure, procedures and performance (more efficient methods for investigating and disciplining practitioners); (b) enhanced agency accountability (better management of the agency); (c) a closer alignment between regulation and public interest (inclusion of public members on boards) and (d) financial savings to consumers (elimination of restrictions on open competition). Even in those states that repealed Sunset, the process was relatively effective in terms of its impact on state agencies.

Montana terminated five agencies ... and implemented over 150 modifications. Connecticut scored 29 terminations, Arkansas 28, Rhode Island 17 and New Hampshire 15. Illinois eliminated more than 50 agencies before pulling the shade on Sunset. (Kearney, 1990, p. 55)

Licensure versus registration and certification

Although this chapter is entitled, "What is Licensure?", it is important to mention that two other forms of regulation exist with licensure being the most restrictive. Unfortunately, many people use the term licensure to reference all forms of credentialing[3] rather than just to mean title and practice protection. The frequent misuse of the term adds to the confusion already surrounding the actual definition of licensure.

Licensure, certification and registration can each be conferred upon individuals and institutions by states. Certification is, however, more traditionally considered a voluntary mechanism implemented by a nongovernmental entity for the purpose of recognizing more advanced or specialized skills. Certification is frequently granted to individuals who specialize within a profession such as medical doctors who are certified as Neurologists, Pediatricians, or Obstetricians. Specialists often indicate that they are "Board Certified", which simply means they have met the requirements of a state or, more frequently, private agency. Licensure, on the other hand, is mandatory and must be obtained from state government in order for individuals to practice specified occupations or professions.

These distinctions, however, are not always accurate and as mentioned previously, certification may be used by states at the entry level. Even the legal use of these terms can create confusion; "Registered" Nurses are actually licensed as are "Certified" Public Accountants. In a number of instances, one of the entry requirements for licensure includes passing an examination offered by a private certifying agency. Michigan, and a few other states, require dentists who specialize in only one field of dentistry (Prosthodontics, Oral Surgery, Periodontics, etc.) to be state certified in their specialty as well as to remain licensed as general dentists.

Registration provides, at most, title, rather than practice, protection. That is, unregistered individuals can perform the same functions as those who are registered provided that they do not use a designated title. Registration would be appropriate when the "threat to life, health, safety, and economic well–being is relatively small and when other forms of legal redress are available to the public" (Shimberg & Roederer, 1994, p. 5). In its basic form, registration merely requires individuals to "register" their names with the appropriate state agency. Minimum entrance requirements or practice standards are typically not established for the profession.

Certification is also title protection and grants recognition to individuals who have met predetermined requirements. Noncertified individuals may offer similar services to the public provided they do not describe themselves as being "certified"

---

[3]Credentialing is a generic term that subsumes licensing, certification, registration, and institutional licensure by the states, as well as standards of competence where no licensure is required and certification by private organizations where it is required for practice by reference in state law. (McCready, 1982, p. 74)

or hold themselves out as someone who is certified. For instance, dentists may practice as pediatric dentists in Michigan without being certified provided they do not call themselves pediatric dentists or indicate that their practice is limited to this specialty.

A precise distinction among registration, licensure, and certification will probably never be achieved because of the way in which the meanings of the terms have been interchanged. Table 2 is provided to assist in understanding the two factors—mandatory versus voluntary and competency standards versus no competency standards—that are *generally* employed in the definition of the terms. Competency standards include specified education, experience, and/or examination requirements prior to licensure.

Table 2. Distinction Among Registration, Certification and Licensure

	Competency Standards	No Competency Standards
Mandatory	LICENSURE	REGISTRATION
Voluntary	CERTIFICATION	

Critics of licensure are also critical of certification and believe that neither form of regulation accomplishes the stated goal of public protection. Rather, both mandatory licensure and voluntary certification are viewed as self–serving to those who are able to meet the imposed standards. According to Hogan (1979), "associational policies tend to promote precisely the same harmful effects of licensure [restricting the supply of practitioners; decreasing mobility; increasing the cost of services, etc.] although their effects are probably not as pervasive" (p. 336).

Competency Examinations

Whether individuals are licensed by a state or certified by a private association,[4] everyone has to demonstrate competency by passing an approved examination prior to being granted a license or certificate. An individual may have been administered an oral, written, or practical examination or any combination of these examination formats. Regardless of the adherence to standards and quality assurance, examinations are often viewed by candidates as unnecessary, tricky, and inappropriate barriers to practice.

In 1961, John Gardner, Secretary of Health, Education, and Welfare during the Johnson administration, made the following statements about tests. Although he was not specifically referencing credentialing examinations, the sentiments expressed are nevertheless applicable.

The fact that tests may have high statistical reliability and validity does not quiet the apprehension over their use. ...Apprehension is fostered by the fact that it is very hard for those without professional training in psychology to understand the process of mental measurement. No one wishes to be judged by a process he cannot comprehend. ...there is not only fear of the tests but fear of the unknown bureaucracy that handles the test and acts on the results.

---

[4]There are a number of registered professions that do require an examination, although this situation is not typical.

No one concerned with the future of testing can afford to ignore these sources of anxiety. On the other hand, even if these sources of concern were to disappear, the hostility toward the tests would probably remain. *The tests are designed to do an unpopular job.* ...As the tests improve and become less vulnerable to present criticism, the hostility to them may actually increase. A proverbial phrase indicating complete rejection is "I wouldn't like it even if it were good." With tests, the more appropriate phrase might be "I wouldn't like them *especially* if they were good." (Gardner, 1961, pp. 47–48)

During the 30 plus years since Mr. Gardner's comments, tests have definitely improved and the hostility towards them has definitely not lessened. Tests will not disappear as they are an essential component of ensuring initial competence. Enhancements to test development, administration, and scoring have been and will continue to be made. The remaining chapters in this book detail where we have been, where we are now, and where we are going with examinations.

Federal Involvement in Licensure

According to the Constitution of the United States, states have the authority for establishing requirements for and ensuring compliance with occupational and professional regulation as an exercise of their police power. Prior to the 1970s, with the exception of the mandate for states to license Nursing Home Administrators, the federal government viewed state regulation in this area with, at most, a passive interest. However, in 1971 and again in 1973, the then U. S. Department of Health, Education, and Welfare (HEW) recommended that states observe a 2–year moratorium on legislation establishing new licensed health care personnel.

Ironically, however, at the same time a moratorium was being urged, the federal government imposed a requirement that health care reimbursement could only be paid to providers who were licensed by a state or certified by an approved national organization. Contradictory messages, such as this, have caused state legislators and regulators to question whether the federal government accurately understands the statutory responsibilities of states in terms of deciding who should be regulated and how it should be accomplished.[5]

In 1977, the HEW issued a report entitled *"Credentialing Health Manpower"* which urged the adoption of national standards to be developed jointly by states and professions with limited involvement by the federal government. In fact, the following position was taken by HEW.

It is important to emphasize that the development and adoption of national standards should not be confused with federal licensure. Licensure is presently, and will continue to be, a function of state government. (p. 11)

Various publications by the Office of the Inspector General, Department of Health and Human Services during the late 1980s continued to emphasize that licensure is a function of states, yet federal actions seem to convey a different attitude. It is beginning to appear that the states' *traditional* responsibility for the

---

[5]There are a number of professions regulated at the federal level (airline pilots or coast guard masters), but the regulation of these individuals has been retained by various federal agencies and states have not been told to assume responsibility for the professions.

licensure and regulation of professions is being slowly eroded by the intrusion of federal action.

Although it is true that some action taken by the federal government has improved states' regulatory efforts, this has not always been the case. In a number of instances, regulatory actions taken by the federal government appear to have been predicated on monetary issues (third party payments; Medicare or Medicaid funding) rather than on the need for better public protection or improvements in the quality of service delivered.

Perhaps part of the reason for increased federal involvement is that they perceive states as not meeting the needs of the public. Often the laws of politics resemble the laws of physics. If a vacuum exists, something or someone will intervene to fill the void. The federal government's apparent perception that states are unable to enact or enforce essential regulatory programs, whether due to insufficient resources, insufficient collaborative efforts, or a lack of will on the part of states, has fostered increased federal involvement in regulatory activities (Schmitt, 1989, p.33). The Congress may perceive that they are being responsive to their constituents by instituting regulatory mandates on states. But is the public demanding the regulation or are lobbyists for various organizations starting to apply pressure on congressmen in the same way they have been applying pressure on state legislators?

In terms of federal legislation, several major laws have been enacted that have created a financial and staffing burden on states. One of these laws, the *Omnibus Budget Reconciliation Act of 1987* mandates that states evaluate the competence of nurse aides employed by nursing homes, establish mandatory training, maintain a register of those who pass the required examination, establish a mechanism for handling complaints, and restrict practice if aides are found guilty of abuse, neglect, or theft.

The actual implementation date of this requirement was pushed back on several occasions because the federal government failed to recognize fully the impact the law would have on states. When the legislation was initially enacted, it created a frenzy of activity and innumerable headaches as states attempted to implement overly vague or overly specific requirements. The language included in this Act exemplifies the concept of micro–management. The Act specified the state agency to regulate nurse aides (at least 11 states fought this requirement and won) and placed a prohibition on states from collecting any registration fees from nurse aides. Although the legislation provided no assurance that the quality of care would be raised, it did raise the costs incurred by nursing homes and subsequently by patients.

It is interesting to note that once an individual's name is placed on the register, there is no requirement to remove the nurse aide's name following disciplinary action. An aide found guilty of abuse, neglect, or theft of a resident's property can, however, never work in a facility receiving Medicare or Medicaid funds. Thus, the aide remains registered, but cannot work. Another unique aspect of the legislation is that nurse aides who work in hospitals are not required to be registered. Many hospitals have, however, established their own requirement that an aide must be registered before being hired. Nurse aides who work in home health care organizations are not required by the federal government to be registered, but they are required to have the same training and pass the same competency evaluation required of aides who must be registered.

Two companion legislative acts, the *Health Care Quality Improvement Act of 1986* and the *Medicare and Medicaid Patient and Program Protection Act of 1987*, were intended to initiate and then expand upon a National Practitioner Data Bank (NPDB). The concept behind the creation of a data bank was excellent; the manner in which the data bank was implemented was less than what many had hoped for. The first set of proposals to administer the data bank, submitted in 1987, were all rejected because there was no appropriation of funds for the NPDB. The contract was bid twice due, in part, to the funding problems. Multiple delays were necessary before the NPDB was finally implemented on September 1, 1990. Initially, only medical doctors and dentists were to be included in the bank; then legislation was created so that most health care providers would be included; then a decision was made that funding was unavailable for such a massive project. Presently, the data bank contains information only on medical doctors and dentists.

Since the NPDB was made active in 1990, there have been continual complaints about the manner in which information is obtained, the cost of retrieving information, the threat to privacy and due process, as well as the lack of accessibility of information to the public. It should be noted that the NPDB contains a report on *any* payment made in response to a claim by a patient which is causing considerable controversy about the data bank. In fact, during the 1993 meeting of the American Medical Association, members voted to seek the abolition of the NPDB. As part of his health care reform initiatives, President Clinton has, however, called for public access to the bank regarding practitioners with repeated reports.

The 1989 Savings and Loan Bailout Bill included a section mandating that states license two different classes of real estate appraisers. The argument for incorporating this requirement was that poorly trained and unqualified appraisers were partially to blame for the Savings and Loan fiasco. States had to have a licensure mechanism in place by July 1, 1991 (subsequently delayed for 6 months). The oversight responsibility for this mandate was given to The Appraisal Foundation, a non–governmental, national appraisal organization. The licensing requirements (education and experience) were dictated to the states and any examination used not only had to adhere to the required test specifications (not based on generally accepted testing standards), but also had to be approved by a private testing organization selected by the Appraisal Foundation. New classifications of appraisers and expanded requirements for initial and continuing licensure, with which states will have to comply, are currently being proposed by the Foundation. According to a September 10, 1993 proposal to revise the appraiser qualifications criteria, the justification cited for these changes is the need to *elevate* appraisers and appraisals to a professional level. The suggested revisions appear to be based on professional need rather than public need.

The Americans With Disabilities Act (ADA) of 1990 has also affected the manner in which state regulatory agencies function. The ADA requires that facilities used by agencies be able to accommodate the disabled, that all documents prepared by agencies include a telecommunication device for the deaf (TDD) phone number, that policies and procedures relating to accommodations for the disabled be developed, and that test administration accommodations be made available. In the latter instance, most states, particularly those with centralized testing divisions, were providing necessary accommodations prior to the enactment of the ADA.

The requirements of this Act are, in general, reasonable and accommodations should certainly be made so that disabled individuals are not discriminated against. A number of extensive technical manuals have also been prepared to assist states in their efforts to comply. Nevertheless, there is still considerable confusion as to what is a "reasonable" accommodation versus too little or too much.

Testing personnel, at the state level and with national testing companies, concur that many of the questions they have raised will be answered in court rather than by the Department of Justice. No one at the federal level has been able to answer questions such as "at what point do reasonable accommodations change the validity of an exam?" or "how much latitude do testing agencies have in trying to provide reasonable accommodations for a candidate?" As an example of the lack of assistance provided, a letter requesting clarification as to whether Michigan would be required to waive one section of a validated practical examination (as requested by a candidate) was sent to the Department of Justice in December, 1992. Several years later, the only response was a letter acknowledging receipt of the initial inquiry.

In addition to Congress mandating that states regulate certain professions or report disciplinary action to a central data bank, other federal agencies have become more actively involved in state regulation. The Federal Trade Commission (FTC) has investigated the laws and rules of a number of professions to determine whether they promote an anti–competitive environment. Based on the FTC's recommendations, several professions, either at the state level or nationally, have revised their policies. Although many of the FTC recommendations have been challenged by the respective professions, the eventual implementation of these recommendations has been beneficial to the public.

During the latter half of the 1980s, the Office of Inspector General, Department of Health and Human Services, evaluated the licensure and disciplinary activities related to five or six health professions. The recommendations offered could have been more beneficial had there been different, specific recommendations for each of the professions. Instead, the primary recommendations were the same across all of the reviews.

Future regulatory actions by the federal government are certain to occur. For example, the United States and Canada Free Trade Agreement, as well as the North American Free Trade Agreement, will undoubtedly have a direct impact on the operation of regulatory agencies. If enacted, the health care reform measures proposed by various individuals may also have a significant, yet unknown, impact on regulation.

It appears clear that the federal government, either through Congress or federal agencies, will continue to oversee the operations of states in terms of their regulatory functions. In some instances, this oversight may prove beneficial; in other instances, it may only create additional work for states without producing demonstrable benefits to citizens.

Future of Licensure

Even though state regulatory efforts may not be optimal and many criticisms about regulatory inefficiency are justified, major improvements have been made in the regulatory arena during the last decade. Boards are no longer composed solely of licensees; legislators are taking a more critical look at the reasons why various groups want regulation; barriers to practitioner mobility are being eliminated; communication among states is being enhanced; unnecessary regulation and requirements are being eliminated; examinations are becoming more valid, reliable, and relevant to practice; and enforcement efforts are being improved. Even with all of these enhancements and improvements, additional changes must take place if licensure and regulation is to better serve and protect the public.

Continuing efforts must be made to clearly and concisely convey to legislators the meaning of and purpose for licensure and other forms of regulation, in order for the haphazard proliferation of occupational and professional regulation to stop. This does not mean that no new regulation should be enacted or that a total deregulation of the 1,000 or so professions should occur. Rather, better communication among all interested parties—legislators, regulators, professions, and the public—should occur so that essential regulation is maintained or enacted and unessential regulation is eliminated or not enacted.

Purpose of licensure. One of the first steps that should be taken is redefining the purpose for licensure. The current justification of "protection of the health, safety and welfare of the public" should be revised so that fewer occupations and professions can claim that they need licensure to accomplish this nebulous goal. A better goal of licensure might be the "protection of the public from *imminent* or *significant* threat or harm economically, physically or psychologically." Although the basic premise for licensure still exists, the intent is more clearly defined.

Legislative evaluations. All state legislatures, and even Congress, need to become more active in their scrutiny of professions that wish to achieve licensure status. Although each and every legislator wants to be viewed favorably by constituents, lawmakers are going to have to make some difficult decisions that, in turn, may anger professional organizations.

The concept of Sunrise, either formal or informal, must be expanded to all states. The prelegislative review procedure must become more critical of the underlying reasons why occupations and professions desire regulation. The questions posed earlier in the chapter, as well as the following guidelines, must be incorporated into the decision–making process in order for legislators to make accurate evaluations of the need for additional regulation.

1. Regulation should meet a public need.
2. Government should provide only the minimum level of regulation.
3. If an occupation is to be licensed, its scope of practice should be coordinated with existing statutes to avoid fragmentation and inefficiency in the delivery of services.

4. Requirements and evaluation procedures for licensure should be clearly related to safe and effective practice.
5. Every out–of–state licensee or applicant should have fair and reasonable access to the credentialing process.
6. Once granted, a credential should remain valid only for that period during which the holder can provide evidence of continued competency.
7. Complaints should be investigated and resolved in a manner that is satisfactory and credible to the public.
8. The public should be involved in the regulatory process.
9. The regulatory structure should promote accountability and public confidence. (Shimberg & Roederer, 1994, pp. 3–19)

Additionally, consideration must be given to the length of time between each Sunset review. Currently, many reviews are conducted every 5 to 10 years. Although this time frame may be appropriate for some agencies, less standardization in the timing of reviews may be necessary. Agencies that are newly created or that have frequent changes in their laws, rules and practices may need to be reviewed more often than every 5 years. On the other hand, old established smoothly working agencies may need to be reviewed less often than every 10 years.

Restructuring of current laws. Greater attention must also be focused on those occupations and professions currently licensed. Again, formal or informal Sunset reviews need to occur on a periodic basis. If the profession no longer needs to be regulated, deregulation should occur. If changes are needed to the profession's law and rules, these changes should be made. If administrative improvements are necessary, they should be incorporated.

Situations such as the following should not be allowed to continue. A 1943 Michigan law, as amended, stipulates that horologists (watch makers) must be registered. In the early 1980s, consensus was reached by the profession and the regulatory agency that this law was no longer necessary. During the past 10 years, no entrance examinations have been given, no licensure applications have been distributed or filed, no disciplinary action has been taken, no board meetings have been held, and no list of registrants has been maintained. In essence, the regulation of horologists in Michigan has ceased *except* for one small problem—the law still exists. In fact, amendments were made to it in 1989 as part of a series of amendments made to other sections of the Occupational Code. Even though there is total agreement on the deregulation of horologists, legislators have not eliminated the requirement from the statutes! Should situations such as this continue to occur, the public may begin to view all forms of regulation as nothing more than a joke.

Entrance requirements. Legislators must also focus on the profession's entrance requirements included in new or existing regulation. Licensure is intended to ensure that individuals entering a profession possess the *minimally acceptable* level of knowledge, skills, and abilities necessary to protect the public. It is not the purpose of state government to impose stringent requirements so that only the best can obtain licensure or that only a limited number of individuals can become licensed.

Obviously, professions want their members to be viewed as competent and able to provide quality service, but this does not mean that unrealistic entrance requirements should be implemented. One of the legislators at the 1975 workshops conducted by Shimberg expressed this problem quite succinctly:

> I see this all the time. Every year they [licensing board members] come back to raise them [entrance requirements]. I'm not saying the minimum today should be the minimum 50 years from now, but every year they want something more stringent. (Shimberg, 1976, p. 38)

Regulatory boards and agencies must assume a greater responsibility for the development and administration of their examinations. Whether examinations are developed by a board or a central testing agency within state government, or developed by a private testing company, boards are ultimately responsible for the validity and reliability of their examinations. Board members must become knowledgeable about proper testing practices and must devote sufficient time to be certain the examination used to measure competence meets required psychometric standards. Too often boards transfer their authority to an outside testing organization and therefore "assume" the examinations are appropriate. This attitude must change if examinations are to truly measure a candidate's competency.

Training. Newly appointed board members, both professional and public, must receive adequate training so that they know what is expected of them. They need to recognize that their function on a board is to make decisions that will be of benefit to the public and not just to the profession. This includes an understanding of the level of appropriate entrance requirements as well as appropriate disciplinary action. Both independent boards and central agencies need to devote sufficient funds and time to accomplish the necessary training of new members as well as periodic retraining of current board members.

Continuing competency. In addition to more closely scrutinizing the entrance requirements, greater concern for continuing competency must occur. Reliance on continuing education to ensure competency should be replaced with more accurate periodic assessments of an individual's competence after initial licensure. Certifying agencies are presently implementing continuing competency requirements for their members and, therefore, may be doing a better job of ensuring continuing competency than are the states. Peer reviews, enhanced course evaluations of knowledge obtained, follow–up evaluations of course participants, practice audits, and even periodic, comprehensive examinations should be required in order for practitioners to retain their license or certification.

There is no question that because of the rapidly changing environment, expansion of new technologies, enhancement of procedures, and the ever–increasing body of knowledge that must be maintained, there is a need for individuals to continually learn. This is true for both the health and nonhealth professions. It is also true that technological changes in some professions are more rapid than in other professions. Accordingly, the format required for continued competency in some professions may be more stringent or require more frequent assessment than would be required in other professions. Continued competency assessment should not be mandated just because it sounds like a good thing to do. (Presently, continuing education for some occupations has been instituted just because other occupations have required it and without any other justification.)

Sitting in a classroom for one or more hours does not, however, guarantee learning; it only guarantees attendance. If specific hours of continuing education remain a condition for license renewal, the education must become more than just a classroom experience. Continuing education must evolve into a system that ensures a person has mastered, over the short and long term, the necessary knowledge, skills, and abilities to maintain competence.

Mobility. States must initiate better procedures for ensuring that the incompetent practitioner is unable to cross state lines in an attempt to escape discipline, while at the same time eliminate the unnecessary barriers that restrict the competent practitioner from moving from state to state. Greater communication among the states as well as viable, effective disciplinary data bases are needed. States should license an individual only after obtaining conclusive evidence that no disciplinary action has been taken or is pending against that individual in other states.

States should review their entrance requirements for individuals who have been licensed in another state and eliminate arbitrary barriers that are unrelated to legitimate consumer protection. States need to focus on the competency of the licensee, not on historical minutia. Is it really necessary for an individual who has been in practice for 10 years and who has had no disciplinary action taken to be required to pass an initial licensure examination? Does it really matter if a competent licensee received only 3 hours credit in a particular subject rather than 4 hours?

At the same time, states should avoid the concept of "I'll license all of your licensees, if you license all of my licensees." Reciprocity, in the strictest sense, does not really provide for easy mobility of competent individuals. Endorsement, on the other hand, permits a state to evaluate whether the initial licensure requirements in another state were *substantially*, not exactly, equivalent to its requirements. To further aid in the mobility of licensees, states should work together to establish standards (educational, experiential, examinations and continuing competency) that would be acceptable to ensure competency. Once standards were obtained, there would be more freedom for licensees to practice in different states and not be restricted in where they can work.

As a result of an agreement among the European Economic Community, licensed professionals are now able to practice freely in any of the member countries. Language competency is not required as a condition for reciprocity. The member countries have agreed that meeting the requirements for licensure in one country is sufficient for practice in any of the others. If the various countries in Europe can reduce the barriers across countries and diverse cultures, shouldn't it be possible to reduce barriers across states?

The Free–Trade Agreement between Canada and the United States has caused a number of the national associations of professional boards to re–examine some of the restrictions placed on licensees who may be interested in practicing in the other country. Both countries are beginning to assess their individual national licensure examinations to determine what differences, if any, exist and whether such differences are significant. With the enactment of the North American Free Trade Agreement (NAFTA), states are required to eliminate questionable restrictions placed on licensees from Canada as well as Mexico who may wish to practice in the United States and vice versus.

Alternative forms of recognition. One potential change is that government would no longer regulate individuals per se, but rather would regulate the specific tasks performed. This concept has already been explored in Ontario, Canada for a number of the health professions and legislation formalizing this concept was passed in 1991. The Ontario plan is based on the concept that, among the health professions, it is the performance of certain acts (i.e., improper manipulation of joints and muscles) that pose a threat to the public and accordingly it is those acts, rather than individuals, that should be licensed.

Professions want to be recognized as having achieved certain standards or qualifications. There may, however, be other methods to obtaining recognition rather than through licensure.

One idea being considered is the use of Trademarks. Legislation would require a profession to specify the title, letters, or insignias reserved for persons having the specified education, examination results, or work experience. Only those persons meeting the standards would be permitted to use the title, letters, or insignias. The specific criteria for recognition would be established by a national professional association, a national certifying agency, a multi certifying agency, or a state agency. There would be no provision for the evaluation of an individual's credentials, but rather, the individuals who held themselves out as a member of the profession would bear the responsibility for establishing, if a complaint was received, that they did indeed meet the criteria. Civil or criminal penalties would be included in the legislation for anyone who claimed to possess the education, examination, or experience when they did not.

A similar concept was proposed by the California Board of Medical Quality Assurance (McCready, 1982). Title licensure would permit anyone to perform health care, but people who wished to use a particular title in their practice would have to meet certain standards and would have to be licensed. Care providers would be "required to give prospective patients detailed information about their training, competencies and proposed treatments and to secure informed consent prior to treatment" (p. 75). Proponents of this form of recognition believe that it would introduce greater competition and more freedom of choice into health care. Critics claim that this would only create greater confusion for the public as they would be unable to make a "comparative study of health care alternatives" (p. 75).

A third option would be to concentrate more on the licensure of institutions rather than individuals, particularly in the health care arena. For instance, hospitals, nursing homes, or other facilities would be responsible for the regulation of individuals who have privileges in the facility. It would be the responsibility of the institution to establish standards for being admitted to practice in the institution as well as to remain with the institution. Objective, pre–established criteria would have to be applied uniformly if this option were to work. One negative aspect of institutional licensing is that not all licensees are associated with an institution and a separate system would still have to be established for these individuals. Another potential problem is that there have been antitrust cases against hospitals for refusing to grant privileges to licensed physicians. Delegating licensing authority to an institution may not necessarily change the darker side of the licensing culture.

Regulation of a single profession by a single board might need to be changed. A number of *super boards,* each of which regulated a number of similar professions, could be created. This might solve some of the problems associated with the ever increasing number of allied health professions. Rather than a separate board for each group, which is a significant cost to states, comparable professions would be licensed under a single law and be regulated by a single board. A concept initiated in Colorado is the creation of a Mental Health Grievance Board. The four licensed mental health professions (Psychology, Counselors, Social Workers, and Marriage and Family Therapists) each maintain their individual licensing boards, but the Grievance Board is responsible for all complaints and disciplinary actions associated with both licensed *and* unlicensed psychotherapists. The Grievance Board is composed of members from each of the licensed professions as well as the unlicensed psychotherapists.

As a result of the California Board of Medical Quality Assurance's 2–year study (1980–1981), the most extreme proposal for solving the plethora of regulation was deregulation of all health care practitioners. Proponents for this option state that the:

> existing regulatory system is not effective either at assuring initial or continuing competence of licensees or at protecting the public from incompetent or unethical practitioners. Furthermore, it is argued that licensure creates a governmentally sanctioned monopoly that inevitably increases the cost of health care by limiting access and freedom of choice. In a free market consumers can choose the kinds of care they want and the costs they are willing to pay. Mediocre care would be driven out by competition, and exceptional care would be appropriately rewarded. (McCready, 1982, p. 76)

Deregulation of many professions is certainly an option that should be considered and instituted, but whether it would ever be implemented for the entire health care system is dubious.

Enforcement. Not only must there be revisions to the methods of determining the need for regulation and ensuring initial competence, there must also be revisions to enforcement activities. If government is serious about the licensing of individuals, it must also be serious about its enforcement activities. Additional funding will have to be allocated by the legislature or fees from licensees will have to be increased in order to provide greater assurance to the public that regulation is truly intended for the protection of the public and not the profession.

If additional resources are not made available to state regulatory agencies, complaints by consumers will continue to not be investigated and pursued or will be investigated in an inefficient manner. Regardless of the state or profession, there is currently a large number of practitioners who should have been disciplined, but who continue to practice simply because there are too many cases for the agency to handle efficiently. Decisions have had to be made as to which complaints should be investigated immediately and which should be postponed or even ignored. If states are unable to take the appropriate disciplinary action, other organizations will have to assume the responsibility.

Institutions themselves will have to do a better job of policing their employees or practitioners. Insurance companies will need to enhance their role and more closely review the reasonableness of claims filed, the quality of services provided, as well as the frequency of complaints against certain individuals. Professional associations will need to become more aware of the quality of service provided by their members as well as the behaviors exhibited (i.e., impaired practitioners).

If the enforcement role of nongovernmental entities is expanded, it will necessitate better communication between the private sector and the regulatory agency. Currently, someone can be dismissed from a hospital or office for incompetence and the licensing agency is never informed. The licensee merely moves to another state, establishes practice, and continues to practice in an unprofessional or incompetent manner. Unless the regulatory agency is informed of this situation, nothing can be done to stop the individual. It is critical that organizations eliminate the notion that they must "keep their dirty linen hidden" if appropriate enforcement is to occur. Mandatory reporting laws may need to be enacted to reduce or eliminate protection of colleagues in the professions.

Another group that will need to assist government is the consumer. They need to become better educated about what they should expect from providers as well as the appropriate procedures for filing complaints. Consumers need to be less willing to accept poor quality and more willing to voice their concerns. In order to do this effectively, they need to receive clear, understandable, yet detailed information about practitioners' responsibilities and their rights. This information should be distributed by both the public and private sectors as well as by individual practitioners. States need to develop and institute creative, yet informative, procedures and methods to help consumers become more aware, informed, and active in the regulatory process.

Even if discipline is maintained by government, alternatives to formal administrative hearings will need to be instituted. Mediation and informal compliance conferences will need to become more prevalent. Another optional enforcement technique might be the issuance of tickets, similar to parking tickets. If violations are observed during an inspection, a ticket is issued and a fine assessed. Rather than requiring a formal hearing, the practitioner merely pays the fine. If the same or similar violations are repeated, it might then be necessary for an investigation and hearing.

By achieving a closer working relationship among regulatory agencies, the private sector, and consumers, the enforcement process will be enhanced. The incompetent or unethical practitioner will no longer be able to escape unnoticed.

Conclusion. Reaching consensus on how to best serve the public will be a major task facing states. The increased interest by the federal government in occupational and professional regulation will add to the states' financial and staffing problems. Given the pressures being placed upon states, it appears that they have two viable options:

develop a closer, more unified working relationship with each other or relinquish regulatory control to the federal government or the professions themselves. While consumers are requesting stronger regulatory control, others, including some of the professions, are suggesting that standards be relaxed or are discussing the concept of self–regulation. (Brinegar & Schmitt, 1992, p. 571)

Should self–regulation be granted, licensure would return to the way it was in the 17th and 18th centuries.

Whether the changes mentioned will actually occur is difficult to predict. One thing, however, is certain, and that is that change must and will occur. Legislators, regulators, members of professional organizations, those who are regulated as well as those seeking regulation, and consumers need to recognize and accept the impending change. As we approach the 21st century, everyone who has an interest in regulation must begin to recognize the positions of others. With a change in attitude, perhaps the various groups will no longer "rail on in utter ignorance of what each other mean, and prate about an Elephant not one of them has seen."

B.F. Skinner, a noted psychologist, once said that if people don't change, they become prisoners of their own experience. Reliance on "we've always done it that way" will not enable improvements to be made in the future. Regulatory legislation may have flourished in the 1970s and 1980s, but will the trend continue into the 21st century? Will new and improved methods of regulation emerge? Will the critics be heard and changes made? Only time will tell.

REFERENCES

Blair, R. D., & Rubin, S. (Eds.). (1980). *Regulating the professions: A public–policy symposium.* Lexington, MA: D.C. Heath.

Brinegar, P. (Ed.) (1990). *Occupational and professional regulation in the states: A comprehensive compilation.* Lexington, KY: The National Clearinghouse on Licensure, Enforcement and Regulation.

Brinegar, P. L., & Schmitt, K. L. (1992). State occupational and professional licensure. Deborah A. Gona (Ed.) *The book of the states* (pp. 567–580). Lexington, KY: The Council of State Governments.

Credentialing health manpower. (1977). Washington, DC: Department of Health, Education and Welfare.

Douglas, B. (1988, August). *Sunrise/Sunset: Can it work? Does it work?* Paper presented at the meeting of the National Council of Engineering Examiners and Surveyors, Albuquerque, NM.

Friedman, M. (1962). *Capitalism and freedom.* Chicago: University of Chicago Press.

Gardner, J. W. (1961). *Excellence: Can we be equal and excellent too?* New York: Harper and Brothers.

Gross, S. J. (1984). *Of foxes and hen houses.* Westport, CT: Quorum Books.

Guralnik, D. B. (Ed.). (1976) *Webster's new world dictionary of the American language.* Cleveland: William Collins & World Publishing.

Hogan, D. B. (1979). *The regulation of psychotherapists, Volume I.* Cambridge, MA: Ballinger Publishing Company.

Kearney, R. C. (1990, January/February). Sunset: A survey and analysis of the state experience. *Public administration review*, *50*(1), 49–57.

McCready, L. A. (1982, Fall). Emerging health care occupations: The system under siege. *Health Care Management Review*, 71–76.

Parsons, M. B. (1952). *The use of the licensing power by the city of Chicago*. Urbana, IL: University of Illinois Press.

Paxton, A. (Ed.). (1993, April/May). Dental association makes "euthanasia" pact to kill Texas board. *Professional licensing report*, 3.

Paxton, A. (Ed.). (1993, April/May). Special Report: Sunset in Texas. *Professional licensing report*, 4–8.

Rogers, C. (1973, May). Some new challenges. *The American Psychologist*, *28*(5), 379–387.

Saxe, J. G. (1949). The blind men and the elephant. In *Childcraft, Vol. 2*, 122–123, Chicago: Field Enterprises.

Schmitt, K. L. (1989, Summer). Licensing and regulation: States v. the federal government. *Intergovernmental perspective*, *15*(3), 33–35.

Shimberg, B. (1976). *Improving occupational regulation*. Princeton, NJ: Educational Testing Service.

Shimberg, B. (1991). *Regulation in the public interest: Myth or reality?* (Resource Briefs, 91–1). Lexington: The Council on Licensure, Enforcement and Regulation.

Shimberg, B., & Roederer, D. (1994). *Questions a legislator should ask*. Kara Schmitt (Ed.). Lexington, KY: The Council of State Governments.

Shryock, R. H. (1967). *Medical licensing in America, 1650–1965*. Baltimore, MD: The Johns Hopkins Press.

The Council of State Governments. *Occupational licensing legislation in the states*. (1952). Chicago: The Council of State Governments.

The Council of State Governments. *Occupational and professional licensing by the states, Puerto Rico, and the Virgin Islands*. (1968). Lexington, KY: The Council of State Governments.

Young, S. D. (1987). *The rule of experts*. Washington, DC: Cato Institute.

LEGAL AND PROFESSIONAL BASES FOR LICENSURE TESTING

William A. Mehrens

Michigan State University

In this chapter the author presents the legal setting for licensure testing,[1] discusses the role of various professional standards and codes (i.e., the EEOC *Uniform Guidelines*, 1978, and the AERA/APA/NCME *Standards*, 1985), presents some of the pertinent rulings from several court decisions, and makes inferences about future changes in professional standards and their potential impact on licensure test development.

There necessarily is some minor overlap with the material in this chapter and some other chapters in this book. There is a brief discussion of the differences between licensure, certification. and employment testing and how those differences relate to the professional standards and court cases. It is necessary to mention some concepts such as task analysis, validity, and cut scores when discussing the professional standards and the court cases. However, these concepts are not dealt with in the depth that occurs in later chapters.

THE LEGAL SETTING

Licensure and certification tests are high-stakes tests and those considering using or constructing such tests should be aware of previous case law regarding

Portions of this chapter have been adapted from an article by Mehrens, W.A. and Popham, W.J. (1992). How to evaluate the legal defensibility of high-stakes tests. *Applied Measurement in Education, 5*(3), 265-283. Permission of the publisher and Dr. Popham to use those portions has been obtained. Special appreciation is given to Dr. Kara Schmitt and Susan Boston for their assistance in tracking down many of the legal documents used in writing this chapter.

[1]The words "test" and "testing" are to be interpreted broadly as including a variety of assessment procedures.

such testing. Some generic legal issues are discussed first. In subsequent sections, the various professional standards and some court decisions are presented.

Generic Legal Issues

Existing case law is based on constitutional requirements—primarily the 14th Amendment—and statutory requirements—primarily Title VII of the 1964 Civil Rights Act.

Constitutional Requirements: The 14th Amendment

Two basic requirements of the U.S. Constitution's 14th Amendment are discussed: equal protection and due process. For a plaintiff to win under the equal protection analysis, it must be shown that there was intent to discriminate. In *Village of Arlington Heights v. Metropolitan Housing Development Corp.* (1977), the court stated that the following factors could be considered in establishing discriminatory intent: (a) historical background, (b) the specific sequence of events leading up to the challenged decision, (c) departures from normal procedural sequences, and (d) the legislative or administrative history. Nevertheless, to prove discriminatory intent, one court has ruled that it must be shown that the user of the test "selected or reaffirmed a particular course of action at least in part `because of' not merely `in spite of,' its adverse effects upon an identifiable group" (*Personnel Administrator v. Feeney*, 1979, at 4656). Another court has stated that:

> An action does not violate the equal protection clause simply because the decision maker knows that it will have a disparate impact on racial or ethnic groups. (*United States v. LULAC*, 1986, p. 646)

It is difficult to *prove* intent. As a consequence, most plaintiffs would prefer basing their cases on the Civil Rights Acts, which do not require proof of discriminatory motive.

The due process provisions of the Constitution relate to substantive and procedural due process. Substantive due process requires a legitimate relationship between a requirement and the purpose. This legitimate relationship is easier to establish than the business necessity requirement of the Civil Rights Acts. In fact, for licensure and certification challenges Herbsleb, Sales, and Overcast (1985) concluded that:

> the rationality standard is so lenient that we were unable to find a single case where an examination was successfully challenged on this basis. (p. 1169)

Procedural due process requires fairness in the way things are done. In testing cases, this means that there must be advance notice of the requirement, an opportunity for hearings/appeals, and that the hearings must be conducted fairly. A licensure or certification testing program should not be implemented without paying careful attention to these procedures. It should be pointed out that if a plaintiff wins on procedural grounds, he/she does not necessarily get a license. However, some additional procedure—such as a hearing—must be applied.

Statutory Requirements: The Civil Rights Acts

The 1964 Civil Rights Act was a general federal statute prohibiting discrimination in employment. When first enacted it pertained to employment in the private sector, but it was extended in 1972 to employment practices in educational institutions. The Civil Rights Act of 1991 was passed to reverse parts of several U.S. Supreme Court decisions that were unfavorable to employment complaints. There is some debate about whether licensure and certification procedures are to be considered employment practices and whether the Civil Rights Acts apply to such processes. This is discussed in more detail later.

The Acts prohibit two kinds of discrimination: disparate treatment and disparate impact. Disparate treatment involves overt discrimination—where employers treat some people less favorably than others because of their race, color, religion, or national origin. The plaintiff has the initial burden of establishing that disparate treatment occurred. Most case law related to the Civil Rights Acts regarding testing is based on disparate impact rather than disparate treatment.

Disparate impact does not require evidence of subjective discriminatory *intent*, but refers to employment practices that are ostensibly neutral in their treatment, yet result in protected groups being hired at a lower rate than unprotected groups. It is the plaintiff's responsibility to show disparate impact, but it is the responsibility of the user (e.g., employer or licensure board) to maintain documentation regarding disparate impact (see *Chance v. Board of Examiners*, 1971, 1972). The Civil Rights Act of 1991 states that the plaintiff must demonstrate that each *particular* challenged process (e.g., written test, subtest, oral exam, performance appraisal) causes a disparate impact unless the plaintiff can demonstrate that the decision-making elements cannot be analyzed separately. (This emphasis on each component may have implications for scoring procedures—should one use part scores or total scores—and conjunctive versus compensatory decision making.)

There exists some debate about what statistics to use and what groups should be considered in the statistical analysis to show disparate impact. Regarding the relevant groups, the general conclusion is that the proper comparison is between the proportions of the groups in the qualified population in the relevant job market (*Wards Cove Packing Co.*, 1989; Civil Rights Act of 1991). For the statistical analysis, the *Uniform Guidelines*[2] (EEOC, 1978) suggest a four-fifths rule. This means that the percent of protected group applicants hired should be at least 80% of the percent of unprotected group applicants hired. Others prefer a statistical inference test to discern if an observed disparity between protected and unprotected groups is statistically significant (e.g., Hazelwood, 1977). Because the issue of impact is not one of test construction and use, per se, we will not discuss it further. However, interested readers may wish to consult the literature concerning this issue (see, e.g., Meier, Sacks, & Zabell, 1984).

In cases where there has been a showing of disparate impact on members of a protected group for a particular employment practice, the burden of proof shifts to the defendants and requires them to demonstrate that the use of the test (or other assessment procedure) constitutes a *business necessity*. (Employers do not need to defend those parts of the process that do not show disparate impact.) This means that the particular challenged tests (or subtests) must be shown to be job-related and

---

[2]The *Guidelines* is a single work. However, for smoothness in reading it will be treated as a plural noun.

to have been professionally developed. If a test is job-related and professionally developed, it can be used even if there is disparate impact unless the plaintiffs can show that there exists an equally effective alternative selection procedure that results in less adverse impact. Although there were some Supreme Court decisions in 1988 and 1989 that lessened the burden of proof of the defendants to show business necessity, the 1991 Civil Rights Act reestablished this requirement.

Title VII and Employment, Licensure, and Certification Testing

As discussed in the previous chapter, the purposes of licensure and certification tests are different from the purpose of employment tests. The function of licensure is to protect the health, safety, and welfare of the public. There is some debate about whether Title VII of the Civil Rights Act applies to licensure tests. Some attorneys (e.g., Phillips, 1991; Pyburn, 1990; Rebell, 1986) have suggested that Title VII does not apply to state licensing agencies and their tests. Rulings in bar examination cases such as *Tyler v. Vickery* (1975, 1976) and *Woodward v. Virginia Board of Bar Examiners* (1976, 1979) support this position. For example, one court stated that:

> Title VII does not apply by its terms...because the Georgia Board of Bar Examiners is neither an "employer," an "employment agency," nor a "labor organization" within the meaning of the statute. (*Tyler v. Vickery*, 1976, p. 1096)

Smith and Hambleton (1990) concluded that:

> Most courts have been unwilling to extend Title VII...to licensure examinations. (p. 8)

Shimberg (1990) reached the same conclusion.Others believe that at least for teacher licensure, the State can be viewed as an employer (see Kuehn, Stallings, & Holland, 1990). Freeman, Hess, and Kasik (1985) discuss why teacher licensure may be unique. They suggest that:

> the history of certification in most states indicates that certification has been intimately interwoven in the employment process. (p. 14)

They argue further that:

> Teaching as a profession is somewhat peculiar because teachers are certified or licensed to work exclusively in institutions that are created, maintained, and more or less financed by the state. (p. 23)

The above quote is not precisely true because many private school, parochial school, and home school teachers are licensed. Nevertheless, some courts may view it as a relevant argument.

Based, in part, upon the number of teacher certification test cases *filed* under Title VII, and the number of employment testing cases *cited as relevant* precedent in teacher certification test litigation, Kuehn, Stallings, and Holland (1990) believe Title VII does apply to *teacher* licensure. They suggest that:

> If the Courts treat teacher certification tests as employee selection procedures, we are compelled to construct them and defend them as employee selection procedures. (p. 21)

The problem with the above quote is that it is widely recognized that licensure tests serve different purposes from employment tests and this *should* result in different test construction and validation procedures. One difference is that a person is employed to do a specific job whereas a license allows the person to engage in *diverse* jobs. Freeman et al. recognized this problem and concluded that:

> examining certification requirements to determine their job-relatedness becomes an almost hopeless task. (1985, p. 25)

The EEOC *Uniform Guidelines* address this whole issue, but the statements are not decisive. The *Guidelines* state that "licensing and certification are covered 'to the extent' that licensing and certification may be covered by Federal equal employment opportunity law" (Equal Employment Opportunity Commission [EEOC], 1978, p. 38294). They further state that:

> Voluntary certification boards, where certification is not required by law, are not users ... with respect to their certifying functions and therefore are not subject to these guidelines. If an employer relies upon such certification in making employment decisions, the employer is the user and must be prepared to justify, under Federal law, that reliance as it would any other selection procedure. (1978, p. 38294)

Thus, if an employer used the results of a certification test for promotion, or a differential salary, it would be used as an employment exam and be subject to Title VII. For example, consider the proposed certification tests of the National Board of Professional Teaching Standards. These are intended to be voluntary in the sense that licensed teachers will not have to take them to maintain their licenses. However, if a state or local district chose to reward certified teachers with additional salary, that may be considered an employment decision and the Civil Rights Acts (Title VII) might apply. But it would apply to the state or local unit that uses the test for decision making.

The issue of the relevance of Title VII to licensure and certification tests is important because Title VII calls for a business necessity requirement, which is considered harder to demonstrate than the legitimate relationship requirement that would otherwise apply to licensure tests. Because there is some disagreement about whether (or under what circumstances) licensure and certification testing programs are subject to the Civil Rights Acts requirements, this chapter discusses guidelines for both types of settings. This author's view is that most licensure and certification testing programs should *not* be ruled as employment programs, but others, used in different fashions, might be.

PROFESSIONAL STANDARDS AND CODES

There are several sets of professional standards and codes that should be considered when constructing a licensure or certification examination. The two major ones are the *Standards for Educational and Psychological Testing* (American Educational Research Association, American Psychological Association, & National Council on Measurement in Education [AERA/APA/NCME], 1985), hereafter referred to as the *Standards*; and the *Uniform Guidelines on Employee Selection Procedures* (EEOC, 1978), hereafter referred to as the *Guidelines*.

Prior to discussing these standards and codes, it should be emphasized that both the *Standards* and the *Guidelines* are somewhat dated. Both documents explicitly recognize that they need to be interpreted keeping this datedness factor in mind. The *Standards*[3] note that they are concerned "with a field that is evolving" (AERA/APA/NCME, 1985, p. 2) and the *Guidelines* point out that "they will have to be interpreted in light of changing factual, legal, and professional circumstances" (EEOC, 1978, p. 38292). In a later section, current psychometric views and potential future directions in the field and how they may impact legal issues and future revisions of the *Standards* and *Guidelines* are discussed.

AERA/APA/NCME Standards

The 1985 *Standards* constitute the fifth in a series of documents from the three sponsoring organizations regarding the development and use of tests and they supersede the previous documents.

> In general, the *Standards* advocates that, within feasible limits, the necessary technical information be made available so that those involved in policy debate may be fully informed. The *Standards* does not attempt to provide psychometric answers to policy questions. (AERA/APA/NCME, 1985, p. 1)

The *Standards* are divided into four parts. Part I covers technical standards for test construction and evaluation. Included in this part are chapters on such topics as validity, reliability, and norming, score comparability, and equating. Part II covers standards for test use. The chapter on licensure and certification testing is of major importance to readers of this volume although the chapter on employment testing is mentioned. Part III covers standards for particular applications and the chapter on testing the disabled is particularly important. Finally, Part IV presents standards for administrative procedures.

The *Standards* point out that their use in litigation is inevitable, but that "professional judgment ... always plays an essential role in determining the relevance of particular standards in particular situations" (AERA/APA/NCME, 1985, p. 2). Further, it is stressed that:

> evaluating the acceptability of a test or test application does not rest on the literal satisfaction of every primary standard in this document, and acceptability cannot be determined by using a checklist. (AERA/APA/NCME, 1985, p. 2)

Although the *Standards* represent an "official" guideline to be judgmentally followed, it should be recognized that there is less than consensus in the psychometric community about various components of the *Standards*. For example, regarding the concept of test validity, Linn, comments on the Joint Committee's attempt

> to carry this unified view of validity a bit further, but not, I might add, without significant objection from a number of people. ... A number of reviewers considered such a requirement to be overly demanding. (Linn, 1984, p. 4)

Shimberg has stated that the writers of the *Standards* did not obtain consensus "among all those who prepare and use licensing and certification tests

---

[3]The *Standards*, like the *Guidelines*, is a single work. However, for smoothness in reading it also will be treated as a plural noun.

regarding what constitutes acceptable professional practice in these areas" (1990, p. 13).

In spite of the above comments, the *Standards* are (correctly in my opinion) used as a guide in the development of a licensure or certification test, and one should try to follow the *relevant* standards. The subsections that follow discuss some of the most pertinent standards from various chapters of the *Standards*.

Validity Standards

The validity chapter of the *Standards* states that "validity is the most important consideration in test evaluation" (AERA/APA/NCME, 1985, p. 9) and presents 25 different standards regarding validity.

Certainly many of the standards in this chapter are relevant. However, it is clear that not even all of these are relevant for any given test development/use project. For example, in the validity chapter, Standard 1.1 states that "evidence of validity should be presented for the major types of inferences for which the use of a test is recommended" (AERA/APA/NCME, 1985, p. 13). By implication, and by the comment following the standard, it is obvious that one would not have to gather all the types of validity evidences that are addressed in the *Standards* for any particular use. The separate chapters in Part II on various uses of tests make that clear also.

Validity is a technical area where the field has changed its nomenclature, if indeed not its approach. The *Standards* state that validity

> refers to the appropriateness, meaningfulness, and usefulness of the specific inferences made from test scores. Test validation is the process of accumulating evidence to support such inferences. (AERA/APA/NCME, 1985, p. 9)

Although, as the *Standards* point out, validity is a unitary concept, evidence may be accumulated in many ways and psychometricians have traditionally categorized the various ways into content-related, criterion-related, and construct-related evidence of validity although "rigorous distinctions between the categories are not possible" (p. 9). As the *Standards* suggest:

> evidence identified usually with the criterion-related or content-related categories ... is relevant also to the construct-related category. (AERA/APA/NCME, 1985, p.9)

Because content-related validity evidence is likely to be one type of validity evidence that will be gathered, it seems important to consider the validity standards that relate particularly to content-related evidence. Standard 1.3 relates indirectly and Standard 1.6 directly to content-related evidence.

> Standard 1.3: Whenever interpretation of subscores, score differences, or profiles is suggested, the evidence justifying such interpretation should be made explicit. Where composite scores are developed, the basis and rationale for weighting the subscores should be given. (Primary) (AERA/APA/NCME, 1985, p. 14).

> Standard 1.6: When content-related evidence serves as a significant demonstration of validity for a particular test use, a clear definition of the universe represented, its relevance to the proposed test use, and the procedures followed in generating

test content to represent that universe should be described. When the content sampling is intended to reflect criticality rather than representativeness, the rationale for the relative emphasis given to critical factors in the universe should also be described carefully. (Primary) (AERA/APA/NCME, 1985, p. 14)

The last sentence in the above quoted standard is particularly important because, as will become more clear when discussing Chapter 11 of the *Standards*, one often wishes for a critical rather than representative domain in licensure testing.

Reliability Standards

The reliability chapter of the *Standards* presents 12 different standards. Some of the more important reliability standards that should be attended to are as follows:

Standard 2.1: For each total score, subscore, or combination of scores that is reported, estimates of relevant reliabilities and standard errors of measurement should be provided... (Primary) (p. 20)

Standard 2.10: Standard errors of measurement should be reported at critical score levels. Where cut scores are specified for selection or classification, the standard errors of measurement should be reported for score levels at or near the cut score. (Secondary) (p. 22)

Standard 2.12: For dichotomous decisions, estimates should be provided of the percentage of test takers who are classified in the same way on two occasions or on alternate forms of the test. (Conditional) (AERA/APA/NCME, 1985, p. 23)

Test Development and Revision Standards

The chapter on test development and revision presents 25 different standards. The standards primarily relate to building a test in a correct fashion. The major overriding standard in this chapter is Standard 3.1, which states that "Tests and testing programs should be developed on a sound scientific basis" (p. 25). Standard 3.2 states that the definition of the universe or domain must be described. Many of the other standards in this chapter would also be appropriate for licensure and certification examinations.

Scaling, Norming, Score Comparability, and Equating Standards

It is certainly important that there be score comparability and equating of tests given at different times for licensure and certification exams, and the nine standards presented in this chapter relevant to those issues should be considered in test development. The standard most relevant for licensure tests is Standard 4.8 which speaks to the content and statistical requirements for anchor test items if an anchor test design is used for equating.

Setting the Cut Score

For licensure tests, the precision of the equating at the cut store is of primary importance. There is no chapter in the *Standards* directly related to this issue and the *Standards* do not make any recommendation regarding specific standard setting procedures. However, they do suggest that the method and rationale of setting the cut score, as well as the qualifications of the judges, should be documented (see *Standards* 6.9 and 10.9).

Standards Specific to Employment Testing

Chapter 10 of the *standards* is on employment testing. If a developer/user of a licensure or certification test believes that it will be regarded by the courts as an employment examination, then attention should be given to the standards in this chapter. As mentioned above, this author does *not* consider licensure tests to be employment tests, but some *uses* of *certification* tests (promotion, differential tasks or differential salaries based on the tests) may place them in that category. The major difference between the standards for employment testing and licensure and certification testing is that employment testing standards place more emphasis on criterion-related validity evidence.

Professional and Occupational Licensure and Certification Standards

Chapter 11 of the *Standards* focuses directly on professional and occupational licensure and certification examinations. As the *Standards* point out, "several hundred occupations are now regulated by state governments. Many other occupations are certified by nongovernmental agencies" (p. 63). The *Standards* discuss the different purposes of employment and licensure examinations already discussed in this book, and point out the implications of those differences for various issues of validity. For licensure and certification, the focus is on necessary skills and knowledge, whereas the employer may wish to maximize productivity. The *Standards* make clear that:

> Investigations of criterion-related validity are more problematic in the context of licensure or certification than in many employment settings. Not all those certified or licensed are necessarily hired; those hired are likely to be in a variety of job assignments with many different employers, and some may be self-employed. These factors often make traditional studies that gather criterion-related evidence of validity infeasible. ... For licensure and certification, ...primary reliance must usually be placed on content evidence..." (AERA/APA/NCME, 1985, p. 63)

Another distinction is that although an employment test typically should cover the totality of the knowledge, skills, and abilities desirable on the job, the content domain of a licensure test should be limited to the "knowledge and skills necessary to protect the public" (p. 64). Note that "abilities" was left out of this quote. Linn (1984) and Kane (1984) have made the same point. There is at least some legal precedent to suggest that a licensure examination need not evaluate the full range of skills desirable to practice a profession (Eisdorfer & Tractenberg, 1977, p. 119).

Although the *Standards* appropriately emphasize the importance of content-related validity evidence over criterion-related or construct validity evidence for licensure tests, builders or users of licensure tests should not think they "have it easy" in constructing licensure tests that meet the *Standards*. The requirements of content validity are quite explicit and demanding.

> Standard 11.1: The content domain to be covered by a licensure or certification test should be defined clearly and explained in terms of the importance of the content for competent performance in an occupation. A rationale should be

provided to support a claim that the knowledge or skills being assessed are required for competent performance in an occupation and are consistent with the purpose for which the licensing or certification program was instituted. (Primary) (AERA/APA/NCME, 1985, p. 64)

The comment for Standard 11.1 points out that "job analyses provide the primary basis for defining the content domain," that "the emphasis for licensure and certification is limited appropriately to knowledge and skills necessary to protect the public," and that "skills that may be important to success but are not directly related to the purpose of licensure (i.e., protecting the public) should not be included in a licensing exam" (AERA/APA/NCME, 1985, p. 64).

Two final standards from this chapter seem particularly relevant.

Standard 11.4: Test takers who fail a test should, upon request, be told their score and the minimum score required to pass the test. Test takers should be given information on their performance in parts of the test for which separate scores or reports are produced and used in the decision process. (Primary) (p. 65)

Standard 11.5: Rules and procedures used to combine scores or other assessments to determine the overall outcome should be reported to test takers preferably before the test is administered. (Secondary) (AERA/APA/NCME, 1985, p. 65)

The comment for Standard 11.5 points out that:

In some cases candidates may be required to score above a specified minimum on each of several tests. In other cases the pass-fail decision may be based solely on a total composite score. (AERA/APA/NCME, 1985, p. 65)

These last two standards and the comment for Standard 11.5 need to be considered along with Standard 2.1 quoted above. If the test is not unidimensional, the subscores provide potentially useful information for failing candidates who wish to direct their subsequent review and study to their areas of weakness. If these subscores are reported for remediation purposes and are not used in a conjunctive model but are simply used in a total composite score in a compensatory model, it is debatable whether the scores have been used "in the decision process." They have not been used in the licensure decision, but may be used by the failed candidate for remediation purposes. In writing specifically about teacher licensure examinations, Mehrens has suggested that:

Because subscores are not typically used in teacher licensure decisions they would not need to be reported. If they are reported they might be used as study guides by candidates who failed and thus it would be useful to report their reliabilities and standard errors. The reliabilities are frequently low and candidates should recognize their limitations as study guides. However, *it should be stressed that low subscore reliabilities are irrelevant in litigation regarding the legality of using the total score for licensure decisions* [emphasis added]. (1990, p. 85)

It seems reasonable to generalize from this point to any licensure examination use where the decision is based on a total composite score. One final point deserves emphasis. The quoted comment accompanying Standard 11.5 suggests that it is appropriate to base pass-fail decision "solely on a total composite score." Although this author agrees with that position, a common statement heard from expert witnesses for plaintiffs is that one should not make a decision on only a single piece of data. Obviously, that stated opinion ignores the fact that there was probably a sequential decision-making model employed requiring other acceptable data on additional variables prior to being allowed to sit for the licensure examination, and it ignores this specific standard that specifically accepts making a decision solely on a composite score.

Standards on Testing Individuals with Disabilities

Chapter 14 of the *Standards* presents eight standards for testing individuals with disabilities. With the passing of the Americans with Disabilities Act (1990), which became effective in 1992, there has been much discussion regarding what accommodations need to be made for individuals with claimed disabilities. This issue has been considered in depth in other publications. For example, Millman, Mehrens, and Sackett address this issue for the New York Bar Examination in detail (1993). Clearly, there is some obligation to allow individuals with physical disabilities to be accommodated when the knowledge and skills needed for licensure are not the specific physical skills which are being accommodated. Probably the biggest areas of concern are with those who claim learning disabilities. These are hard to classify and most classification schemes result in a large number of false positives. Whether correctly or incorrectly classified, there is the issue of what is a fair accommodation for individuals with a cognitive disability when the job in question demands cognitive functioning. The largest specific issue probably relates to the amount of time extension that should be given to individuals with disabilities. If the job in question demands primarily physical skills, then it would be reasonable to grant accommodations to those with learning disabilities, but it may not be reasonable to grant them to those with physical disabilities.

Some of the major points made in the eight standards are as follows:

Standard 14.1: People who modify tests for handicapped people should have available to them psychometric expertise for so doing. (p. 79)

Standard 14.2: Until tests have been validated for people who have specific handicapping conditions, test publishers should issue cautionary statements in manuals and elsewhere regarding confidence in interpretations based on such test scores. (p. 79)

Standard 14.5: Empirical procedures should be used whenever possible to establish time limits for modified forms of timed tests rather than simply allowing handicapped test takers a multiple of the standard time. (p.79)

Standard 14.6: When feasible, the validity and reliability of tests administered to people with various handicapping conditions should be investigated and reported by the agency or publisher that makes the modification. (AERA/APA/NCME, 1985, p. 80)

EEOC Uniform Guidelines

The *Uniform Guidelines* (EEOC, 1978) are a set of guidelines on employee selection procedures that have been adopted by the Equal Employment Opportunity Commission, the Civil Service Commission, the Department of Justice, and the Department of Labor. In addition to being quite dated, there is, as has been mentioned, some debate about whether (or when) they might apply to licensure and certification exams. As is stated:

> These guidelines apply to tests and other selection procedures which are used as a basis for any employment decision. Employment decisions include but are not limited to hiring, promotion, demotion, membership (for example in a labor organization), referral, retention, and licensing and certification, to the extent that licensing and certification may be covered by Federal equal employment opportunity law. (EEOC, 1978, p. 38296)

They also state that:

> Voluntary certification boards, where certification is not required by law, are not users as defined...with respect to their certifying functions and therefore are not subject to these guidelines. If an employer relies upon such certification in making employment decisions, the employer is the user and must be prepared to justify, under Federal law, that reliance as it would any other selection procedure. (EEOC, 1978, p. 38294)

Whether or not the *Guidelines* apply in licensure, it is important to realize that they "have been given great weight by the courts in Equal Protection as well as Title VII cases" (Eisdorfer & Tractenberg, 1977, p. 121; see also, Rebell, 1990a, p. 347).

Under the *Guidelines*, to use a measure that produces adverse impact, the employer

> must justify the use of the procedure on grounds of 'business necessity.' This normally means that it must show a clear relation between performance on the selection procedure and performance on the job. (EEOC, 1978, p. 38291)

Although users need not validate procedures which do not have an adverse impact,

> if one way of using a procedure (e.g. ranking) results in greater adverse impact than another way (e.g. pass/fail), the procedure must be validated for that use. (EEOC, 1978, p. 38294)

There are no major contradictions between the *Guidelines* and the *Standards*, however, the *Guidelines* are more explicit than the *Standards* on some dimensions (e.g., they require that any cutoff score be justified by reference to the "need for a trustworthy and efficient work force" [EEOC, 1978, p. 38291], and that when "cutoff scores are used, they should normally be set so as to be reasonable and consistent with normal expectations of acceptable proficiency within the work force" [EEOC, 1978, p. 38298]). The *Guidelines* terminology of "normal expectations" clearly suggests a judgmental approach for setting a cutoff score. However, the *Guidelines* suggest that rank ordering requires substantial evidence of validity and a reasonable expectation that small differences in scores would reflect real differences in job performance.

The *Guidelines* address the three types of validity evidence and state that "users may rely upon criterion-related validity studies, content validity studies or construct validity studies" (EEOC, 1978, p. 38298). They recognize the lack of a clear distinction between types of validity evidence and try to address the borderline between content validity and construct validity. As an example, the *Guidelines* state that for typing, a typing test:

> is justifiable on the basis of content validity because it is a sample of an important or critical part of the job...but [the *Guidelines*] do not allow the validation of a test measuring a construct such as "judgment" by a content validity strategy. (EEOC, 1978, p. 38292)

Other quotes from the *Guidelines* relevant to validity are as follows:

> Any validity study should be based upon a review of information about the job for which the selection procedure is to be used. (p. 38300)

> A selection procedure can be supported by a content validity strategy to the extent that it is a representative sample of the content of the job. (p. 38302)

> A selection procedure based upon inferences about mental processes cannot be supported solely or primarily on the basis of content validity. (EEOC, 1978, p. 38302)

Finally, it should be mentioned that the *Guidelines* stress the importance of record keeping and documentation.

> Users of selection procedures...should maintain and have available for each job information on adverse impact of the selection process for that job and, where it is determined a selection process has an adverse impact, evidence of validity...Where a total selection process for a job has an adverse impact, the user should maintain and have available records or other information showing which components have an adverse impact. (EEOC, 1978, 38303).

STATE AND FEDERAL COURT DECISIONS

There are differences in case law and test construction processes between employment and licensure testing and the case law precedents will be discussed separately. For each type of test, some of the pivotal cases are identified and what made those cases important is described. In generalizing from the rulings in these cases, it should be pointed out that a legal case is binding only on lower courts in the same jurisdiction. For example, Federal Supreme Court rulings are binding on all other Federal Courts, but an Appeals Court ruling in, for instance, the 5th Circuit would be binding only on lower courts in that circuit. Also, the decisions are binding only on cases that are factually similar. Nevertheless, even cases not binding may be broadly instructive.

Employment Cases

The *Griggs v. Duke Power Company* case (1971) was the first landmark case dealing with job-related testing. The court ruled that in employment testing in private industry the defendants must show the job relatedness of the test. "Broad and general testing devices ... as fixed measures of capacity" were barred in employment testing (Griggs, 1971, p. 433). In *Albermarle Paper Company v. Moody* (1975), it was held that the EEOC *Guidelines* (revised in 1978) were the fundamental benchmark for assessing Title VII of the 1964 Civil Rights Act job relatedness requirements. These *Guidelines* constituted the administrative interpretation of the act by the enforcing agency and "consequently are entitled to great deference" (*Griggs v. Duke Power Company*, 1971, 401 U.S., at 433-434). *Chance v. Board of Examiners* (1972) established a job relatedness precedent for tests used with public employees as well as private employees.

Thus, it is clear that employers can be challenged regarding the job-relatedness of their employment practices. When challenged, employers must show that their test development procedures followed acceptable professional practices, with the EEOC *Guidelines* being considered an important guide. However, in *Guardians Association of N.Y. City v. Civil Service Commission* (1980), the court ruled that the *Guidelines* adopted too rigid an approach in the selection of validation techniques and that it was inconsistent with Title VII's endorsement of professionally developed tests. The Court basically considered content validation strategies to be acceptable for a test that assessed *observable* abilities. The court stated that content validation should *not* be rejected just because the abilities measured could be classified as constructs.

In an earlier decision (*Washington v. Davis*, 1976) the Supreme Court accepted the use of a verbal skills test for entry into police training even though its use had adverse impact because the scores correlated with performance in the training program and that training program completion is a prerequisite to employment. It should be mentioned that:

> Title VII standards were not applied in *Washington v. Davis* because the statute was not applicable to federal employees when the case was initially filed. (Cohen, 1989, p. 240)

However, the Court commented that had the job-relatedness requirements of *Griggs* or *Albermarle Paper* been applied, the correlation with the training program would have been sufficient validation.

In a fairly recent court decision (*Richardson v. Lamar County Board of Education*, 1989, 1991) a school district was challenged for using the Alabama Initial Teacher Certification Test. This test was originally intended as a licensure examination. Thus, although the case was technically an employment case, it may have implications for licensure examinations. The judge ruled against the district's use of the test. Judge Thompson's decision contained a fairly extensive analysis of perceived problems in test development and standard setting processes in the Alabama Initial Teacher Certification Test. Judge Thompson ruled that:

- first try failure statistics can be used for determining the extent of adverse impact because initial failure is a discrete injury (even though another court had previously ruled otherwise—see *United States v. LULAC*, 1986);
- outside experts should have been retained to monitor the test developer's work;
- all items should have been reviewed by committee members and suggested changes in items should not have been ignored by the test developer;
- the developer should have conducted empirical bias studies (even though for many of the tests the sample sizes were small);
- the cut scores were too high;

- failure to use a backup cut score method was *not* unprofessional;
- a developer *may* change methodology across time without this constituting an admission of error; and
- a court should not eschew an idealistic view of test validity evidence, but neither should it apply an "anything goes" approach.

Although this author does not agree with all of Judge Thompson's interpretations of the data in the case, the ruling does suggest that test developers should carry out their test construction tasks very carefully.

Two recent U.S. Supreme Court rulings relate to the requirements for subjective assessments. Basically, the rulings in both cases were that nonobjective assessments are subject to legal scrutiny under the disparate impact analysis of Title VII. In *Watson v. Fort Worth Bank and Trust* (1988), it was ruled that the Griggs standards would apply to subjective testing processes such as interviews. The court wished to prevent employers from circumventing the *Griggs* standard by replacing tests with subjective assessments. However, there was sharp dispute among the Justices on how to apply the standards. A plurality of the court said the standards should be applied in a less rigorous manner in subjective testing. In the *Wards Cove Packing Co. v. Atonio* (1989), a majority of the court agreed to less rigorous standards. Rebell (1990b) has suggested that:

> The net effect of Watson/Wards Cove might be said to constitute a broadening of Title VII's reach but also a modification of its bite. (p. 5)

Nevertheless, courts will not accept an "anything goes" approach in subjective assessments. (See the discussion in the next section of a licensure case [*Musgrove et al. v. Board of Education for the State of Georgia et al.*], which was a case involving a subjective assessment process.)

Licensure Cases

Licensure testing may involve a conflict between two rights: social and individual. The tension between societal and individual rights is both a legal and a moral issue (McDonough & Wolf, 1988). No one denies that the public has a legitimate right to have competent individuals practicing in various occupations and professions. No one denies that individuals have the right to be protected from unfair employment practices. The trade-off between the two is where the controversy lies.

As mentioned, there is debate about the applicability of the Civil Rights Acts to licensure tests. However, there is a strong constitutional basis for licensing. Reeves (1984) states that:

> The constitutionality of requirements to take and pass qualifying examinations is firmly entrenched. (p. 65)

This basis is stated in *Goldfarb v. Virginia State Bar* (1975) as follows:

> The States have a compelling interest in the practice of professions within their boundaries, and that as part of their power to protect the public health, safety, and other valid interests they have broad power to establish standards for licensing practitioners and regulating the practice of professions. (p. 792)

Although a constitutional basis is well established, licensure tests must have a rational relationship to the occupation. However, as mentioned, this is relatively easy to establish.

There are several court precedents for licensure. Most of these are for licensure to the Bar although in recent years there have been several teacher licensure cases. We begin our review of licensure cases with a very early decision on the licensure of doctors. In *Dent v. State of West Virginia* (1881), ruling in favor of the licensure requirement, the court declared, in part:

> The power of the state to provide for the general welfare of its people authorizes it to prescribe all such regulations as in its judgment will secure or tend to secure them against the consequences of ignorance and incapacity, as well as of deception and fraud....The nature and extent of the qualifications required must depend primarily upon the judgment of the state as to their necessity. If they are appropriate to the calling or profession, and attainable by reasonable study or application, no objection to their validity can be raised because of their stringency or difficulty. (1881, p. 114)

In a massive review of the literature, Eisdorfer and Tractenberg (1977) suggested that: "In the post-1937 period, the standard of review has become even more relaxed than that stated in the *Dent* case" (p. 117).

Given the thorough review by Eisdorfer and Tractenberg in their 1977 chapter, this review jumps to a more recent case: *United States v. State of North Carolina* (1975, 1977). The United States brought a Title VII complaint against North Carolina for requiring a minimum score on the National Teacher Examination (NTE). The court record revealed that at least one teacher training institute had

> graduated functional illiterates and the court acknowledged that the state should have "the right to adopt academic requirements and written achievement tests designed and validated to disclose the minimum amount of knowledge necessary to effective teaching." However, the NTE was not designed for use in assessing inservice teachers, the cut-off score chosen was not validated for job performance, and the result was a disparate impact on blacks. (Cohen, 1989, p. 239)

The court ruling was vacated in 1977 following the Supreme Court's ruling in *Washington v. Davis* regarding correlation with training programs and because a validation study was conducted for the NTE in North Carolina.

The *Tyler v. Vickery* (1975, 1976) case was a challenge against the constitutionality of the Georgia Bar Examination. The decision is important for several reasons. First, as mentioned, it rejected the view that the EEOC *Guidelines* were appropriate for a bar examination. Related to cutoff scores it was ruled that:

> While the minimum passing score of 70 has no significance standing alone, it represents the examiners' considered judgment as to "minimum competence required to practice law." (p. 1102)

The court also rejected the plaintiffs' complaint that the examinations did not cover the full range of skills needed to practice law and it held that no review procedure was necessary because there was an opportunity to retake the examination within a reasonable time.

An important early teacher licensure case was the *United States v. the State of South Carolina* (1977, 1978). In this case, it was ruled that the National Teacher Examination (NTE) could be used for *both* teacher certification (licensure) and determination of salary levels. This case followed *Washington v. Davis*, and the NTE was validated against teacher training programs and not actual job performance. It was held that the content validity study was adequate under Title VII (and constitutional) guidelines. One way this case differed from the original (prior to vacating) North Carolina case was that the state did both an extensive cutoff score study and content validation study. Cohen (1989) has concluded that:

> When teacher certification tests are professionally developed in good faith to insure teacher competency and are then validated as to content, they will be upheld by courts. The public interest in having at least minimally competent teachers seems to outweigh the disparate impact that has often resulted. (p. 242)

An Alabama teacher licensure case was an example of a prolonged, complex litigation. A Basic Professional Studies Test and 45 tests for different teaching specializations were constructed and administered by the National Evaluation Systems (NES). A class action suit was brought against the state on behalf of all African-Americans who had been (or would be) denied certification because of failure to pass the tests. After considerable discussion, a settlement was approved by the court. Subsequently, the Alabama State Board of Education wished to back out of the settlement. After much legal manipulation, the United States Court of Appeals ruled that the original agreement was enforceable. The settlement incorporated the idea of the *Golden Rule* (1980) settlement that required items with minimum racial differences to be used first in any test. (The *Golden Rule* approach to choosing items has been almost unanimously viewed by measurement professionals as one that will result in psychometrically inferior examinations.) At any rate, the Alabama case was decided on procedural grounds rather than on the merits of the proposed certification programs. Nevertheless, while the settlement issue was being debated in the courts, the case was tried on its merits, but the judge never issued a ruling. Although the *Richardson* employment case discussed earlier may provide some clues regarding how the judge might have ruled, it is possible that previous legal precedent for licensure cases may have caused the judge to rule differently in a licensure case than he would have in the employment case.

Two licensure cases with important implications for testing are the *State of Texas v. Project Principle* (1987), and *United States v. LULAC* (1986). In the *Project Principle* case, use of the Texas Examination of Current Administrators and Teachers (TECAT) was ruled constitutional. It was held that there was no impairment of a contract right because teaching certificates are licenses, not contracts; state legislatures may change licensing requirements retroactively; and that teacher testing was a rational means of achieving legitimate State objectives, hence was not fundamentally unfair. Also, it was ruled that due process was not violated because applicants had a right to retake the test prior to being decertified. The court ruled that:

> teacher testing is a rational means of achieving the legitimate state objective of ensuring that public school educators meet specified standards of competency. (1987, p. 391)

In the *LULAC* case, the use of the Pre-Professional Skills Test (PPST) was upheld. The court noted that the state had considered other alternative tests before selecting the PPST, and that a validation study had been conducted which surveyed Texas educators regarding their beliefs about whether the skills measured by the PPST were necessary for success in teacher education programs and in teaching. The court agreed with the *Washington v. Davis* (1976) decision that a test only need show a relationship to the effects of a required training program, not the eventual competence of individuals on the job. Further, as noted earlier, the court held that because applicants are permitted to retake the test, and that the passing rate for minority-group students was increasing, "the ultimate impact of the PPST on the number of minority teachers in the State has not been assessed" (*United States v. Lulac*, 1986, p. 643). With respect to the issue of due process, the court held that the legislative process gave adequate notice:

> When the legislature enacts a law, or a state agency adopts a regulation, that affects a general class of persons, all of those persons have received procedural due process by the legislative process itself and they have no right to individual attention. (*United States v. Lulac*, 1986, p. 647)

Finally, the court ruled that institutions of higher education were not required to lower standards to accommodate students who had been inadequately educated due to the state's historical dual school system.

> In administering its higher education systems...a state...has no constitutional or statutory obligation to suspend or lower valid academic standards to accommodate high school students who may be ill-prepared because of prior constitutional violations by its local and elementary school systems (*United States v. Lulac*, 1986, p. 7015).

Musgrove et al. v. Board of Education for the State of Georgia, et al. (1991) was a case involving use of the Teacher Performance Assessment Instrument (TPAI) for teacher licensure. Several points were made in that ruling that have important implications for licensure testing. One issue pertained to the rule that candidates were only allowed six attempts to pass the test. The court ruled that:

> a [sic] irrebuttable lifetime presumption of unfitness after failure to pass six "TPAI"s was arbitrary and capricious because no further education, training, experience, maturity or higher degree would enable such persons to become certified in Georgia. (*Musgrove*, 1991, p. 3).

Further, the court found that two competencies ("Interpersonal Skills" and "Helps Learners Develop Positive Self-Concepts") had indicators that were "so vague, ambiguous, indefinite, arbitrary and subjective as to fail to place a reasonable person on notice of the standards of conduct expected" (Musgrove, 1991, p. 6). This court ruling focused on a performance instrument that had been carefully constructed and heavily researched. Those who are developing performance assessment instruments for high-stakes decisions should consider this court decision very carefully.

Although the ruling not limiting the number of attempts to six is different from those to be discussed in the next paragraph, consideration should be given regarding whether additional education should result in additional attempts being permitted. Performance standards should be defined with great care to minimize the possibility of their being considered vague, arbitrary, and subjective.

Four courts have ruled in favor of limiting the number of chances an individual may have to take an exam. In *Younger v. Colorado State Board of Law Examiners* (1980) the court ruled in favor of limiting the number of examinations to three, and in *Poats v. Givan* (1981) a rule limiting the number of times an applicant could sit for the bar exam to four was declared legal. In *Jones v. Board of Commissioners* (1984) an Alabama rule limiting the number of times an applicant could take the bar exam did not create an irrebuttable presumption of incompetence. In *Yu v. Clayton* (1986) it was ruled that an RN applicant who had failed a licensure exam six times was ineligible for another chance until after recompleting an entire course of nursing studies. These four rulings are at odds with the *Musgrove* decision cited earlier.

Several other cases are worthy of brief mention. One relates to the review of exams. In *Balaklaw v. American Board of Anesthesiology, Inc.* (1990) a plaintiff who failed brought suit requesting he be allowed to review his exam and answer sheet. The request was denied. This ruling was similar, in this respect, to the *Tyler v. Vickery* decision mentioned earlier.

Finally, in *Millet v. Hoisting Engineers' Licensing Div.* it was ruled, for an *oral* exam, that:

> Failure to keep a record of the questions and answers has been held to be a constitutional violation because this deprives the failed applicant of any chance of showing that the examination was irrational and arbitrary or that the grading was in error. (1977, 1171)

Conclusions Regarding Court Decisions

A general conclusion seems to be that if tests are constructed according to procedures advocated in the *Guidelines* and *Standards*, they should withstand legal scrutiny. For employment cases, the key issue is validity. Rossein summarizes case law as follows:

> Courts readily uphold an employment practice if the employer can show that the practice actually enables the employer to screen out unqualified or less qualified candidates. (1992, p. 11)

The issue, of course, is what kinds of, and how much, evidence is required. Content validity evidence has generally been considered sufficient. For example, in *Jones et al. v. New York City Human Resources Administration* (1975) it was stated that *no* case in that Circuit had held that criterion-related evidence was required to prove job-relatedness.

Although, the Court argued in the *Richardson* decision that it should not eschew an idealistic view of test validity nor apply an "anything goes" approach, it is clear that the decision employed standards on the idealistic side of a middle position. That can perhaps be seen most clearly by looking specifically at the cut score issue. In general, the courts have accepted judgments regarding the cut score. In *Tyler v. Vickery* (1975) the court ruled that the cut score had been validated even though there was no empirically demonstrated evidence because the score represented the examiners' "considered judgments" as to minimum competence required. In *Guardians Association* the exam was ruled as invalid, but regarding the cut score the court stated that:

> As with rank-ordering, a criterion-related study is *not* necessarily required: the employer might establish a valid cutoff score by using a professional estimate of the requisite ability levels, or, at the very least, by analyzing the test results to locate a logical "breakpoint" in the distribution of scores. (from Byham, 1983, p. 107)

Pyburn (1984) concluded that a state may set the passing grade where it chooses because it is empowered to require high standards. He references *Schware v. Board of Bar Examiners of State of New Mexico* (1957) and *Chance v. State Bar of California* (1967). The *Dent* decision was quoted above. Although all these cases suggest that professional judgment is acceptable as a means of setting cut scores, if a judge is convinced the cut scores are too high, the ruling may be unfavorable. In the *Richardson* case discussed earlier, the court ruled that:

> the developer's procedure yielded cut scores that were so astoundingly high that they signaled, on their face, an absence of correlation to minimum competence. (1989, p. 28)

> an inference as to competence will be meaningless if the cut score, or decision point, of the test does not also reflect *what practitioners in the field deem to be a minimally competent level of performance on that test.* Again, the test developer's role in setting a cut score is *to apply professionally accepted techniques that accurately marshal the judgment of practitioners.* (1989, p. 32)

One interesting point about the above quotes is that the judge seemed to support judgmental methods. Yet, when the test developers did apply what some supported as a professionally accepted technique, the judge contended that the cut scores were "astoundingly high." Certainly the attempt by the test constructors was to marshal the judgment of practitioners. Experts for the defendants did not believe the cut scores were too high. However, experts for the plaintiffs argued that the standards were too high. The judge obviously agreed.

Rebell, in discussing three recent challenges that were settled or withdrawn, pointed out the very high pass *rate* for these tests. As he suggested:

> To the extent that fear of judicial intervention caused a lowering of otherwise valid and appropriate cut scores, increased court involvement in evaluation matters is a worrisome prospect. (1990a, p. 351)

Thus, although some judges will set very high (unrealistic?) standards for test quality, the bulk of the case law suggests most judges are reasonable in their expectations and rulings. In concluding this section, it seems appropriate to quote Pyburn:

> To date, there have been very few successful challenges to licensing examinations on the grounds that the tests were "discriminatory" or were not "rationally related" to the purpose for which they were being used. (1990, p. 14)

FUTURE DIRECTIONS

The *Guidelines* are quite out of date, but no revision is being planned; the *Standards* are somewhat dated and a revision is being planned; the 1991 Civil

Rights Act, at the time of this writing, has had little chance to impact court rulings; and the *Watson* and *Wards Cove* rulings regarding subjective assessments are too recent to have had much impact on subsequent rulings. Thus, a variety of factors may impact how one should construct licensure tests and how courts may rule on their legality. Although the future is always difficult to predict, some discussion of possible future directions seems worthwhile.

New Standards

The revision of the *Standards* is being planned and, by the time this book is published, the individuals on the committee will be appointed and specific changes for the *Standards* will likely have been proposed. No revised standards are anticipated before 1996. As was mentioned, there was not total agreement among psychometricians regarding the 1985 *Standards*. Some thought they were not "tough" enough whereas others thought they set unrealistically high standards. Whether the revised standards will be more or less rigorous regarding tests used for licensure or certification will depend, in part, upon the views of the particular individuals appointed to the committee.

Although the political/social interests and psychometric views of the individuals on the new *Standards* committee will likely have an impact on the *Standards*, just what that impact will be is unknown. What is known is that some views of the psychometric profession have changed and there is likely some general agreement on the wisdom of the changes. The 1985 *Standards* predicted some specific areas where

> new developments are particularly likely, such as gender-specific or combined-gender norms, cultural bias, computer based test interpretations, validity generalization, differential prediction, and flagging test scores for people with handicapping conditions. (AERA/APA/NCME, 1985, p. 2)

Some of these new developments have been influenced by legislation. For example, the Civil Rights Act of 1991 prohibits ethnic or gender norming for employment tests. Some of the other areas have not developed as much as was surmised when the 1985 *Standards* went to print.

In my view, the major writings likely to influence the revised *Standards* are in the area of validity. As reported earlier, there was a movement in the 1985 *Standards* to unify the notion of validity under the heading of construct validity. There has been continued writing in that area and the new *Standards* may well go further in that unifying direction than the current ones do. Whether there will be any major changes in the methodologies used to establish validity is more questionable. In my view, the methodologies available for gathering validity evidence have not, in fact, expanded much. One is still likely to use the methodologies that heretofore have been referred to as content, criterion-related, and construct validity evidences. There may, in fact, be a change in that all these methodologies are referred to as providing evidence regarding the construct validity of the measures.

In addition to wishing to call all validity construct validity, there has been some suggestion that the notion of validity should extend beyond the accuracy of inferences made from the scores to encompass the social consequences of testing

(Messick, 1989; Shepard, 1993). It is unclear at the time of this writing whether that expansion of the meaning of the word "validity" will be widely accepted by the measurement community. For example, Wiley (1991) prefers to focus on the psychological processes intended to be measured rather than the use of the tests. In general, there is some concern that broadening the concept of validity into a consideration of social concerns will cause it to lose some of its scientific meaning. Nevertheless, whether consequences of test use become a part of the connotation of "validity," the measurement community has long noted the importance of considering the costs of false positives and false negatives and the new *Standards* are almost sure to emphasize the consideration of these costs more explicitly. It is hard to imagine that the costs of false positives would be taken lightly for licensure decisions.

New Legislation

Some aspects of the *Civil Rights Act of 1991* and the *Americans with Disabilities Act* have been discussed. Because both are reasonably recent, there is little legal precedent regarding what the impact of these will be. In this author's view, there will be little impact on licensure from the *Civil Rights Act of 1991* because it relates primarily to employment testing and it basically reaffirms the business necessity requirement that was the basis for many of the previous decisions. The only two decisions that would have allowed for a lessening of the business necessity requirement were the *Watson* and the *Wards Cove* cases. There will likely be some consideration of the *Americans with Disabilities Act* in the new *Standards*. Whether or not that occurs, test constructors and test users do need to attend to the necessity of providing *appropriate* accommodations for individuals with documented disabilities.

Subjective Assessments

Although portions of the *Watson* and *Wards Cove* cases have been made impotent as precedents due to the 1991 Civil Rights Act, the act did not address the issue of subjective assessments. It is reasonable to assume that many more cases will arise where subjective assessments are being challenged. Both Rebell (1990b) and Phillips (1993) have pointed out that the testing issues in *Watson* were less complex than those posed by some of the currently proposed performance tasks.

> The question remaining is whether it is reasonable and technically feasible to apply
> the EEOC Guidelines to such performance (subjective) tasks. (Phillips, 1993, p.
> 735)

It is too soon to know how demanding the courts will be regarding the psychometric properties of subjective assessments. However, it would seem that the psychometric community would desire high quality assessments whether they be considered objective or subjective. Thus, one should not anticipate support from the psychometric community for subjective assessments that have low reliability, low validity, inadequate equating procedures, etc. (It is true that the specific operational definitions of validity and reliability may be somewhat different for subjective assessments.)

SUMMARY

The general legal setting within which employment and licensure tests are judged has been described in this chapter. Generic legal issues include the constitutional requirements (primarily of the 14th Amendment) and the statutory requirements of the Civil Rights Acts. Basically the Constitution requires equal protection and due process. The Civil Rights Acts prohibit disparate treatment and disparate impact.

A distinction was made between employment and licensure/certification testing. The purposes of these types of testing are quite different and logically should lead to different test development procedures. There is some uncertainty about whether the Civil Rights Acts and the EEOC *Guidelines* are applicable to licensure tests. This is an important issue because the Civil Rights Acts call for a business necessity requirement, which is considered harder to demonstrate than the legitimate relationship requirement that the 14th Amendment calls for.

The more relevant portions of a variety of professional standards and codes for licensure tests were summarized. Although both the AERA/APA/NCME *Standards* and the EEOC *Guidelines* are somewhat dated, they have been used extensively in previous court cases (the *Guidelines* for employment tests) and, thus, there is some legal precedent based on these standards.

Several of the more important employment and licensure court decisions were discussed. In general, it would appear that higher test development/validation standards have been set for employment decisions than for licensure decisions. The courts have accepted a variety of kinds of validity evidence and are (generally) reluctant to second-guess cut scores that have been established by obtaining the judgments of individuals in the profession/occupation in question.

Future directions with respect to legal precedents will be somewhat dependent upon the upcoming revision of the *Standards*. It is unclear what recent legislation such as the *Civil Rights Act of 1991* and the *Americans with Disabilities Act* will have on court decisions. Basically, the new Civil Rights Act reaffirms the business necessity requirement that was the basis for many previous decisions. The *Americans with Disabilities Act* may result in increased accommodations for those with claimed disabilities. The movement to more subjective based assessments coupled with the *Watson* and *Wards Cove* rulings that subjective assessments are subject to test development standards should result in some interesting court cases.

Although an agency can always be sued, and one can never predict how a judge will rule, there has been enough precedent to suggest that if one develops an exam with professional care, there should be a good chance that the test will be declared legally acceptable.

REFERENCES

Albermarle Paper Co. v. Moody, 422 U.S. 405, 431 (1975).

American Educational Research Association, American Psychological Association, & National Council on Measurement in Education. (1985). *Standards for educational and psychological testing*. Washington, DC: American Psychological Association.

Americans with Disabilities Act, 42 U.S.C. Section 12101 *et seq.* (1990).

Balaklaw v. American Board of Anesthesiology, Inc., 562 N.Y.S. 2d 360 (Sup. 1990).

Byham, W. C. (1983). *Review of legal cases and opinions dealing with assessment centers and content validity.* Monograph IV, Pittsburgh: Development Dimensions International.

Chance v. Board of Examiners, 303 F. Supp. 203, 209 (SDNY, 1971) aff'd, 458 F. 2d 1167 (2nd Cir., 1972).

Chance v. State Bar of California, 386 F. 2d 962, 964 (9th Cir., 1967).

Civil Rights Act of 1991. (1991). Washington, DC: The Bureau of National Affairs, Inc.

Cohen, J. H. (1989). Legal challenges to testing for teacher certification: History, impact and future trends. *Journal of Law and Education, 18*(2), 229-265.

Dent v. State of West Virginia, 129 U.S. 114, 122 (1881).

Eisdorfer, S., & Tractenberg, P. (1977). The role of the courts and teacher certification. In W.R. Hazard, L.D. Freeman, S. Eisdorfer, & P. Tractenberg (Eds.), *Legal issues in teacher preparation and certification* (pp. 109-150). Washington, DC: ERIC Clearinghouse on Teacher Education.

Equal Employment Opportunity Commission, Civil Service Commission, Department of Labor and Department of Justice. (1978, August 25). Uniform guidelines on employee selection procedures. *Federal Register, 43* (166), 38290-38315.

Freeman, L. D., Hess, R., III, & Kasik, M. M. (1985, March). *Testing teachers and the law.* Presentation made at the American Educational Research Association annual meeting, Chicago, IL.

Golden Rule Insurance Co. et al. v. Mathias et al. 86 Ill.App 3d 323, 326, 41Ill. Dec. 888, 891, 408 N.E. 2d 310, 313 (1980).

Goldfarb v. Virginia State Bar, 421 U.S. 773 (1975).

Griggs v. Duke Power Company, 292 F. Supp. 243 (MD NC, 1968), 420 F.2nd 1225 (4th Cir., 1970) and 401 (U.S. 424, 1971).

Guardians Association of New York City v. Civil Service Commission, 431F. Supp. 526 (Southern District of New York, 1977); U.S. District Court of Appeals, Second Circuit (No. 849), July 31, 1980.

Hazelwood School District v. United States, 97 S.Ct. 2736 (1977).

Herbsleb, J. D., Sales, B. D., & Overcast, T. D. (1985). Challenging licensure and certification. *American Psychologist, 40*(11), 1165-1178.

Jones v. Board of Commissioners, 737 F. 2d (11th Cir. 1984).

Jones et al. v. New York City Human Resources Administration, U.S. District Court, Southern District of New York, January 10, 1975; 73 (1) 3815; U.S. Court of Appeals, Second Circuit (New York), January 26, 1976.

Kane, M. T. (1984, April). *Strategies in validating licensure examinations.* Paper presented at the annual meeting of the American Educational Research Association, New Orleans, LA.

Kuehn, P. A., Stallings, W. M., & Holland, C. L. (1990). Court-defined job analysis requirements for validation of teacher certification tests. *Educational Measurement: Issues and Practice*, 9(4), 21-24.

Linn, R. L. (1984, April). *Standards for validity in licensure testing*. Paper presented at the "Validity in Licensure Testing" symposium at the annual meeting of the American Educational Research Association, New Orleans, LA.

McDonough, M. W., Jr., & Wolf, W. C., Jr. (1988). Court actions which helped define the direction of the competency-based testing movement. *Journal of Research and Development in Education, 21*(3), 37-43.

Mehrens, W. A. (1990). Assessing the quality of teacher assessment tests. In J. V. Mitchell, Jr., S. L. Wise, & B. S. Plake (Eds.), *Assessment of teaching: Purposes, practices, and implications for the profession* (pp. 77-136). Hillsdale, NJ: Lawrence Elbaum Associates.

Meier, P., Sacks, J., & Zabell, S. L. (1984). What happened in Hazelwood: Statistics, employment discrimination, and the 80% rule. *American Bar Foundation Research Journal, 1*, 39-164.

Messick, S. (1989). Validity, In R.L. Linn (Ed.), *Educational Measurement* (3rd ed., pp. 13-103). New York: American Council on Education and Macmillan.

Millet v. Hoisting Engineers' Licensing Div., 377 A.2d 229 (R.I. 1977).

Millman, J., Mehrens, W. A., & Sackett, P. R. (1993, May). *An Evaluation of the New York State Bar Examination*. A study commissioned by the New York State Court of Appeals. Albany, NY.

Musgrove et al. v. Board of Education for the State of Georgia et al. (Feb., 1991). Civil Action File No. D-62016.

Personnel Administrator v. Feeney, 442 U.S. 256, 279, 99 S.Ct. 2282, 2296, 60 L.Ed.2d 870 (1979).

Phillips, S. E. (1991). Extending teacher licensure testing: Have the courts applied the wrong validity standard? *Thomas M. Cooley Law Review, 8*(3), 513-550.

Phillips, S. E. (1993, March 11). Legal issues in performance assessment. *Education Law Reporter, 79*, 709-738.

Poats v. Givan, 651 F. 2d 495 (7th Cir. 1981).

Pyburn, K. M., Jr. (1984, April). *Legal challenges to licensing examinations*. Paper presented at the AERA-NCME Annual Meeting, New Orleans, LA.

Pyburn, K. M., Jr. (1990). Legal challenges to licensing examinations. *Educational Measurement: Issues and Practice, 9*(4), 5-6, 14.

Rebell, M. A. (1986). *Pre-Trial Memorandum of Law on behalf of Amicus Curiae National Evaluation Systems, Inc.* Margaret T. Allen et al. and Board of Trustees for Alabama State University and Eria P. Smith v. Alabama State Board of Education et al., Civil Action No. 81-697-N.

Rebell, M. A. (1990a). Legal issues concerning teacher evaluation. In J. Millman & L. Darling-Hammond (Eds.), *The new handbook of teacher evaluation: Assessing elementary and secondary school teachers* (pp. 337-355). Newbury Park, CA: Sage.

Rebell, M. A. (1990b). Legal aspects of subjective assessments of teacher competency. In NES (Eds.), *The assessment of teaching: Selected topics* (pp. 1-10). Amherst, MA: National Evaluation Systems.

Reeves, R. (1984). *The law of professional licensing and certification*. Charlotte, NC: Publications for Professionals.

Richardson v. Lamar County Board of Education, et al., Civil Action No.87-T-568-N (1989); U.S. Court of Appeals, Eleventh Circuit, Nos.90-7002, 90-7336 (July 17, 1991).

Rossein, M. (Feb., 1992). *Disparate Impact Theory After the Civil Rights Act of 1991: Restoring the Job Performance Standard.* 429 PLI/Lit 155 PLI Order No. H4-5127.

Schware v. Board of Bar Examiners of State of New Mexico, 353 U.S. 232, 238-239 (1957).

Shepard, L. A. (1993). Evaluating test validity. In L. Darling-Hammond (Ed.), *Review of research in education: 19* (pp. 405-450). Washington, DC: American Educational Research Association.

Shimberg, B. (1990). Social considerations in the validation of licensing and certification exams. *Educational Measurement: Issues and Practice, 9*(4), 11-14.

Smith, I. L., & Hambleton, R. K. (1990). Content validity studies of licensing examinations. *Educational Measurement: Issues and Practice, 9*(4), 7-10.

State of Texas v. Project Principle, Inc., 724 S.W. 2d 387, 391 (Tex. 1987).

Tyler v. Vickery, 517 F.2d 1089 (5th Cir. 1975), cert. denied, 426 U.S. 940 (1976).

United States v. LULAC, 793 F.2d 636, 640 (5th Cir. 1986).

United States v. North Carolina, 400 F. Supp. 343 (E.D.N.C. 1975), *vacated*, 425 F. Supp. 789 (E.D.N.C. 1977).

United States v. State of South Carolina, 445 F. Supp. 1094 (DSC), (1977), *aff'd.* 434 U.S. 1026 (1978).

Village of Arlington Heights v. Metropolitan Housing Development Corp., 429 U.S. 252, (1977).

Wards Cove Packing Co. v. Atonio. 490 U.S., 109 S. Ct. 2115 (1989).

Washington v. Davis, 348 F. Supp. 15 (D.C., 1972), 512 F. 2d 956(D.C. Cir., 1975) and 426 U.S. 229, 250. (1976).

Watson v. Fort Worth Bank and Trust. 487 U.S. 977 (1988).

Wiley, D. E. (1991). Test validity and invalidity reconsidered. In R. E. Snow & D. E. Wiley (Eds.), *Improving inquiry in social science: A volume in honor of Lee J. Cronbach* (pp. 75-107). Hillsdale, NJ: Erlbaum.

Woodward v. Virginia Board of Bar Examiners, 420 F. Supp. 211, 18 FEP 836 838 (E.D. Va 1976), *aff'd per curiam*, 598 F.2d 1345 (4th Cir. 1979).

Younger v. Colorado State Board of Law Examiners, 625 F.2d 372 (10th Cir. 1980).

Yu v. Clayton, 497 N.E. 2d 1278 (Ill. App. 1 Dist. 1986).

POLICY ISSUES WITH PSYCHOMETRIC IMPLICATIONS

Michael Rosenfeld

Educational Testing Service

Richard J. Tannenbaum

Educational Testing Service

Scott Wesley

Educational Testing Service

Testing candidates with disabilities, testing repeaters, and coaching involve issues of fairness, the validity of the inferences made from test scores, and protection of the public. Licensing boards must develop policies to deal with each of these issues. It is interesting to note that although all three are of concern to licensing agencies, little of the research on these topics has been conducted in licensure settings. This chapter discusses the results of research conducted on each topic, considers the psychometric implications for policy of each, and suggests steps licensing boards can take when formulating policy.

TESTING CANDIDATES WITH DISABILITIES IN LICENSURE SETTINGS

Disabled examinees take tests to apply for college, graduate school, and to be licensed or certified. Their ability to perform well on these examinations can be severely limited if the testing conditions or test format interact with their disability, but are not required for performance in school or on the job.

Most licensing agencies have been providing examinations in facilities accessible to disabled candidates, and have been providing alternative forms of examinations for many years (Schmitt, 1991). Accommodations for college-entrance examinations have been made since the 1930s (ETS, 1988). In 1937, a version of the Scholastic Aptitude Test was developed for students who are visually impaired. The College Board, with the assistance of the American Foundation for the Blind, developed a braille booklet containing 100 antonyms, 50 analogies, and 50 reading comprehension items. A "talking book" record was also introduced which contained additional reading comprehension passages and questions. A braille practice booklet was developed to provide an opportunity for blind students to review the concepts covered by the test prior to taking the examination. Testing agencies had been providing accommodations to candidates from special populations, based primarily on the agencies' commitment to fairness and equal opportunity. The passage of the Americans with Disabilities Act (ADA) PL 101-336 now requires licensing agencies to provide appropriate accommodations for disabled test candidates. This legislation is likely to result in increased numbers of candidates requesting accommodations, and in licensing agencies providing them. The following section focuses on the requirements of the ADA that are related to testing, and the psychometric implications of these requirements.

The ADA

The ADA was enacted on July 26, 1990. It contains five major parts or titles. The act provides comprehensive civil rights protection to disabled individuals in the areas of employment, public accommodations, state and local government services, transportation, and telecommunications. Its intent is to increase job opportunities and access for disabled individuals. The testing requirements of the ADA took effect on January 26, 1992.

Title II of the ADA describes the responsibilities of state licensing agencies. It extends the prohibition of discrimination in federally assisted programs established by Section 504 of the Rehabilitation Act of 1973 (PL 93-112) to all activities of state and local governments, including those that do not receive Federal financial assistance. Title III delineates the responsibilities of private certification agencies. In general, the ADA emphasizes the need for (a) access to examination and course presentation facilities, (b) examination results that accurately reflect candidates' levels of knowledge or skill rather than their disabilities, and (c) administration of examinations for disabled candidates as often, and in as timely a manner, as examinations for nondisabled examinees. The section on examinations is quoted at length to provide examples of the language included in the ADA.

Section 36.309. This section delineates the ADA requirements for examinations and courses. It is part of Title III but also applies to state licensing agencies. The law reads:

    A. *General.* Any private entity that offers examinations or courses related to applications, licensing, certification, or credentialing for secondary or postsecondary education, professional, or trade purposes shall offer such examinations or courses in a place and manner accessible to persons with disabilities or offer alternative accessible arrangements for such individuals.

    B. *Examinations.*

        (1) Any private entity offering an examination covered by this section must assure that—

(i) The examination is selected and administered so as to best ensure that, when the examination is administered to an individual with a disability that impairs sensory, manual, or speaking skills, the examination results accurately reflect the individual's aptitude or achievement level or whatever other factor the examination purports to measure, rather than reflecting the individual's impaired sensory, manual, or speaking skills (except where those skills are the factors that the examination purports to measure);

(ii) An examination that is designed for individuals with impaired sensory, manual, or speaking skills is offered at equally convenient locations, as often, and in as timely a manner as are other examinations; and

(iii) The examination is administered in facilities that are accessible to individuals with disabilities or alternative accessible arrangements are made.

(2) Required modifications to an examination may include changes in the length of time permitted for completion of the examination and adaptation of the manner in which the examination is given.

(3) A private entity offering an examination covered by this section shall provide appropriate auxiliary aids for persons with impaired sensory, manual, or speaking skills, unless that private entity can demonstrate that offering a particular auxiliary aid would fundamentally alter the measurement of the skills or knowledge the examination is intended to test or would result in an undue burden. Auxiliary aids and services required by this section may include taped examinations, interpreters or other effective methods of making orally delivered materials available to individuals with hearing impairments, brailled or large print examinations and answer sheets or qualified readers for individuals with visual impairments or learning disabilities, transcribers for individuals with manual impairments, and other similar services and actions.

(4) Alternative accessible arrangements may include, for example, provision of an examination at an individual's home with a proctor if accessible facilities or equipment are unavailable. Alternative arrangements must provide comparable conditions to those provided for nondisabled individuals. (pp. III-100-103)

Definitions of disability. Section 36.104 contains the ADA definition of disability. This is quite broad, and describes which individuals are covered under the ADA. The law reads:

Disability means, with respect to an individual, a physical or mental impairment that substantially limits one or more of the major life activities of such individual; a record of such an impairment; or being regarded as having such an impairment.

(1) The phrase *physical or mental impairment* means—

   (i) Any physiological disorder or condition, cosmetic disfigurement, or anatomical loss affecting one or more of the following body systems: neurological; musculoskeletal; special sense organs; respiratory, including speech organs; cardiovascular; reproductive; digestive, genitourinary; hemic and lymphatic; skin; and endocrine;

   (ii) Any mental or psychological disorder such as mental retardation, organic brain syndrome, emotional or mental illness, and specific learning disabilities;

   (iii) The phrase physical or mental impairment includes, but is not limited to, such contagious and noncontagious diseases and conditions as orthopedic, visual, speech, and hearing impairments, cerebral palsy, epilepsy, muscular dystrophy, multiple sclerosis, cancer, heart disease, diabetes, mental retardation, emotional illness, specific learning disabilities, HIV disease (whether symptomatic or asymptomatic), tuberculosis, drug addiction, and alcoholism.

   (iv) The phrase *physical or mental impairment* does not include homosexuality or bisexuality.

(2) The phrase *major life activities* means functions such as caring for one's self, performing manual tasks, walking, seeing, hearing, speaking, breathing, learning and working.

(3) The phrase *has a record of such an impairment* means has a history of, or has been misclassified as having, a mental or physical impairment that substantially limits one or more major life activities.

(4) The phrase *is regarded as having an impairment* means—

   (i) Has a physical or mental impairment that does not substantially limit major life activities but that is treated by a private entity as constituting such a limitation;

   (ii) Has a physical or mental impairment that substantially limits major life activities only as a result of the attitudes of others toward such an impairment; or

   (iii) Has none of the impairments defined in paragraph (1) of this definition but is treated by a private entity as having such an impairment.

(5) The term *disability* does not include—

   (i) Transvestism, transsexualism, pedophilia, exhibitionism, voyeurism, gender identity disorders not resulting from physical impairments, or other sexual behavior disorders;

(ii) Compulsive gambling, kleptomania, or pyromania; or

(iii) Psychoactive substance use disorders resulting from current illegal use of drugs. (Equal Employment Opportunity Commission and U.S. Department of Justice 1991, pp. II-16-20)

Discussion of board responsibilities. As can be seen, the ADA describes disabilities quite broadly. It also describes two general types of accommodations. The first involves the accessibility of facilities to individuals (e.g., wheelchair accessibility); the second involves modifications to the examination itself or the examination process (e.g., providing additional time to take the examination or using of large-size print). The ADA requires that decisions concerning accommodations be tailored to the individual needs of the candidate and the essential functions of the job. The decision made by the licensing or certification board should be designed to provide the candidate an opportunity to demonstrate his or her knowledge and skill on as equivalent a basis as possible. (In many instances, the request for a particular accommodation will initially be made by the candidate and then verified by an appropriately licensed professional or a certified specialist selected by the candidate.)

A board must make several types of decisions when considering an applicant with a disability. First, the candidate must have the same qualifications to take the examination as all other candidates. Examples of such qualifications include educational attainment and work experience. This is consistent with the ADA's concept of a qualified individual with a disability (p. II-26). The Act clearly states that a person must be qualified to perform the job in question, with or without a reasonable accommodation. Second, the board must decide if the disability will affect the candidate's ability to perform the essential functions of the job. For example, it would be unreasonable to expect a candidate who cannot see to perform surgery or function as a building inspector because both jobs are heavily dependent on visual ability. Once the board has decided a candidate is qualified to take the examination and can perform the essential functions of the job, it must determine what modifications in the examination or the examination process it is willing to make to allow the candidate a fair opportunity to demonstrate relevant knowledge or skills.

ADA regulations provide two criteria licensing and certification boards can use in making decisions about accommodations for disabled candidates. The first would require the board to determine whether it believed the accommodation would fundamentally alter the measurement of the construct being assessed. For example, if a test were designed to measure reading comprehension and the accommodation requested was to allow someone to read the test aloud to the candidate, the accommodated test would measure listening comprehension, not reading comprehension. The inferences made about the test score would thus be invalid. The second criterion involves whether the board believes the accommodation represents an "undue burden" because of the cost or difficulty in developing or administering the modified examination. Clearly, applying the ADA to individual situations requires sound professional judgment.

Types of Accommodations. Paragraph 36.104 of the ADA delineates the types of physical and mental disabilities covered by the Act. These definitions are, for the most part, taken from Section 504 of the Rehabilitation Act of 1973. Many licensing, certification, and admission-testing agencies already provide accommodations to candidates who are physically disabled, blind or visually impaired, deaf or hard of hearing, learning disabled, or mentally disabled. In many of these categories the nature and severity of the disability varies greatly from candidate to candidate. Therefore, no single accommodation is likely to be appropriate for all members of any group of disabled candidates. Listed below are some testing accommodations that are commonly made available to disabled test candidates.

Alternative Test Versions. Many tests can be provided in braille, large print, and audiocassette versions. Sometimes test questions in the print version may have to be reformatted, substituted, or dropped from the examination because they are not appropriate for the specific disability (e.g., a visual stimulus or test question that cannot be translated into braille). Alternative ways to record answers to test questions have also been provided. These include allowing the use of typewriters or computers rather than the typical machine-scorable answer sheets. Answers can be written on the test booklet itself and on large-print answer sheets.

Assisting Personnel. When special versions of a test are not available, it is not uncommon for testing agencies to provide or allow for candidates with disabilities to use a reader. Amanuenses may be used by disabled candidates to help them record their answers. Deaf or hard-of-hearing candidates whose primary mode of communication is sign language may need an interpreter.

Assisting Devices. Some assisting devices can be used. These might include an Opticon, Visualtek, or a braille typewriter for a print test, or a voice synthesizer or a special keyboard for a computer-based test.

Separate Testing Locations. Tests that are usually group administered have frequently been provided to disabled individuals in a separate room or at a separate site. This is particularly true if extra time is needed, a reader or amanuensis is used, or if the test is in braille or on a cassette. A separate room could also provide a disabled examinee an opportunity for more space, the use of enhanced lighting, special seating, and provisions for rest periods.

Extra Time. Most standardized tests are administered so all candidates have the same amount of time to respond to the test questions. Some accommodations provided to disabled candidates, such as the use of a cassette or braille version of the test, or the use of a reader, may require more testing time. In addition, some individuals with physical or mental disabilities may require time to rest during the examination or between sections of the examination. Extra time is the accommodation most frequently provided in licensing as well as other testing contexts.

Appropriate and Inappropriate Accommodations. Accommodations provide an accessible alternative way for the disabled candidate to demonstrate the desired skill. Accommodations are intended to provide an equally accurate assessment of the knowledge, skill, or ability that the test is designed to measure for both disabled and nondisabled candidates. For example, a candidate with a visual disability may take a reading comprehension test in braille or using large print, and the test would still measure reading comprehension. This accommodation provides a format change that allows the disabled candidate to demonstrate the desired ability unimpaired by the candidate's disability. This would be considered an appropriate or, as Phillips (1993) refers to it, a valid accommodation. The inference made concerning reading ability would be similar for candidates taking the braille version of the test and those taking the test in its standard print version.

An inappropriate or invalid accommodation is one in which the accommodation changes the construct being measured. As in a previously mentioned example, if the purpose of a test was to assess a candidate's reading comprehension, and the candidate requested that the test be read to him or her, the accommodated test would measure listening comprehension, not reading comprehension.

Boards should exercise care when deciding which accommodations to offer or allow. They must keep clearly in mind the purpose of the test, what it is designed to measure, and the inferences that are to be made from the test scores. Before making a final decision, the board might do well to consult with psychometric and legal professionals.

Many accommodations can be provided that will not affect the underlying construct being measured. Boards have the right to deny requests they believe could alter the construct, however. Licensing boards have the dual responsibility to provide reasonable and appropriate accommodations to disabled examinees while providing protection for the health, safety, and welfare of the general population.

Psychometric Implications of Test Accommodations. Accommodations for disabled candidates called for in the Rehabilitation Act of 1973 and the ADA reflect the first instances in which testing organizations have been required to modify testing conditions or the format of an examination for a particular subgroup of test takers. This raises a number of measurement issues. For example, can the scores obtained from an accommodated and a standard administration be equated? Do the scores have the same meaning as in a standard administration? Should the scores obtained from an accommodated test administration be noted or "flagged" so those responsible for using test scores are aware that an accommodation has been provided to a disabled candidate? These concerns are discussed below.

Equating Scores. Can the scores obtained from a test administered with special accommodations be equated with those from a standard test administration? This issue is discussed in "The Score" (APA, 1993), the newsletter of the Division of Evaluation, Measurement, and Statistics of the American Psychological Association. It discusses various equating strategies and the technical difficulties associated with each approach.

One major problem is that the two groups being compared are not random samples from the same population. Secondly, the two groups are not as nearly equivalent as could be desired; the disability may have affected the educational experience and learning of one of the groups. Thirdly, the testing conditions differ: The accommodation may have provided more time, or a different item format. Under these "new" conditions, the construct being measured may have changed even though the nature of the change may not be as obvious as the example noted earlier of shifting from the measurement of reading comprehension to the measurement of listening comprehension.

These problems make it very difficult to equate the scores of examinees taking a test under standard conditions with those of examinees taking the same test with special accommodations. "The Score" concludes, "There is no standard technical solution available for precisely equating a modified administration of a cognitive test, which has itself been modified, to the standardized form—at least, in those situations where the modification is one that will have an effect on test scores" (APA, 1993, p. 8).

Meaning of Scores. The second issue is whether scores on a modified test have the same meaning in terms of what they measure and how they measure it. Standard 14.6 of the *Standards for Educational and Psychological Testing* (AERA, APA, & NCME, 1985) states that "When feasible, the validity and reliability of tests administered to handicapped people, with and without accommodation, should be investigated" (p. 80). However, such studies have rarely, if ever, been conducted in the areas of licensing and certification. There are usually too few candidates requesting accommodations in any one program to make it feasible to conduct studies of this sort within a short time span. Often, it takes the accumulation of data over many years to answer questions of this type. Data are available, however, from the area of college admissions testing. A report from a National Academy of Sciences Panel (Sherman & Robinson, 1982) called for research to clarify whether tests modified for examinees with disabilities are comparable to standard tests, and whether they give valid estimates of the academic abilities of disabled people.

A series of studies on the Scholastic Aptitude Test (SAT) and the Graduate Record Exam (GRE) General Test were undertaken jointly by the College Board, Educational Testing Service, and the Graduate Record Examination Board in response to the National Academy of Science Panel report (Willingham, Ragosta, Bennett, Braun, Rock, & Powers, 1988). The studies cover four major groups of people with disabilities (deaf and hard of hearing, learning disabled, physically disabled, and visually impaired students). Several indicators of score comparability were discussed. Those judged relevant for licensing and certification are summarized below:

The internal consistency reliability of individual subscores for the standard SAT and GRE tends to be approximately .90. The reliability of these tests when administered with accommodations to disabled students was approximately the same. The standard error of measurement was virtually the same for the disabled groups and for those taking the tests under standard conditions.

The factor structure of the SAT and GRE were very similar for several different groups of disabled and nondisabled examinees. This result indicates that nonstandard tests (tests with accommodations) have comparable meaning for the cognitive abilities they measure.

There was little evidence of differential item difficulty. It appears the SAT and GRE are largely free of item types that are unusually difficult for students with particular disabilities compared with other items measuring the same ability.

The use of test scores was studied as another aspect of comparability, namely, admission decisions of colleges and universities using the SAT. Although admissions decisions are not directly relevant to licensing, the use of flagged test scores should interest licensing boards. Willingham et al. concluded that the nature of the selection process seemed comparable for nondisabled and disabled applicants submitting flagged scores, based on an analysis of decisions using test scores and school grades. The probability of admission increased for both groups of applicants as test scores and grades increased. The weight placed on these measures seemed similar for both groups.

When academic performance was predicted using both test score and prior grades, there was little consistent over- or underprediction for the four categories of disabled students. However, the academic performance of some categories of disabled students was less predictable than that of nondisabled students from test scores, from previous grade-point averages, or from both combined. The performance of three of the four groups of disabled students was significantly under- or overpredicted when predictions were based on test scores alone. Deaf and hard-of-hearing students were underpredicted by the SAT; physically disabled and learning-disabled students were overpredicted.

There was evidence that nonstandard timing versions of the SAT and GRE were not comparable to the standard version. All groups of disabled candidates were more likely to complete the test. Some items near the end of the test were easier for three of the four disabled groups studied; and some instances of overpredicted college performance suggested that extended testing time may have contributed to inflated test scores.

Another study (Laing & Farmer, 1984) conducted by the American College Testing Program (ACT), investigated the equivalency of examination formats for examinees with disabilities (physical, learning, visual, and auditory) and nondisabled examinees using standard examination formats. Data from high school students taking the ACT assessment for college admission were used in the study. ACT identified 880,040 examinees who were tested on national test dates in 1982–83, of which 1% (6,289) indicated they had a disabling condition that might require related services. Visually impaired examinees obtained the highest test scores, and deaf and hard-of-hearing examinees obtained the lowest test scores of the disabled groups. These findings are consistent with those from other studies (Bennett, Ragosta, & Stricker, 1984; Ragosta & Kaplan, 1986) which found that visually impaired students and physically disabled students obtained higher mean SAT scores than did learning disabled students, who obtained higher mean scores than deaf and hard-of-hearing students. Scores for disabled examinees in the ACT study, even with accommodations, were lower than those received by nondisabled examinees. This was true for all groups except for visually impaired examinees given accommodations during testing. The prediction of grades was generally lower for disabled examinees. However, caution was recommended in interpreting the results, given small sample sizes and the reliability of self-reported high school and college grades.

The results provided above indicate that nonstandard versions of the SAT and GRE were comparable to standard versions with respect to reliability, factor structure, and item functioning. For the SAT, the use of test scores and grades for admissions decisions was also comparable. (Because of limited sample size, a similar study could not be conducted using GRE scores.) Although there seemed little systematic over- or underprediction of academic performance when both SAT score and previous grades were used, there were instances of over- and underprediction for three of the four disabled groups when test scores were used alone. There was also evidence that nonstandard timing versions of the SAT and GRE were not comparable to the standard version. Although the results from admissions testing provide some indications of comparability, the findings are not definitive.

What are the implications of the research for licensing boards? The results cited above were obtained within an admissions-testing context by organizations that have some of the largest examinee populations in the world. Even these organizations had difficulty conducting some aspects of their studies because of limited sample size and problems with criterion measures. The results presented are based on the best data currently available to investigate the comparability of test scores of disabled candidates taking examinations under nonstandard conditions with nondisabled candidates under standard conditions. It should be noted that these studies were conducted with multiple-choice items and were predominantly measures of verbal and quantitative abilities. There were no results presented on performance assessment, computer-based assessment, or constructed-response measures. In terms of their usefulness for the licensing context, these studies can only be considered suggestive. Comparability studies will be extremely difficult for licensing boards to conduct, however, given the relatively small number of candidates tested overall and the still smaller number who are tested with particular types of disabilities and different accommodations. We do not have definitive answers now about the comparability of test scores obtained under standard and nonstandard conditions for these two groups of examinees, and we are not likely to have them in the near future. It is important that licensing boards collect data in order to accumulate enough information over time to conduct research studies on this issue.

Flagging Test Scores. Because we do not know whether scores obtained for disabled examinees in a licensing context are directly comparable to the scores obtained by nondisabled examinees under standard conditions, should the scores obtained by disabled examinees under nonstandard conditions be flagged? Standard 14.2 of the *Standards for Educational and Psychological Testing* (AERA, APA, & NCME, 1985) states that "until tests have been validated for people who have specific handicapping conditions, test publishers should issue cautionary statements in manuals and elsewhere regarding confidence in interpretations based on such test scores" (p. 79). This is stated as a primary standard. Although the ADA does not prohibit the practice, many candidates with disabilities perceive flagging as discriminatory. It seems that licensing boards may have a responsibility to flag test scores until validity studies have been conducted. The questions licensing boards must answer include:

- Should test scores be flagged?
- If so, under what conditions?
- Who should have access to this information?

The purpose of flagging a test score is to inform and caution users that the score was obtained under nonstandard conditions and might not have the same meaning as other scores obtained under standard conditions. The board should consider who uses the test score other than the board itself, and whether the flag would prevent an inappropriate decision being made with that score.

One rationale for flagging a test score would be research purposes, because it is clear that more research must be conducted on the comparability of test scores taken under standard and nonstandard conditions. As numbers of candidates with various types of disabilities accrue, it is important for licensing boards to investigate the comparability of scores. The possibility of future litigation presents another reason for boards to keep records of the number of disabled examinees who have received accommodations and the type of accommodations provided. Flagged scores could be kept secure at the licensing board and used only for research and record keeping.

Because one of the major responsibilities of licensing boards is to protect the public from practitioners who lack the minimum qualifications for competent performance (Shimberg, 1985), boards should consider if flagging would help protect the public. In this regard, a board has responsibility for deciding who is eligible to take its licensing examination (Shimberg, 1985). If applicants requesting a particular accommodation are required to specify the nature of their disabilities, the board must decide whether candidates will be able to perform the essential functions of a given job, and whether the proposed accommodation would fundamentally alter the construct being measured. This action would be consistent with the content validity model used to support most licensing examinations (Impara & Stoker, 1985; Kane, 1982; Shimberg, 1981). If the board believes the nature and extent of the disability will not allow the examinee to perform essential functions of the job, or that the accommodation will alter the construct being measured, it is the board's responsibility to inform the examinee that he or she is ineligible to take the licensing examination. If the board decides the candidate is eligible to take the examination and the accommodation is acceptable, the board has agreed that this is an appropriate way for the examinee to demonstrate possession of the knowledge and skill necessary to perform the essential functions of the job for which the license is being issued. Under these conditions, it would seem there is little or no basis for flagging the score other than for the board's own records as described above.

Boards should carefully decide whether they believe it necessary to flag scores and, if so, to document the rationale for their decision. If scores are flagged, the board should develop policies and procedures designed to protect the rights of disabled candidates and insure that the scores are kept secure from unauthorized personnel and uses. Flagged scores should not be used in a way that discourages eligible candidates from requesting accommodations, nor that harms their opportunity for employment.

Summary and Implications for Licensing Boards

On July 26, 1992 the ADA went into effect, requiring licensing boards to modify testing conditions and/or formats for disabled individuals requesting accommodations. This was clearly a social policy decision, but it does raise a number of psychometric issues regarding how to implement this policy while maintaining standards and test score comparability. Unfortunately, the quality and quantity of research data on disabled examinees are very limited. As a result, the possibility of establishing the comparability of nonstandard test scores on the basis of empirical studies alone is also limited. It appears that licensing boards will need to use logical analysis and sound judgment to decide what constitutes a comparable task for a disabled examinee, taking into account the purpose of the test as well as the degree of the disabling condition.

Standardization was developed to increase the likelihood that all examinees would have an equal opportunity to demonstrate the relevant knowledge and skills and to provide a common basis for interpreting test scores. Thus, the purpose of standardizing the testing task was to make it more objective and fair for all candidates. If for some examinees, however, the task has extraneous sources of difficulty because of their disability, the test would be unfair. The goal of the accommodation, then, is to eliminate or greatly reduce the extraneous sources of difficulty. One can consider a special accommodation as an attempt to modify the test or the testing condition so it provides comparable information about the individual on the construct the test is designed to assess. In the absence of a great deal of empirical data, this will require the exercise of sound professional judgment.

Boards must balance their responsibility to provide access and accommodations to disabled examinees with their responsibility to protect the health, safety, and welfare of the general population.

In addition, the board must decide, for each disabled examinee requesting an accommodation, whether the:

- Candidate has met all qualifications to take the examination.
- Disability will affect the candidate's ability to perform essential functions of the job.
- Accommodation would alter the measurement of the construct being assessed.
- Accommodation is available and feasible without placing an undue burden on the board.

Boards must make good-faith efforts to meet both sets of demands and, as case law evolves under the ADA, must track rulings and modify their policies and procedures accordingly.

Table 1 presents some steps boards can follow to assist in making these decisions.

TESTING REPEATERS

It is probably safe to say that not all candidates who take a licensure test will pass. Some candidates may not pass the test because they lack the requisite knowledge or skills being measured by the test. Others may not pass because of chance factors unrelated to the purpose of the test (e.g., high test anxiety, temporary illness, or fatigue). Although the reasons for candidates not passing may be varied (and, no doubt, readers have thought of many more than we listed), one thing all such candidates have in common is the need to repeat, that is, to take the licensure test again (provided, of course, that they still want to enter the particular profession).

Table 1. Suggestions for Setting Policy on Disability Issues

1. Prepare up-to-date job analysis information that can be used to establish the essential functions of the particular job or profession in question.

2. Develop and publish a policy on examination accommodations with the advice of psychometricians and legal counsel.

3. Decide on the written documentation necessary to request an accommodation. It would be wise to request an adequate description of the disability, evidence that the disability currently exists, and a rationale for the accommodation requested. This documentation should be provided by an appropriate licensed professional or certified specialist.

4. Establish procedures for responding to requests for accommodations in a timely manner.

5. Identify consultants expert in various disabilities to assist in reviewing and assessing documentation and to perform applicant evaluations when necessary.

6. Develop procedures for board review of all requests for accommodations, or at least those requests which are denied.

7. Keep a record of all requests for accommodations and the response to each request.

8. Decide whether to flag scores, and document the rationale for the decision.

9. Track the emerging court cases under the ADA to determine whether board policies and procedures are consistent with case law.

10. Produce additional program materials and procedures needed to develop special test editions, to administer tests, and to provide services for disabled examinees. Steps should also be taken to develop practice test materials for disabled examinees.

11. Maintain records for possible use in research activities or litigation.

Simply letting those who do not pass take the licensure test again—after all, we all deserve at least a second chance—like most life events is not without complications. In this section, we focus on one potential measurement confound associated with testing repeaters: the practice effect.

Practice Effects and Validity Implications. A practice effect is defined as a gain in test performance resulting from previous experience with the same test or a parallel (alternate) form of the test (Weiss, 1961). Unlike coaching (discussed in a later section of this chapter), in which candidates participate in test preparation activities specifically to improve their test scores, the benefit from practice is derived solely from familiarity with the test and the testing situation. (Candidates who have repeated and/or who have been coached have a greater advantage than first-time test takers who have not been coached. To reduce this advantage as well as to promote test fairness, many testing organizations provide all candidates with a pre-examination booklet that includes sample test items and general test-taking strategies.)

As with all testing applications, at issue here is validity, or accuracy of the inferences drawn from the scores obtained on the licensure test. Licensure tests are designed to ensure that candidates who seek to enter a profession possess knowledge and skills necessary to protect the public's health, safety, and welfare (*Standards for Educational and Psychological Testing*, AERA, APA, & NCME, 1985). The objective is to determine whether candidates have minimal competence; licensure testing, as such, is a selecting-out process (Madaus & Mehrens, 1990). In the vernacular of decision theory (Cronbach & Gleser, 1965), licensure testing also attempts to minimize the incidence of both false acceptances and false rejections; that is, to reduce the granting of licenses to those who lack minimal competence and to avoid withholding licenses from those who possess minimal competence.

The validity of test scores will be compromised to the extent that practice effects are large. A gain in a test score, due only to the effects of practice, would incorrectly be attributed to increased knowledge or improved skills. The social consequence of this false inference takes on much greater import if the spurious gain results in a test score that exceeds the cut score established for the licensure test. The explicit intention of licensure testing would be circumvented if a professional license was granted to a candidate who did not possess the knowledge and skills necessary to safeguard the welfare of the public. It is critical, therefore, that the effects of practice on licensure testing and the factors that contribute to and moderate these effects be better understood. To this end, we will attempt to delineate the domain of practice effects as it relates to licensure testing, bearing in mind that in doing so, we may raise more issues than answers.

Practice Effects: A Brief Review. Researchers investigated the effects of practice on intelligence tests as early as the 1920s (e.g., Dunlap & Snyder, 1920; Richardson & Robinson, 1921; Thorndike, 1922). Though the explanations for the obtained results were not always consistent, the general finding was. Test scores increased upon retesting.

One of the first reviews of literature on the effects of practice was carried out by Weiss, who reviewed 17 studies conducted in Great Britain and the United States on tests of mental ability and scholastic aptitude (1961). He concluded that: (a) practice improved performance; (b) significant practice effects occurred on a first and second retest, but the effects diminished after that; (c) practice effects varied with the time between test administrations—significant effects were obtained for time intervals of 2 weeks to 3 months; and (d) practice effects interacted with mental ability—more intelligent test takers appeared to benefit most from practice.

Since the time of the Weiss review, other studies have attempted to explicate more fully the domain of practice effects. Attention began to focus on characteristics of the test and the testing process that practice affected. As was the case with previous studies, however, the preponderance of tests included in these studies were either mental aptitude or achievement tests. None were used for professional licensure. And most, if not all, used a traditional multiple-choice item format.

Rock and Werts (1980) examined the effects of practice on the Graduate Record Examinations (GRE) Aptitude Test. They were particularly interested in the effects of time and gender on repeaters' performance. They found, in general, that test scores on both the verbal and quantitative components increased upon retesting, regardless of the gender of the test taker. Slightly greater gains after one retest were observed on the verbal component (about 26–27 points) compared with the quantitative component (about 23 points). Both men and women single-repeaters showed greater gains in their verbal scores as the length of time between test administrations increased. This was attributed to growth in verbal abilities over time, not just to the effects of practice. The same result was not observed, however, for the quantitative component. As noted by Rock and Werts, verbal skills would appear to increase throughout adulthood, whereas quantitative skills would appear to be relatively stable.

Wing (1980) examined the effects of practice on five abilities (verbal, judgment, induction, deduction, and number) as measured by the Professional and Administrative Career Examination (PACE), a test used by the federal government to select entry-level employees. Data were collected from more than 60,000 test takers. The effects of practice were found to vary depending upon the ability being measured, the order of presentation of the items, the difficulty of the items, and the speededness of the items.

Wing concluded that practice effects were (a) largest for item types (e.g., letter series, geometric classifications, arithmetic reasoning) that were solvable by systematic application of general problem-solving skills; (b) next largest for test parts subject to speededness; and (c) smallest for item types (vocabulary, comprehension) solvable by application of previously acquired general information.

In 1984, Kulik, Kulik, and Bangert conducted a meta-analysis of 40 studies to identify variables that had an impact upon practice effects. Among the variables of interest were the ability level of the subjects (high, medium, or low); the grade level of the subjects (elementary, high school, postsecondary); and the type of test used (aptitude versus achievement).

Their analyses revealed that practice effects (as measured by an effect-size statistic) were larger when the tests were identical than when the tests were parallel forms of one another (though the effect was still significant in the latter case). The effects of practice were also positively related to the number of practice tests. The average effect size increased from .42 from one practice on an identical test to 1.89 for seven practice tests. For parallel forms, the average effect size increased from .23 to .74. Lastly, the magnitude of practice effects was related to the ability level of the test takers. High-ability test takers gained more from a single practice test (effect size = .82) than did middle-ability test takers (effect size = .40) and low-ability test takers (effect size = .17). Neither grade level nor type of test significantly affected the magnitude of practice effects.

The most recent synthesis of the literature on within-test practice effects for aptitude tests was conducted by Powers (1986). Within-test practice refers to previous exposure to item types that appear later in the same test. Powers coded studies according to the seven characteristics of test items: (a) number of response options, (b) option format, (c) item difficulty, (d) time per item, (e) length of test directions, (f) examples, and (g) overall complexity of directions and/or task. He then related practice effects (as measured by an effect-size statistic) to the item characteristics.

Practice effects were found to be highly related to both the length of directions ($r = .49$) and the complexity of directions ($r = .63$). Likewise, practice effects were related to option format ($r = .42$). In particular, fixed-format items (those in which the same set of alternative answers was used for each question) were associated with the larger effects. In addition, significant relationships were obtained between the number of response options and practice effects ($r = .40$) and between the time allotment per item and practice effects ($r = -.40$). In the latter case, the greater time per item was associated with smaller practice effects (cf. Wing, 1980).

Perhaps the only study to examine the effects of special test preparation on constructed-response items was conducted by Powers, Fowles, and Farnum (1993). Though actually a study of coaching effects, its results are noteworthy, and may be viewed as an upper limit of the effects of practice alone. A pool of 10 essay topics was disclosed and used for coaching purposes by instructors at four different colleges or universities. Following the coaching, students wrote two essays—one on a previously disclosed topic and the other on a topic that was not included in the disclosed set. Scoring of the essays was done by trained readers who independently assigned holistic scores on a 6-point scale. The results indicated relatively small differences between the scores on the disclosed essay and the new essay topics (across all students, the effect size was .15). Furthermore, using a cut score of 3.0, Powers et al. found little increase in the pass rate as a result of students writing on a disclosed topic compared to a new topic.

Summary

Several generalities may be culled from research on the effects of practice (also see Bond, 1989; Hopkins, Stanley, & Hopkins, 1990):

- Practice effects are greater on identical forms of a test than on parallel forms of a test.
- The average practice effect for a group of test takers is approximately .20 standard deviation units.
- Test takers of high ability benefit most from practice.
- Practice effects are more pronounced on speeded tests than they are on power tests.
- Less-experienced test takers benefit most from practice.
- The longer the time interval between the test and the first retest, the smaller the effects of practice (exclusive of growth effects).
- The more complex the item, the greater the effects of practice.

- Certain types of items (e.g., constructed-response) may be more resistant to practice effects than traditional multiple-choice items.

Practice Effects and Licensure Testing

Tests of professional licensure are noticeably missing from the research on practice effects. We can only speculate this may be because of the smaller numbers of test takers compared, for example, to Scholastic Assessment Test takers; or because the failure rate in licensure testing may not be high enough to prompt the concern of licensing agencies.

We would rather err on the side on conservatism and assume that licensure tests are prone to the effects of practice, at least to some degree. The interpretation of the significance of these effects, however, may need to be viewed differently for licensure tests. Unlike most aptitude or achievement tests, licensure tests are criterion referenced. That is, test scores are compared to an external cut score; test takers' scores are not compared to one another. The real issue, then, is not whether there is a practice effect per se, but whether the effect is strong enough, on average, to push the test taker above the cut score on repeated administrations of the licensure test or alternate forms thereof. This question awaits empirical investigation.

Psychometrically Based Issues Related to Testing Repeaters

Conjoined with the issue just raised are a variety of psychometrically based concerns. In this section we will acquaint the reader with some of these concerns. (Where appropriate, the reader will be directed to other chapters in this book for more in-depth discussions of these psychometric issues.)

Cut Scores (also see chapter 10). A cut score or passing score is typically set by a committee of subject-matter experts using any of a number of standard-setting procedures (e.g., Angoff, Jaeger, Nedelsky, contrasting groups). In order to diminish the effects of practice, emphasis must be placed on setting a cut score that unambiguously differentiates between those candidates who do and do not possess minimal competence. Measurement error should be explicitly considered during the standard-setting process. The standard error of the cut score should be such that the rates of false rejections and false acceptances are minimized.

Regression Effects. It is probable that upon retesting, a candidate's test score will increase, due, in part, to simple regression effects (Campbell & Stanley, 1966). That is, candidates who have scored very low on the initial test will, on average, score higher upon retesting (i.e., their scores will regress towards the mean score of the second test). This phenomenon occurs because of the imperfect correlation between the two tests. Without recognizing the potential impact of regression effects, the inference drawn from a test score above the cut score—that a candidate possesses minimal competence—may be suspect.

Equating (also see chapter 11). Testing repeaters may also affect both the methods used for equating and the outcomes of equating studies. Essentially, equating refers to statistical procedures designed to ensure that scores from alternate forms of a test will be directly comparable (Angoff, 1971). A frequently used equating design for licensure testing is the nonequivalent groups-common item method. In this design, an identical subset of test items appears in each form of a test along with a distinct subset of test items. Two groups of test takers receive each form of the test. The comparability of the test scores is based upon the results obtained for the common (equated) subset of test items. If a large proportion of repeaters were included in the equating study, however, their previous exposure to the equated subset of test items would introduce an unwanted source of error.

The presence of a large number of repeaters in the second test administration would most likely lead to a gain in scores on the equated subset of test items. This could lead to the erroneous conclusion that the test takers in this administration have higher abilities than the group in the previous administration. A related confound arises if the nonequated items in the second test administration now appear to be more difficult than the nonequated items in the first test administration. A likely, though erroneous, outcome would be that the cut score for the second test administration is adjusted downward to compensate for the perceived greater difficulty of the items that constitute the second test.

Another form of equating, section pre-equating (Holland, 1981) does not require the use of two complete forms of a test; rather, multiple sections of items for equating are embedded across operational tests. Not all candidates, therefore, receive the same equating sections. The placement of the equating sections also varies across the operational tests; and the equating sections do not count toward the candidate's test score. Though promising, this method of equating may be prone to within-test practice effects. That is, because each pre-equating section is parallel to some operational section of the test, candidates may receive practice on particular item types that will affect their performance on the scored sections. The magnitude of these effects may vary depending upon the types of items (see Leary & Dorans, 1985, for a review of within-test effects).

Test Security. According to Burns (1985), for licensure testing to be considered secure, all candidates should have the same testing experience, and some candidates should not gain advantage by prior knowledge of the test. Repeaters clearly gain advantage by their prior exposure to and experience with either the same test or an alternative form of the test, however. And, as Burns notes, licensure tests may be particularly vulnerable to breaches of security because their specialized content may not readily lend itself to the construction of large item pools. It would appear, then, that part of maintaining the security of licensure testing is reducing the effects of previous exposure to the test (i.e., practice effects).

Time between test administrations. One of the easiest ways to reduce the effects of practice and to enhance test security is for the licensing agency to set a minimum interval before a candidate is eligible to repeat. Candidates may be required to wait a minimum of 6 months before being allowed to repeat, for example. Safeguards, such as verifying candidates' identities, could be implemented to ensure that candidates are not taking the licensure test before they are officially permitted to do so.

Item types. As we have seen, research has indicated that practice does not affect all item types similarly. Items that are not speeded are less prone to practice effects, for example, as are items not solvable by the application of specific rules.

Less complex items also appear more resistant to the effects of practice. Using constructed-response types of items may reduce the effects of practice. Continued efforts are needed to clarify the characteristics of items that make them resistant to the effects of practice.

Alternate forms. The effects of practice may be reduced, (though as noted earlier, not eliminated) by using multiple forms of the licensure test. Practice effects are less pronounced when alternate forms of a test are used. One effective variant of alternative forms testing is called spiralling. This refers to the packaging and subsequent distribution of multiple forms of a test to an administration site. By spiralling the tests, essentially random groups of test takers receive an alternate form of the test. The chances of a repeater receiving the same form more than once are thus dramatically reduced.

Computerized adaptive testing. Computerized adaptive testing (CAT) is a fairly recent technological development that may prove useful to reduce the effects of practice and increase test security. Adaptive testing was designed to enable more accurate and more efficient determinations of a test taker's true ability by matching the difficulty level of each presented item to the estimated true ability level of the test taker (Lord, 1980).

In CAT, as described by Wainer (1990), a test taker begins the test with an item in the middle of a prospective range of difficulty. Then, depending upon the correctness of the response, the next item is either harder or easier. If the item was answered correctly, the next item would be harder; if, however, the item was answered incorrectly, the next item would be easier. After each response to an item, the test taker's current ability level is estimated. Based upon the current ability estimate, a new test item of appropriate difficulty is then selected. Testing continues in this manner until a predetermined level of measurement precision is attained, a preselected number of items has been given, or a predetermined amount of time has elapsed (Thissen & Mislevy, 1990). The most recent estimate of a test taker's ability level is used as the test score.

A particularly appealing feature of CAT is that it is possible—though not necessarily easy—to establish exposure parameters or decision rules that control the selection of test items (Thissen & Mislevy, 1990). By incorporating these item exposure controls, each test taker could be presented with a completely unique set of test items. Clearly, this capability greatly reduces, if not eliminates, threats to test security.

Additionally, as noted by Green (1983), CAT enhances security because the computer contains the item pool, rather than just the specific subset of items that will comprise the actual test. This makes it very difficult for test takers to spuriously improve their scores by learning a few items. Still, every effort should be made to ensure that the item pool is secure.

Summary and Recommendations

It is very likely that a candidate's test score will increase upon retesting, particularly if the same test is administered on each occasion. This gain, however, cannot be attributed exclusively to growth in a candidate's knowledge or skill base;

part of this gain may simply be due to a candidate's previous familiarity with the test—a practice effect. One potential consequence of this is granting a license to someone who does not possess the knowledge and skills necessary to protect the public's health, safety, and welfare. Licensing boards must, therefore, try to minimize the effects of practice on licensure test performance. The following suggestions are offered to help boards mitigate the effects of practice:

- Use alternate forms. Alternate or spiralled test forms help safeguard against item-specific practice effects. A candidate's recall of the item from a previous administration cannot come into play because the same items are not included on the alternate forms.
- Extend the time between test administrations. Few studies have examined the stability of practice effects over long periods of time. Nevertheless, a reasonable expectation is that the effects of practice will be less pronounced when the interval between test administrations increases.
- Use non-multiple-choice items. To our knowledge, no research has been conducted examining the effects of practice on non-multiple-choice items. The study by Powers et al. (1993), indicates, however, that coaching (viewed as an upper limit on practice) does not signifi-cantly affect constructed-response items. The use of non-multiple-choice items to reduce the effects of practice should be explored.
- Use computerized adaptive testing. The allure of computerized adap-tive testing is its capacity to develop, on the spot, unique forms of a licensure test, thus potentially eliminating the effects of practice. The technical requirements to see this to fruition are not trivial, however. As work continues in this area, the use of this testing option should become more feasible.

COACHING

The preceding discussions of testing accommodations and practice effects treated broad questions of fairness in the context of high-stakes licensure tests. The question of fairness arises again on the issue of coaching, a technique some have embraced in attempts to improve their test scores.

The term "coaching" covers a wide variety of test-preparation activities that some view in a negative light. Clearly, research on the effects of coaching deserves the same thoughtful discussion we have given studies dealing with testing accommodations and practice effects—and for many of the same reasons, as we shall see.

Although coaching in athletics is generally thought a positive and often necessary activity, coaching for tests sometimes has negative connotations, in that test coaching is perceived as an illicit or, at least, nebulously inappropriate activity (Cole, 1982). Nevertheless, test coaching is a widespread enterprise. Many high schools provide in-class, instructional preparation for college entrance examina-tions. An ever-growing commercial industry provides test preparation courses for college, graduate school, and professional examinations. Test preparation books and software packages are available in almost every library and bookstore in the country.

As Powers (1993a) notes, test preparation today is most often associated with high-stakes tests. These include assessments that are used either to select students for undergraduate and graduate study; to determine that they have demonstrated sufficient knowledge and/or skills to leave formal instructional settings; or to certify or license them in their professional careers. In some situations, such as those in which tests are used for accountability, both educators and administrators often have an interest, albeit somewhat vested, in making sure students are well prepared to take tests (Powers, 1993a).

Test publishers are also paying more attention to preparation. They are taking more responsibility to ensure that all test candidates are on as nearly equal ground as possible with respect to the methods required for good test taking. As Powers (1993a) notes, their rationale is straightforward.

> To be valid indicators, test scores should reflect the substance of the assessment much more than the method of assessment. Simply put, tests should reflect more than just the ability to take tests. (p. 2)

What is Coaching? Anastasi (1981) distinguishes three broad types of test preparation and discusses their implications for test taking. The first, test-taking orientation, entails test practice, which may help instill confidence and relieve anxiety by providing opportunities to learn appropriate test-taking strategies. The rationale for this intervention is that it can put all examinees on an equal footing with respect to their sophistication about test taking. A second type of preparation involves instruction in broad cognitive skills designed to develop intellectual skills and problem-solving strategies that may have broad application. This intervention, which might best be termed education, should improve both test scores and criterion performance. The third type of intervention concentrates on the specific knowledge and skills covered by the test, rather than more broadly on the larger domain that the test is intended to reflect. This type of intervention, according to Anastasi, is coaching. Bond (1989) espouses a similar definition of coaching. In his view, any instruction given primarily to increase test scores on a particular examination and only incidentally to improve the more general skills that the test is designed to measure can be considered coaching. Other writers (e.g., Slack & Porter, 1980) have argued that coaching includes any intervention, including full-time instruction for periods of 6 months or more, that results in improved test scores. The dictionary also presents a broadly inclusive definition, "to train intensively by instruction, demonstration, and practice" (Webster, 1974, p. 213). For the purposes of this paper, we will adopt Messick's (1982) definition: Coaching is "any intervention procedure specifically undertaken to improve test scores, whether by improving the skills measured by the test or by improving the skills for taking the test, or both" (p. 70). Therefore, "coaching" and "test preparation activities" will be used interchangeably in this chapter.

A list of test preparation activities is provided by Cole (1982). She lists the following six components of test preparation: (1) supplying correct answers (cheating), (2) taking the test for practice, (3) maximizing motivation, (4) optimizing test anxiety, (5) instructing in test wiseness, and (6) instructing in test content.

Components 5 and 6 are further delineated. Instruction in test wiseness includes: (a) general test-wiseness instruction (being careful, following directions, using good guessing strategies); (b) instruction in identifying test construction flaws and cues; and (c) use of special strategies for a novel or complex question format. Test wiseness may be generally defined as "a subject's capacity to utilize the characteristics and formats of the test and/or test-taking situation to receive a high score" (Millman, Bishop, & Ebel, 1965, p. 707). Instruction in test content, Component 6 in Cole's list, also has three subcomponents: (a) instruction in areas related to the interpretation of scores (the content domain for an achievement measure, the ability being measured, requisite skills or knowledge for eventual success for an admissions or selection measure); (b) review of previous instruction in areas related to score interpretation; and (c) instruction in test-specific content unrelated to score interpretation.

Test Preparation and Validity. Test preparation raises questions regarding test validity. Each individual enters the testing situation with his or her own assortment of skills, knowledge, experience, and characteristics. The testing situation is intended to produce a *sample* of performance in order to infer something more general about the individual. The extent to which such samples of performance (i.e., test scores) lead to correct interpretations of the more general domain is validity. Test preparation activities can have different effects on validity. These activities can give rise to three broad outcomes: (a) criterion performance overprediction, (b) predictor noise reduction, and (c) criterion and predictor performance gains. The particular outcome is entirely dependent on the nature of the test preparation activity.

Criterion Performance Overprediction. Efforts to improve the performance sample in the test without concomitant energy on the more general domain being measured poses a serious threat to validity. If coaching raises test performance above ability levels, then scores cannot be interpreted as accurate measures of ability. In Cole's (1982) scheme, the first component, supplying correct answers (cheating), would lead to this negative outcome. The result is that the test candidate may move from what Bond (1989) terms a "valid rejection" category to a "false acceptance" category. What is learned for the test is not transferred to the criterion; criterion performance is overpredicted as a result.

Cheating, once confined to glancing at your neighbor's bubble sheet, has advanced significantly in recent years. Technology and ingenuity have combined to present formidable challenges to test security. Testing companies and agencies regularly expose schemes involving paid and unpaid imposters. Some paid imposters may be hired (at additional cost) to resemble a candidate. The information age has also aided and abetted the cottage industry of test cheating. Facsimile machines, high-speed transoceanic and transcontinental flights, and tape recorders have been exposed recently as tools used to circumvent the testing process.

Subcomponent 5b, instruction in identifying test construction flaws and cues, may also result in test scores that overestimate knowledge and skills. Consequently, test developers should be careful to screen assembled tests for item cue and overlap. Similarly, Subcomponent 6c represents instruction in content that is important to know in order to do well on the test, but is unrelated to criterion performance. For many kinds of test content, it is difficult to imagine an example of this subcomponent. Some item types, however, such as verbal analogies are rarely seen outside a test. Specific instruction in verbal analogies might improve test performance, but probably would not result in an increase in a student's academic performance. A licensure test, assuming a good job analysis and a specification plan that closely matches test content to job requirements, should be less susceptible to this type of overprediction.

Predictor Noise Reduction. Components 2–4 in Cole's scheme may also affect test validity. Unlike techniques that lead to overprediction of criterion performance, preparation activities that include test practice and that promote individual motivation and optimize test anxiety should allow candidates to better show their true ability. These activities would seem to be in the best interest of the test candidates, the test publishers, and all users of test scores. Further, Subcomponents 5a, instruction on general test wiseness, and 5c, use of special strategies for novel or complex question formats, might also enable the test-anxious student to be more relaxed and efficient during the test. In this instance, test performance would be improved and should be a more accurate reflection of ability. Such instruction does not enable students to achieve scores that overestimate their true level of knowledge and skills. Rather, it reduces the chances of underperforming (Jones, 1986). Such test preparation might result in a candidate moving from a "false rejection" category to a "valid acceptance" classification, an indisputably positive outcome (Bond, 1989).

If, however, test preparation of this type is only available to some candidates, the differences in the extent to which near-maximal performance is achieved could affect the validity of interpretation of the scores (Cole, 1982). This situation has social implications as well. If candidates who can afford special test preparation and coaching schools gain an advantage on admissions and professional licensure or certification tests, then testing could contribute to a sharper economic stratification in society. This result runs counter to testing's traditional goal of offering opportunity to the most capable regardless of economic background. For a test like the College Board SAT, for which there are a large number of books, software packages, and special preparation programs, the potential for unfairness is significant. As of 1988, there were at least 20 books and 30 software packages designed specifically to help students prepare for this single test (Powers, 1988). The greatest threat to equity, however, comes from the differential availability of formal commercially offered coaching programs. These programs may require substantial investments of time (up to and exceeding 40 hours of in-class instruction plus a large amount of time for homework and practice) and money. As these programs generally guarantee substantial score improvements but are not accessible to all, the public perception is that unfairness exists (Powers, 1993a). This persists despite the fact that the coaching-school claims for large score gains on the SAT have not been substantiated (cf. Messick & Jungeblut, 1981; DerSimonian & Laird, 1983; Kulick, Bangert-Drowns, & Kulick, 1984; Becker, 1990, Powers, 1993b).

Some authors (e.g., Downey, 1977; Sarnacki, 1979, 1990) have suggested general instruction in test wiseness for all test takers in order to attempt to eliminate or minimize the test-wiseness variable. Test publishers and agencies seem to have heeded this advice. Candidate information bulletins containing test descriptions, general test-taking strategies, and sample questions are generally provided to test candidates well in advance of the test date. More detailed information that might include the test specifications or body of knowledge, practice tests, and disclosed tests are often provided as well, particularly for tests with relatively large volumes. It should be noted, however, that Stricker (1982) found no discernible influence from disclosed tests on the SAT.

Criterion and Predictor Performance Gains. A third situation in which coaching can affect validity applies to strategies that focus on the criterion domain. Subcomponent 6a, instruction in areas related to the interpretation of scores, is such a strategy. For professional certification, 6a involves instruction in the knowledge and skills required for practicing the profession. For standardized achievement testing, it involves instruction in the knowledge and skills taught in the classroom. For admissions and selection, 6a involves instruction in the requisite knowledge and skills required for college, graduate, or professional education or a job (Cole, 1982). This strategy is a legitimate and defensible form of coaching, as it would raise both the level of test performance and facility within the domain being assessed. Assuming the test measures knowledge and skills that take time to acquire, this strategy must be associated with a reasonably long-term educational effort. In contrast, reviewing previously learned material relevant to the criterion, Subcomponent 6b requires much less time, but can also lead to performance improvements on both predictor and criterion. For the borderline candidate, coaching activities that focus on the criterion domain should have the effect of moving the student from the "valid rejection" category to the "valid acceptance" category.

The sole difficulty with strategies that focus on the criterion domain is that they rely heavily on the test as an authentic and representative sampling of that domain. If the test misses the mark, then well-prepared candidates will be underpredicted. They will be moved from a "valid acceptance" to a "false rejection" classification. This is one reason job analysis is critical for licensure and certification testing.

Coaching and New Forms of Assessment. Assessment is currently undergoing some very dramatic changes. The trends toward an emphasis on performance assessment, authentic assessment, computer-based assessment, and constructed-response item types will, no doubt, have ramifications for test coaching. It is too early to tell, however, just what the effects will be. Certainly, some measures might be less susceptible to illicit coaching, whereas others might be more so. For example, short-answer, open-ended items presented and scored by computer should resist coachability. Computerized adaptive tests, which by matching items with ability estimates are shorter and therefore expose fewer items, should also be less vulnerable to various forms of cheating (see Chapter 12).

The coachability of performance assessments is uncertain, but will likely depend upon fidelity of simulation and sufficiency of instruction. An oft-spoken criticism about standardized testing—that teachers end up "teaching to the test"— ironically seems relevant here. The argument against teaching to the test seems based on the assumption that the test is not worthy of teaching to; that the educational experience will have little positive outcome as the test does not reflect the real world. In apparent contrast, performance assessments, which are supposed to simulate important criterion behavior, should be worthy of instruction. Therefore, if the assessment has high fidelity and the instruction is comprehensive, then the assessment should predict and the instruction should transfer to the criterion.

Recommendations for Licensure and Certification Programs. What is the relevance of coaching for "high-stakes" licensure and certification programs? What can be done to reduce threats to validity? A brief list of recommendations follows:

- Understand the criterion domain so that the test is a true reflection of the profession in question. Any test preparation activities that focus on the test content should thus provide at least some relevant education. The best way to maintain a strong link between the test and the profession is through periodic job analysis, followed by systematic test development.
- Provide adequate test information to all candidates in advance of the test. To help ensure candidates are on the same level playing ground, adequate test information should be provided in a candidate information bulletin. The bulletin should include: an overall description of the test, test-taking strategies, policy information about guessing and other relevant scoring issues, sample test items (particularly if they are at all novel), and information about the specifications for the test.
- Promote worthwhile educational activity. Licensure and certification programs might undertake several activities to promote education via testing. They could promote education by providing lists of reference texts and articles, publishing study manuals, and conducting review courses, for example.
- Maintain secure tests. Test security is the only safeguard against cheating. The initial stages of test development through test scoring and reporting must be secured. Further, item pools must be replenished on a regular basis.
- Review test items and forms for possible test-construction flaws. Test items should be carefully screened for flaws that might cue the correct answer. Assembled tests should be reviewed to minimize item overlap.
- Conduct item analysis. Even careful review may not identify all possible test-construction flaws prior to administration. Item analysis, however, may identify misbehaving items that may be flawed.

CONCLUSION

Testing special populations, testing repeaters, and coaching all have implications that can affect the validity and fairness of licensing examinations. This chapter has presented some important issues related to each of these topics as well as their psychometric implications. In addition, we have provided advice licensing boards can consider when establishing or reviewing related policy issues. It is important that policies encourage equal access and fairness, and do so in a way that assures confidence in licensing as one way of protecting the public from incompetent practitioners.

Our review of the literature indicated that very little research on these topics was conducted within the context of licensure testing. This requires that boards set policy based on information and research findings from other contexts. Researchers and licensing boards must conduct studies to guide board policies on these topics.

REFERENCES

American Educational Research Association, American Psychological Association, & National Council on Measurement in Education. (1985). *Standards for educational and psychological testing*. Washington, DC: American Psychological Association.

American Psychological Association, Division of Evaluation, Measurement, and Statistics. (1993, January). Psychometric and assessment issues raised by the Americans with Disabilities Act (ADA). *The Score, 15*(4), 1-15.

Anastasi, A. (1981). Coaching, test sophistication, and developed abilities. *American Psychologist, 36*(10), 1086-1093.

Angoff, W. H. (1971). Scales, norms, and equivalent scores. In R. L. Thorndike (Ed.), *Educational measurement* (2nd ed., pp. 508-600). Washington, DC: American Council on Education.

Becker, B. J. (1990). Coaching for the Scholastic Aptitude Test: Further synthesis and appraisal. *Review of Educational Research, 60*, 373-417.

Bennett, R. E., Ragosta, M., & Stricker, L. (1984). The test performance of handicapped people (Research Rep. No. 84-32). Princeton, NJ: Educational Testing Service.

Bond, L. (1989). The effects of special preparation on measures of scholastic ability. In R. L. Linn (Ed.), *Educational measurement* (3rd ed., pp. 429-444). New York: Macmillan.

Burns, R. L. (1985). Guidelines for developing and using licensure tests. In J. C. Fortune (Ed.), *Understanding testing in occupational licensing* (pp. 15-44). San Francisco, CA: Jossey-Bass.

Campbell, D. T., & Stanley, J. C. (1966). *Experimental and quasi-experimental designs for research*. Chicago: Rand McNally.

Cronbach, L. J., & Gleser, G. C. (1965). *Psychological tests and personnel decisions* (2nd ed.). Urbana: University of Illinois Press.

Cole, N. (1982). The implications of coaching for ability testing. In A. Wigdor & W. R. Gardner (Eds.), *Ability testing; Use consequences and controversies, Part 2: Documentation sections* (pp. 389-414). Washington, DC: National Academy Press.

DerSimonian, R., & Laird, N. M. (1983). Evaluating the effect of coaching on SAT scores: A meta-analysis. *Harvard Educational Review, 53*, 1-15.

Downey, G. W. (1977, January). Is it time we started teaching children how to take tests? *The American School Board Journal, 164*, 26-31.

Dunlap, K., & Snyder, A. (1920). Practice effects in intelligence tests. *Journal of Experimental Psychology, 3*, 396-403.

ETS Committee for Testing Handicapped People. (1988). *Sourcebook for testing handicapped examinees.* Princeton, NJ: Educational Testing Service.

Equal Employment Opportunity Commission and the U.S. Department of Justice. (Oct. 1991). *Americans with Disabilities Act Handbook.* Washington, DC: Equal Opportunity Commission and the U.S. Department of Justice.

Green, B. F. (1983). The promise of tailored tests. In H. Wainer & S. Messick (Eds.), *Principals of modern psychological measurement* (pp. 69-80). Hillsdale, NJ: Erlbaum.

Holland, P. W. (1981). *Section pre-equating the Graduate Record Examination* (Program Statistics Research Tech. Rep. No. 81-13). Princeton, NJ: Educational Testing Service.

Hopkins, K. D., Stanley, J. C., & Hopkins, B. R. (1990). *Educational and psychological measurement and evaluation* (7th ed.). Angled Cliffs, NJ: Prentice Hall.

Impara, J. C., & Stoker, H. W. (1985). Determining reliability and validity of licensure examinations. In J.C. Fortune (Ed.), *Understanding testing in occupational licensing* (pp. 65-86). San Francisco, CA: Jossey-Bass.

Jones, R. F. (1986). The effect of commercial coaching courses on performance on the MCAT. *Journal of Medical Education, 61*, 273-284.

Kane, M. A. (1982). The validity of licensure examinations. *American Psychologist, 37*. (8), 911-918.

Kulik, J. A., Bangert-Drowns, R. L., & Kulik, C. C. (1984). Effectiveness of coaching for aptitude tests. *Psychological Bulletin, 95*, 179-188.

Kulik, J. A., Kulik, C. C., & Bangert, R. L. (1984). Effects of practice on aptitude and achievement test scores. *American Educational Research Journal, 21*, 435-447.

Laing, J., & Farmer, M. (1984). *Use of the ACT assessment by examinees with disabilities* (ACT Research Rep. No. 84). Iowa City, IA: American College Testing Publications.

Leary, L. F., & Dorans, N. J. (1985). Implications for altering the context in which test items appear: A historical perspective on an immediate concern. *Review of Educational Research, 55*, 387-413.

Lord, F. M. (1980). *Applications of item response theory to practical testing problems.* Hillsdale, NJ: Erlbaum.

Madaus, G., & Mehrens, W. A. (1990). Conventional tests for licensure. In J. Millman & L. Darling-Hammond (Eds.), *The new handbook of teacher evaluation: Assessing elementary and secondary school teachers* (pp. 257-277). Newbury Park, CA: Sage.

Messick, S. (1982). Issues of effectiveness and equity in the coaching controversy: Implications for educational and testing practice. *Educational Psychologist, 17*, 67-91.

Messick, S., & Jungeblut, A. (1981). Time and method in coaching for the SAT. *Psychological Bulletin, 95*, 191-216.

Millman, J., Bishop, C. H., & Ebel, R. L. (1965). Analysis of test-wiseness. *Educational and Psychological Measurement, 25,* 707-726.

Phillips, S. E. (1993). Testing condition accommodations for disabled students. *West's Education Law Quarterly, 2,* (1), 366-389.

Powers, D. E. (1986). Relations of test item characteristics to test preparation/ test practice effects: A quantitative summary. *Psychological Bulletin, 100,* 67-77.

Powers, D. E. (1988). *Preparing for the SAT: A survey of programs and resources* (College Board Rep. No. 88-7 and ETS Research Report No. 88-40). New York: College Entrance Examination Board.

Powers, D. E. (1993a). Coaching for tests and examinations (Research Memorandum No. 93-7). Princeton, NJ: Educational Testing Service.

Powers, D. E. (1993b). Coaching for the SAT: A summary of the summaries and an update. *Educational Measurement: Issues and Practice, 12,* 24-39.

Powers, D. E., Fowles, M. E., & Farnum, M. (1993). Prepublishing the topics for a test of writing skills: A small-scale simulation. *Applied Measurement in Education, 6,* 119-135.

Ragosta, M., & Kaplan, B. A. (1986). *A survey of handicapped students taking special test administrations of the SAT and GRE* (Research Rep. No. 86-5). Princeton, NJ: Educational Testing Service.

Richardson, F., & Robinson, E. S. (1921). Effects of practice upon the scores and predictive validity of the alpha intelligence examination. *Journal of Experimental Psychology, 4,* 300-317.

Rock, D., & Werts, C. (1980). *An analysis of time-related score increments and/or decrements for GRE repeaters across ability and sex groups* (GRE Board Rep. GREB No. 77-9R). Princeton, NJ: Educational Testing Service.

Sarnacki, R. E. (1979). An examination of test-wiseness in the cognitive domain. *Review of Educational Research, 49,* 252-279.

Sarnacki, R. E. (1990). Test-wiseness. In H. J. Walbert & G. D. Haertel (Eds.), *The international encyclopedia of educational evaluation* (1st ed.; pp. 124-125). New York: Pergamon Press.

Schmitt, K. (1991). Testing across the nation. *Clear Exam Review, 2*(1), 4-6.

Sherman, S., & Robinson, N. (Eds.) (1982). *Ability testing of handicapped people: Dilemma for government, science, and the public.* Washington, DC: National Academy Press.

Shimberg, B. (1981). Testing for licensure and certification. *American Psychologist, 36.* (10) 138-1146.

Shimberg, B. (1985). Overview of professional and occupational licensing. In. J.C. Fortune (Ed.), *Understanding testing in occupational licensing* (pp. 1-14). San Francisco, CA: Jossey-Bass.

Slack, W. V., & Porter, D. (1980). The Scholastic Aptitude Test: A critical appraisal. *Harvard Educational Review, 50,* 154-175.

Stricker, L. J. (1982). *Test disclosure and retest performance on the Scholastic Aptitude Test* (College Board Rep. No. 82-7). New York: College Entrance Examination Board.

Thissen, D., & Mislevy, R. J. (1990). Testing algorithms. In H. Wainer (Ed.), *Computerized adaptive testing: A primer* (pp. 103-135). Hillsdale, NJ: Erlbaum.

Thorndike, E. L. (1922). Practice effects in intelligence tests. *Journal of Experimental Psychology, 5,* 101-107.

Wainer, H. (1990). Introduction and history. In H. Wainer (Ed.). *Computerized adaptive testing: A primer* (pp. 1-21). Hillsdale, NJ: Erlbaum.

Webster's new collegiate dictionary. (1974). Springfield, MA: G. & C. Merriam.

Weiss, R. A. (1961). *The effects of practicing a test: A review of the literature* (ETS Rep. No. RM-61-12). Princeton, NJ: Educational Testing Service.

Willingham, W. W., Ragosta, M., Bennett, R. E., Braun, H., Rock, P. A., & Powers, D. E. (1988). *Testing handicapped people.* Needham Heights, MA: Allyn and Bacon.

Wing, H. (1980). Practice effects with traditional mental test items. *Applied Psychological Measurement, 4,* 141-155.

Section Two

Overview of the Procedures for Developing a Licensure Examination

James C. Impara

Buros Institute of Mental Measurements

There are a variety of strategies that may be employed in the development of a licensure examination. The following list of activities illustrates typical procedures. Depending on the needs and conditions of the particular occupation, certain variations in specific activities may take place or changes in the sequence may be appropriate. In addition to the procedures listed, many decisions will be made that may add activities. For example, the decision to use a computerized item bank or to enter into a computerized adaptive testing format will require procedures in addition to those described briefly below.

1. Conducting a job (or practice) analysis. Often practitioners in the occupation are surveyed to assess the nature of the job; the essential knowledge, skills, and abilities (KSAs) associated with the job; the extent that the KSAs are critical to performance in the profession for the purpose of protecting the public; and the extent that these critical KSAs are at the entry level of practice. An initial list of KSAs is often developed by a committee (perhaps supplemented by "shadowing" some practitioners and seeking additional insights from interviews with others) and a survey questionnaire is drafted and piloted. The pilot testing leads to expansion and development of the questionnaire that is then sent to a sample of practitioners. Responses may be analyzed by staff or a consultant.

2. Developing test specifications based on the job analysis. The licensure board, or a test committee, determines the specific content dimensions and nature of the test by examining the job analysis (often assisted by quantitative analyses of the survey done by staff or a consultant). It may be possible to obtain a copy of the test specifications (or even the job analysis) of the tests currently being used in the same or related fields in other states or nationally and compare them with each other to assess the essential differences among the occupations of interest.

3. Making a decision about test development. Strategies at this stage include: (a) develop an original test from scratch, (b) use a test already developed by another state or a national organization, or (c) attempt to collaborate with other states to develop a new test. Test development is an arduous and long-term project that has far-reaching implications and costs. If the occupation to be licensed is unique this may be the only available option. If original test development is the decision, the development process could be expected to take up to 2 years and it should be done with the advice of a test specialist/consultant.

Ideally, test development includes such activities as drafting original test items, reviewing the items by a testing committee, revising the items, pilot testing the items, assessing the psychometric properties of the items (DIF analysis) and the total scores (reliability and validity studies), refining the items based on the pilot test results, assembling the items into a final form (and having one or more alternate forms is desirable).

4. Arranging for test administration. The examination must be administered and scored. Various decisions need to be made (e.g., distributing the tests, employing test proctors, insuring test security, compliance with the ADA legislation) before the testing program can become operational.

5. Arranging for test scoring and data analysis. Reports need to be developed for the Board as well as for candidates who were tested. Reports to the Board often include various statistics about the test (e.g., item analyses, DIF analyses, reliability estimates, overall and subgroup score distributions). Examinees will need to know their test results, licensed or not, and the Board may decide to provide some diagnostic feedback to candidates who failed the test.

6. Setting a passing score. This is one of the most important aspects of the process and one of the most frustrating. There are several ways to set such scores, but only a few of these ways are considered by the testing profession to be defensible in the context of licensure. The nature of licensure precludes certain mathematical procedures—regression analyses that relate test score to future competency is virtually impossible; and arbitrary criterion-referenced ("70%" of the total score) and norm-referenced (scores above the "national average") methods may not hold up in court. Among the most often used methods is one reported by Angoff (1971). His method involves a panel of judges who independently examine each item and estimate the proportion of minimally competent examinees who will answer correctly. These proportions are averaged across panelists and the sum of the average proportions represents the cut score (often some adjustments are made to the derived cut score based on sampling error or measurement error or both). There are other similar methods that rely on expert judgment and an examination of the test items, and there are some variations on the Angoff method.

7. Equating the test across test forms. The test form should be reconstituted by replacing all or most items for each administration of the test (for reasons of security—there will be candidates who are repeating the test who may be unfairly advantaged by having seen the items previously). This will require equating each different form of the test to some base form. There are several ways to accomplish this, but the decision about how it will be done is needed before the first test form is developed (the method used has implications for how the test is constructed).

The above model for organizing a licensure testing program is fairly standard for any testing program. Many important steps have been mentioned only in passing (e.g., conducting reliability and validity studies) yet these are critical steps and involve much time and energy if they are done properly. Section Two of this book describes the means for accomplishing these steps.

REFERENCES

Angoff, W. H. (1971). Scales, norms, and equivalent scores. In R. L. Thorndike (Ed.), *Educational Measurement* (2nd ed.; pp. 508-600). Washington, DC: American Council on Education.

PRACTICE ANALYSIS: BUILDING THE FOUNDATION FOR VALIDITY

Joan E. Knapp

Lenora G. Knapp

Knapp and Associates

INTRODUCTION

A review of the literature associated with job analysis reveals two extremes of opinion as represented by the following provocative quotes:

> Historically job analysis has been a relatively soporific area of industrial and organizational psychology, characterized by neither heated controversy nor prominent visibility in the research literature. (Harvey, 1991, p. 71)

> Validation was once a priestly mystery, a ritual behind the scenes with the professional elite as witness and judge. Today it is a public spectacle combining the attraction of chess and mud wrestling. (Cronbach, 1988, p. 3)

Both our evaluation of practice analysis research and our professional experience with licensure programs indicate that practice analysis as a validation strategy is somewhere in between the two extremes described above.
Practice analysis:

- is a very important tool for validating licensing tests
- has become more interesting and visible than in the past
- can indeed provoke controversy (see Nelson, 1994; Schoon, 1985; Shimberg, 1990;)

DEFINITION OF PRACTICE ANALYSIS

Whether one views the process as soporific or a public spectacle, the fact remains that the systematic collection of data describing the responsibilities required of a professional and the skills and knowledge needed to perform these responsibilities is the foundation upon which to build a viable and legally defensible licensure examination.

A variety of terms have been used to refer to the collection of this type of job-related data, including job analysis, role analysis, role delineation study, process analysis, and practice analysis. This chapter will use the latter term for several reasons. First, the term may be viewed as more accurately reflecting the comprehensive nature of professional practice, as opposed to the narrowly focused activities covered in a traditional job analysis (Smith & Hambleton, 1990). Second, traditional job analysis differs from licensure-related practice analysis, in that the former assesses responsibilities and knowledges necessary to successful job performance (McCormick, 1976), whereas the latter focuses on minimal though critical competencies required to protect the public (Kane, 1982b). Thus, when a practice analysis is conducted for purposes of validating licensure examinations, the professional responsibilities examined are those of an entry level, rather than advanced practitioner and these competencies may or may not be related to professional success.

LEGAL AND PROFESSIONAL STANDARDS PERTAINING TO PRACTICE ANALYSES

Professional licensure examinations are not developed in a vacuum. The increasingly heated political and legal climate in which these examinations are designed and administered demands knowledge of legal and professional standards and court decisions pertaining to the appropriate use of practice analyses.

Legal Standards

Uniform Guidelines on Employee Selection Procedures (1978). Although the *Guidelines* pertain to the use of job analyses in employment selection, these laws and the subsequent court cases based on them also are relevant to licensing because they characterize which types of procedures are viewed by the court as being appropriate for defining professional responsibilities and knowledges. The *Guidelines* clearly establish the importance of using job analyses to demonstrate the validity of selection procedures, but describe only in very general terms what constitutes acceptable job analysis methodologies. Any method of job analysis may be used if it provides information appropriate for the type of validity to be demonstrated (i.e., content-, construct-, or criterion-related validity). Procedures to be used for establishing each type of validity are outlined, again only in very general terms. With respect to establishing content validity—which is the goal of most practice analyses conducted within the context of licensure—the *Guidelines* require that the job analysis focus on observable work behaviors and tasks and work products, as opposed to personality and other individual characteristics that are not directly observable.

Professional Standards

Professional standards that pertain to practice analyses include: *Standards for Educational and Psychological Testing* (American Educational Research Association, American Psychological Association, & National Council on Measurement in Education, 1985) and the *Principles for the Validation and Use of Personnel Selection Procedures* (Society for Industrial and Organizational Psychology, 1987). Although the *Standards* and *Principles* are not legal documents, they frequently have been used by the courts to determine the appropriateness of validation procedures (Harvey, 1991). Perhaps it is for this reason that many licensing agencies have elected to develop procedures that are in accordance with these professional standards, despite the fact that there have as yet been no Supreme Court cases regarding the validation of occupational tests.

Standards for Educational and Psychological Testing (1985). The *Standards* emphasize that job analysis is the primary basis for determining the content, and assessing the validity, of licensure examinations. Moreover, only responsibilities and knowledges crucial to protecting the public are to be included in licensing examinations. This, in turn, implies that practice analyses conducted in conjunction with licensing efforts also must focus on these minimal but crucial competencies. Responsibilities and knowledges important to successful job performance, but unrelated to protecting the public, are not appropriate to the domain of licensing.

Although the *Standards* stress the importance of conducting job analyses, no guidelines are provided for determining which procedures are appropriate for a given situation. These decisions are to be guided by professional judgement.

Principles for the Validation and Use of Personnel Selection Procedures (1987). The *Principles* also point out the importance of job analysis in establishing content validity, but like the *Standards*, do not specify when particular procedures should be used. However, some general recommendations are provided that would pertain to licensure-related practice analyses:

- sources of job-related information should be credible
- rating scales should have reasonable psychometric characteristics
- lack of consensus among subject matter experts regarding tasks, knowledges, skills, and abilities should be noted and carefully considered

Court Decisions Related to Practice Analyses

As noted previously, court decisions have helped to determine what does and does not constitute legally defensible practice analyses procedures. In their review of cases arising between 1971 and 1981, Thompson and Thompson (1982) state that a trend toward requiring job analysis has been evident beginning with the landmark case of Griggs v. Duke Power Co. (1971), which established the importance of the concept of job relatedness and thereby implied a legal need for conducting job analyses.

Subsequent cases (e.g., Albermarle Paper Co. v. Moody, 1975) found that validation procedures that did not include job analyses were insufficient. A more recent review, examining court cases dating from 1982, suggests that the courts have continued to point out the necessity of conducting job analyses and that emphasis on adherence to professional testing standards has increased (Kuehn,

Stallings, & Holland, 1990). This review identified three requirements for job analysis that have emerged in court cases during the last decade:

1. Job incumbents are knowledge specialists and should be part of the job analysis (Gillespie v. State of Wisconsin, 1985).
2. Performing an adequate job analysis does not ensure test validity. The failure to demonstrate a link between job analysis tasks and test content also can result in invalid tests (United States v. City of Chicago, 1984).
3. Regional or job context variability must be considered and, therefore, the incumbents sampled in the job analysis must be representative (Burney v. City of Pawtucket, 1983; Allen v. Issac, 1988).

It can be concluded that measurement experts and the courts are in agreement with the position taken in the *Standards* that content validity is the type of validity that is most relevant to licensure testing (Council on Licensure, Enforcement and Regulation, 1993). This type of validity, which can be established through practice analysis studies, provides a strong underpinning of quality and defensibility for assessment for licensure as well as meeting testing industry standards. Although other types of validity studies, such as those demonstrating construct- or criterion-related validity also may be relevant, they rarely are required as evidence for validity.

Other Legal and Professional Considerations

Smith and Hambleton (1990) have noted that the criterion by which the courts have assessed validation procedures for licensing examinations is not as rigorous as that of the *Standards*, creating a climate in which a licensing board can develop a licensing exam that is legally defensible, but does not meet testing community standards. They conclude that it is professionally inappropriate to maintain that legal defensibility can serve as the sole basis for developing and validating licensure examinations, but remark that:

> except for the legal and political pressures created by social systems, sponsors of licensure examination programs are under no obligation to conduct validation studies or to make public the results of their investigation . . . In today's litigious society, sponsors of licensure examination programs seem to feel that they must estimate the dangers associated with conducting, or not conducting, various kinds of validity investigations. (Smith & Hambleton, 1990, p. 8)

Members of the testing community have pointed out that despite the existence of legal and professional standards and a substantial number of court cases elaborating on the importance of job analyses, there still remains a certain degree of ambiguity regarding appropriate practices for validating assessment procedures. Shimberg (1990) laments that the *Guidelines* and *Standards* do not give test developers and users sufficient guidance in assuring valid and fair assessment and suggests that the regulatory and testing community take a proactive stance. One positive approach has been developed by Madaus (1988). He proposes the creation of a non-governmental, self-regulatory agency to establish standards and monitor testing practices within the testing industry. Under such a plan, testing agencies would voluntarily seek to be "accredited."

PRACTICE ANALYSIS METHODOLOGIES

A variety of methodologies are available for conducting job and practice analyses. This section outlines the most frequently used methodologies and discusses their applicability within the context of licensure.

Functional Job Analysis

The Functional Job Analysis (FJA) (Fine & Wiley, 1971) methodology has been used by the United States Employment Service to categorize jobs for the *Dictionary of Occupational Titles* (U.S. Department of Labor, 1977). The first step taken in conducting a FJA is defining the purpose and goals of the occupation. A trained job analyst then identifies what must be done to accomplish the purpose and goals, by determining what the worker does (i.e., processes or procedures used to perform a task) and how it is done (i.e., physical, mental, interpersonal skills required during the processes and procedures). Job information is obtained through interviews with job incumbents and supervisors and direct observation of job-related activities. The goal of FJA is to analyze an occupation in terms of the degree to which it deals with data (e.g., numbers, narrative information), people (e.g., customers, co-workers), and things (e.g., computers, machinery).

Considerations. The FJA involves a very fine-grained analysis of occupational responsibilities and far exceeds the level of specificity required to describe a profession for licensing purposes. Indeed, by describing a profession in terms of data, people, and things, one may lose the essence of the profession and critical responsibilities and competencies may be overlooked.

Position Analysis Questionnaire

The Position Analysis Questionnaire (PAQ) (McCormick, Mecham, & Jeanneret, 1977) was developed to compare job characteristics across occupations. The questionnaire categorizes job activities into six major areas: Information Input (how job-related information is received), Mediation Processes (decision-making, reason and judgement, and planning), Worker Output (activities performed to accomplish a task), Interpersonal Activities (communication and interpersonal relationships), Work Situation and Job Context (physical working conditions and social environment), and Miscellaneous (methods of pay, type of work schedule, etc.). The questionnaire is completed by job incumbents or a trained job analyst.

Considerations. Because it was designed for the purpose of making comparisons across occupations, the items on the PAQ are very general and consequently, responses to the items may not accurately profile the unique aspects of the profession under study. The generality of the questionnaire also may make it difficult for respondents to determine how the items might apply to the specifics of their own professional activities (Landy, 1989). Another consideration is the large number of items on the PAQ that pertain to machine and equipment use. It has been suggested that because of this emphasis, the instrument may not be appropriate for analyzing professional, managerial, or some technical jobs (Cornelius, Schmidt, & Carron, 1984; DeNisi, Cornelius, & Blencoe, 1987).

Critical Incident Technique

During the first phase of the critical incident technique (CIT) (Flanagan, 1954), job incumbents or supervisors are asked to provide examples of actions they have engaged in or witnessed that were especially effective or ineffective in carrying out the responsibilities of the profession. These "critical incidents" include descriptions of the setting in which the action occurred, the specifics of the action itself, and the positive or negative consequences that occurred as a result of the action. The incidents are obtained via structured questionnaires or individual or group interviews conducted with incumbents, and sometimes, supervisors. Generally, hundreds of incidents are needed to accurately describe a professional's role.

In the second phase of the process, the critical incidents are examined to derive categories of behavior or job dimensions into which the incidents can be classified. Subsequently, a panel of subject matter experts (SMEs) sorts the incidents into the newly created categories. Taken together, the classifications and critical incidents provide a composite of professional practice. Primoff (1975) found that CIT yielded job analysis data of a higher quality than FJA, PAQ, or standard task analysis and that the methodology was particularly useful in developing performance measures.

Considerations. The critical incident technique is a highly labor intensive, and thus costly, methodology that may not completely capture the full breadth of professional practice. No matter how many incidents are developed, some information regarding the profession may be omitted. Furthermore, the data collected via critical incidents often cannot be replicated, due in part to the fact that professionals performing the same responsibilities may have different ways of correctly and incorrectly engaging in these activities (Harvey, 1991). For these reasons, the role of critical incidents in licensure-related job analyses may best be limited to that of supplementing information previously obtained through SME panels and surveys of incumbents (Harvey, 1991; Robinson, 1981). Using this approach, critical incidents could be developed for each of the specific responsibilities, rather than being used as the basis for determining these responsibilities a priori.

DACUM (DEVELOP A CURRICULUM)

A structured brainstorming process, led by a trained facilitator, is at the core of the DACUM (Norton, 1985) method for conducting practice analyses. A panel of 8–12 expert professionals, representing the range of specialties within a field, is assembled to provide practice-related data through participation in the brainstorming process. To reduce potential bias, the panel facilitator should be an individual who has had no experience with the profession. Initially, the brainstorming process emphasizes doing rather than knowing or understanding (Faber, Fangman, & John, 1991; Norton, 1985). That is, task statements focus on observable behaviors.

Once the general responsibilities of the profession are identified, the panel develops task statements for each duty. Panelists then order the statements in a learning sequence, based on which responsibilities are learned and performed first on the job. The process of identifying responsibilities is completed when the panelists reach consensus regarding the accuracy and sequence of the task statements produced. Typically, a DACUM process will result in 8–12 responsibilities and 50–200 tasks. After this has been accomplished, panelists proceed to generate lists that identify knowledge and skills, traits and attitudes, and tools and equipment necessary to the performance of the identified tasks.

Considerations. To date, DACUM primarily has been used to develop training programs for workers and professionals. As such, the information obtained is generally broader than what is required for licensing (i.e., minimal competencies). In its standard form, the usefulness of DACUM for deriving content validation data for licensure examinations may be limited, because the process is time-consuming and the information obtained comes from only a small sample of incumbents. However, the procedure could be adapted for licensure purposes by changing the focus of the brainstorming process to the critical knowledge, skills, and abilities necessary for competent practice and using this information to create a survey to be distributed to a larger group of incumbents.

A GENERAL METHODOLOGY FOR LICENSURE-RELATED PRACTICE ANALYSES

In response to increased concern regarding legal issues pertaining to validation and emphasis on adherence to professional standards, we recommend a general methodology for conducting licensure-related practice analyses that has the potential of providing defensible documentation and meeting legal challenges that may arise. We use the word "potential" because the methodology itself is not what assures a valid and defensible approach to the development of licensing specifications. Rather, it is the manner in which the methodology is executed that will provide the assurance that licensing boards seek. In addition to addressing important legal considerations, this practice analysis methodology is:

- relatively easy to conduct
- more cost effective than other approaches
- easily replicated as occupational and professional knowledge and competency requirements change
- useful for obtaining "buy-in" from key stakeholders in the licensing process

This is not to say that the methodology outlined below should be the model of choice for all licensing agencies. In some circumstances, it may simply be used as a point of departure for boards charged with the important function of establishing the validity of their assessment procedures. The methodology includes a number of processes and procedures that are important to developing defensible licensure procedures, regardless of which practice analysis technique the board ultimately chooses to utilize. Many components of the methodology can be combined with other practice analysis procedures, such as those mentioned previously, to create a practice analysis study that is tailored to the specific needs of the licensing board and the profession it represents.

Establishment of a Practice Analysis Advisory Committee

Perhaps no step in the practice analysis process is as critical to achieving credible and rigorous evidence for content validity as the appointment of an advisory committee of experts to assist in the implementation of the study. The members of the committee must be licensed individuals, recognized by their peers as qualified practitioners in the field, and whose licenses are valid and reputations unblemished by consumer complaints. If the program is new and there are as yet no licensees, the committee should consist of leaders in the field, who are active in the professional community and recognized by their peers for their expertise. At times, it may be appropriate to have other groups, such as consumers and educators (as opposed to practitioners), represented on the committee.

The overall role of the advisory committee is to guide the entire practice analysis process and to recommend the responsibilities, skills, and knowledges necessary for competent practice and the protection of the public from financial or physical harm. More specifically, committee members, usually with the assistance of a technical consultant:

- provide references and other documents as needed to develop the lists of responsibilities, skills, and knowledges related to the practice of the profession or occupation under consideration
- assist in the design of a survey instrument
- advise on sample selection and ways of reaching the population under study
- review all materials developed for, and data resulting from, the practice analysis study

Committee members must be willing and able to commit sufficient time to participate actively in the process. This participation includes attending several days of meetings, engaging in work assignments as preparation and follow-up to meetings, and providing technical and political and professional support for the entire research process.

Advisory committees typically comprise 12–15 members. This number is necessary to obtain the diverse representation required for broad input from the field and to develop the consensus necessary for the advisory process. The literature of group process suggests that an 8-to-10-member committee is optimum for a working committee; however, in the case of practice analysis committee work, it is important to balance the need for appropriate representation with the ability of the group to work together. In fields in which there is little variability in theoretical orientation or professional practice (e.g., hearing aid dispensers) 10 people may be excessive, whereas, in other more diverse fields (e.g., psychology), that number may be barely enough.

Literature/Document Review

One of the first responsibilities assigned to the advisory committee is to supply the technical consultant with documents and materials related to the profession. These materials might include any or all of the following: competency statements, training curricula, job descriptions, results of manpower studies, research reports, journal articles, specifications of previous examinations, previous state practice analyses, and studies conducted in other states or by national agencies. The document review helps the technical consultant to:

- learn how others expect individuals to practice
- become familiar with the language and vocabulary of the occupation or profession under study
- develop a preliminary list of responsibilities, skills, and knowledges without using the committee members' valuable time

These materials will serve as a resource for determining whether the board should build on previous work that has been done in its home state, in other states, or by a national organization.

At this stage of the practice analysis process, the goal is to obtain a comprehensive picture of the profession and, therefore, all information relevant to professional practice is included in the document review and development of a preliminary list of responsibilities, skills, and knowledges. During later stages of the process, advisory committee members and other subject matter experts narrow the list of responsibilities, skills, and knowledges considered to those critical to competent performance, based on survey data and their professional experience.

Because the document review process can be time-consuming and the materials for some disciplines can be quite extensive, it is suggested that advisory committee members and/or the technical consultant first evaluate the usefulness of the materials collected by the committee. Criteria for determining which documents are critical include (Wolf, Wetzel, Harris, Mazour, & Riplinger, 1991):

- Is the document recent?
- Is it clearly written?
- Can essential information be uncovered easily?
- Has it been useful to the audience for which it was intended?
- Has it been used to develop test specifications?

Not all occupations and professions have a foundation of previous work and information of the quality and rigor required by boards. If the review of existing materials does not reveal an appropriate content validity alternative, the next step is to develop a survey to be administered to a group of incumbents. Even when there exists adequate documentation regarding the profession, the advisory committee may choose to conduct a survey of incumbents to confirm and supplement the information produced in the document review.

Practitioner Interviews

A first-hand verification of what tasks an incumbent actually performs, obtained through telephone or face-to-face individual interviews, is an essential part of the practice analysis process and the first step in developing a practice analysis survey (Blum & Naylor, 1968). Typically, 5–10 practitioners should be interviewed. The size of the sample is dependent on the diversity in the field, the degree of the relationship of the scope of practice to related disciplines, and the number of practicing incumbents in the state.

The interview questionnaire is based on information gathered from the literature/document review process described above. Although the technical consultant has acquired knowledge of the field through the document review process, it is important that he/she not impose any biases regarding the inclusion of various responsibilities, knowledges, and skills and the organization of this information. Consequently, interview questions are open-ended and general. However, knowledge of the field is helpful in understanding the interviewee's responses and may assist the consultant in formulating any probes necessary to elicit further elaboration or clarification.

During the interview process, particular care is taken to discern the major practice dimensions of the role of the practitioner and the tasks that would be subsumed under these dimensions. Then information is gathered about the knowledge, skills, and abilities required to perform these tasks. Where possible and appropriate, interviewers may observe the practitioner performing on the job (e.g., delivering client services, performing engineering or construction tasks, handling real estate transactions).

Draft Survey Instrument

Following completion of the practitioner interviews, the technical consultant develops a preliminary list of: the major responsibilities of the profession, the tasks subsumed within these responsibilities, critical skills required to carry out the tasks, the major knowledge areas required for competent performance of critical skills, and the specific knowledges included in these areas. A survey instrument is drafted based on these lists.

For licensing purposes, the survey instrument is typically designed so that the responsibilities, skills, and knowledges are targeted for the entry-level practitioner. In some cases, a board may wish to distinguish between the types of practitioners in a profession (i.e., nurse aide vs. nurse assistant vs. LPN vs. RN) by conducting a role delineation study. These studies are designed to tease out the scopes of practice for various levels of responsibility while at the same time disclosing any common job content across these levels.

Occasionally, boards question the need for conducting a document review and practitioner interviews prior to devising a draft of the survey instrument. They consider the review and analysis and synthesis of information by technical consultants to be time-consuming and expensive and instead, offer the alternative of the board or a committee nominated by the board sitting down at a meeting to develop the list of responsibilities and knowledges in vivo. However, there is empirical evidence that without the impartial and objective preparatory work of consultants, the phenomena of selective perception, beliefs, and value systems will subvert the "expert judgment" of the most well-meaning group of professionals (Pottinger, 1979). That is, no matter how large the size of the committee, how professional the members are, or how broad the diversity in viewpoints represented, the group may still fall victim to subjectivity.

Upon completion of the draft survey, committee members are brought together to review the document. They are asked to consider the responsibilities, skills, and knowledges included in the draft survey and determine if terminology is used correctly and whether any deletions or additions are needed. The instructions for completing the survey are evaluated for clarity and rating scales (e.g., importance, frequency, and criticality) are selected. Having a draft inventory prepared in advance for committee review reduces the amount of time needed for the meeting and the amount of bias that might emerge if the instrument were created on the basis of committee input only.

The advisory committee also selects survey items that will be used to determine the demographic characteristics (e.g., age, gender, education, years of professional practice) of the survey sample. Obtaining a profile of the sample allows the board to determine the extent to which the sample responding to the survey is representative of the licensing population at large. If the sample size is large enough, respondent characteristics also can be used as analytic categories for determining if any meaningful differences occur between and among the various subgroups.

Following the review of the document, the committee determines how practitioners will be sampled for the survey. It is important that individuals selected for the survey sample are licensed incumbents in good standing. Other subgroups that might be included in the survey sample are educators, consumers, and incumbents in a related discipline. Educators are one of the most common subgroups selected to participate in the survey because education requirements typically are part of the candidate eligibility process. Analyses comparing the ratings of practitioners with educators will assist the state and educational institutions in ensuring that critical practice requirements are included in training and educational offerings.

Pilot Test of Draft Survey

After the survey instrument has been revised, based on the comments and suggestions of the advisory committee, it is sent to advisory committee members for review and approval for the pilot test. Subsequently, the survey instrument is piloted with a small sample of professionals recommended by the committee or the board. The pilot sample should consist of practitioners who have not been involved in the development of the survey. Sample size for the pilot depends on the number of professionals in the field. For fields in which there are a large number of practitioners (500–1000), a pilot test of as many as 30-40 professionals can be conducted. However, there are many professions, particularly those that are highly specialized, in which the number of practitioners is relatively small (100-200). In these situations, a smaller pilot sample (e.g., 10-15 professionals) can be used.

The individuals in the pilot sample are interviewed to discuss their reactions to the survey, whether the directions and items are clear, and if the survey content is both accurate and complete. This feedback is discussed with the advisory committee and the final revisions to the survey instrument are made.

Administration of Practice Analysis Survey

Upon the final approval of the advisory committee, the survey is distributed to the survey sample. The survey is accompanied by a cover letter explaining the purpose of the practice analysis and requesting the cooperation of the addressee. Typically, the letter is signed by the chair of the board and perhaps a well-regarded leader in the profession who might be known to licensees in the state or across the country.

Analysis of Survey Data and Preparation of Practice Analysis Study Report

Data analyses are designed to identify the core tasks and core knowledge areas judged to be most critical to competent performance. If the sample is large enough, subgroup analyses can be performed using the demographic variables selected by the committee. These analyses will assist the committee in determining whether there are significant differences in responses among various subgroups. If any response biases or differences are revealed, the committee will be advised to take this information under consideration when interpreting the survey data.

After the data analyses are conducted, a meeting of the advisory committee is convened to review the results of the practice analysis study. At this time, decision rules are formulated for determining which responsibilities, skills, or knowledges can be eliminated. Kane (1984) suggests that the specification of content for licensing tests does not require an exhaustive listing of the knowledge, skills, and abilities required to practice. Instead, the advisory committee should focus on selecting those skills and knowledges most critical to competent entry-level performance, based on their professional judgement and data from the survey. In other words, the key objective is to select those knowledge and skill areas that are "need to knows" rather than "nice to knows." Rationales for all decisions made by the committee are documented.

The final phase of the practice analysis is the drafting of a report, describing the methodology of the study, the data analyses, and the decision-making rules used by the advisory committee to select the critical responsibilities, skills, and knowledges. After the draft is reviewed and revised by the advisory committee, a final report is issued to the board by the committee. The report provides a solid foundation for both the development of assessment procedures and the documentation of a content-valid licensing process.

DEVELOPMENT OF SPECIFICATIONS FOR ASSESSMENT PROCEDURES

Conducting a practice analysis is not sufficient for ensuring the content validity of a licensure examination. The manner in which the survey data are used to develop specifications for assessment procedures also is crucial to validation efforts. This process begins with the selection of a specifications development committee with essentially the same characteristics as those of the advisory committee described previously. Although this committee should be independent of the advisory committee, it is advisable to have some overlap in members. This allows the new specifications committee to benefit from the expertise and lessons learned by the advisory committee, while opening up the process to another set of expert judgements that can confirm and expand upon previous efforts.

The first step in the development of examination specifications is a review of the advisory committee's report on the practice analysis process and study findings. The specifications committee then proceeds to confirm and refine the most critical responsibilities, skills, and knowledge to be examined based on the results of the practice analysis, the advisory committee's recommendations, and their professional experience.

Although the practice analysis data play a key role in guiding decisions regarding the critical responsibilities, skills, and knowledges, the consensus of the subject matter experts represents "the last word" on the matter. For example, an emerging knowledge area in the field may receive low importance ratings, but if the committee believes the knowledge to be critical to competent professional practice in the future, they may elect to include the knowledge area in the examination specifications. Also, it must be kept in mind that for licensure purposes, the responsibilities, skills, and knowledges selected to be measured by the assessment procedures must be critical in the sense that they have a significant impact on client outcomes. In other words, the relationship between that which is measured and client outcomes should be explicit (Kane, 1982b).

After determining the most critical responsibilities, skills, and knowledges, the committee links each specific knowledge and skill to the appropriate responsibility area, thereby producing a specifications matrix (see Figure 1).

This is accomplished by determining, through group consensus, whether the knowledge or skill is crucial to competent performance of the responsibility.

A key decision to be made by the committee regards the form the assessment procedures will take (i.e., written, oral, and/or performance examinations). The

Figure 1. Example of a test specifications matrix.

	I	II	III	IV
I. SOCIO-CULTURAL SYSTEMS (35% of exam)				
A. Language/Language Use (20% of exam)				
Aspects of English language:				
1. Structural properties (e.g., grammar, semantics, pragmatics)	1 item	2 items		1 item
2. Socio-linguistic factors (e.g., register, dialect variances, context)	1 item	2 items		1 item
Aspects of American Sign Language:				
3. Structural properties (e.g., grammar, semantics, pragmatics)	1 item	4 items		1 item
4. Socio-linguistic factors (e.g., register, dialect variances, context)	1 item	4 items		1 item

Note. Knowledge areas are listed on the vertical axis; responsibilities are listed on the horizontal axis. For responsibilities, I = Preparation for Service Delivery, II = Provision of Service, III = Post-Service Closure, and IV = Professionalism.

most common form of assessment for licensure is the written multiple-choice examination. The assumption is that this format is the most reliable, valid, and cost-effective. Although used much less frequently, clinical simulations (i.e., case scenarios that branch into different questions depending on the answers given for previous questions), performance testing (i.e., trained assessors evaluate the candidate's performance of critical professional tasks) and other written test formats, such as matching and multiple true-false, also are promising formats.

In the 1980s, many agencies dropped performance testing because of the expense associated with it and the high correlation between performance scores and scores on written tests. However, Hambleton and Rogers (1986) believe there is validity evidence to support the added utility of performance examinations. Indeed, in recent years, there has been an increasing trend toward adding performance testing to licensing and credentialing procedures (e.g., teacher certification, nurse aides, massage therapists).

Schoon (1985) provides a framework that specifications development committees may find useful when evaluating which assessment procedures should be used for licensure. He argues that professions should be analyzed and classified according to a continuum that is anchored at one end by purely cognitive skills (e.g., philosopher) and by manual skills (e.g., meat packer) at the other end. Competency measures should reflect the profession's position in this continuum. On a less theoretical level, the committee should also be guided by their response to the following question: "What critical factors would the performance test, oral examination or other techniques measure that cannot be measured effectively with more cost-efficient examination formats?"

Once a determination has been made regarding the assessment procedures to be used, the committee must decide on the relative weights of the various competencies to be measured by each procedure. It is important to recognize that the weighting of various components should not be based solely on importance or frequency ratings derived from practice analysis data. There may be a number of problems that fall into the "uncommon, but harmful if missed" category that should be given greater emphasis than might be indicated by the study data (Rakel, 1983).

The final phase of specifications development is the formulation of operational definitions for the responsibilities, skills, and knowledges to be measured by the assessment procedures (Yalow & Collins, 1985). These definitions expand upon the specifications by citing the actual situations and knowledge to be tested and will serve as detailed guidelines for item writers and test developers. Operational definitions also provide a framework for assessing the content validity of the examination (Hambleton & Rogers, 1986).

FREQUENTLY ASKED QUESTIONS BY LICENSING BOARDS

Who should be involved in overseeing the practice analysis process?

Pottinger (1979) has branded the expert consensus validation technique as the most dangerous approach for defining competence. Although this may be true when it is used as the sole method of validation, this is not the case when experts are used as part of a broader validation strategy, which also involves the collection of survey data. Indeed, the appointment and active participation of subject matter experts is an essential part of a comprehensive practice analysis study.

Aside from being licensees in good standing or in the case of new programs, leaders in their field, committee members should represent diverse settings and interests. Most important to industry standards of quality and fairness, committee members should be representative of diversity in the profession in terms of geographic region, ethnicity, educational and experiential backgrounds, and practice settings. The recent passage of the Americans With Disabilities Act points to the importance of also including on the committee individuals who represent practitioners with disabilities.

An angry failing candidate will not only subject the test construction and administration procedures to question and scrutiny, but also may request the names of individuals who have been involved in the process. If these individuals are not respected, do not represent various subgroups within the profession, or are not active practitioners, the validity of the examination could be called into question.

Can the results of national practice analyses be used as validation for individual state licensure examinations?

Each jurisdiction granting licensure is legally responsible for determining examination content; however, this does not mean that each state must conduct a unique practice analysis. Many national organizations have assumed the burden of content validation, test construction, and administration. Although this has been at the cost of states giving up some control over content or jurisdictional issues, these boards have not lost the opportunity to participate in the process and ensure that the national procedures are valid for their jurisdiction. State boards can fulfill their legal responsibilities by reviewing the final practice analysis report for appropriateness to their jurisdiction, setting their own passing scores, or having practitioners from their jurisdiction included in the practice analysis used to develop the national examination (Smith & Hambleton, 1990). If desired, a jurisdiction also can conduct its own practice analysis and compare findings with the national study. The involvement of national organizations has improved the quality and consistency of state licensing efforts and encouraged reciprocity, thereby enabling licensees to move more freely across borders to pursue their careers.

One example of the successful involvement of a national organization in licensure and certification is that of The Council on National Certification of Massage Therapists, which was formed to provide a national voluntary certification program for massage therapy. The foundation of the program was a national practice analysis that involved a large nationally representative sample. Even prior to the inaugural administration in 1992, several states were reviewing the practice analysis and the examination specifications to determine whether they would adopt the program for use in their licensing process. To date, six states have adopted the new program.

Another example of states using practice analyses conducted by national organizations comes from the activities of The National Council of State Boards of Nursing (NCSBN), which is charged with the responsibility of developing licensure examinations for its state member boards. Each year, the program licenses approximately 170,000–180,000 nurses. The foundation of this program is a series of national role delineation studies that are conducted periodically by the NCSBN. These studies are major endeavors; they are costly, require over a year to conduct, and typically, are performed by a respected technical consulting firm. The NCSBN provides state boards with a quality service that is more cost-effective than performing validation studies in-house. Such a service also assures reciprocity for licensed individuals and allows for the mobility needed in the highly dynamic healthcare environment.

In some cases, national testing agencies have developed testing programs for licensure. The testing agency assists states in adopting the program by conducting validity studies. States can then determine if the program and its offerings meet their needs and regulatory requirements.

What rating scales should be used in the survey?

Ratings of frequency of task performance, amount of time spent engaged in a task, and the importance and criticality of a task, knowledge, or skill are the most commonly used scales on practice analysis surveys (see Figure 2 for examples of rating scales).

In selecting the rating scales to be used, it is important not to have too many ratings per item on the inventory. Using more than two ratings for each item (e.g., frequency and importance) is tedious and confusing for the survey taker. This is likely to decrease both the response rate and the accuracy of the data collected.

Figure 2. Examples of practice analysis rating scales.

EXTENT OF COMPETENCE AT LICENSURE
0   Not performed
1   Competence not essential at time of licensure
2   Some degree of competence essential
3   Full competence is essential

TIME SPENT ON RESPONSIBILITY
Taking into account all of the things you do on the job during the course of a year, what is your best estimate of the amount of time spent dealing with this responsibility?
0   I do not have this responsibility
1   I spend very little time on this responsibility
2   I spend some of my time on this responsibility
3   I spend a lot of my time on this responsibility

EXTENT OF COMPETENCE AT ENTRY-LEVEL
0   Not necessary for a beginning practitioner
1   Not necessary—is learned on the job
2   Desirable but not necessary
3   Some degree is necessary, however, performance should improve on the job
4   Full competence is necessary for a beginning practitioner

Figure 2 (continued)

IMPORTANCE
Regardless of the amount of time you spend, how important is this responsibility to your practice?
0   I do not have this responsibility
1   Of little or no importance
2   Moderately important
3   Very important
4   Of extreme importance

CRITICALITY
How important is competence in this responsibility for an entry-level practitioner if he or she is to adequately serve and protect the public?
O   Of no importance
1   Of little importance
2   Moderately important
3   Very important
4   Extremely important

EXTENT OF KNOWLEDGE
To what extent must an entry-level practitioner master this specific knowledge if he or she is to adequately serve and protect clients?
0   NONE REQUIRED—Knowledge of this area is not required
1   BASIC CONCEPTS—Ability to understand basic concepts and information encompassed by the knowledge area
2   APPLICATION—Ability to use and apply concepts from the knowledge area to conventional practice situations
3   IN-DEPTH MASTERY—In-depth mastery of the knowledge area and the ability to apply it to complex or unique practice situations

---

The degree to which rating scales are redundant or highly correlated also must be considered. Research has shown that relative time spent and frequency ratings are highly correlated with importance ratings when both scales are applied to each item (Harvey, 1991). Similarly, Friedman (1990) found that time spent and importance ratings on a task inventory for managers were redundant. Thus, using highly correlated rating scales adds little additional information to the results of practice analysis and the subsequent development of test specifications, but may increase the burden on the survey respondent.

Another factor to consider when selecting rating scales is the unique goal of a licensure examination—to protect the public from harm. Kane (1982a) recommends that practice analyses not depend solely on frequency data or even weight this data heavily. He argues that the gravity of the consequences to the public of an incompetent practitioner dictates that analyses of survey data should place the greatest emphasis on ratings of criticality or importance.

How should the sample for the survey be selected?

Farrell, Stone, and Yoder (1976) suggest that three basic factors be taken into consideration in any sampling design: (a) the sample should be representative of the population from which it is being drawn, (b) it should be as small as considerations of precision and dependability permit, and (c) it should be obtained by some systematic probability process (e.g., sampling every fifth name on the current membership list of a professional association).

Determining whether sufficient representation has been obtained in the sample is not as straightforward as it would seem at first glance. Ethnic/minority representation provides a good illustration of this point. Many records on licensees do not have ethnic information and answers to questions on the survey related to ethnicity are voluntary. If data on ethnic representation in the field are unavailable, boards must determine, based on their experience and best judgement, the approximate proportion of individuals in ethnic subgroups they believe to be practicing in the profession. If a professional association of minority practitioners exists, they should be contacted by the board to provide input on the matter.

When survey returns appear to fall short of estimates of representation by various subgroups within the profession, the board may wish to take additional measures to ensure input from these population segments. For example, in a national practice analysis of psychologists, it was found that the size of the overall survey sample and the low percentage of African Americans in the profession resulted in a very low number of African American respondents. A decision was made to oversample this segment by including the entire membership of a national association of African American psychologists in a special mailing of the survey. This procedure was successful in yielding a sufficient number of responses to provide adequate representation in the survey sample (Rosenfeld, Shimberg, & Thornton, 1983).

Characteristic patterns of responding by various groups within a sample also have a bearing on sample selection. Landy and Vasey (1988) found that the frequency ratings of experienced police officers differed significantly from less experienced officers; however, there were no differences between the reported tasks of white, black, and Hispanic officers and no differences were found when the educational levels of the incumbents were contrasted. These results were supported by a subsequent study in which ratings by subject matter experts varied depending on their job experience, but were only minimally affected by educational level and race (Landy & Vasey, 1991).

In contrast to the Landy and Vasey (1988, 1991) findings, research conducted by Schmitt and Cohen (1989) revealed ethnic and gender differences in the ratings of middle managers on time spent and difficulty scales for various job tasks. There is also some question as to whether job experience plays a significant role in ratings for all occupations. Silverman, Wexley, and Johnson (1984) found that job incumbent age and job experience did not affect the ratings of secretaries and clerks.

Given the mixed findings in research on respondent characteristics, it is recommended that the sample surveyed include the full range of professional experience and demographic characteristics in order to get an accurate picture of the relative values for different scales used in the survey. It should also be noted that legal guidelines dictate that certain sample parameters must be adhered to, regardless of whether research findings indicate the absence of significant differences in ratings (e.g., ethnicity, gender).

The size of the sample required is a question frequently raised by boards. There is no magic number for the size of the sample necessary to obtain good data; however, it is clear from the discussion above that fulfilling the requirements of broad representation in the field is more important than sheer numbers. At times, because of controversy in the profession or a highly vocal subgroup, it may be important to survey the entire population so that each licensee has an opportunity to provide input to the process.

How can I ensure a high response rate for the practice analysis?

First, one must consider what an acceptable response rate might be for the survey. Unless the survey is large enough to allow a statistical determination of this number, the desired response rate will be determined subjectively (Fowler, 1988). Response rates for practice analysis surveys generally range from 20% to 60%, with most falling in the range of 25% to 35%. Rates of 50-60% are considered to be excellent. Nonetheless, the risk of bias with response rates of this size is high. With the guidance of the technical consultant, advisory committee members can assess potential biases by determining whether: (a) the sample was representative (based on demographic data on respondents) and (b) the results of the survey are consistent with their impressions of professional practice.

Boards must balance the desire for a high response rate with the limited resources (i.e., time, labor, and funding) available to devote to the project. However, there are a number of strategies that are easy to implement and can help to increase the return rate of respondents. Pilot testing during the earliest phases of the practice analysis improves response rates by eliminating potential sources of difficulty, such as poorly worded items, an excessive number of items, and confusing rating scales (Fowler, 1988). A compelling cover letter from a respected practitioner, asking for respondents' to provide their support and share their professional expertise can be very effective in boosting returns. Follow-up post cards are effective reminders to those who are slow to respond and have put the survey aside to fill out at a later date. Finally, in surveys that have relatively small samples, personalizing contact with respondents may optimize response rates. The board can contact a network of key professionals who in turn will enlist others to call incumbents and encourage them to complete and return their surveys (for further information on maximizing response rates, see Dillman, 1978).

What types of analyses should be performed on the data?

Sophisticated data analyses on practice analysis data are not required. A decade ago it was common for consultants to run factor analyses on data to determine if job dimensions and knowledges could be clustered in a meaningful way (Goodfellow, 1977; Rosenfeld & Thornton, 1976). These complex analyses were difficult to interpret and did not prove to be useful in uncovering core tasks, knowledges, and skills. For example, factors that emerged from the analyses typically were not interpretable as important to the dimensions of the profession and dimensions that subject matter experts agreed were important did not emerge as factors (Cranny & Doherty, 1988). Today, these types of analyses are seldom performed. Data can be analyzed by examining the means and standard deviations of survey ratings. If unusual patterns are discerned in the data, additional analyses can be conducted to determine if any notable subgroup differences exist.

How can the cost-effectiveness of practice analyses studies be improved?

The primary factors that influence the cost of a practice analysis are the size of the sample and whether the practitioners involved in the process are paid or volunteer. Cost savings can be accomplished in several ways. Selection of the most parsimonious sample size will reduce survey administration and processing expenses (e.g., postage, printing, data entry). If the sample to be surveyed is very large, survey booklets that can be optically scanned may reduce data entry costs. Performing certain tasks "in-house" (e.g., data entry) also may reduce costs. The expenses of advisory committee members and other professionals involved in reviewing the draft survey may be reduced if they volunteer their time. Travel expenses also may be reduced if committee meetings can be held the day before or after professional conferences and conventions that the members would otherwise be attending. Finally, savings may be achieved if the board relies on the interest and professional responsibility of the survey sample to motivate their completion of the instrument, rather than providing payment for doing so.

How often should a licensing board conduct a practice analysis?

Experts in the field—practitioners—are the best judge of this and their decision is highly dependent on the nature of their profession. For example, the field of opticianry is not changing as rapidly as oncology nursing. If the research and knowledge base or technology of a profession is changing rapidly, or if new specialties are emerging in shorter periods of time, the time between practice analysis updates should reflect this momentum. Werner (1990) cautions that practice analyses can be very costly so their updates should not be planned just because a set period of time has elapsed. However, he suggests that the need for re-analysis be considered at least every 5 years.

When is a technical consultant needed and what should I look for in a consultant?

In most cases, licensing boards use technical resources provided by state licensing agency staff or if the state does not have staff resources, the board typically will hire a technical consultant to direct and facilitate the practice analysis process. Although members of the board may be involved in the technical process by gathering information, nominating content and practice experts, and reviewing documents, generally they do not feel that they have the expertise and/or the time to be actively involved in conducting technical studies. Board members also may utilize technical consultants to avoid any appearance of bias or conflict of interest (i.e., the appearance that the practice analysis is an intentional effort to exclude members of a profession or occupation from licensure, rather than an effort to define the profession).

Technical consultants, whether they be internal or external to the licensing agency or board, should be experts in educational and psychological measurement or industrial/organizational psychology. However, it is important that this expertise also has been supplemented by professional experience in the development of certification and/or licensing programs. As noted previously, the types of job analysis techniques typically used in the development of selection and promotion procedures are not always appropriate to the development of licensure examinations. Moreover, licensure-related practice analysis must be conducted with an awareness of the intricacies of the legal and political climate in which a licensing board must operate. The checklist in Figure 3 can assist boards in evaluating previous or current work conducted for the board by technical consultants (Knapp, 1991).

Figure 3. Checklist for evaluating the practice analysis services of technical consultants.

YES   NO

_____ _____   1.   Are the goals/purposes of the practice analysis study clear and shared by key players or subgroups in your organization or profession?

_____ _____   2.   Is the validation strategy consistent with the *Uniform Guidelines* and the *Standards for Educational and Psychological Testing*?

_____ _____   3.   Are the experts involved appropriate in background, number, and expertise? Can they provide the most accurate picture of the field?

_____ _____   4.   Are the experts committed to the project and willing to dedicate the time necessary for the project?

_____ _____   5.   Have all essential documents concerning responsibilities, skills, and knowledges necessary for practice been collected?

_____ _____   6.   Is the survey instrument designed around the level of practice to be studied?

_____ _____   7.   Are the responsibilities, skills, and knowledges in the instrument strongly linked to professional outcomes and everyday practice?

_____ _____   8.   Are the responsibilities, skills, and knowledges within the profession's scope of practice?

_____ _____   9.   Has the appropriate sample been selected?

_____ _____ 10.   Is there a strategy in place to achieve the best possible return rate?

_____ _____ 11.   Will the data lead to weighting responsibilities, skills, and knowledges according to their importance for practice?

_____ _____ 12.   Are the study methods and results communicated to the profession in an accurate and easily understood manner?

REFERENCES

Albermarle Paper Co. v. Moody. (1975). 422 U.S. 405.

Allen v. Isaac. (1988). 39 F.E.P. Cases 1142.

American Educational Research Association, American Psychological Association, & National Council on Measurement in Education. (1985). *Standards for educational and psychological testing*. Washington, DC: American Psychological Association.

Blum, M. L., & Naylor, J. C. (1968). *Industrial psychology: Its theoretical and social foundations* (rev. ed.). New York: Harper & Row.

Burney v. City of Pawtucket. (1983). 559 F. Supp. 1089.

Cornelius, E. T., Schmidt, F. L., & Carron, T. J. (1984). Job classification approaches and the implementation of validity generalization results. *Personnel Psychology*, *37*(2), 247-260.

Council on Licensure, Enforcement and Regulation. (1993). *Development, administration, scoring and reporting of credentialing examinations: Recommendations for board members* (1st ed.). Lexington, KY: Author.

Cranny, C. J., & Doherty, M. E. (1988). Importance ratings in job analysis: Note on the misinterpretation of factor analyses. *Journal of Applied Psychology*, *77*(2), 320-322.

Cronbach, L. J. (1988). Five perspectives on the validity argument. In H. Wainer & H. I. Braun (Eds.), *Test validity* (pp. 3-17). Hillsdale, NJ: Erlbaum.

DeNisi, A. S., Cornelius, E. T., & Blencoe, A. G. (1987). Further investigation of common knowledge effects on job analysis ratings. *Journal of Applied Psychology*, *72*(2), 262-268.

Dillman, D. A. (1978). *Mail and telephone surveys: The total design method*. New York: John Wiley.

Faber, D., Fangman, E. J., & John, L. (1991). *DACUM: A complete model for curriculum development*. Baltimore: The DACUM Resource Center.

Farrell, W. T., Stone, C. H., & Yoder, D. (1976). *Guidelines for sampling in marine corps task analysis*. (Evaluation of Marine Corps Task Analysis Program, TR No. 11). Los Angeles: California State University.

Fine, S., & Wiley, W. W. (1971). *An introduction to functional job analysis*. Washington, DC: Upjohn Institute for Employment Research.

Flanagan, J. C. (1954). The critical incident technique. *Psychological Bulletin*, *51*, 327-358.

Fowler, F. J. (1988). *Survey research methods*. Newbury Park, England: Sage.

Friedman, L. (1990). Degree of redundancy between time, importance, and frequency task ratings. *Journal of Applied Psychology*, *75*(6), 748-752.

Gillespie v. State of Wisconsin. (1985). 771 F. 2d 1035.

Goodfellow, R. A. H. (1977). *Job analysis of the K-12 teaching position* (California Educator Selection Project Report No. 11). Sacramento, CA: Selection Consulting Center.

Griggs v. Duke Power Co. (1971). 401 U.S. 424.

Hambleton, R. K., & Rogers, H. J. (1986). Technical advances in credentialing examinations. *Evaluation and the Health Professions*, *9*(2), 205-229.

Harvey, R. J. (1991). Job analysis. In M. D. Dunnette & L. M. Hough (Eds.), *Handbook of industrial and organizational psychology* (2nd ed., vol. 2; pp. 71-163). Palo Alto, CA: Consulting Psychologists Press.

Kane, M. T. (1982a). A sampling model for validity. *Applied Psychological Measurement, 6*(2), 125-160.

Kane, M. T. (1982b). The validity of licensure examinations. *American Psychologist, 37*(8), 911-918.

Kane, M. T. (1984, April). *Strategies in validating licensure examinations.* Paper presented at the annual meeting of the American Educational Research Association, New Orleans, LA.

Knapp, J. E. (1991, April). *Conducting a job/task analysis.* Paper presented at the regional conference of the National Organization in Competency Assurance, Washington, DC.

Kuehn, P. A., Stallings, W. M., & Holland, C. L. (1990). Court defined job analysis requirements for validation of teacher certification tests. *Educational Measurement: Issues and Practice, 9*(4), 21-24.

Landy, F. J. (1989). Psychology of work behavior (4th ed.). Pacific Grove, CA: Brooks/Cole Publishing.

Landy, F. J., & Vasey, J. (1988). *The effects of demographic variables on job analysis results.* (Unpublished manuscript).

Landy, F. J., & Vasey, J. (1991). Job analysis: The composition of SME samples. *Personnel Psychology, 44*(1), 27-50.

Madaus, G. F. (1988). *Monitoring high stakes tests: A proposal.* Unpublished manuscript.

McCormick, E. J. (1976). Job and task analysis. In M. D. Dunnette (Ed.), *Handbook of industrial and organizational psychology* (pp. 651-696). Chicago: Rand McNally.

McCormick, E. J., Mecham, R. C., & Jeanneret, P. R. (1977). *Technical manual for the Position Analysis Questionnaire (PAQ) (System 2).* West Lafayette, IN: University Book Store.

Nelson, D. S. (1994). Job Analysis for Licensure and Certification Exams: Science or Politics? *Educational Measurement: Issues and Practice, 13* (3), 29-35.

Norton, R. E. (1985). *DACUM handbook.* Columbus, OH: Ohio State University National Center for Research in Vocational Education.

Pottinger, P. S. (1979). Competence testing as a basis for licensing: Problems and prospects. In M. A. Bunda & J. R. Sanders (Eds.), *Practices and problems in competency-based education* (pp. 28-46). Washington, DC: National Council on Measurement in Education.

Primoff, E. S. (1975). *How to prepare and conduct job element examinations.* Washington, DC: U.S. Government Printing Office.

Rakel, R. E. (1983). Defining competence in specialty practice: The need for relevance. In J.S. Lloyd and D. Langsley (Eds.), *Evaluating the Skills of Medical Specialists.* Chicago IL: American Board of Medical Specialties, 85-91.

Robinson, D. D. (1981). Content-oriented personnel selection in a small business setting. *Personnel Psychology, 34*, 77-87.

Rosenfeld, M., Shimberg, B., & Thornton, R. F. (1983). *Job analysis of licensed psychologists in the United States and Canada.* Princeton, NJ: Educational Testing Service, Center for Occupational and Professional Assessment.

Rosenfeld, M., & Thornton, R. F. (1976). *A case study in job analysis methodology.* Princeton, NJ: Educational Testing Service.

Schmitt, N., & Cohen, S. A. (1989). Internal analyses of task ratings by job incumbents. *Journal of Applied Psychology, 74*(1), 96-104.

Schoon, C. G. (1985). Methods for defining and assessing professional competence [Special Issue: The Measure of Competence]. *Professional Practice of Psychology, 6*(1), 144-155.

Shimberg, B. (1990). Social considerations in the validation of licensing and certification exams. *Educational Measurement: Issues and Practices, 9*(4), 11-14.

Silverman, S. B., Wexley, K. N., & Johnson, J. C. (1984). The effects of age and job experience on employee responses to a structured job analysis questionnaire. *Public Personnel Management, 13*(3), 355-359.

Smith, L. E., & Hambleton, R. K. (1990). Content validity studies of licensing examinations. *Educational Measurement: Issues and Practices, 9*(4), 7-10.

Society for Industrial and Organizational Psychology. (1987). *Principles for the validation and use of personnel selection procedures* (3rd ed.). College Park, MD: Author.

Thompson, D. E., & Thompson, T. A. (1982). Court standards for job analysis in test validation. *Personnel Psychology, 35*(4), 865-874.

Uniform Guidelines on Employee Selection Procedures. (1978). *Federal Register, 43,* 38290-38315.

United States v. City of Chicago. (1984). 38 EPD P35,606.

U.S. Department of Labor. (1977). *Dictionary of occupational titles* (4th ed.). Washington, DC: U.S. Employment Service.

Werner, E. (Winter, 1990). The answer key. CLEAR Examination Review. Clearinghouse for Licensure Enforcement and Regulation.

Wolf, P., Wetzel, M., Harris, G., Mazour, T., & Riplinger, J. (1991). *Job task analysis: Guide to good practice.* Englewood Cliffs, NJ: Educational Technology Publications.

Yalow, E. S., & Collins, J. L. (1985, April). Meeting the challenge of content validity. In *The assessment boomerang returns: Competency tests for education.* Symposium conducted at the annual meeting of the American Educational Research Association, Chicago.

SYSTEMATIC ITEM WRITING AND TEST CONSTRUCTION

Anthony LaDuca

National Board of Medical Examiners

Steven M. Downing

American Board of Internal Medicine

Thomas R. Henzel

National Board of Medical Examiners

Standardized objective testing remains the most popular mode of licensure testing. Even where other types of tests are incorporated, it is often the case that they are provided as complimentary to standardized, multiple-choice (MC) tests. Moreover, scoring theories and standard-setting procedures have been developed over the years in the context of standardized MC testing. At the same time, critics have pointed to limitations of contemporary MC testing practices, including lack of fidelity to real-life challenges and emphasis on recall of factual minutiae. In our view, testing professionals should make conscientious attempts to modify test development procedures so as to address valid criticisms. In this chapter we offer several suggestions for improving licensure test development, although it may not be feasible to adopt the entire array of recommendations we make. We are providing an intentionally wide selection in the hope that testing professionals will find something of use in their field of practice. Our discussion emphasizes careful design and systematic item-writing methods. We describe types of test items and make suggestions for development and maintenance of an item pool. Later we discuss test-construction procedures.

OPERATIONAL ASSUMPTIONS

We assume that the testing program is intended for use in licensing persons who are entering an occupation or profession in a U.S. jurisdiction. Our discussion assumes further that the program is new; however, the implications for already established licensure programs may be clear to the reader. The testing programs we consider are those that rely on paper-and-pencil techniques generally associated with standardized testing. These imply having examinees fill in spaces on answer sheets that are optically scanned at a later time. We are also assuming that the standards for passing the licensure test will be established using one or more of the content-based approaches that are presently available. Such standards are fixed and maintained through equating proceduresusing the appropriate statistical methods. Details of these procedures are provided elsewhere in this volume. In this chapter we assume that systematic pretesting of newly written multiple-choice questions (MCQs) will be implemented as part of the testing program.

Much of our experience has been in the context of licensing and certifying physicians and our examples are largely restricted to medical applications. We believe that the features we outline will be effective with nonmedical professions as well.

IMPORTANCE OF TEST DESIGN

Test development comprises the full array of activities associated with bringing a standardized assessment into operation. The particulars of what we designate as *design* are of special significance in development of licensure tests for two reasons. First, the imperative to assemble evidence in support of the content validity of the examination is heightened in the licensure context. Second, the logical and procedural linkages between the design and the test items must withstand close scrutiny.

Job Analysis, Job Relevance and Content Validity

Content validity retains a somewhat controversial character among measurement specialists. Much contemporary commentary relegates content validity to an inferior status because it is described as emerging from the apparent fit between the test content and the persons (i.e., experts) involved in the development of the test. This version of content validity places it outside the preferred paradigm of interpretations of examinee scores. In our view this disparagement of content validity is unwarranted in licensure testing. Validation of licensure tests may rely heavily on evidence of unimpeachable "job relevance" of test content, but there is no reason to exclude empirical processes from content validation, including interpretations of scores. More to the point, the imperative to establish the unimpeachable job relevance of the licensure test enhances the importance of design because it is at the level of test design that the issue of relevance is first addressed.

The job relevance perspective implies that the test items in the licensure examination must be linked through systematic means to a well-defined representation of the demands of the occupation or profession. The *Standards for Educational and Psychological Testing* (American Educational Research Association, American Psychological Association & National Council on Measurement in Education, 1985) call for a "job analysis" in licensure test development (Fine, 1986) and this has come to be a well-accepted element of the process (see chapter 4). Although we prefer an alternative method to conventional job analyses, the more significant point is the imperative to start with a representation of the target occupation or profession. The purpose of such a representation is to establish a definition of knowledge and skill that is essential to competent practice. It is possession of the candidate's knowledge and skill that the licensing examination is intended to establish or confirm, and the presumption is that the public is protected by such an assessment.

Among the available alternatives for job analysis, we prefer representing the target profession by devising a model of the situations that comprise the professional domain. This strategy has evolved from a social constructionist view of professions, which argues that the knowledge and skill possessed by competent practitioners is displayed in response to the demands posed by encounters in a real-world (i.e., social) environment (LaDuca, 1980; LaDuca, 1994; LaDuca & Engel, 1994). Therefore, an effective means of laying out the knowledge and skill demands of an occupation or profession begins best by defining the situations that constitute the domain of the occupation or profession.

This approach is responsive to the special context of physician licensure, wherein there is tension between the increasing specialization of physicians during their extended training, on the one hand, and the language of licensure laws, which usually emphasizes the credentialling of *undifferentiated* practitioners, on the other hand. Our response to this dilemma has been to devise a method for representing the generalist practitioner, although such persons are largely hypothetical. For other professions this dilemma may not exist. Nevertheless, we are impressed that the approach we have devised over the years retains significant advantages for other professions as well.

Our approach involves constructing a *practice model* based principally on log-diary surveys of practitioners in which they report their activities. It is important to note that the practice model captures crucial elements of professional situations in order to describe them. There is no attempt to presume modalities of intervention in the professional situations. In professions where alternative interventions are available, (e.g., psychotherapy), the practice model approach only asserts the imperative that qualified practitioners engage successfully with, for example, married couples considering a divorce, or treatment of a child displaying school phobia. Different and acceptable modes of treatment are defined in the subsequent analysis of the allowed situations.

Decisions about the content of the licensure test are made by a committee of recognized experts in the field, but in this approach their decision making is informed by the structure of the description of the practitioner's work as derived from empirical data. The design of the licensure test then results from the informed judgments of content experts who have evaluated the data underlying the practice model.

For example, surveys of selected office-based physicians, supplemented by other data bases, lead to a practice model that identifies the character of the patient population and the nature of clinical problems encountered. These data have shown that a large majority of physicians' office-based clinical encounters are with patients who have been diagnosed previously and who are presenting in the context of continued care. In the face of these data, content experts have agreed that the test blueprint should incorporate a continued care frame in a majority of test items. At the same time, the expert committee has not endorsed a simple one-to-one correspondence between the blueprint and the specific clinical problems and diseases reported in the surveys, because that would imply a physician licensure test focused on patients seen for general physical examinations and upper respiratory infections (i.e., "colds"). There may be instances where rarely occurring, but high-impact problems may be preferred over frequently occurring, low-impact conditions. Thus, the practice model approach retains reliance on expert judgment about the weighting of content on the licensure examination. The logic of that process puts the experts in the position of interpreting data descriptive of the professional domain and devising rationales for appropriate departures from the weightings implied by the empirical data. (For a more complete treatment of the manner in which this process leads to test specifications, see LaDuca, Taylor, & Hill, 1984.)

The composite of expert decisions, informed by an empirically derived practice model, establishes the main points of the content of the licensure test, although the benefits of these analyses would be diminished if the writing of test items was not carried out in a systematic manner. In the following sections we describe several approaches to systematic item writing. In the section on "Developing the Initial Item Pool" and in the appendices we illustrate the ways in which the job analysis, evaluative objectives, and test items are connected. We begin by identifying types of objective items used in licensure and certification examinations. Examples of these item types are provided and their strengths and limitations described. In the interest of complete-ness, constructed response items also are discussed.

SELECTED RESPONSE ITEMS

Objectively scored selected response items are the most frequently used item type on standardized licensure and certification examinations. Selected response items require examinees to choose an answer from possible answers supplied as a list of options. This family of item types has been in use for at least the past 50 years and, at its introduction, virtually replaced the constructed response item.

There are several types of selected response items currently in use: *single-best-answer* questions, *true-false* questions, *matching* questions, and *extended-matching* questions. Single-best-answer items require examinees to choose the one best answer from among a list of options or possible answers supplied by the test writer. The various matching formats are variations of the single-best-answer format. The most popular item type in use today is the multiple-choice question (MCQ) with four or five options and one option keyed as correct (Type A). The alternate-choice (AC) item, a special case of the MCQ, presents a stem question with only two possible answers (Downing, 1992; Ebel & Frisbie, 1986). The strength of the AC item is that it can test content that does not require absolute truth or falsity, such that the more correct option is selected. Matching and extended-matching items are also used in large-scale examinations.

Current practice is to designate ("key") only one option as correct in high-stakes examinations using selected response items, although it is possible to create good test items that involve more than a single correct response. In some contexts these may be preferable, as when equally attractive treatment options may exist for selected illnesses, or several appropriate diagnostic studies should be pursued. Classical test theory is most efficient for single-best answer items (e.g., Ebel & Frisbie, 1991); it is less well suited to items with more than one keyed response. The literature shows efforts to develop scoring methods that accommodate items with more than one correct response, principally item-response theory and polychotomous response models (e.g., Embretson, 1984). Testing professionals also must be sensitive to validity problems that may arise because of examinees' lack of familiarity with this response format.

True-false questions require examinees to respond to the truth or falsity of statements or questions. The stand-alone true-false item is rarely used in standardized examinations, but multiple true-false (MTF) items are employed. MTF items present a statement or open-ended question in the stem and require examinees to respond "true" or "false" to each of the varying number of options presented. Each true-false item in the set is generally scored as right or wrong, although some testing programs use various "cluster" scoring procedures for these items.

In the next section these selected response formats are discussed in turn, with an example of each item type given, and the format's strengths and limitations noted.

Multiple-Choice Questions

Where multiple-choice questions are used for licensure and certification examinations, the single-best-answer MCQ is the format of choice. The MCQ format presents a question or incomplete statement in the item stem and several (typically four or five) options as possible answers; only one option is keyed as the correct answer.

The most useful test for following the activity of disease in a patient with rheumatoid arthritis is

        (A) erythrocyte sedimentation rate
        (B) serum antinuclear antibody titer
        (C) serum protein electrophoresis
        (D) serum rheumatoid factor concentration
        (E) synovial fluid antiglobulin titer

Strengths

Multiple-choice items permit efficient and straightforward measurement of cognitive knowledge and educational achievement. Because responses are easily machine scored, large-scale testing can usually be accomplished in a cost-effective manner. Although MCQ testing has been criticized for emphasis on simple recall and trivia, it is possible to measure complex knowledge, such as judgment, decision making, and synthesis of knowledge (Maatsch, Huang, Downing, & Munger, 1984). MCQs are time-efficient for both the item writers and test developers, and also for examinees challenged by these items. The research base and psychometric theory for MCQs is very rich.

Principles of MCQ construction are discussed widely (e.g., Haladyna, 1994; Haladyna & Downing, 1989a; LaDuca, Staples, Templeton, & Holzman, 1986; Roid & Haladyna, 1982). However, the empirical research on aspects of these item-writing principles is somewhat less rich. (See Haladyna & Downing, 1989b, for a good summary.)

MCQ Weaknesses

MCQs require examinees to recognize and select correct answers that are supplied. Presentation of answers may clue the correct answer, making this task less difficult than constructing responses to questions. Some research supports this belief (e.g., Ebel, 1972), but recognizing correct answers and constructing correct answers are very highly correlated. Nevertheless, implications for validity of using MCQ testing for licensing continue to receive constant scrutiny.

All selected response formats allow the possibility of the examinee guessing the keyed correct answer when the correct answer is unknown. In general, providing a larger number of options lowers the probability of randomly guessing the correct answer. Because of the possibility of guessing, MCQs traditionally have four or five options.

In our view, psychometric concerns about guessing are excessive. If guessing were a large source of error variance for MCQs, reliability estimates would be much lower than typically reported for such examinations. When sufficient numbers of items are used, the guessing issue becomes trivial. Licensure and certification examinations should use large numbers of test items for content validity and high reliability. Lord (1944) reported that the three-option format is the optimum for high-ability examinees. Lord (1977) replicated these findings using item-response theory. Haladyna and Downing (1993) report that even well-written four- or five-option MCQs used in national certification and standardized college admissions examinations have only two distractors that perform as expected, effectively creating a three-option MCQ.

Other potential weaknesses of MCQs include ambiguity, bias, reading level problems, security problems, testwiseness clues, and test anxiety. Ambiguity is reduced by careful and thorough editing by both content experts and professional test editors. Various techniques to identify and reduce test bias are available (Cole & Moss, 1989). Reading level must be appropriate to the examinee population and is controlled by careful editorial review and pretesting. Test security is problematic for MCQs; to ensure the valid interpretation of test scores, MCQ examination materials must be secured throughout the test development process including test administration and scoring.

Much heat and little light have been generated by issues of testwiseness, coaching and its effects, and test anxiety issues. Examinees must be familiar with MCQ formats. The *Standards* (AERA, APA, & NCME, 1985) require that examinees have the opportunity to practice with item formats prior to the certification and licensure examination. Coaching probably has some small effect, (see Chapter 3, Rosenfeld et al.) but far less effect than thorough study of the content measured by the examination and a smaller effect than the statistical effect of regression toward the mean (e.g., Becker, 1990; Smith, 1991). Test anxiety may affect test scores for some examinees, but this phenomenon, if it exists, is not limited to the selected response formats.

Matching Items

Matching questions present several test items that are answered by selecting from a set of (usually) four or five options. Matching sets may be very useful for testing examinees' knowledge of related concepts and conditions. In contrast to single-best-choice items, matching items should have options that are of apparently equal likelihood. In the medical context, selecting the most likely diagnosis is a good example. (It is possible to use more than two stems for each matching set.)

> *The most likely explanation is:*
> *(A) Conversion disorder*
> *(B) Dysmorphic body image*
> *(C) Malingering*
> *(D) Normal behavior*
> *(E) Panic disorder*
>
> *1. A 66-year-old woman comes to the clinic requesting evaluation for breast cancer after a close friend and neighbor was diagnosed with the disease. Mammography is arranged. Later, the patient is relieved when results of her mammogram are negative.*
>
> *2. A 21-year-old woman comes to the clinic. She says that she was on the way to an acting audition when "I got a racing heart, I couldn't breathe, I got dizzy and I was afraid I was going to die!" She says that this type of episode has happened three times before but never this bad.*

Matching Item Strengths

For the most part, matching items share the strengths noted for MCQs. Traditional matching items may be most efficient for testing comparisons and relational concepts across broad topic areas.

Matching Item Weaknesses

Recall of facts and their relationships may also be the limitation of traditional matching items. The focus is narrowed by the theme (e.g., diagnosis) and the items must pose classic presentations if examinees are to make the distinctions. It also is difficult to write matching items that measure higher-order knowledge because of the possibility of word associations cuing the examinee to the correct response. The comparison of concepts usually requires that their distinctions be less subtle; it may be imperative to limit the contrasts to black-and-white distinctions.

Extended-Matching Items

Matching items are a variation of the single-best-answer question format. In the traditional matching item, questions are to be answered by selecting from a lettered list of possible answers. A newer variation is the extended-matching item (Case, Swanson, & Stillman, 1988; Case & Swanson, 1993). Extended-matching items have four essential components: a common theme, a lead-in, a list of options, and two or more item stems.

COUGH

The most likely diagnosis is:

(A) *Acute bronchitis*   (F) *Chronic obstructive pulmonary disease*
(B) *Atelectasis*   (G) *Cystic fibrosis*
(C) *Bronchial asthma*   (H) *Pneumococcal pneumonia*
(D) *Bronchiectasis*   (I) *Pulmonary embolus*
(E) *Cancer of the lung*   (J) *Pulmonary tuberculosis*

1. An afebrile patient complains of "tightness or pressure" in the chest. He has dyspnea, a cough and expiratory wheezing.

2. During the past 5 years, a patient who smokes two packs of cigarettes a day has developed progressive dyspnea accompanied by coughing and wheezing.

Extended-Matching Strengths

The extended-matching format encourages item stems that provide more detail (e.g., in medicine, stems that present extensive clinical descriptions of patients) and provide for a longer list of options. The research data (e.g., Case & Swanson, 1989) suggest that this item format is more difficult than MCQs, with higher item discriminations, and higher reliability estimates; however, these findings probably are not universal. The item format lends itself best to diagnostic questioning, and therefore, probably assesses "higher" cognitive levels than the traditional matching format. Item authors seem able to produce large numbers of extended-matching items efficiently (Case & Swanson, 1993) and the format lends itself to the item-modeling principles outlined in this chapter.

Extended-Matching Weaknesses

In general, the limitations of matching items may be amplified when a larger number of options are used. Because a common theme is needed for the format, it is possible to oversample in some content areas while overlooking other content areas. Such over- and undersampling could reduce the content validity of the examination. Also, attempts by item writers to capitalize on the longer options list may lead them to develop questions that make trivial distinctions. Longer lists may allow for subsets to function as distractors for different questions, permitting more capable examinees to reduce the functionality of the entire array.

Multiple True-False Items

The multiple true-false (MTF) item presents a statement or open-ended question, followed by two or more related true-false items. The examinee is instructed to respond to each option as true or false. (This item type is sometimes referred to as the Type-X item.) Frisbie (1992) presents a comprehensive review of this item type and a summary of the research reports on this item type. An example follows.

The table shown below represents the performance of Test A for Disease X in 100 patients.

TEST A	DISEASE X	
	Present	Absent
Positive	50	8
Negative	12	30

Correct statements include:
(A) The sensitivity of the test is 81%
(B) The specificity of the test is 79%
(C) The positive predictive value of the test is 86%
(D) The negative predictive value of the test is 28%
(E) The prevalence of Disease X in this population is 58%

Multiple True-False Item Strengths

MTF items are consistently more reliable than single-best response MCQs, when reliabilities are adjusted for equal amounts of testing time (Frisbie, 1992). MTF items have been shown to be more difficult than MCQs in some studies (e.g., Albanese, Kent, & Whitney, 1977; Kreiter & Frisbie, 1989). Concurrent validity evidence (correlations of MCQ and MTF item data) shows that the two formats measure about the same knowledge (e.g., Frisbie & Sweeney, 1982). Criterion-related validity evidence for the MTF item is sparse. Albanese, Kent, and Whitney (1977) found that MTF items predicted GPA as well as other formats, such as MCQs.

MTF items are time-efficient for both examinees and item authors. Although there are exceptions, most timing studies (Frisbie, 1992) suggest that the ratio of MTF items to MCQs answered per minute of testing time ranges from about 2.3 to 3.4. Hence, MTF items are very efficient.

Multiple True-False Weaknesses

Downing, Grosso, and Norcini (1994) showed that, compared with MTF items, MCQ items had higher criterion-related validity for an independent external rating of competence. The MTF format typically lends itself to assessment of facts and other so-called "lower" cognitive taxonomic levels. For example, Baranowski, Downing, Grosso, Poniatowski, and Norcini (1994) show that in subspecialty certifying examinations in Internal Medicine, 40% to 80% of MTF items are classified as measuring knowledge, rather than judgment or synthesis.

CONSTRUCTED RESPONSE ITEMS

Constructed response items require the examinee to supply an answer rather than select an answer from a listing of possible answers. Constructed response items are currently used in some large-scale testing programs, such as the Medical College Admissions Test and the College Board's Advanced Placement Program.

Examples of constructed response items range from the familiar "fill in the blanks" items and short- and long-answer essay tests to complex computer-scored natural language items and computer administered and scored problem-solving exercises (Martinez & Bennett, 1992). Another example of a constructed response item is math problems that require the examinee to grid the computed answer on a special optical-scan sheet, which can be computer scored. Bennett (1991) offers a taxonomy of constructed response items ranging from the simple to the very complex.

Constructed Response Strengths

The principal strength of the constructed response item format is that examinees must supply answers rather than identify answers from a list. It is widely thought that supplying answers is a more complex task than recognizing answers. The research evidence for this advantage of constructed response items is sparse, but constructed response is believed to require different skills than selected response formats (Bennett, 1991).

The constructed response item format eliminates clueing of answers, because the examinee must formulate an original response. This formulating of a response is believed to be a more complex cognitive task than merely recognizing the correct answer from a list of possible answers. Constructed response items also appear to pose more authentic real-life problem-solving assessments, because real-life problems rarely come with a ready-made set of possible answers. Also, constructed response items are often easier to construct than selected response items because there is no need to devise plausible distractors.

Constructed Response Weaknesses

Constructed response items are difficult to score reliably. Development of machine-scoring methods for these items is only in its infancy (Martinez & Bennett, 1992). In order to score paper-and-pencil constructed response items reliably it is generally necessary to use multiple raters or scorers and then average their ratings. Interrater agreement is the essential reproducibility required in this context. Raters must be trained and "calibrated" to their task and their performance must be tracked over time. Sample answers, that make explicit the range of correct and incorrect answers, must be developed. Obviously, the rating process itself is expensive and time-consuming. Expert judgment is often required, in which case raters may need to be skilled professionals in the content area, which may be even more expensive and logistically complex.

Much development is currently taking place in constructed response formats, including work in the higher technology areas of computer scoring of these items. For example, Martinez and Bennett (1992) describe a natural language computer-scoring system being developed by Kaplan (1992). In this system, constructed response short answers are scored by a pattern-matching computer program; high agreement is reported for the computer scoring and human judges. Another example of development in this area is the computer-administered "figural response" items used in architecture examinations. Martinez (1993) reported that the figural response item performed well, but was less reliable than parallel MCQs.

Another area of development using currently available technology is the so-called uncued item format (Veloski, Rabinowitz, & Robeson, 1993). Although not strictly a constructed response item, the uncued format uses multiple choice stems as questions, but the answers are selected from a very long list (1,000 or more options) of possible answers that are available for all items. Answer codes are then gridded on a special optical-scan answer sheet for machine scanning. This format may be considered a hybrid between selected and constructed response items, utilizing the strengths of both while minimizing the limitations.

Using Item Sets

The matching formats usually call for several items associated with a list of some sort. However, sets of items may also be used effectively in non-matching formats. This tactic allows assessment of several aspects of the same general topic. A familiar example is the reading comprehension test, which presents a paragraph for the examinee to read, followed by several related questions that challenge the examinee to interpret what was read. This general format has been described by Haladyna (1992) as "context-dependent item sets," although there are other names.

Item sets are helpful in promoting assessment of higher-order thinking, because a richer problem or situation can be presented and several aspects tested. For example, in medical licensure testing, Dillon, Henzel, Klass, LaDuca, and Peskin (1993) have reported on their experience with the *case cluster*. This format consists of a series of four to nine single-best-answer MCQs related to a specific patient encounter. (See Appendix 3.) This format permits advancing the narrative of the encounter and posing challenges that reflect multiple aspects of the case such as initiating therapy, modifying therapy, making referrals to other clinical specialists, admitting the patient to the hospital, monitoring for progressive deterioration, detecting new problems in an established patient, and exploring ethical aspects of managing patients and their families.

DEVELOPING THE INITIAL ITEM POOL

The following section describes approaches to writing MCQs for assessing the knowledge of practitioners and students. The origins of this work reside in development of MCQs for tests used in evaluating the clinical knowledge of physicians and, for the most part, the examples cited are medical. The approach recommended here is believed to be equally appropriate for use with testing programs for other professionals.

Although the history of MCQs in standardized testing extends back more than 50 years, it has been only during the past two decades that systematic methods for writing MCQs have been advocated vigorously (e.g., Haladyna, 1991, 1994; Haladyna & Downing, 1989a, 1989b; Popham, 1978). Collectively, these methods have been described as an item- writing "technology" (Roid & Haladyna, 1982) that is intended to assist in production of larger numbers of higher quality MCQs. We will describe two methods that rely on making linguistic linkages between items and objectives. Separately, we will describe another method that permits development of large numbers of items based on exemplary items.

OBJECTIVES-BASED METHODS

All objectives-based item-writing methods start with a statement pertaining to an important aspect of knowledge or skill. These statements are assumed to have emerged from the job analysis procedure selected to support the design of the licensure examination. Our approach relies on content analysis of scenarios describing details of professional situations located in the practice model. We prefer this to soliciting knowledge and skill statements from expert practitioners in the target profession, but what follows is applicable to such descriptive statements as well.

In some applications, an objective is recommended for each item. However, this strategy may lead to an overabundance of objectives without commensurate gain in numbers of items or in quality of measurement. It is better to think of an *evaluative* objective as broad enough to encompass a set of at least 10 related items. Such objectives may be thought of as domain descriptions. In this context, item writing becomes part of domain-referenced test construction (Baker, 1974). What is crucial to effective objectives-based item writing is making explicit connections between the language of the objective and the words comprising the item.

Preparing Objectives

Objectives-based item writing requires the identification of the content reference, or topics, eligible for inclusion. In the two approaches described here, the content reference is a separate listing, such as clinical problems or diseases. Strictly speaking, development of evaluative objectives (or domain descriptions) is separate from the process of objectives-based item writing. In fact, developing objectives probably should involve a different group of experts, though there may be overlap.

An effective method of preparing evaluative objectives has been used in selected examinations developed by the National Board of Medical Examiners (NBME). The method begins with a practice model or other framework for situations that the competent target practitioner is expected to encounter (Burg, Lloyd, & Templeton, 1982; LaDuca, Taylor, & Hill, 1984). These situations may be described in a brief scenario, written and reviewed by content experts. Content analysis of the scenarios identifies important objectives. In our test development work, the objectives have been related to a physician task (e.g., performing a physical exam; using diagnostic aids; managing therapy). The items written to assess these objectives generally require a clinical vignette that describes a specific patient. Because the goal of the physician licensure testing is to evaluate the examinee's readiness to practice medicine, this focus on patient management seems warranted. Other evaluation contexts may require alternative perspectives, but whatever the context of evaluation, the advantages of developing relatively few objectives with broad content boundaries remain. Examples of items written in an objectives-based manner are found in Appendix 1.

THE LEAD-IN METHOD

The *lead-in* is the name given to the sentence or phrase that ends the item stem. Functionally, the lead-in puts the question to the examinee. Therefore, the lead-in serves as the direct link between the evaluative objective and the test item. A lead-in may be in the form of a question (*"What is the most likely diagnosis?"*), or it may be in sentence-completion form. For example, if the objective relates to knowledge of appropriate diagnostic tests, then one reasonable lead-in might state, *"The most appropriate diagnostic study is. . ."*

It is recommended that one or more lead-ins be prepared when objectives are developed. With experience, additional lead-ins may emerge and these should be made available. Writing test items using evaluative objectives and lead-ins should proceed as follows:

1. Identify a clinical problem AND a related objective.
2. Select a specific lead-in that is associated with the assigned objective. If available, sample items should be provided as additional aids to effective item writing.

3. Confirm that the item's lead-in poses the question that relates to the referenced evaluative objective.

4. Write an appropriate stem preceding the lead-in addressing the selected clinical problem and including sufficient clinical detail (e.g., patient age, history, complaints, history).

5. Write the correct answer and distractors that are logically and grammatically consistent with the lead-in.

Appendix 2 contains a brief selection of evaluative objectives associated with physician tasks. In addition, one or more lead-ins are provided as examples.

THE AMPLIFIED OBJECTIVE METHOD

The amplified objective (Baker, 1974) is the most systematic method described here. It is also the most demanding. Amplifying objectives works best where objectives are plentiful and large pools of items are needed. It is effective when groups are responsible for instruction or evaluation, because the process emphasizes clear explication of content relationships. An amplified objective has four parts. They are:

1) General Evaluative Objective;

2) Sample Item—illustrates the results of the amplifying process;

3) Content Limits—identifies appropriate content by defining key terms in the objective;

4) Response Limits—describes item formats and testing conditions; states criteria for correct and incorrect responses.

The following section describes a modified process for amplifying evaluative objectives. Assessing cognitive aspects of clinical competence is emphasized, and so, in general, the items are clinical vignettes.

Amplifying Evaluative Objectives

1. Identify the focal *Evaluative Objective*. Use wording that states (a) what information will be provided to the examinee, (b) what action the examinee will take, and (c) what information the examinee will be acting upon. For example, the objective should have this structure:

Assesses severity of patient condition and makes judgment as to current status, prognosis, or need for further action. (Response options are inferences or conclusions referenced to the patient in complete sentences.)

2. Prepare a *Sample Item*. Write or select at least one very good example of an item conforming to the amplified objective. Identify the keyed (correct) response.

3. Develop *Content Limits*. Begin by highlighting specific terms in the objective that identify, or imply, important clinical content. In the objective cited above, these would include *patient, acute but limited problem, ambulatory setting,* and *likely diagnoses.*

4. Establish *Response Limits*. Specify item formats (e.g., A-type, four-option). Also, elements of stem content should be delimited (e.g., patient age, presenting complaint, signs and symptoms, setting, etc.), and variations on lead-ins should be specified.

5. Define the correct responses, usually by referring to a content reference, such as a list of eligible diseases, drugs, laboratory studies, etc. Also, you should stipulate the character of incorrect responses. For example, if the correct response is a respiratory infection, you must decide if all distractors must be respiratory infections. You may insist that distractors be varieties of pneumonias, or that other etiologies may be represented.

THE ITEM MODELING METHOD

Pioneered at the NBME, this method is helpful when the goal is rapid expansion of a small item pool. The process begins with a high quality MCQ that can serve as a model for many similar items. The assumption is that a well-written item, relating to a complex content topic or domain, is only one instance of a larger "family" of equivalent items (Haladyna, 1994; LaDuca, Templeton, Holzman, & Staples, 1986; Shea, Poniatowski, Day, Langdon, LaDuca, & Norcini, 1992). Other members of the "family" can be developed by imitating, or modeling, the *source* item. To guide the modeling process, a set of specifications for new items is based on a content analysis of the source item. Item modeling produces large numbers of items, but in a limited content area. Item modeling is more successful with MCQs that have longer stems, especially clinical vignettes. Modeling basic science items has been less successful.

Item Modeling Process: Preparing Modeling Specifications

1. Select a *source item.* It should be a well-written MCQ, preferably a clinical vignette, on a topic for which you want additional items. Use a single-best choice (A-type) with 4 or 5 options as the source item.

2. Highlight the specific terms in the stem that are important clinical content, (e.g., clinical setting; patient age, sex, and race; medical history; presenting complaint(s); signs and symptoms; and results of diagnostic studies).

3. Identify the correct (keyed) response, and the *content category* to which it belongs. For example, the answer to the question may be a diagnosis; a follow-up diagnostic study; a decision to admit the patient to the hospital; a referral; a modification in the patient's medications; etc.

4. *Review the available wrong options (distractors),* and discard any that are inconsistent or flawed. List additional plausible alternatives, and, if possible, stipulate rules for combining choices in new items. These "distractor rules" should guide item writers by delimiting options that should, or should not, appear together.

5. *For each clinically important term in the stem,* list several significant alternatives. The alternatives should be "differences that make a difference" in the clinical context. For example, how would the clinical situation be different

- if the patient were a young child instead of an adult?
- if the patient were a woman instead of a man?
- if the patient had significant family history of disease?
- if the diagnostic studies produced different results?
- if the patient's prior treatments were different?

6. *Prepare complete specifications for each new item.* Identify the content of the new stem by labeling one clinically reasonable combination of the alternatives. Then, for each new stem, identify or provide a keyed response. Finally, for each keyed response, specify the desired distractor rule. Figure 1 shows a sample specifications table for a modelling procedure.

TEST CONSTRUCTION

In describing this systematic test development process, we have assumed that the examination is new and intended for a high-stakes decision; that the test specifications have been developed through a defensible and systematic design process; that content experts will develop the test items and create all the test materials; that a committee structure is in place to create and approve examination policy and plans, to review and approve content specifications, to write and/or review test items, and so on; that items will be pretested for all future forms of this examination; and, that items will be stored in an item pool to access for future examinations. (We must omit from this discussion the critical issue of content validation of test items, although it has great significance for checks of adequacy of test items as measures of important knowledge and skill. This topic, so crucial in licensure testing, is addressed more fully in chapter 4.)

It should be noted that test security is needed from the very outset of test development for high-stakes examinations such as those examinations used for licensure and certification. Procedures for securing the examination items while they are being developed and reviewed should be as thorough as those security measures used during and after examination administration. Secure mail should be used to move items from author to test agency to reviewers; computer systems must be as secure as possible and access to items must be limited to those with a need to know. The security plan for the examination should be developed together with and as an integral part of the test development plan.

Appointing Expert Panels

Because individual test items are the building blocks for examinations, a primary task is to select and train item authors. Several defensible models are possible, but selecting item writers who are expert in the content to be measured and who are invested in the success of the testing program are key elements. Item authors must be willing to follow item writing guidelines established for the testing program and make a reasonable effort to accommodate the timelines established for test development and review. The lead-in method and the item modeling techniques discussed in this chapter provide highly efficient means of generating large quantities of high-quality test items. Item authors can be readily trained in these techniques and typically find these methods useful. Generally, about one-half to two-thirds of the items written will ultimately survive all content and editorial reviews and pretesting.

Item-Writer Training

Item writers for the testing program must be thoroughly familiar with the guidelines for item development and all the procedures established for submission and review of items. Test security requirements for authors should also be well

| STEM ATTRIBUTES | | | | OPTION ATTRIBUTES | | |
PATIENT	SYMPTOMS	PHYS EXAM	STUDIES	OPTIONS	KEY	DISTRACTORS
0. 10-yr-old boy previously healthy	10-day progressive cough, low-grade fever, dyspnea on exertion	diffuse rales bilaterally	Chest x-ray (perihilar infiltrate)	A) Pneumonia due to respiratory syncytial virus B) Pneumonia due to *streptococcus pneumoniae* (Pneumococcus) C) Pneumonia due to *mycoplasma pneumoniae* D) Pneumonia due to staphlococcus E) Congestive heart failure F) Tuberculosis	C	1. Any four others. 2. Include all pneumonias 3. Include only two other pneumonias
1. Same as 0 above.	10-day progressive cough, 24 spiking fever and dydpnea on exertion	diffuse rales bilaterally; egophony on right	Chest x-ray (two small air fluid levels on right)	Same as 0 above	D	Follow rule 2
2. Same as 0 above	Same as 1	fine crackling rales in right posterior base with impaired resonance	Chest x-ray (infiltrate in right lower lobe, fluid in right fissure); WBC = 38,000; 96% PMN	Same as 0	B	Follow rule 3
3. 2-mo-old boy; normal delivery	10-day persistent cough, afebrile, alert, rapid breathing	red eyes with purulent discharge from both; diffuse rales bilaterally	Chest x-ray (hyperinfiltration, diffuse interstitial infiltrates	G) Group B beta-hemolytic Streptococcus H) Hemophilus influenzae I) Pseudomonas J) Chlamydia pneumonia K) Pertussis	J	4. Include cited options
4. Same as 3 above	10-day mild cough with choking episodes, low-grade fever, profuse mucoid nasal discharge	conjunctival injection; normal chest sounds	Chest x-ray (perihilar infiltrate, scattered atelectasis); WBC = 30,000; 70% lymphocytes	Same as 3 above	K	Follow rule 4

Figure 1. Sample Item Modeling Specifications.
(Adapted from LaDuca, Templeton, Holzman, & Staples [1986] Item modelling procedure for constructing content-equivalent choice questions. Medical Education, 20, 53-56.)

understood (for example, authors may not keep copies of their items; secure mail should be used to ship questions; FAX and electronic mail transmissions are not secure).

Generally, specific item-writing assignments to individual authors are helpful. Such assignments will specify the number of items to be produced, the type of item format, and the exact content domains in which items are to be produced (from the test specifications). Sometimes it is helpful to tailor the assignment to the specific content expertise and interest of the authors. Authors could reasonably be asked to produce 25 to 50 MCQs over a period of several months.

Typically, item authors can be trained to the item-production task in about a one-half to full-day workshop, during which time clear written instruction is given, with many good and bad examples of the item types to be used presented. New authors also should have the opportunity to actually write items, receive feedback on their attempts, and receive some practice in review and critique of other authors' items.

Item Production

Timelines of sufficient length should be established to allow adequate time for item writing, review, rewriting, editing, and approval cycles. Generally, a minimum time of 18 months is needed to initiate a new high-stakes testing program (from the start of the test development process to the first testing date).

Each item should be subjected to a systematic development process that includes initial development, review, revision, and pretesting (Hambleton, 1980). One such sequence is shown in Figure 2. According to this sequence, the item is produced by the author, following the guidelines and content assignments established. The assigned items are received by the test development agency, generally logged in, and then entered into a computer system (ideally tied to an item-banking system). Subsequently, newly written items are edited by skilled professional test editors who are familiar with test construction technology. All items should be reviewed for potential bias and insensitivity to population subgroups.

ITEM WRITER PRODUCES TEST ITEM
ITEM SUBMITTED TO TEST DEVELOPMENT AGENCY
BIAS/SENSITIVITY REVIEW AND INITIAL EDIT
ITEM RETURNED TO WRITER FOR APPROVAL/EDIT
ITEM RETURNED TO AGENCY
ITEM REVIEWED BY ITEM WRITING COMMITTEE
ITEM APPROVED/REJECTED/ MODIFIED BY ITEM WRITING COMMITTEE
ACCEPTED ITEM ENTERED IN ITEM POOL
ITEM USED IN PRETEST FORM
ITEM APPROVED BY EXAMINATION COMMITTEE
ITEM USED IN SCORED FORM
ITEM RETURNED TO POOL FOR LATER USE

Figure 2. Life cycle of a test item

Edited items are then returned to authors for comment, clarification of questions raised by editors, and final author approval. Such items are then returned to the test development agency and prepared for content review. Content reviewers must be expert in the discipline and willing to review test items critically. It is preferable that reviewers have had experience as item writers because it will increase their sensitivity to the task confronting the item writers. Batches of test items can be securely mailed to content reviewers for critique and/or all items produced can be reviewed by a content committee charged with examination development. Reviewers, just like item authors, must be familiar with test security procedures and willing to follow all explicit security guidelines.

Item Pool

Once an item is accepted by a test development committee, the item is entered into the item pool and awaits pretesting. It is helpful to have rated the items for priority in pretesting. All identifying information about the items is entered with the item to facilitate test construction. An item pool can range in complexity from a simple paper system on which items and identifying information are stored on index cards to sophisticated, tailor-made computer software designed for an individual application. Many commercially produced software systems are currently available. Essential features of an item pool include: easy item storage and retrieval; the capability to store, sort, and retrieve items based on all relevant variables such as content classification, author, item statistics, and so on; integration with word processing and/or editing systems; and the flexibility to be modified easily as requirements change. (For more details about item banking, see Chapter 8).

Test Construction

Test construction refers to the actual process of building test forms from the item pool of approved items. For this discussion, we assume that we are building a new high-stakes examination to be administered in one day of testing time. The examination will contain a total of 200 MCQs for scoring and an additional 160 items for pretesting only. The examination is to be administered to 1,000 examinees. Four test booklets containing the same 100 scorable items, but including 20 unique pretest items, will be produced for the 4-hour morning session. The pattern will be repeated for the 4-hour afternoon testing session. Figure 3 illustrates this design.

This test booklet design allows 2 minutes of testing time per MCQ and permits a sufficient number of examinees (e.g., 250) to take each pretest item. For programs using traditional item and test statistics, about 100 examinees is minimum for each pretested item. For programs using IRT methods, the number of examinees may need to be much higher. Test booklets will be "spiraled" so that they will be distributed to examinees in the sequence Form 1, 2, 3, 4, 1, 2, 3, 4....n.

The purpose of pretesting is to generate score performance data on test items— to try out the item with examinees who are similar to those examinees who ultimately will be challenged by the item for "credit." Pretesting allows the test developers to select items that have the most desirable psychometric characteristics, thereby enhancing test validity and reliability. It is important to restrict the number of pretested, unscored items seen by each examinee, but about 10% is a reasonable target.

Examination Administration, Scoring, and Evaluation

Once the examination is administered, answer sheets and all test materials are returned to the test development agency (using secure shipping methods) for scanning and scoring. Test materials are first checked in and any missing materials are traced and located. Answer sheets are machine scanned to produce an electronic file of the responses recorded by the examinee on the answer sheet. Scoring is accomplished by applying the approved scoring key to the response. (It is assumed that scoring programs are available and that all psychometric issues such as passing score determination, scaling, score reporting, choice of psychometric model, and so on, have been made prior to examination administration.)

A preliminary scoring and item analysis takes place, using carefully con-structed and approved answer keys. A process of "key validation" may be completed prior to the final examination scoring. Key validation refers to a final verification of the scoring keys' accuracy by a group of content experts. (When all items have been previously pretested the key already has been validated; under these circumstances "key confirmation" may be a better name for this procedure.) This final key review is facilitated by reference to the preliminary item analysis data for each item. Criteria for item statistics such as item difficulty and discrimination are used to "flag" items for content review and key accuracy. For example, items that are very difficult and/or that do not discriminate well between those who score

TIME	TEST FORM	COMMON SCORED ITEMS	UNIQUE PRETEST ITEMS
Morning			
	A1	100	20
	A2	100	20
	A3	100	20
	A4	100	20
Afternoon			
	P1	100	20
	P2	100	20
	P3	100	20
	P4	100	20

Figure 3. Test booklet design for accommodating item pretesting.

highest on the test and those who score lowest may be flagged for evaluation. Content experts may decide to delete (score as correct for everyone) the item, change the key, or score the item as it was administered.

After final scoring, pretested items are evaluated. Item analysis data are examined for each pretested item using some predetermined criteria of item difficulty and discrimination. If the item meets the criteria, it is retained in the item pool for possible use on a scorable form of the examination in the future. (Items will be reviewed by content experts prior to use on a scorable examination.) Items that fail the statistical criteria for inclusion in the item pool may be discarded or returned to item authors or test development committees for evaluation and possible rewriting.

The performance of examination items is useful feedback to item authors. Some systematic method of item tracking should be included in the specifications of the item pool, such that the performance of items can be summarized for individual authors. Simple statistics such as the average difficulty of an author's items and the proportion of items passing the pretest criteria may be useful to authors as feedback.

Items used on a scored portion of an examination have some shelf life for possible reuse if the test remains secure. Shelf life depends on several variables: how rapidly the content and/or the test specifications change and evolve and how restrained content committees are in editing or otherwise modifying "used" questions.

Item pooling for high-stakes examinations require maintaining good items for possible reuse because creating new test material is expensive and labor intensive. As a general rule no more than 50% of items might be reused together from a previously scored examination (pretest items are not included, because these are "new" items); however, reusing about one-third of items is preferable.

One very basic reason for reusing items on an examination is to allow for the statistical procedure known as "equating." Examination equating (discussed in detail in Chapter 11) refers to the process of adjusting test scores on a current version of an examination in order to maintain the identical interpretation of the passing score from administration to administration. Equating allows one to interpret test scores in exactly the same way from administration to administration; it is as though all examinees took the same examination. Hence, when examination scores are properly equated, the meaning of the passing score is the same from administration to administration. No matter how carefully examinations are constructed (even from pretested and used items) it is impossible to maintain the identical average difficulty of the test from administration to administration. Equating solves this problem so that examinees are neither benefitted nor penalized by getting a slightly easier or more difficult examination.

A design of a typical classical measurement equating model used by many high-stakes examinations requires the use of a common set of used items (often referred to as "anchor" items). Because these common items are used to anchor the equating, such items must be unchanged from administration to administration. When the equating is carried out, the performance of examinees on these common items is compared from the first to the second administration. This performance is used to adjust scores on the current administration of the examination to maintain the identical score scale.

Common items used for equating cannot be edited or changed in any way. Although there is always some creative tension between content experts and test development agencies around editing anchor items, the logic of equating requires that items be repeated in exactly the same presentation from administration to administration. Some effort should be made to retain as much common context as well (i.e., use in the same book). If used items are edited substantially (and this is where the debate often occurs), then such items should not be used as part of the equating link.

Conclusion of Testing Program

At the end of each testing cycle, it may be very useful to prepare a technical report of all relevant test development, administration, standard setting, scoring, and reporting activities. Such a report is an attractive method for maintaining records of activity in support of the program's defensibility. Summary psychometric analyses should be reported, including average item difficulty and discrimination, estimates of score and decision reproducibility, and mean scores and pass rates for important examinee subgroups. Specific recommendations and plans for improvement of the program should be included in the final technical report.

Program Audits

Madaus (1992) has advocated routine external review as a further guarantee that high-stakes testing programs are fulfilling their obligation to protect the public. The fundamental argument is that all testing programs can be improved by systematic and independent inspection by qualified professionals. The consequences to the public and to the profession may be too serious to restrict responsibility for quality assurance to persons who may have vested interests.

The auditors' primary responsibility is to the protection of the public. Therefore, it is imperative that auditors be independent of all interested parties and without any stake in the outcome of the audit. External, independent auditors should be highly qualified measurement professionals, with experience in the specific type of examinations being reviewed.

The *Standards* (AERA, APA, & NCME, 1985) provide the basis for all testing program audits. Schmeiser (1992) provides additional guidance concerning the ethical obligations of measurement professionals. The auditor should collect systematic data about all important aspects of the testing program; test development, item quality, item review and editing, content validity evidence, and test security should be examined. Additionally, it is important to evaluate psychometric data, including item analysis, statistical evidence of validity, estimates of reliability, procedures for determining passing scores, and score reporting. The evaluator should make specific recommendations for program improvements, with implementation of recommendations included in subsequent audits.

SUMMARY

We have covered substantial ground in this chapter. We have discussed several critical elements of test development for assessments used in licensing. We remain cognizant that the purpose of licensure is protection of the public and the profession from unqualified practitioners. Because these are high-stakes decisions, the developer is obliged to give priority to issues of quality, defensibility, and validity in all components of the testing program.

We have restricted our discussion to conventional methods of standardized testing, with emphasis on multiple-choice formats. Irrespective of the formats used, we have recommended systematic item-writing methods, relying on committees of content experts appointed especially for this purpose. We have assumed that the design of the program has been conducted in accord with current requirements as summarized in the *Standards*, with particular attention to the imperative to assess in areas of knowledge that are of unimpeachable relevance to the demands of professional practice. The content specifications for the examination must be delineated carefully and based on the implications arising from an appropriate job analysis. Detailed discussion of the methods for accomplishing this phase of the program development is beyond the scope of this chapter.

We have recommended that item pools be developed, consisting of large numbers of test items that have been pretested successfully. In addition we have urged the use of content-based standard-setting methods for establishing criteria for adequacy of performance. We have suggested maintaining fixed standards through application of statistical equating methods described elsewhere in this volume. Finally, we have admonished test developers and licensing agencies to exercise extreme caution in the maintenance of test security.

We began by acknowledging that critics of standardized testing make valid arguments in some instances. We believe that the overall quality of standardized licensure testing will be enhanced greatly by attention to the techniques and procedures detailed in this chapter.

REFERENCES

Albanese, M. A., Kent, T. H., & Whitney, D. R. (1977, November). *A comparison of the difficulty, reliability, and validity of complex multiple choice, multiple response and multiple true-false items.* Paper presented at the Annual Conference on Research in Medical Education, Washington, DC.

American Educational Research Association, American Psychological Association, & National Council on Measurement in Education. (1985). *Standards for educational and psychological testing.* Washington, DC: American Psychological Association.

Baker, E. (1974). Beyond objectives: Domain-referenced tests for evaluation and instructional improvement. *Educational Technology, 14*, 10-16.

Baranowski, R. A., Downing, S. M., Grosso, L. J., Poniatowski, P. A., & Norcini, J. J. (1994, April). *Item type and ability measured: The validity of multiple true-false items.* Paper presented at the Annual Meeting of the National Council on Measurement in Education, New Orleans, LA.

Becker, B. J. (1990). Coaching for the Scholastic Aptitude Test: Further synthesis and appraisal. *Review of Educational Research, 9,* 179-190.

Bennett, R. E. (1991). *On the meanings of constructed response.* Princeton, NJ: Educational Testing Service.

Burg, F. D., Lloyd, J. S., & Templeton, B. (1982). Competence in medicine. *Medical Teacher, 4(2),*: 60-64.

Case, S. M., & Swanson, D. B. (1989, April). *Evaluating diagnostic pattern: A psychometric comparison of items with 15, 5, and 2 options.* Paper presented at the Annual Meeting of the American Educational Research Association, San Francisco, CA.

Case, S. M., & Swanson, D. B. (1993). Extended-matching items: A practical alternative to free-response questions. *Teaching and Learning in Medicine, 5*, 107-115.

Case, S. M., Swanson, D. B., & Stillman, P. L. (1988). *Evaluating diagnostic pattern recognition: The psychometric characteristics of a new item format.* Paper presented at the Annual Conference on Research in Medical Education, Washington, DC.

Cole, N. S., & Moss, P. A. (1989). Bias in test use. In R. L. Linn (Ed.), *Educational measurement* (3rd ed; pp. 201-219). New York: American Council on Education.

Dillon, G. F., Henzel, T. R., Klass, D. J., LaDuca, A., & Peskin, E. (1993, April). *Presenting test items clustered around patient cases: Psychometric concerns and practical implications for a medical licensing program.* Paper presented at the Annual Meeting of the American Educational Research Association, Atlanta, GA.

Downing, S. M. (1992). True-false, alternate-choice, and multiple-choice items. *Educational Measurement: Issues and Practice, 11*, 27-30.

Downing, S. M., Grosso, L. J., & Norcini, J. J. (1994, April), *Multiple true-false items: Validity in medical specialty certification.* Paper presented at the Annual Meeting of the National Council on Measurement in Education, New Orleans, LA.

Ebel, R. L. (1972). *Essentials of educational measurement.* (2nd ed.). Englewood Cliffs, NJ: Prentice-Hall.

Ebel, R. L., & Frisbie, D. A. (1991). *Essentials of educational measurement (5th ed.).* Englewood Cliffs, NJ: Prentice-Hall.

Embretson, S. E. (1984). A general latent trait model for response processes. *Psychometrika, 49*(2), 175-186.

Fine, S. A. (1986). Job analysis. In R. E. Berk (Ed.), *Performance assessment: Methods and applications (pp. 53-81).* Baltimore: Johns Hopkins University Press.

Frisbie, D. A. (1992). The multiple true-false item format: A status review. *Educational Measurement: Issues and Practice, 11*(4), 21-26.

Frisbie, D. A., & Sweeney, D. C. (1982). The relative merits of multiple true-false achievement tests. *Journal of Educational Measurement, 19*, 99-105.

Haladyna, T. M. (1991). Generic questioning strategies for linking teaching and testing. *Educational Technology: Research & Development, 39*, 73-81.

Haladyna, T. M. (1992). Context-dependent item sets. *Educational Measurement: Issues and Practice, 11*, 21-25.

Haladyna, T. M. (1994). *Developing and validating multiple-choice test items.* Hillsdale, NJ: Lawrence Erlbaum.

Haladyna, T. M., & Downing, S. M. (1993). How many options is enough for a multiple-choice test item? *Educational and Psychological Measurement, 53*, 999-1010.

Haladyna, T. M., & Downing, S. M. (1989a). A taxonomy of multiple-choice item-writing rules. *Applied Measurement in Education, 2*, 37-50.

Haladyna, T. M., & Downing, S. M. (1989b). Validity of a taxonomy of multiple-choice item-writing rules. *Applied Measurement in Education, 2*, 51-78.

Hambleton, R. K. (1980). Test score validity and standard-setting methods. In R. A. Berk (Ed.), *Criterion-referenced measurement: State of the art (pp. 80-123).* Baltimore: Johns Hopkins Press.

Kaplan, R. M. (1992). Scoring natural language free-response items—A practical approach. Proceedings of the 33rd Annual Conference of the Military Testing Association (pp.514-518).

Kreiter, C. D., & Frisbie, D. A. (1989). Effectiveness of multiple true-false items. *Applied Measurement in Education, 2*, 207-216.

LaDuca, A. (1980). The structure of competence in health professions. *Evaluation & the Health Professions, 3*, 253-288.

LaDuca, A. (1994). Validation and professional licensure examinations: Professions theory, test design, and construct validity. *Evaluation & the Health Professions, 17*, 178-197.

LaDuca, A., & Engel, J. D. (1994). On the neglect of professions theory in professions education. *Professions Education Researcher Quarterly, 15* (4), 8-11.

LaDuca, A., Taylor, D. D., & Hill, I. K. (1984). The design of a new physician licensure examination. *Evaluation & the Health Professions, 7*, 115-140.

LaDuca, A., Templeton, B., Holzman, G. B., & Staples, W. I. (1986). Item-modelling procedure for constructing content-equivalent multiple choice questions. *Medical Education, 20*, 53-56.

Lord, F. M. (1944). Reliability of multiple-choice tests as a function of number of choices per item. *Journal of Educational Psychology, 35*, 175-180.

Lord, F. M. (1977). Optimal number of choices per item—A comparison of four approaches. *Journal of Educational Measurement, 14*, 33-38.

Maatsch, J. L., Huang, R. R., Downing, S. M., & Munger, B. S. (1984). The predictive validity of test formats and a psychometric theory of clinical competence. *Proceedings of the 23rd Conference on Research in Medical Education.* Washington, DC: Association of American Medical Colleges.

Madaus, G. F. (1992). An independent auditing mechanism for testing. *Educational Measurement: Issues and Practice, 11*, 26-31.

Martinez, M. E. (1993). Problem-solving correlates of new assessment forms in architecture. *Applied Measurement in Education, 6* (3), 167-180.

Martinez, M. E., & Bennett, R. E. (1992). A review of automatically scorable constructed-response item types for large-scale assessment. *Applied Measurement in Education, 5*, 151-169.

Popham, W. J. (1978). *Criterion-referenced measurement*. Englewood Cliffs, NJ: Prentice-Hall.

Roid, G. H., & Haladyna, T. M. (1982). *A technology for test-item writing*. New York: Academic Press.

Schmeiser, C. B. (1992). Ethical codes in the professions. *Educational Measurement: Issues and Practice, 11*, 5-11.

Shea, J. A., Poniatowski, P. A., Day, S. C., Langdon, L. O., LaDuca, A., & Norcini, J. J. (1992). An adaptation of item modelling for developing test item banks. *Teaching and Learning in Medicine, 4* (1), 19-24.

Smith, M. L. (1991). Meanings of test preparation. *American Educational Research Journal, 28*, 521-542.

Veloski, J. J., Rabinowitz, H. K., & Robeson, M. R. (1993). A solution to the cuing effects of multiple choice questions: The un-Q format. *Medical Education, 27*, 371-375.

Chapter 5 Appendix 1

EXAMPLES OF OBJECTIVES-BASED ITEMS

Encounter: Diabetes mellitus
Objective: Recognizes new signs and symptoms in patient with established diagnosis

A 55-year old man has had insulin-dependent diabetes mellitus for most of his life. He is in the hospital recovering from a gastrointestinal operation and he is receiving regular insulin on a sliding scale. He has no glycosuria, but he has persistent ketonuria. The most appropriate management is to

(A)   increase the dose of insulin
(B)   decrease the dose of insulin
(C)   increase his caloric intake
(D)   decrease his caloric intake
(E)   substitute an oral hypoglycemic drug

Encounter: Diverticula of intestine
Objective: Knows to counsel patient or family regarding current and future problems or self-care

A 34-year-old woman who is otherwise asymptomatic had an upper gastrointestinal roentgenographic study because of a 6-month history of abdominal pain. A duodenal diverticulum was found. She should be advised that

(A)   the duodenal diverticulum is the cause of her pain
(B)   the duodenal diverticulum should be removed surgically
(C)   the duodenal diverticulum will cause gallstones
(D)   long-term treatment with tetracycline will be initiated
(E)   no treatment is necessary for the duodenal diverticulum

Encounter: Various diseases of the gallbladder
Objective: Recognizes new signs and symptoms in patient with established diagnosis and adjusts therapy

A 50-year-old woman, who is scheduled for elective cholecystectomy, has been taking eight aspirin tablets daily for pain caused by arthritis. In preparing for the operation, it would be best to

(A) give her a 4-donor platelet pack on the morning of the operation
(B) operate, but have platelets available if bleeding occurs during the operation
(C) discontinue her aspirin therapy and wait 2 weeks before proceeding with the operation
(D) discontinue her aspirin therapy and wait 24 hours before proceeding with the operation
(E) give the patient fresh-frozen plasma if bleeding occurs during the operation

Encounter: Osteoarthritis and allied conditions
Objective: Interprets laboratory or diagnostic studies as to underlying patho-physiology

A 73-year-old woman who has degenerative joint disease develops pain and swelling in her left knee. An x-ray film of the knee shows a narrowed joint space and linear calcifications within the joint space. The most likely finding in the joint fluid will be

(A) decreased serum glucose concentration
(B) gram-negative organisms
(C) leukocyte count > 100,000 mm^3
(D) negatively birefringent (needle-shaped) crystals
(E) positively birefringent (rhomboid) crystals

Encounter: Gout
Objective: Interprets results of diagnostic studies as to the impact on diagnosis or management

A 41-year-old man has an acute attack of gout involving his right great toe. He had one attack 8 months ago, but he has not been taking any medication. An x-ray film of the affected area would most likely show

(A) calcification of cartilage
(B) sharply marginated bone erosions
(C) subchondral osteopenia
(D) subperiosteal bone resorption
(E) no abnormality

Encounter: Prostate gland
Objective: Knows to counsel patient or family regarding current and future problems or risk factors

Two days ago, a 69-year-old man had a suprapubic prostatectomy during which 85 g of hyperplastic tissue were easily enucleated. Microscopic examination shows a 2-mm focus of adenocarcinoma. In addition to providing supportive care, he should be advised that he will also benefit from

(A) no further specific therapy
(B) total prostato-seminal-vesiculectomy
(C) hypophysectomy
(D) orchiectomy
(E) estrogen therapy

Chapter 5   Appendix 2
SELECTED EVALUATIVE OBJECTIVES AND ASSOCIATED LEAD-INS

History-Taking

Recognizes physician's best choice of words or interprets patient's own words
The best opening question is
The most appropriate initial question would be
The (physician's) most appropriate response would be
Interprets elicited history; vignette description is limited to history information
The most likely explanation (of presented case history) is

Physical Exam

Knows appropriate directed physical exam or required technique
During the physical examination, particular attention/special consideration should be given to
The physical examination should specifically focus on
The physical examination should be directed toward

Using Diagnostic Aids

Selects appropriate routine laboratory or diagnostic studies (study of choice, usually initial)
The most appropriate initial diagnostic study is
At this time, the most appropriate diagnostic study/procedure is
The best initial diagnostic step/study is
The most appropriate next step is to (response options list diagnostic studies)
Evaluates utility of diagnostic and invasive, special, non-routine studies
NOTE: The studies of choice are usually follow-up and more invasive than initial studies (e.g., biopsies). Results of prior diagnostic studies are usually described in the stem.
The most reliable next diagnostic test is
The most appropriate next step is (response options list, invasive diagnostic studies)

Making Diagnosis & Defining Problems

Selects most likely diagnosis or evaluates differential in light of history and/or physical and/or diagnostic test findings
The most likely diagnosis is (given diagnostic vignette in stem)
These findings are most likely a result of (response options are diagnoses)
Interprets vignette and identifies the indicator for consultation or further diagnostic assessment (Response options are indications)
Which of the following findings should prompt referral to a (specialist)?
In this patient, which of the following requires consultation with a specialist?
Further diagnostic assessment is mandated by
The most important indication for consultation (with a particular specialist) is the presence of

Assesses severity of patient condition and makes judgment as to current status, prognosis or need for further action (Response options are inferences or conclusions referenced to the patient in complete sentences)

At this time it is most appropriate to conclude that

The most accurate statement concerning the patient is

The most likely explanation for this patient's worsening condition is

Managing Therapy

Knows priorities for, or immediate consequences of, selecting among various interventions or therapies

Priorities in management include

(Therapy/intervention) will be appropriate for this patient if/when

The most appropriate next step is (response options focus, for example, on whether to obtain more details of the history or physical or order more studies or observe or begin treatment)

Knows indications (based on signs and symptoms) for immediate medical intervention (Emergency situations)

The most appropriate immediate management would be to

Knows appropriate present management of selected conditions (excludes all-drug options); often "wait and see" or other benign intervention

At this time, the most appropriate management is to

The most appropriate initial management is to

The most appropriate next step is to (response options are management-oriented, not diagnostic studies)

Recognizes indications for use of medications or prophylactic drugs or vaccines (e.g., drug of choice)

The most appropriate pharmacotherapy (for specific patient) is

In managing a patient with (condition), the medication most appropriate is

Knows indications for hospital admission or other appropriate setting, including moving patient to ICU, CCU

The factor most influential in deciding if the patient should be admitted to the hospital/special care unit is

The most appropriate next step is to (correct response option is to admit the patient to the hospital or special care unit)

Knows importance of educating patient or family regarding self-care, therapeutic regimen (e.g., BP measurement, home glucose monitoring) (Focus is on behavior regarding the specified therapy)

The patient (receiving a specific medication/therapy) should be told to avoid/be told to expect/be warned about

The patient should be told to/advised to (response options include, for example, home blood glucose measurement, self-examination)

Chapter 5   Appendix 3

SAMPLE CASE CLUSTER

A 45-year-old nurse sticks herself with a needle after it was used to draw blood from a 35-year-old jaundiced patient. The nurse is in good health when she comes to your office for a work-up of the incident. She takes only lovastatin for hyperlipidemia. Her last tetanus toxoid injection was 8 years ago. Laboratory studies done on the nurse and patient show:

TESTS	NURSE	PATIENT
Serum		
AST, GOT	16 U/L	450 U/L
ALT, GPT	8 U/L	560 U/L
Alkaline phosphatase	50 U/L	200 U/L
Serologies		
HbsAg	Negative	Positive
Anti-HBc	Negative	Negative
Anti-HAV (IgM)	Negative	Negative
Anti-HAV (IgG)	Negative	Positive
HIV	Negative	Negative

1. Other persons who should be tested are:
   - (A)   the nurse's household contacts
   - (B)   the other emergency department staff who were exposed to the patient
   - (C)   the patient's child's playgroup
   - (D)   the patient's household contacts
   - (E)   no one else needs to be tested
2. The nurse should receive
   - (A)   hepatitis B vaccine
   - (B)   hyperimmune B globulin
   - (C)   hyperimmune B globulin and hepatitis B vaccine
   - (D)   immune serum globulin
   - (E)   tetanus toxoid
3. The patient should receive
   - (A)   hepatitis B vaccine
   - (B)   hyperimmune B globulin
   - (C)   hyperimmune B globulin and hepatitis B vaccine
   - (D)   immune serum globulin
   - (E)   none of these

The nurse and patient are treated appropriately. Two weeks later the nurse develops right upper quadrant pain, low-grade fever, and dark urine.

4. The LEAST likely explanation for her symptoms is
   - (A)   hepatitis A
   - (B)   hepatitis B from the needle-stick contact with the patient
   - (C)   hepatitis C
   - (D)   gallbladder disease
   - (E)   reaction to lovastatin

The nurse admits to heavy intake of alcohol. Testing shows no other abnormalities and her symptoms resolve with abstinence from alcohol. Six months later she has a routine examination as part of an application for life insurance coverage. She is asymptomatic. Laboratory test results are:

Serum

AST, GOT	100 U/L
ALT, GPT	110 U/L
Alkaline phosphatase	100 U/L
Bilirubin, total	1.0 mg/Dl

5. Which of the following statements concerning these findings is correct?
   - (A)   Her lack of symptoms is a favorable prognostic sign
   - (B)   It is unlikely that she has chronic hepatitis because she is female
   - (C)   These values are expected as a consequence of her history of alcohol ingestion
   - (D)   The results represent a laboratory error
   - (E)   The results are most likely an early sign of AIDS

Repeat testing done the next day shows the following:

HBsAg	Negative
Anti-HBc	Positive
Anti-HAV (IgG and IgM)	Negative

6. Based on these findings, the most appropriate next step is
   - (A)   administration of immune serum globulin to her family members
   - (B)   administration of hyperimmune B globulin
   - (C)   liver biopsy
   - (D)   repeat liver chemistry profile in 6 months
   - (E)   test for antibodies to smooth muscle

Chapter 5   Appendix 4
SAMPLE AMPLIFIED OBJECTIVE

Evaluative Objective

Assesses severity of patient condition and makes judgment as to current status, prognosis, or need for further action.

Sample Item

Encounter: Cranial or ocular injury
Objective: Assesses severity of patient condition

A 55-year-old woman, who is an established patient, has been returned to the office by her adult son because of continuing complaints following an auto accident. At that time she suffered severe laceration when she was hit in the occipital skull by a piece of metal. For the past six weeks she has complained of headaches and she has had difficulty seeing. During this period, her family has noticed that she is behaving strangely. She does not seem to recognize objects even though her vision appears to be intact. She is forgetful, especially of recent events. She appears somewhat indifferent to friends and family members, and is described as "socially inappropriate." The greatest concern is that this patient

- (A)   has experienced an exacerbation of the occipital injury
- (B)   has experienced a major psychiatric illness, with the experience of the auto accident as a precipitating factor
- (C)   has had a major bilateral stroke in the anterior cerebral arteries
- (D)   has suffered damage to the anterior temporal lobes and frontal lobes in her initial auto accident
- (E)   is having episodes of atrial fibrillation or other cardiac problems

Answer: D

General Description

Given a description of an existing clinical problem or condition in a specific patient, the examinee will assess severity of illness by making appropriate judgments about clinical status, prognosis, or therapeutic options.

Faceted General Description

A

Given a {description of an existing clinical problem or condition}

B

in a {*specific patient*}, *the examinee will make a judgment about appropriate*

C   *D*   *E*

{*clinical status*}, or {*prognosis*}, or {*therapeutic options*}.

Content Limits

A:{*description of an existing clinical problem or condition}*

Use clinical problems/conditions in appropriate domain reference.

B:{specific patient}

b_1:   adult, black, female

b_2:   adult, white, male

b_3:   elderly, black, male

b_n: age, race, sex

C:{clinical status}

c_1:   admission to the hospital is required

c_2:   specific infectious agent is responsible

c_3:   no further follow-up is required

D:{prognosis}

d_1: patient is at risk for _____

d_2: the most likely consequence will be _____

d_3: the complication most likely to arise is _____

E:{therapeutic option}

e_1: surgical valve replacement will be required

e_2: serology is essential for further evaluation

e_3: no change in pharmacotherapy is needed

e_4: referral to _____ is needed

Response Limits

1. Use 4-, or 5-option, A-type MCQ preferably.

2. Response options are declarative sentences stating various assessments of severity.

3. Response options may be drawn from ONE facet (e.g., C or D or E), or from SEVERAL facets (e.g., one each from C and D and E).

4. Correct therapeutic option responses need only be preferable to incorrect responses.

DEVELOPING AND USING CLINICAL EXAMINATIONS

Jimmie C. Fortune

Virginia Tech

Theodore R. Cromack

Consultant

INTRODUCTION

Generally, clinical examinations for licensing (sometimes called performance tests) involve the candidate completing one or more tasks (in licensing this is thought of as "services for a client") that have been selected from the supervised practice (job analysis) of an occupation or profession. The clinical examination may exist in contexts (occupations) that do not require client interactions. Such contexts include building trades, automobile repair, accounting, etc. The tasks may range from fixing brakes, to preparing a body for burial, to wiring a house, or auditing a set of business interactions.

Other contexts require the candidate to perform services or tasks while interacting with a client. Such tasks include filling a tooth, counseling, fitting contact lenses, hair removal, and similar services. These tasks would then be graded as part of the licensure examination. Supervision or scoring of the tasks in the context where interaction is not required is easier than those requiring the presence of the client. Interaction with clients makes the second type of tasks harder to supervise and to grade. In recent practice, some boards have moved from using live clients to using simulations (Yaple, Metzler, & Wallace, 1992). Oral interviews may be required prior to issuance of a license in some contexts, but such entry orals or group interviews are not considered here as clinical examinations as they seldom are tasks germane to the job analysis of these occupations or professions.

Tests are used as a proxy to judge the ability of an individual relative to actual performance of a task. It might be useful to consider a continuum of faithfulness to the task ranging from a paper-and-pencil (multiple-choice) test to actual performance of the task. This continuum describes the concept of fidelity, or the degree to which the test requires the same behaviors as those required by the task. Unfortunately, this faithfulness to the task is only half of the equation, the other half is accuracy of the inference made about the candidate's ability to complete the task. This dimension speaks to the measurement concept of validity. Both fidelity and validity are complex, thus making a judgment about ability a complex activity.

Human judgment is complex and so intertwined with previous experience that total objectivity is virtually impossible to achieve. So called "objective tests," such as multiple-choice tests, generally moderate judgment by being constructed using multiple judges to determine content and to set cut scores, and by being scored in such a manner that individuals who perform the same task in the same way will attain the same score (often scoring is possible by machine or template). Moving along the continuum toward actual performance (i.e., from multiple-choice tests through essay tests, oral tests, and simulations, to actual clinical performance), the potential gain in fidelity can be offset by loss in objectivity.

Clinical tests appear on the side of the continuum closest to the actual performance of the task. The discussion which follows offers suggestions for enhancing the objectivity in the development and use of the clinical tests. Making scoring judgments explicit, reducing compounding of judgments, utilizing multiple judges in scoring individual performance, and providing statistical evidence of reliability, validity, and fidelity are among the topics discussed.

Performance on a clinical examination generally requires the candidate to use a combination of knowledge gained in training, skills acquired in the education or training program, physical attributes demanded in practice, interpersonal interaction skills, and attitudes. The clinical examination is believed to require candidates to demonstrate their ability to master and apply these different elements in concert. In a discussion with the Advisory Board to Southern Regional Testing Agency (SRTA) at Fort Walton Beach, Virginia, August, 1991, one dentistry board member explained that the clinical examination requires diagnosis, treatment, and patient education cast in the context of dealing with a fearful and uncomfortable patient. It requires practice of the profession along with human management. In dentistry, it was suggested that clinical examination required the candidate to work in the hard-to-reach areas of the mouth without compounding the patient's problems by injury of the areas that make access difficult. Common dental clinical examinations include: one or more types of restoration, prosthetics, and endrodentics.

Historically, these examinations were graded without psychometric analysis. In clinical examinations such as these, the complexity resulting from the joint application of several measurable actions, each of which could alone or in combination cause the service to be unsatisfactory, led the scorers to make single, global judgments of the degree of satisfaction of the candidate's performance of the service. When civil rights became an issue in the early 1960s, efforts to guarantee fair treatment of the candidates brought about increasingly sophisticated psychometric treatment of clinical examinations (Weiss, 1987). Among efforts to improve practice are methods to: (a) make scoring judgments explicit; (b) display the criteria associated with these judgments; (c) control the objectivity and uniformity of these judgments; and (d) measure agreement in these judgments (Schroeder, 1993). In other words, a methodology of clinical testing is now under development.

"Getting items" for clinical examinations differs from standard (i.e., multiple-choice) test development procedures in both conceptual and practical ways even though both start from the same body of information: the job analysis. In building multiple-choice tests, standard practice is to build from an inductive perspective using a "table of specifications" (or test blueprint) framework and the notion of domain sampling from the critical dimensions of the job. In clinical examinations, scorable dimensions, or items, must be extracted from a task within the clinical process. Hence, the test is developed in a more deductive manner. First comes the task, then critical elements of the task are identified and defined as criteria to be scored, hence items.

Many times clinical tasks result in an end product, a dental plate or a properly fitted pair of eye glasses. In such cases, evaluation of the product may be the most appropriate assessment of adequacy of performance by a candidate. Conversely, some clinical tasks are more aptly referred to as process tasks and do not yield a readily assessable product. Among such tasks might be ability to reduce a dental patient's anxiety concerning use of the drill. Such process tasks require observation and evaluation of the process as opposed to assessment of a product.

DEVELOPMENT OF SCORING PROCEDURES

When scoring a clinical examination, there is a tendency to avoid a systematic set of procedures and to make an overall global judgment of "pass/fail" for the whole task. The global score is unsatisfactory because it fails to: distinguish between degrees of successful completion of the task, provide the candidate with adequate feedback, make explicit the judgment process, and permit an opportunity to look at the degree of agreement among the judges. The scoring process becomes mystical without a systematic means of arriving at an estimate of the accuracy and quality of completion of the task. Of course, if the judgment is based on a single step or performance, then a single judgment is appropriate.

Beyond the overall judgment or single "pass/fail," scoring procedures are usually designed to describe the adequacy with which the task is completed or the quality of performance of each step in the process of performing the task. Three strategies appear in use, the first strategy is a 100-point system, which we do not recommend. This system involves subtracting a fixed value for each error, usually 1 or 2 points from the customary 100 points assigned to the candidate at the beginning of the examination. Our objections are based on the arbitrary handling of points and on the lack of identification of the number of potential errors. The second strategy is the dichotomous scoring of each process step or criterion point and the summation of the scores for correct steps. The third strategy is similar with regard to scoring the process steps, but weights are assigned to each step in accordance to some rule such as importance or criticality.

Making Scoring Judgments Explicit

Two strategies have been used to make grading judgments explicit. The first strategy breaks the performance of the clinical examination into explicit steps to be performed or skills to be displayed. This method appears most appropriate for process-based clinical examinations, especially those requiring the candidate to interact with a client. The second strategy is to define scoring criteria for the rating of accuracy or quality of the result. This method is most appropriate for product-producing clinical examinations. The first strategy involves a process similar to that of job analysis and the second strategy involves a process of deductive valuing, such as is done in consumer rating of different makes of automobiles.

The National Board performance test in optometry is an excellent example of the explicit step strategy (Gross, 1993). In this examination, 18 clinical skills are performed and evaluated using real patients. The performance of the skills occurs at five examination stations and each skill is scored independently by two judges. Two to six skills are performed at each station. At four of the stations the candidate is faced with a different patient and set of tasks to perform. At the fifth station an examiner portrays a patient from whom the candidate takes a case history.

For scoring, each skill is subdivided into its component items and each item is scored as pass or fail. Although one may observe that this process still requires subjective judgment, this judgment is made on a much narrower, well-specified area of performance. This specific performance can be addressed in the rater calibration process and is more directly linked to the final result. The performance test requires approximately 3 hours, each skill has 9 to 42 items and across the 18 skills there are 279 items scored independently by each judge. Criticality weights have been determined for each item. These weights reflect the consensus judgment of the nine-person examination committee of the relative importance of each item. It is hoped this criticality is related to the job analysis.

To obtain a candidate's score, each judge, for each item, multiplies the dichotomous item score by its criticality weight to get the weighted score for that item. Weighted item scores are then summed for each judge to get a skill subscore for each of the 18 skills. From the sum of these subscores, a pass-fail decision is made for the skill subtest. The process used to determine pass-fail for the skill subtest is based on the amount of error that can be "tolerated" for the skill. Gross (1993) reports that the tolerance level for a skill subtest is one point less than the highest weighted (most critical) item in the set of items associated with the skill. "Therefore, the pass-fail index for a clinical skill is designed to identify all candidates who perform all items correctly except for the most critical item" (Gross, 1993, p. 20). Gross points out that the pass-fail score for the whole examination is the sum of the pass-fail scores for the subtests. In cases where the skill subtests are not "Go No-Go" decisions, the candidate can make up poor subtest scores with high scores on other skill subtests. The dichotomous scoring of the items that go into a skill score is designed to promote interrater agreement. Mock examinations are used to estimate interrater agreement. Gross reported no attempt at estimating intrarater agreement.

The six clinical examinations of the licensing tests for dentists administered by the Southern Regional Testing Agency, Inc. (SRTA) provide excellent examples of the product-producing clinical examination and of the method of making judgments explicit by identifying criteria to assess success. The SRTA clinical examinations include: a non-metallic restoration, a metallic restoration, a gold restoration, two prosthetics (casting and fitting), and endrodentics (Minnich, 1992).

Scoring for each examination was devised by working backwards and deciding what would prevent a work sample from being acceptable. A panel of seven experts met and agreed on criteria to score each clinical examination. The criteria were very specific with descriptions to help pinpoint critical degrees of correctness. For instance, the criteria for the nonmetallic restoration were categorized for scoring as to cavity preparation and then as to finishing. Included in the cavity preparation were five decisions:

1. Was the cavity cleaned of decay?
2. Were the cavity walls prepared so as to facilitate the restoration staying in the cavity?
3. Was the cavity prepared with an anatomy that would permit a solid restoration?
4. Was the depth of the cavity handled appropriately (cement or treatment used if depth is too severe)?
5. Was the preparation properly cleaned and connecting teeth and tissue protected?

Prior to each test administration, slides are used to calibrate the judges on these criteria. Similar criteria are specified for the finishing of the restoration (Minnich, 1992).

Establishing Rater Agreement and Estimating Reliability

Two concepts of agreement are important in a scoring system. One concept is agreement across raters for an examinee or set of examinees for each item, referred to as interrater agreement. This concept could be thought of as one examinee and multiple raters: stability over raters. A second concept is that of internal reliability, or the agreement within a clinical examination for one rater. This is often called intrarater agreement and refers to stability of judgments. To maximize the extent of inter- and intrarater agreement, judges receive training, sometimes referred to as calibration. Calibration represents the degree to which several judges identify the same level of correctness for a given clinical performance or the degree to which a single judge identifies the same level of correctness for the same clinical performance over several examinees.

In 1951 Ebel proposed an analysis of variance format to estimate the reliability of ratings. Medley and Mitzel (1964) expanded the process to study multiple types of agreement using a single analysis of variance (ANOVA) framework. This model was then translated into the Winer (1971) repeated measures concept of reliability analysis. The extent that the judges are equivalent and the extent that intrarater scoring processes are uniform across test administrations determine the overall comparability of scores across test administrations and sites. Feldt and Brennan (1989) demonstrate the thoroughness with which generalizability theory addresses the multiple agreement and reliability needs of clinical examinations.

Feldt and Brennan (1989, p. 115) present a reference page of methods to address internal consistency using different types of data and different theoretical models. A coefficient and formula can be found to fit most clinical examination cases. In addition to the ANOVA to establish interrater agreement of two or more judges across several performances of the same clinical examination, Pearson product-moment correlation coefficients may be used for interval data or phi correlation coefficients for dichotomous data.

Reliability of the scoring process should be studied during pretesting of the clinical examinations and during the actual test administrations. Kenyon and Stansfield (1991) recommend and demonstrate the utility of pretesting in refining tasks for performance assessments. Their work is generalizable to clinical examinations in licensing. The double-blind process discussed in protection of candidates, if used, permits the estimation of interrater agreement on the scores used for licensure. Butzin, Finberg, Brownlee, and Guerin (1982) provide a model for the study of reliability of grades from oral examinations that can be used for other forms of clinical examinations. In many cases slides or simulations are used to establish agreement needed for calibration (Minnich, 1992). Friedman and Ho (1990) report a study of interjudge consensus and intrajudge consistency in standard setting. Their paper indicates the tradeoff between the two concepts.

Methods of Combining Scores from Standard Tests and Clinical Tests to Determine Eligibility for Licensure

Although there are formulae in measurement theory that allow one to combine the scores from several tests into a combined score taking into account the mean and variances of each test (Hopkins & Antes, 1990), we find that these formulae are seldom used in licensure testing. Instead, three methods of rendering the "pass-fail" decision appear to be the most commonly used in licensure settings. All three assume each test or examination represents an independent score on an essential criterion for practice. In the first method it is not assumed that the candidate must pass all of the examination parts, but the candidate must do well enough on all parts to accumulate enough total points to exceed the preset cut score (based on the combined results). In this first method, points are given to each test, written and clinical, and the points scored on the combined tests are summed to a total score which is compared to a preset cut score. This method permits the candidate to do poorly on one test or examination and to make it up by doing well on the rest. This method is frequently called an unweighted compensatory method.

In the other two decision processes, the candidate takes each examination, often one or more written and one or more clinical examinations, as separate, independent events. Both decision processes require the candidate to pass each of the examinations before eligibility for licensure is established (i.e., a conjunctive model). In the second of these three processes, the candidate must pass all examinations in a single testing, one failure results in the requirement to retake the entire examination. Costs of the examinations have tended to reduce the use of the pass all-in-one-sitting requirement.

In the third method, partial credit is permitted. The candidate must pass all examinations, but credit is given for the passing of one or more parts or examinations and the candidate can return in a future examination period to retake the examinations or subtests not passed earlier. This permits the candidate to accumulate passed examinations and is called the part-credit model. Millman (1989) argues for the setting of higher cut scores if the latter method is used. He feels that the probability of passing is modified and a higher cut score is needed to maintain discrimination or to identify the absence of competence.

ISSUES WITH CLINICAL EXAMINATIONS

Several issues are frequently raised by licensure board members or persons interested in licensure testing. Among these issues are: Why should a clinical examination be given? How close to the task must the clinical measure be? How can testing conditions be made uniform and fair? Does the clinical portion have to be standardized? What procedures are needed to insure standardization of the clinical portion? How do these procedures relate to the scoring procedures? What test statistics are needed for clinical items? Can test statistics be computed in the same way as for paper-and-pencil tests or other kinds of performance tests? What special procedures are needed to set a cut score for the clinical portion and how do these relate to continued testing using part credit? And is there some indication to show that a clinical measure is obsolete?

Absolute and comprehensive answers to many of these questions do not exist. In the following pages we discuss considerations required to develop answers for these questions.

Why Should a Clinical Examination be Given?

Interviews with board members in dentistry, nursing, and several licensed commercial occupations suggest that the clinical examination came about from three conditions: a mistrust of the paper-and-pencil or multiple-choice test, a need to see the candidate work with people, and a need to see the candidate perform in a work setting integrating the physical and cognitive skill areas. Often the services selected for the clinical examination are services commonly performed in practice, in many cases they are among the most frequently performed services, but certainly they are services or tasks perceived as "critical" in the job analysis.

Schroeder (1993) presents a series of questions concerning the use of oral, practical (which we have elected to call clinical examinations), or essay examinations, which may be helpful in making the decision whether or not to use a clinical examination. These questions are:

1. Is the behavior being measured something that could not be evaluated by the use of a multiple choice or objectively scored examination?
2. Are the evaluators thoroughly trained prior to the examination and administration?

3. Are the evaluators free of conflicts of interests concerning the candidates?

4. Are there detailed criteria for evaluating and scoring?

5. Does each evaluator make an independent rating?

6. Are at least two independent evaluations made for each candidate?

7. Is the evaluation free of potentially biasing information about the candidate which is not related to examination performance?

8. Has the examination session been documented (proctored, audio or video taped)? (Schroeder, 1993, p. 19)

The publication then suggests what the answer should be to elect to use a clinical examination.

How Close to the Task Must the Clinical Measure Be?

The actual requirement of clinical examinations (we prefer to address each required task as a single examination) may differ by profession or occupational area. Yet, all clinical examinations should evolve from a job analysis directed toward the identification of potential practices that may threaten to harm the health or safety of the public. Generally, clinical examinations are chosen from job analyses because (a) they define a frequently performed and important activity in the occupation (i.e., primary job activities), or (b) they require a complex coordination of cognitive and physical skills for successful practice, or (c) the professional practice demands complex interpersonal interactions with the "clients", or a combination of these reasons.

The first two reasons, primary job activities and complex multiability tasks, may, though do not specifically have to, result in a product-producing examination. Such a product, resulting from the examination, can be subjected to review or even tried out to determine its adequacy. This was illustrated above in the discussionof the SRTA dentistry examinations (Minnich, 1992). The third reason requiring "client" interactions is likely to lead to a process-performing examination. As was illustrated above in the discussion of the optometry examination (Gross, 1993), "Interaction with a client" is a process, as opposed to "preparation of a partial dental bridge" (p. 20) which is a product. Processes are more subjectively evaluated making it more difficult to establish uniform conditions across candidates and to grade the adequacy of the process.

The reason for using a clinical examination should be embedded in the examination. If the clinical examination is selected because of its importance in defining primary activities, it should contain all of the basic elements of performance required in practice (i.e., diagnosis, treatment, client education, etc.). In optometry such an activity might be an eye examination; the examination in this case may be identical with the task.

However, if the clinical examination is selected because it requires a complex coordination of cognitive and physical skills for success, opportunity to perform in a real or near real situation is necessary. In dentistry, such an activity may be the restoration of a molar using nonmetallic filling. This task must be performed in the patient's mouth so as to see if the candidate can handle the physical challenge of working in an awkward position, the challenge of bleeding, patient reaction, etc.

Clinical examinations selected because of required client interaction skills should deal with actual clients who hold real attitudes and perhaps limited tolerance for pain. In optometry, the fitting of contact lenses and the education of the client may be tasks where the candidate and client patience are taxed and the client's threshold of pain exceeded.

Clinical examinations may be selected because of two or more of the characteristics mentioned: (a) frequently performed or important activities, (b) complex coordination of cognitive and physical skills, and (c) complex interpersonal interactions. All three of these reasons appear operative in the case of the dental clinical examination in endrodentics. It is a common practice in dentistry to have to relieve pressure in the root of a tooth. The process of drilling to relieve pressure requires the coordination of cognitive and physical skills and the "client" needing the service or task performed is certainly in pain.

How Can Testing Conditions be Made Uniform and Fair?

For examinations that do not require the use of patients or "real" tasks, fairness and uniformity concerns focus on the candidate. Addressing these concerns for the candidate requires four steps: (a) Assure that the candidate knows what is to be done; (b) be certain that the candidate receives the correct reaction when the appropriate response is made; (c) make certain that the task required is relevant to the job analysis and is not just an exercise; and (d) equate the differences in tasks with regard to difficulty by avoiding the selection of either overly simple or highly complex tasks. Failing to follow these four steps precludes a fair examination as illustrated by the following case involving licensing of polygraph operators. A candidate for licensing as a polygraph operator who was being observed was subjected to an oral examination for which no script was written and in which the examiners "just winged it." The absence of a script and the spontaneous and potentially arbitrary behavior of the examiners made it impossible for the candidate to know what was to be done or what behavior was expected. Because the questions were ad-libbed and not shared with the candidate or even with other examiners prior to the oral interview, it is unlikely feedback on the candidate's responses was appropriately given. It is difficult to see the relevance of an impromptu set of questions to the administering or scoring of a polygraph. Hence, the oral interview was likely just an exercise and was not based on the job analysis. This became more evident when transcripts of other oral examinations were reviewed. These transcripts revealed lack of uniformity in questions asked and of relevance to the operation of a polygraph (Maust, Callahan, Fortune, & Cromack, 1988).

An important consideration in mounting a clinical examination requiring the participation of actual patients or live clients is making certain that the clinical examination is fair to the candidates and is safe for the participating patients. The fairness issue arises from the fact that amount or complexity of services required by patients varies and may offer more or less challenging cases to the candidates.

Certainly, this variance in severity of the clients' problems does not constitute all of the criteria involved in assessing of the fairness of a test, but it is a major consideration in the use of live clients. Concern for the patients is based on the very threats that give rise to the need to regulate. The Council on Licensure, Enforcement and Regulation (CLEAR) has recently published a monograph entitled, *Principles of Fairness: An Examining Guide for Credentialing Boards* (Gross & Showers, 1993), to assist board members in the examination process.

If the examination is to include live clients, explicit instructions must be provided for choosing a cooperating patient. These instructions will describe the task to be performed by each candidate so that patients will be selected having similar needs to be addressed by each candidate. Tasks performed by each candidate should not only be similar, but should be of similar difficulty. Given that these instructions can create uniform levels of difficulty of tasks to be performed, the next step is to assure that no bias occurs in candidate grading. This is usually taken care of through the use of a double-blind procedure for grading. In the double-blind procedure the clients are disassociated from the candidates and are seen by the judges who score the candidate's work independently. The candidate is not seen by the judges. The client does not know the judges' ratings and the candidate does not know who scored his/her work. There are several ways in which the blinds can be constructed, either by moving clients or by moving judges. Logistics can present a problem, but usually the assignment of a candidate number to a patient or moving the patient to the judge can allow the double-blind procedure to work (Gross, 1993; Minnich, 1992). Most methods to assure fairness either use blinds or multiple judges to average out biases. Regardless, the principles are approximately the same.

The double-blind grading procedure works as a protection for the candidate against several types of discrimination, such as race, gender, age, etc. Yet, this protection is somewhat costly in that opportunities to assess candidates' interpersonal skills and attitudes toward patients are lost. The skills and attitudes appear critical in all but a few incidents where clinical examinations are used.

Does the Clinical Portion Have to be Standardized?

Schroeder (1993) suggests that all clinical examinations be standardized in order to insure that each candidate took approximately the same examination. This standardization also aids in helping the judges look at approximately the same criteria to score the performances. "While there are many differences, oral practical and essay examinations also have much in common with objectively scored examinations. Both forms of examination should be standardized so that all candidates have the same opportunity to demonstrate competence" (Schroeder, 1993, p. 18). Standardization may occur in many ways, among them is the use of standardized patients, or patient simulation, where well-rehearsed "actors" are used to insure that each candidate is provided the same opportunity to perform such tasks as collecting a history. This methodology is reviewed by Vu & Barrows (1994). Standardization is desired in some areas to increase mobility through extended reciprocity (Allen, 1992).

What Procedures are Needed to Insure Standardization of the Clinical Portion?

Standardization involves creating the conditions that assure uniformity of the tests with regard to administration, difficulty, clarity in scoring, and establishing psychometric evidence of the quality of the test. One of the conditions demanded is making the scoring criteria explicit. Explicitness means that the number of judgments are listed and clear scoring instructions are written, thus permitting the judges to be calibrated. By calibrated, we mean that each judge's score has the same meaning as every other judge's score. A second condition demands that more than one task or client be required within a given clinical examination to preclude post-test discussions from giving future candidates an unfair advantage in the examination. Lastly, all of the tasks need to be prestudied in order to assure near equality with regard to difficulty (a fairness concern) and fidelity to the job analysis. Two ways of making criteria explicit are discussed earlier in this chapter.

How Do These Standardization Procedures Relate to the Scoring Procedures?

Most clinical examinations can be scored in a variety of ways. Scoring procedures can include several options for the assignment of numerical values to a performance. Such options range from the global judgment of adequacy to intricate tallying of correctness for every step in a process.

The most important factor to include in scoring procedures to insure standardization is difficulty of tasks (or steps). In many clinical examinations some candidate errors are more important than others. In fact, an error such as severe damage to a tooth adjacent to the one on which a dental procedure is being performed can be deemed by the examiners to be so critical that the candidate is failed immediately. Errors that require immediate failure are referred to as "go no-go" items. Other errors appear as very important, but not so important as to demand immediate failure. In the case of differences in step or task importance, weights may be assigned to assure that passing or failing an important step is more significantly reflected in the score than passing or failing a minor step.

Of the two most common methods for scoring, "points correct" and "points off," the second poses the most potential problems. Scoring by summing values representing the adequacy of performance for each criterion is the "points correct" system. Deducting values assigned to each error from a constant score is the "points off" system. When using the "points off" system, errors may be chained, that is, some errors cause other errors to occur later in the scoring process. There must be a provision to handle these chaining errors. Although chaining of errors may also occur in the "points correct" system, this procedure is more adaptable to assuring independent item scoring. Chaining of errors can occur only when items are not independent.

Standardization mandates careful and uniform administration and scoring of the examination. Hence, administrator instructions must be carefully reviewed, making a well-edited examination guide and explicit scoring criteria a necessity. Making the scoring criteria explicit aids both the candidates and the judges. The candidates are aided through the articulation of examination expectations. The judges are enabled to render more uniform judgments, due in part to calibration or judges' training and in part to simplifying the judgment.

What Test Statistics are Needed for Clinical Items?

Schroeder (1993) treats clinical examinations similarly to objective examinations with regard to psychometric evidence of quality. "Both types of examinations, clinical and objective must have a minimum passing standard, and the validity and reliability of the examination program is crucial for both types of examination" (Schroeder, 1993, p. 18). In objective examinations several statistics attesting to reliability appear interchangeable (e.g., Coefficient alpha and Hoyt's method). We suspect that the same situation is emerging for clinical examinations.

The statistics needed to support the utilization of scores from a clinical examination are those that substantiate the fulfillment of the requirements for standardization such as uniformity of the examination content over candidates. Uniformity is necessary for reliability and for making valid interpretation of the examination results because unless the candidates all receive essentially the same test (i.e., they are tested uniformly), one cannot claim that they meet the minimum qualifications to be licensed.

Statistics are needed to show that the clinical tasks have similar performance profiles across successful candidates, there is interrater agreement among the judges, the examination scores are reliable and yield valid interpretations, there is intrarater agreement, there are no systematic exceptions especially in terms of difficult areas in the examinations, and there are similarities between examinee classes or groups to which the examinations are administered to substantiate interpretation of the statistics. By systematic exceptions is meant that candidates performing a task such as drilling a tooth are all given approximately equal or uniform tasks, there is no evidence of systematically assigned difficult tasks.

Clinical examinations are graded or scored using a fixed set of criteria, which indicate the successful completion of the steps required to complete the task and that are designated a priori to examination administration. Multiple administrations of a given clinical examination should produce similar percentages of correct responses across steps. Similarly, comparable percentages should pass the clinical examinations across testing sites and across different test administrations, or a careful review should be made to assure that administrations were fully standardized. Similarity of percentages can attest to the uniformity as equivalents to the difficulty statistics used with objective tests. Points or steps where the candidates have the most and least difficulty are of interest to the examination analyst as indicators of potentially too much difficulty or too little discrimination (Maust et al., 1988).

Statistics are needed to attest to reliability of the examination results. Several types of reliability are of interest and if the judgments are reduced to dichotomies, there are several options in the choice of reliability methods and statistics. Reliability was discussed earlier as it relates to the design of the scoring procedures as well as in the chapter by Stoker and Impara in this book (Chapter 7).

Statistics are also needed to attest to the making of a valid interpretation of the examination results. Statistics that are helpful here are those: which demonstrate the relationship of the examinations to the job analysis, which show that the clinical tasks have similar performance profiles across successful candidates, and which investigate the similarity between examinee classes or groups to which the examinations are administered.

Statistics are needed to monitor examination performance. Records should be kept on exceptions to prescribed process, frequent examination difficulties, and examination performance across time. Such records of examination performance are useful in identifying trends, signalling out-of-date material that should be replaced, indicating potential bias in tasks or scoring, and other indicators of need for examination review and maintenance.

Can Test Statistics be Computed in the Same Way as for Paper-and-Pencil, Multiple-Choice Tests, or Other Kinds of Performance Tests?

Most test statistics used with clinical tests involve dichotomous analogs to statistics used with objective tests or statistics that can be completed using differential item weights. Interrater and intrarater agreement become statistics needed to assure the scoring process and the work of the judges. Coefficients of agreement such as reliability can be calculated several ways. These were discussed above under "Establishing Rater Agreement and Estimating Reliability."

Clinical examination requirements focus on uniformity of the examination procedures and tasks designed to be equivalent. The most useful statistics in looking at uniformity appear to be frequencies of examination exceptions in administration and the effects of these on examination averages. Difficulty levels of the items making up the examination and of the total examination should be analyzed across tasks within a clinical examination, across examination administrations, and across examination administration exceptions.

Estimating item difficulty levels can be done on the judgments in much the same way as it is done in objective testing (Crehan, 1974), specifically, by calculating the proportion of all examinees who answer the item correctly (or are given positive credit for their performance). The same is true for discrimination indices (Millman & Greene, 1989) (e.g., by calculating the correlation between the item score and the total score). Test analysis can be conducted with simple statistics as described by Schroeder (1993): "mean score ... Changes in the mean score from administration to administration may signal either changes in candidate capability or examination difficulty. Often, large changes in overall score means are associated with scoring errors so it is important that score means are reviewed, and the reasons for the change in the score mean investigated" (p. 30); "*standard deviation* ... When the number of candidates is large, the standard deviation will usually be very stable from administration to administration. Large changes in the standard deviation may signal changes in the nature of the candidate group or errors in scoring" (p. 30); "*standard error of measurement...* A relatively small standard error of measurement means that one can be confident that the test scores have a high degree of accuracy. If the standard error of measurement is high, the associated test scores may have a lower degree of accuracy" (p. 31); and *score frequency distribution* ... By comparing frequency distributions from two or more administrations, changes in the nature of the candidate group can be identified. Large changes in frequency distributions may be indicative of scoring errors or of changes in the nature of the candidate group" (p. 31). For large licensure testing programs, application of item-response theory may also be applicable.

What Special Procedures are Needed to Set a Cut Score for the Clinical Portion and How Do These Relate to Continued Testing Using Part Credit?

(See Chapter 10 by Mills for a complete discussion of setting cut scores.) Although other methods exist, it has been our experience that the most frequently used methods for setting cut scores for licensure examinations are Angoff, modified Angoff, and Ebel methods with the Angoff method being used much more frequently than the other two methods. All three methods are test-centered continuum models using judges and rating of items (Jaeger, 1989). Angoff's method leads the judges to set a score that is expected of a minimally qualified population of candidates. The methods use panels to identify item weights for each item. The Angoff method develops weights on the probability of minimally qualified candidates getting the item correct. The modified Angoff methods get the judges to assign item weights and the Ebel method develops item weights using relevance and difficulty classifications.

In working with performance tests the criterion points (or steps) can be treated as items. Because the task was chosen from the job analysis, and because the steps were determined as essential to the completion of the task, dichotomous scoring greatly simplifies the work of the panel of judges as it transforms the judgments to an analog of a right/wrong item. Complications occur when the steps can be partially correct and still the effort results in a successfully completed task.

When clinical examinations are more complex, such as those involving assessment of a candidates portfolio, standard setting is also much more complex. Several articles appear in special issue of *Applied Measurement in Education*, Volume 8(1) that examine issues related to setting standards in such a situation.

Is There Some Indication to Show That a Clinical Measure is Obsolete?

Usually, the clinical measure becomes obsolete when the task is no longer practiced due to a change in the profession. The harbingers of this need for replacement are usually research reports and workshops designed to have incumbents learn new practices in the occupation. Hence, members of the board who are practitioners would know of the changes and anticipate when a new job analysis should be made to see if the clinical examination should be revised. For instance, in optometry the diagnostic examination would continue, but changes in prescribing glasses for the near sighted may end if the emerging surgical procedures to reshape the cornea become widespread, making eye glass correction for myopia virtually obsolete. (Note: The operation is generally successful and the new laser procedure has proven very successful in Canada.) In dentistry, the molding of gold restorations is no longer an important practice because almost all gold restorations are molded in the laboratory. The latter case was verified through a four-state survey of dental practices conducted for the Virginia Board of Dentistry (Fortune, 1991). With regard to psychotherapy, performance or clinical testing is currently under challenge in several states and in Canada (Trebilcock & Shaul, 1983). Clinical examinations in this area suffer from the lack of clients who can participate in testing without adverse effect. In part, clinical examinations are not used in psychotherapy due to the difficulty in making the tasks standard and in the lack of belief in the oral examination process.

IN SUMMARY

We have provided an overview of the rationale and procedures associated with developing, scoring, and using clinical examinations. Moreover, we have tried to provide answers to the following questions that have been raised by licensure board members:

- Why should a clinical examination be given? Is there some indication to show that a clinical measure is obsolete?

If a clinical examination has been indicated through the job analysis, documentation of its disappearance from practice must be made before it should be removed from use. Board members are often the first to question the continued use of a specific clinical examination.

- How close to the task must the clinical measure be?

A clinical measure should be as nearly identical as possible to the condition that gave rise to its existence. If the examination is given because of human interactions, those human interactions must appear in the clinical examination. If the clinical examination has been developed because of the required joint application of complex psychomotor and cognitive skills, then the candidate should have to exhibit those complex skills. Jointly the choosing of the task to fit the dictates of the job analysis answers a validity question and choosing the tasks to be performed very close to tasks in practice addresses the fidelity issues.

- How can testing conditions be made uniform and fair? Does the clinical portion have to be standardized? What procedures are needed to insure standardization of the clinical portion? How do these procedures relate to the scoring procedures?

Standardization is needed for clinical tests to assure fair and uniform treatment of each candidate. Double-blind grading is recommended as the preferred scoring procedure to assure uniform and fair testing.

- What test statistics are needed for clinical items? Can test statistics be computed in the same way as for paper-and-pencil tests or other kinds of performance tests? What special procedures are needed to set a cut score for the clinical portion and how do these relate to continued testing using part credit?

Reliability as indicated through inter- and intrarater agreement, explicit criteria used in the determination of satisfactory test performance, and cut scores are the primary statistics needed in clinical testing. Logistics may prevent their being calculated in the same manner as paper-and-pencil testing, yet pretesting is encouraged.

REFERENCES

Allen, D. L. (1992). Standardized national dental clinical examinations. *Journal of Dental Education, 56*(4), 258-261.

Butzin, D. W., Finberg, L., Brownlee, R. C., & Guerin, R. O. (1982). A study of the reliability of the grading process used in the American Board of Pediatrics oral examination. *Journal of Medical Education, 57*(12), 944-946.

Crehan, K. D. (1974). Item analysis for teacher-made mastery tests. *Journal of Educational Measurement, 2*(4), 255-262.

Ebel, R. L. (1951). Estimation of the reliability of ratings. *Psychometrika, 16*, 407-424.

Feldt, L. S., & Brennan, R. L. (1989). Reliability. In R. L. Linn (Ed.), *Educational measurement* (3rd ed.; pp. 105-146);. Macmillan: New York.

Fortune, J. C. (1991, July). *Report on the analysis of examination performance across a six state licensing area.* Unpublished report commissioned by the Southern Regional Testing Agency, Virginia Beach, for the Virginia Board of Dentistry.

Friedman, C. B., & Ho, K. T. (1990, April). *Interjudge consensus and intrajudge consistency: Is it possible to have both in standard setting?* Paper presented at the Annual Meeting of the National Council on Measurement in Education, Boston, MA. (ERIC Document Reproduction Service No. ED 322 164)

Gross, L. J. (1993, Winter). Assessing clinical skills in optometry: A national standardized performance test. *CLEAR Exam Review*, pp. 18-23.

Gross, L. J. & Showers, B. (1993). *Principles of fairness: An examining guide for credentialing boards.* Lexington, KY: Council of State Governments.

Hopkins, C. D., & Antes, R. L. (1990). *Classroom measurement and evaluation.* Itasca, IL: Peacock.

Impara, J. C., & Plake, B. S. (Eds). (1995). Standard setting for complex performance tasks [Special issue]. *Applied Measurement in Education, 8*(1).

Jaeger, R. M. (1989). Certification of student competence. In R. L. Linn (Ed.), *Educational measurement* (3rd ed; pp. 485-514). New York: Macmillan.

Kenyon, D., & Stansfield, C. W. (1991, April). *A method for improving tasks on performance assessments through field testing.* Paper presented at the annual meeting of the National Council on Measurement in Education, Chicago, IL. (ERIC Document Reproduction Service No. ED 334 226)

Maust, A. P., Callahan, D., Fortune, J. C., & Cromack, T. R. (1988). *An evaluation of the licensing examination function, Virginia Department of Commerce.* Alexandria, VA: Research Dimensions, Inc.

Medley, D. M., & Mitzel, H. E. (1964). Measuring classroom behavior by systematic observation. In N. L. Gage (Ed.), *Handbook of research on teaching* (pp. 247-328). Chicago: Rand McNally.

Millman, J. (1989). If at first you don't succeed: Setting passing scores when more than one attempt is permitted. *Educational Researcher, 18*(6), 5-9.

Millman, J., & Greene, J. (1989). The specification and development of tests of achievement and ability. In R. L. Linn (Ed.), *Educational measurement* (3rd ed; pp. 335-366) Macmillan: New York, .

Minnich, R., (1992). *Examiner's manual and orientation.* Virginia Beach, VA: Southern Regional Testing Agency, Inc.

Schroeder, L. L. (1993). *Development, administration, scoring and reporting of credentialing examinations: Recommendations for board members.* Lexington, KY: Council of State Governments.

Trebilcock, M. J., & Shaul, J. (1983). Regulating the quality of psychotherapeutic services. *Law and Human Behavior, 7,* 165-278.

Vu, N. V., & Barrows, H. S. (1994). Use of standardized patients in clinical assessments: Recent developments and measurement findings. *Educational Researcher, 23*(3), 23-30.

Weiss, J. (1987). The Golden Rule bias reduction principle: A practical reform. *Educational Measurement: Issues and Practice, 6*(2), 23-25.

Winer, B. J. (1971). *Statistical principles and experimental design.* New York: McGraw Hill.

Yaple, N., Metzler, J., & Wallace, W. (1992). Results of the Ohio non-patient dental board examinations for 1990 and 1992. *Journal of Dental Education, 56*(4), 248-250.

BASIC PSYCHOMETRIC ISSUES IN LICENSURE TESTING

Howard W. Stoker

University of Tennessee

James C. Impara

University of Nebraska-Lincoln

INTRODUCTION

The number of people in the United States who carry some responsibility for the writing of examination questions and the construction of tests is unknown. In the *Preface* to *The Construction and Use of Achievement Examinations,* published by the American Council on Education in 1936, the authors indicated that the number probably exceeded a million. That number has certainly grown in the past 60 years. Questions are posed to students by teachers at all levels of education; the Armed Forces have people whose job it is to construct tests which are used in the promotion of personnel; over 1,000 occupations are regulated by the states and many, ranging from the professions to the trades, require licensure or certification (Brinegar, 1990). Many licensure and certification decisions are based on test performance.

Throughout the years, the types of test questions being used have changed, emphasis has changed from performance testing to multiple-choice testing and back to performance assessment. Apprenticeship programs in the trades—a kind of continuous assessment of performance—have been supplemented, or even replaced, by written examinations, or by a combination of written and performance tests. More recently, the use of technology in testing has begun to come into the picture. For example, computer administration of questions, interactive video, and CD-ROM are beginning to be used.

Regardless of the type of test, whether it was written 50 years ago or last week, there are some important concerns. Fundamental among these concerns are the reliability and validity of the measures. The purpose of this chapter is to focus on the psychometric issues of reliability and validity of measures as they pertain to licensure examinations. In addition, the chapter focuses on the relationship of the measures to various guidelines—those of the Equal Employment Opportunity Commission (EEOC, 1975) and *The Standards for Educational and Psychological Testing*, produced by a joint committee of the American Educational Research Association (AERA), American Psychological Association (APA), and the National Council on Measurement in Education (NCME) and published by the APA (1985). (We will refer to the EEOC document as the *EEOC Guidelines* and the AERA, APA, and NCME document as the *Standards.*)

Frequent references are made to the reliability and validity of examinations when, in reality, it is the scores and the decisions made on the basis of the scores that are, or are not, reliable and valid. In the context of licensure, scores are used to make decisions. Statistical analysis may show that the scores possess properties indicative of reliability. Studies may be conducted to show that the measures have some type of validity. However, reliable and valid scores may be used inconsistently or incorrectly, and when this happens, the *decisions* made on the basis of the scores may not be reliable or valid decisions.

The discussion of reliability and validity in this chapter focuses on the traditional concepts of reliability and validity rather than on a more contemporary approach broadly called generalizability theory. Our reasons for the focus on the more traditional conceptsare simply that most licensure and certification programs with which we are familiar have not yet made the transition to generalizability theory as their basic approach to reporting the psychometric characteristics of their tests.

Reliability

Reliability has both a mathematical and a conceptual definition. The conceptual definition relates to the extent that a particular observed score (the score an examinee makes on a test) is a close approximation of the examinee's "true" score on that test. This concept is operationalized by thinking about testing some hypothetical examinee an infinite number of times and calculating the examinee's average score over all these occasions. That average is the examinee's "true" score. We assume, of course, that each testing occasion is independent of every other occasion. In a perfect world, we might find that this hypothetical examinee obtained the same score on every occasion. Under those conditions, the test would be perfectly reliable! In the real world, however, that would not likely be the case. Virtually all tests are unreliable to some degree.

No matter how hard we try, every licensure examination will produce scores that are less than perfect representations of a candidate's "true" score. Various factors contribute to the random errors that influence a candidate's actual score and make it different from the "true" score. Such factors are related to: the test (e.g., ambiguous items or directions); testing conditions (e.g., lighting, temperature, or other environmental factors that may be more or less similar to conditions on the job); and, the physical attributes of the candidates (e.g., high motivation or illness). All such factors contribute to the generation of random errors in scores that lead to the unreliability of the scores. The larger the number of these random errors, the smaller will be the likelihood that a candidate's score has sufficient levels of reliability.

Our concerns with reliability are twofold. First, reliability is somewhat a technical concern. There are actions that can be taken to enhance score reliability. Second, reliability is a precondition for validity. Scores that are unreliable cannot be valid! Although this can be demonstrated mathematically, it is also logical. If you stood on a scale that showed a weight of 170 pounds, stepped off and back on and the weight shown was 150 pounds, which weight is trustworthy? Neither! If a different scale showed similar weights (e.g., 170, 169), then you may have confidence that the second scale is measuring your weight appropriately and in a consistent manner. Any inference you might want to make about your weight would be made more confidently with the consistent scale than it would with the inconsistent scale. If you wanted to make a decision about the effectiveness of your weight reduction program, using the first scale would be difficult, whereas the data from the second would provide more confidence in the decision.

If one cannot rely on the test scores as accurate representations of the behavior being measured (reliability), then no amount of statistical manipulation of the numbers will lead to good decisions (validity). Not too many years ago, a "good mechanic" listened to the noises a car was making and made decisions about what was wrong with the car. Now, the car is hooked up to a diagnostic machine, operated by a technician (possibly a mechanic), that identifies which "chip" is malfunctioning. It can be hoped that more reliable measures are being obtained from the machines than were obtained from the "good mechanic." More importantly, we hope the decisions made about what is wrong with the car are more valid—they certainly are more expensive!

A fact we must face is that we have not developed any diagnostic machine for constructing licensure examinations and making licensure decisions. A few programs may be using more sophisticated test administration procedures (e.g., computerized testing, interactive videos), but these procedures do not assure more reliable scores nor more valid decisions. Various guidelines and standards have identified the areas of concern, relative to reliability, validity, and safeguarding the public, but have produced no machine or magic formulas for us.

Adequate control of random errors can be maintained through careful construction of the licensure examination. Such control will do much to insure that qualified candidates will be granted licenses and the unqualified ones will be screened out. The guidelines and standards insist on such control for the purpose of protecting the public from unqualified practitioners. Such control will also help insure that candidates are treated equitably and that decisions are not capricious.

There are many sets of guidelines for constructing examinations, whether they are licensure examinations or examinations to be used for other purposes.

This book offers suggestions for developing a variety of types of items. Textbooks, mainly in the field of educational measurement, contain lists designed to guide one in the development of examinations, their administration and scoring, and the setting of cut scores (the scores used to make decisions). The construction of a licensure examination that will yield reliable scores and lead to valid decisions is a long and arduous process—not one to be taken lightly. The processes by which items may be developed are described in chapters 5 and 6 of this book and elsewhere. Any licensure board involved in test development should consider whether the examination should be constructed under the direction of testing professionals employed by the board or by consultants who are testing professionals.

Once the initial development of an examination is complete (i.e., decisions about individual items have been made), a tryout is generally scheduled. The purpose of the tryout is to obtain data to estimate score reliability and, perhaps, make preliminary decisions related to cut scores. The tryout data should be collected from a group that resembles the candidates for licensure as closely as can be managed.

In licensure examinations where the number of candidates is very small (e.g., polygraph examiner, embalmer), tryouts may be difficult, if not impossible, to arrange, due to the small number of candidates involved. Hence, it may be necessary to wait until the first administration of the examination to obtain such data. If no pretest is feasible, then careful test development plays an even more important role. The implications this situation has for decision making are discussed later.

Professional Guidelines

The *EEOC Guidelines*, (EEOC, 1975) and *Principles for the Validation and Use of Personnel Selection Procedures* (Society for Industrial and Organizational Psychology [SIOP], 1987) focus on the validity of measures and decisions for employment tests. Both documents represent the basics of good practice, but both are directed toward tests for employment rather than licensure tests. The relationship between these two different purposes is discussed in chapter 2. The *EEOC Guidelines* reference extensively the *Standards for Educational and Psychological Testing* (AERA, APA, & NCME, 1985).

The *Standards* make direct reference to tests used for both licensure and certification, along with other types of test uses. Explicit in the *Standards* is guidance pertaining to the reliability of tests and the use of the standard error of measurement in the interpretation of individual scores.

> Fundamental to the proper evaluation of a test are the identification of major sources of measurement error, the size of the errors resulting from these sources, the indication of the degree of reliability to be expected between pairs of scores under particular circumstances, and the generalizability of results across items, forms, raters, administrations, and other measurement facets.

> Typically, test developers and publishers have primary responsibility for obtaining and reporting evidence concerning reliability and errors of measurement adequate

for the intended uses. The typical user generally will not conduct separate reliability studies. Users do have a responsibility, however, to determine that the available information regarding reliability and errors of measurement is relevant to their intended uses and interpretations and, in the absence of such information, to provide the necessary evidence.

Reliability coefficient is a generic term. Different reliability coefficients and estimates of components of measurement error can be based on various types of evidence; each type of evidence suggests a different meaning. (AERA, APA, NCME, 1985, p. 19)

It is the responsibility of the licensure board to direct the test developer to obtain the types of reliability estimates most appropriate for the licensure examination. If internal consistency estimates are desired, then a single administration may be all that is necessary, but if either reliability estimates that reflect equivalence (of alternate forms) or stability are appropriate, then two separate test administrations will be needed. These different types of reliability estimates are described in more detail below. Moreover, because of the nature of the decision made on the basis of the test, decision-consistency reliability may be the paramount reliability concern.

Reliability Indices for Test Scores

Internal Consistency, sometimes referred to as *homogeneity*, is the easiest method one can use to estimate reliability. This coefficient estimates the degree to which items are contributing to a common underlying construct. It requires only a single administration of one set of items to a group of candidates. Several methods exist to estimate reliability from a single administration of an examination. Coefficient alpha (Cronbach, 1951), or the less general KR-20, are the most common methods. If one is using a "packaged" scoring program for multiple-choice tests, there is a high probability that one, or both, of these values will be generated as by-products of the scoring process. (Some programs may be using a method called split-half. We do not recommend this method. For most purposes it is obsolete and the result is potentially biased depending on how the decision is made to determine the two halves of the test.)

Coefficient alpha can be used to estimate reliability, no matter what type of items are on the test. When only dichotomous items are included (items scored right or wrong) KR-20 and coefficient alpha are the same. Formulas for calculating these coefficients of reliability can be found in almost any basic measurement text.

Stability is estimated by administering a single set of items to the same group of candidates at different times. The correlation between the two sets of scores is the reliability estimate. Most measurement texts refer to this method as test-retest. The lapse of time between the two administrations will, of course, have an impact on the obtained correlation. Hence, when reporting the reliability estimate, it is necessary to describe the group used to obtain it, and the time interval between the testings. A different coefficient for every time interval is expected. Generally, the interval should be kept short, probably less than a week if possible, to minimize any differential learning or forgetting that might occur during the interval, and long enough to allow the candidates to "forget" how they answered an item the first time.

Equivalence, usually called *alternate forms* reliability, calls for two tests, designed and constructed to be essentially equivalent in their psychometric characteristics and to measure the same skills. As with the test-retest method, the reliability coefficient is the correlation coefficient computed between the scores of one group of examinees on the two tests. A counterbalanced administration is recommended. This means that one-half of the candidates take Form 1 first and the other one-half of the candidates take Form 2 first. The order of testing is reversed in the second administration. The time interval between the first and second administrations should be as short as possible. If several days pass between administrations, the obtained correlation between the test scores could be used as both an estimate of equivalence and of stability.

The *Standards* call for full reporting of data from the administrations of both tests—means and standard deviations, along with errors of measurement and the estimate of alternate forms reliability. In addition, the rationale for selecting the particular time interval should be reported.

How to choose? Whichever method is selected to estimate reliability and calculate the standard error of measurement will depend on several factors. As noted above, *internal consistency* calls for one test and one administration of the test. Hence, that method will produce the quickest results. Because of its ease of computation and because the information provided is useful, some internal consistency measure should be computed each time the test is administered. If the one test form could be administered to the same group at two different times, a coefficient of *stability* could be calculated, in addition to the internal consistency estimates for each administration. This would be preferable to a single administration of the test, but this is difficult to undertake in licensure testing.

We recommend the development of two equivalent forms of the licensure examination. The second form will be needed, eventually, for matters of security and to prevent candidates who repeat the test from "learning items" instead of learning the subject matter. We also recommend that item development be a continuing process. New items can be embedded in test forms and "banked" for later use. Most commercial test publishers use this process for test development.

The number of computer-based programs for storing items and constructing tests is large. A few years ago, one needed a large capacity computer to build tests using computer technology. Now, adequate programs can be purchased for virtually any desktop computer. In chapter 8, a full discussion of item-banking is provided.

As noted above, for almost every examination, an internal consistency estimate of reliability (either coefficient alpha or KR-20) should be calculated. The notable exception is any examination that has a speed factor. In the typical speeded test, the candidate's score is largely dependent on the number of items attempted, rather than on the candidate's range of knowledge. (This is generally not the case in licensure examinations, but forewarned is forearmed.) For speeded tests, alternate forms or test-retest are the only appropriate alternatives for estimating score reliability.

Regardless of the method, a coefficient of reliability is essential. This number will reflect (for the group tested, under stated conditions, etc.) a measure of the random error associated with the scores. A symbol used to represent the reliability estimate is "r_{tt}." Because of the different methods of estimating reliability and because reliability estimates vary across different samples, the reliability estimate alone is not sufficient as a way to characterize or interpret measurement error.

Standard Error of Measurement is another way to represent measurement error. It is computed by using the reliability estimate, r_{tt}, and the standard deviation of the test scores (S_Y):

$$SE_M = S_Y \sqrt{1 - r_{tt}}$$

The standard error of measurement, SE_M, as calculated by this formula, is the average error associated with individual test scores across the range of scores in the distribution. This value is most useful when interpreting individual scores. Because licensure examinations focus on individual scores, careful attention must be given to the standard error of measurement.

Two characteristics of the standard error of measurement are important. First, although reliability estimates will vary with the samples used to estimate them, the standard error tends not to fluctuate as widely. For example, suppose a licensure test was administered to a large sample that had a wide range of scores. The reliability estimate might be high ($r_{tt} = .94$) and the standard deviation might be 8 score points. The error of measurement, $SE_M = S_Y \sqrt{1 - r_{tt}}$, would be:

$$SE_M = 8\sqrt{1-.94} = 1.96$$

If another sample was more homogeneous, the reliability estimate for that group might be reduced to .85 and the standard deviation would be lower (e.g., 5), resulting in a standard error of measurement of:

$$SE_M = 5\sqrt{1-.85} = 1.94$$

This illustration makes two important points: As group homogeneity increases, the reliability estimate will tend to be reduced. This does not mean the test is less reliable for the second group, it is simply a function of the way reliability estimates are calculated; and, even though the reliability estimates differ across groups, the standard errors of measurement are nearly the same.

Second, although the standard error of measurement is interpreted as though it is constant throughout the score distribution, this interpretation has been shown to be false. The standard error is usually largest for high and low scores and at a minimum near the mean of the score distribution. It is extremely important in licensure examinations to know the standard error of measurement at the cut score, the score used to decide if a candidate is to be licensed. Setting the cut score at, or near, the mean of the scores (setting cut scores is discussed in chapter 10) will reduce the number of incorrect decisions that are due solely to measurement error. Note that setting the cut score near the mean does not imply that only half of the candidates will be licensed. It is likely that the score distribution will be skewed and, hence, more or fewer than 50% of the candidates will be licensed.

A formula for estimating the error of measurement at a particular score (e.g., the cut score), is:

$$E_{cs} = SE_M \sqrt{1 + \frac{1}{N} + \frac{(T' - \overline{T})^2}{\sum t'^2}}$$

Where: E_{cs} is the standard error of the score of interest;
          SE_M is the standard error of measurement;
          N is the number of examinees tested;
          T' is the estimated true score associated with the desired observed score. T' is estimated by:

$$T' = r_{tt}(X - \overline{X}') + \overline{X}' ;$$

$\overline{T}' = \overline{X}'$ is the estimated true score mean. The estimated true score mean is equal to the observed score mean; and

$\sum t'^2$ is the sum of the deviation scores of the distribution of estimated true scores (i.e., all $T' - \overline{T}'$ scores).

Decision-Consistency Reliability

Decision reliability is related to the consistency of a decision for licensure; the decision to withhold or grant a license when there is a specified decision rule (e. g., pass candidates with scores greater than some cut score). This is conceptually similar to the reliability of scores, but in the case of licensure, the decision "score" can be thought of as either zero (withhold license) or one (grant a license). Estimating decision reliability takes place following test development, test administration, cut-score determination, and estimation of score reliability. As in estimating score reliability, estimating decision reliability may occur after a single administration of the test, after repeated administrations of the same test form, or after administering alternate forms of the test to the same group of examinees.

Feldt and Brennan (1989) summarized techniques for estimating reliability for criterion-referenced interpretations as in licensure or certification. They describe two squared-error loss methods (those proposed by Livingston and by Brennon and Kane) and four threshold loss methods (those proposed by Cohen, Huyhn, Subkoviak, and Raju). The squared-error loss methods consider "error" to be the distance between an individual's observed score and the cut score. The formulas take into account both measurement error and classification error. The squared-error loss methods require only a single administration of the test. Livingston's coefficient results in decision-consistency estimates that can be interpreted in the same way as coefficient alpha and KR-20 Brennan and Kane's index of generalizability can be interpreted like KR-21 (an estimate of KR-20). Depending on the location of the cut score relative to the mean of the test, coefficient alpha (and KR-20) and KR-21 will be lower limits for the the respective estimates of decision-consistency reliability. (If the cut score is equal to the mean, then the computations will result in the same values as would be obtained with coefficient alpha/KR-20 or KR-21, respectively.)

For the squared-error loss method we recommend using Livingston's (1972) formula, represented as follows:

$$k^2 = \frac{\frac{I}{I-1}[V_X - \Sigma V_i] + (\overline{X} - C)^2}{V_X + (\overline{X} - C)^2}$$

Where: I is the number of items;
          $\overline{X}$ is the mean score for all individuals.
          C is the cut score;
          V_x is the total score variance; and
          V_i is the variance of an item.

Feldt and Brennan (1989) indicate that the threshold loss methods take into account only classification errors and assume that any misclassification is equally serious. They also note that there are methods other than those they discussed and that some of these other methods permit differential weighting of misclassification errors. These other methods are, computationally, quite complex. Early strategies for the threshold loss methods required two administrations of the test. The two dominant methods are a simple coefficient of agreement (the proportion of individuals classified the same way after two administrations of the test) and coefficient kappa (Cohen, 1960).

Because of the opportunity to compute both squared-error and threshold loss coefficients, we believe the optimal determination of decision reliability occurs when scores are available from two administrations (or two forms) of the examination. However, as noted, test-retest and alternate forms administrations are often difficult to arrange in licensure examinations.

For a test-retest or alternate forms situation, we recommend the kappa threshold loss method for estimating decision consistency. For all practical purposes, kappa represents an index of the proportion of agreement of assignment to the license and fail-to-license categories, beyond that expected by chance.

For example, Table 1 illustrates the results which might arise from two administrations of a licensure examination to a single group of candidates.

		First Administration		
		License	Fail to License	
Second Administration	License	75	5	80
	Fail to License	10	10	20
		85	15	100

Table 1. Classifications Resulting from Two Administrations of a Licensing Examination

In this illustration, 75% of the applicants would be licensed based on the scores earned on both tests; 10% would not be licensed by both tests. Hence the proportion of agreement is

$$P_o = .75 + .10 = .85$$

To calculate the proportion of agreement to be expected by chance, marginal totals are used

$$P_c = (.85 \times .80) + (.15 \times .20)$$
$$= .68 + .03 = .71$$

Kappa, then, is an index of the proportion of agreement over and above what might be expected by chance.

$$kappa = \frac{P_o - P_c}{1 - P_c}$$

In this example:

$$kappa = \frac{85 - .71}{1.00 - .71} = .48$$

In general, kappa ranges from zero to one, with the higher values indicating higher agreement. Negative values are possible, indicating "less than chance" agreement, but are probably not interpretable (Huynh, 1976). As the cut score deviates from the mean score, measurement error tends to increase, which would lead to a decrease in kappa. According to Linn (1979), "kappa tends to be lower for criterion scores near the extremes, to increase with test length, and to increase with test variability (p. 100)."

Kappa has some clear limitations that condition its use, especially when the cut score deviates from the mean and when the distribution of passing and failing candidates is highly skewed. Although the theoretical range of kappa is zero to one, the maximum value of kappa depends on the specific marginal values associated with any particular set of data. If the scores represent the most extreme values (all candidates pass or all fail), then although the proportion of agreement is 1.00, kappa cannot be computed (it is undefined because the formula results in dividing zero by zero). In essense, kappa is interpreted as an index that represents the proportion of consistent decisons beyond that expected to occur under conditions of chance (Subkoviak, 1980).

One advantage of using kappa is that it can be calculated in situations where there are more than two decision categories. For example, licensure may be a multiple stage testing situation (i.e., obtaining a "passing score" or a "borderline" score on one test, prior to taking a second test). The passing score for the first test might be the passing score, plus one standard error of measurement, calculated at the cut score. This criterion would set up a three-level condition: clear fail (e.g., scores more than the cut score minus one SE_M), borderline (e.g., scores between plus and minus one SE_M around the cut score), and pass (e.g., scores greater than the cut score plus one SE_M). Such a strategy would reduce the number of candidates incorrectly classified as failing the first examination and give them a second chance at becoming licensed. The second test would also have the same three score categories (of course, this would require some policy decision for dealing with candidates who were borderline on one or both of the tests). For such a situation, coefficient kappa would be quite appropriate for estimating decision consistency of either test or for the combined effects of both tests.

Methods for use when only one score is available (i.e., when the test has been administered only one time) are somewhat complex, computationally. One method, attributed to Subkoviak (1976), is easier to use than the Huynh method mentioned below, but it is still computationally complex. An individual's true score is estimated using one of two methods, and then the probability of that score being above/below the cut score is calculated for the actual test and for a hypothetical parallel test. The resulting coefficient would, of course, depend on the selection of the cut score. A disadvantage of this method is that it tends to be biased for short tests (in that case, it underestimates the level of agreement when cut scores are near the center of the distribution and overestimates the level of agreement when cut scores are near the extremes [Subkoviak, 1980]).

The Huynh (1976) model is based on kappa, and is much more computationally complex. If an examination has more than 10 items, as one would expect in a licensure examination, simpler methods can be used to approximate the calculations (Huynh, 1976). The calculations yield a number between zero and one, representing decision agreement based on the test administered and a hypothetical parallel test. The magnitude of the index depends on test length, the variability of the test scores, and the cut score. This method also tends to produce biased estimates of the level of agreement, but unlike Subkoviak's method, Huynh's method tends to underestimate the level of agreement throughout the distribution when the test is short (Subkoviak, 1980). This conservative approach may be justified in licensure testing.

In some licensure contexts multiple tests are used (either collectively as a total score or sequentially as in multi-stage testing). In these situations, the estimation of the reliability of the decision is not a straight-forward procedure (Raju, 1982).

Additional Reliability Issues

There are two additional reliability issues to be discussed. The first issue is related to the condition when two or more tests (or subtests) are used to make the licensure decision. The second issue is when the licensure decision is based wholly, or in part, on ratings other than (or in addition to) test scores.

Two or More (Sub)tests

The above discussion has assumed that licensure decisions rest solely on the score from a single test. Although this is true for many areas, some procedures include more than one test. The medical, dental, and legal professions have multiple examination procedures, as do CPAs and Certified Professional Secretaries, among others. In such situations, the licensure decision could be made by finding a total score across all (sub)tests—called a compensatory model; attaining a minimum score on each test—called a conjunctive model, or some combination of those options—a disjunctive model. The disjunctive model, we think, has few applications in making licensure decisions, but it may have utility for certification decisions. Thus, when there are multiple tests or subtests used in the licensure testing situation, there are serious implications for the way in which the cut score(s) are set.

Estimating score reliabilities when there are multiple (sub)tests is difficult, because the unidimensionality assumption in the calculation of coefficient alpha and KR-20 is typically violated. Test-retest or alternate forms would be the preferred methods in these cases. A procedure for estimating the reliability of the total score from a single administration is a stratified coefficient alpha in which the total score consists of the sum of the subtest scores. The reliability of such a composite can be estimated by:

$$r_{tt} = 1 - \frac{\Sigma V_i(1 - r_{kk})}{V_t}$$

Where: r_{tt} = reliability of the composite;
          r_{kk} = reliability of a subtest;
          V_i = variance of subtest i; and
          V_t = variance of the total score.

Reliability of Ratings

In many licensure situations, there is a performance or clinical component that is scored by judges' ratings. Measures that rely on human judgment for scoring usually have lower score reliability. The licensing agency must assume responsibility for establishing procedures that maximize the reliability of the judgment scores. Some discussion of the methods for examining reliability and for enhancing reliability are discussed in chapter 6 of this book. A summary of that discussion follows.

To enhance the reliability of ratings, the most critical factor is the training of the observers, scorers, and/or judges. Check lists, rating scales, etc., can help ensure that all the raters are looking for the same thing and, hence, increase interrater reliability. Another factor in enhancing the reliability of ratings is the use of multiple judges, with either a requirement that judges/raters agree on pass/fail decisions, or, if that is deemed too rigid, an averaging of ratings may be used. The need for multiple judges to increase the reliability of ratings is exemplified by the judging of athletic competitions, such as diving, synchronized swimming, gymnastics, etc. At a local meet, two or three judges may be used. As the competition moves to district, state, and national levels the number of judges increases and, in Olympic competition, up to eight judges may be present.

Intense training of judges and the use of multiple judges correspond to the two dimensions of reliability discussed by Ebel (1951). In this landmark discussion, Ebel provides rationale and statistical formulas for estimating the reliability of individual ratings or of average ratings. He suggests that if the decision is made on the average score across a number of judges, then the reliability of the average rating is needed. If, however, the judgment is made by judges working individually, across a number of examinees, then the reliability of individual ratings is appropriate. He argues strongly for the computation of an intraclass correlation to estimate reliability and he also provides formulas for the computation of a coefficient when there are missing data. Many of the formulas Ebel demonstrates are consistent with newer applications of generalizability theory being advocated in estimating the reliability of ratings. Additional discussion of the problem and methods of estimating reliability of raters may be found in Feldt and Brennan (1989).

Validity

About 40 years ago, validity was well defined and understood. There was *content* validity—earlier called face validity—which was necessary to show that the tasks in a test were representative of some domain. *Predictive* validity was needed to show the relationship between performance on the test and some later performance. *Concurrent* validity called for a correlation between the test scores and criterion performance obtained at about the same time. In some measurement texts, predictive and concurrent validity were subsumed under statistical validity. Finally, there was *construct* validity, which called for a conceptual framework, frequently implying some underlying trait and usually considered to be the responsibility of researchers. Licensure examinations relied heavily, if not entirely, on content validity.

About 30 years ago, predictive and concurrent validity merged into *criterion-related* validity. The criterion could exist along some time continuum, but the idea was that there be a relationship between the test scores and some criterion. About 25 years ago, two other types of validity were introduced, largely as a result of court challenges to the use of test scores in making pass or fail decisions about high school students. These two types of validity were called *instructional* validity and *curricular* validity (McClung, 1978). Instructional validity "is the actual measure of whether the schools are providing students with instruction in the knowledge and skills measured by the test" (McClung, 1978, p. 397). Curricular validity is "an actual measure of how well test items measure the objectives of the curriculum" (McClung, 1978, p. 397).

The *Standards* (AERA, APA, & NCME 1985) state, "Validity is the most important consideration in test evaluation. The concept refers to the appropriate-ness, meaningfulness, and usefulness of the specific inferences made from test scores. Test validation is the process of accumulating evidence to support such inferences. A variety of inferences may be made from scores produced by a given test and there are many ways of accumulating evidence to support any particular inference... The *inferences* [italics added] regarding specific uses of a test are validated, not the test itself" (p.9).

The *Standards* add, "Traditionally, the various means of accumulating validity evidence have been grouped into categories called *content-related, criterion-related, and construct-related evidence of validity.* These categories are convenient...but the use of the category labels does not imply that there are distinct types of validity... Evidence identified usually with the criterion-related...categories, for example, is relevant also to the construct-related category."

The consensus today seems to be that validity is a *unitary* concept, and that all evidence to be collected is a part of construct validation. For those who may be interested in the changes in emphasis in test validation, Messick's chapter in *Educational Measurement* (1989), Geisinger's article in *Educational Psychology* (1992), and Shepard's chapter in *The Review of Research in Education* (1993) are highly recommended.

Shepard's proposal (Shepard, 1993) "is that validity evaluations be organized in response to the question, 'What does the testing practice claim to do?'" (p.429). Applying this question to licensure examinations, the primary claims to be considered are: Is the test designed and developed to identify candidates who possess the entry-level knowledge and skills sufficient for licensure? And, does passing the test insure that the public will be protected from incompetent candidates?

The first claim, test design, falls into the areas commonly referred to as content validity. The licensing agency would start with a job, or practice, analysis from which is derived statements of purpose and, perhaps, a listing of objectives, knowledge, or skills that candidates are expected to attain, or display. Following this would be the establishment of what is usually referred to as a test blueprint. The test blueprint will include the domain of knowledge and skills to be sampled and the types of responses candidates will be asked to make (responses to multiple-choice items, constructed responses, performance, etc.). This process is described in some detail in chapters 5 and 6.

The job analysis may indicate the need for some general knowledge and skills all candidates should possess. If a carpenter is to read the plans for a house and estimate the cost of materials, certain reading and mathematics skills will be required (although, with today's emphasis on "precut" homes, the level of these skills may be lower than before). In any case, the list of general knowledge and skills will probably be a long one. Even though the list is long, it is unlikely that the test will provide an estimate of proficiency on such general skills. Instead, those skills specific to the occupation or profession will be tested and scored.

The knowledge and skills specific to the profession and critical to the protection of the public should be identified. In developing a job analysis for electricians, a domain might be the use of tools (observing an electrician at work would reveal a large array of tools in a hip pack). One such tool is probably a "Klein off-set screwdriver." Non-electricians would not be expected to know the use for this particular tool, but an electrician should (and "handy" home owners would be well advised to learn). Job analyses can be accomplished by observing professionals at work, or by surveying them using mail, telephone, and/or personal interviews or some combination of these methods. Any method may be acceptable and, again, will produce a long list of knowledge and skills from which the knowledge and skills needed at the entry level for the protection of the public needs to be identified.

Subsequently, the list of general and specific critical knowledge and skills must be examined and prioritized. The measurement of general knowledge and skills tends to be easier than the measurement of job-specific skills. Care must be exercised in the selection of tasks to be included in the test so that the actual job performance is represented in the test. Even though reading may be required for successful job performance, a reading comprehension test may not be appropriate for licensure.

The level of specificity associated with the identification of critical skills and abilities for an occupation or profession varies greatly. In some licensure settings, it is virtually impossible to obtain a listing of all the "critical" knowledge, skills, and abilities. For example, it might be argued there are domains of knowledge, skills, and abilities needed by a lawyer or physician that are critical, but within these domains it is virtually impossible to identify the specific knowledge, skills, and abilities that are critical. Specifically, a specialist in problems with the feet may not be expected to have much knowledge about throat infections. A specialist is licensed as a physician and at some later time may choose to seek certification in his or her specialty. Because of situations like this, some licensure tests may be undifferentiated in terms of critical knowledge, skills, and abilities (i.e., individual items may be difficult to classify as measuring "critical" things, but the domain from which items are drawn may be considered critical). In such undifferentiated professions it is assumed there is a broad-based, but nonspecific set of critical knowledge, skills, and abilities to be measured on the licensure examination. Law, medicine, elementary school teaching, and real estate sales are but a few examples of such professions.

Job analysis, prioritizing elements, and developing a test blueprint are critical steps in developing content validity evidence. The *Principles* (SIOP, 1987) list several aspects of content validity evidence that should be provided. These principles, as modified to focus on licensure testing, are:

A. *The job content to be sampled should be defined.* The job domain need not be exhaustive, but the definition of the domain should include the most important parts of the job. General knowledge and skills can be thought of as one end of a continuum and job-specific skills as the other end. Between them, one would expect to find blends of general and job-specific skills that the candidates for licensure would be expected to have.

B. *Special circumstances should be considered in defining job content domains.* If there are specific skills that are part of the job description, these should be included in the content domain description. Similarly, if there are parts of the job that would be difficult to test, a substitute method of measurement may be needed. For example, the task may require a piece of equipment that is too heavy or too costly to provide to the candidate in the testing situation. In order to deal with the use of this equipment, the test would have to deal with subordinate skills, related to the operation of the machine. Alternatively a simulation may be substituted (as in using a flight simulator prior to taking an actual flight). When testing subordinate skills or simulations are not feasible, then some other means to determine that skills and knowledge exist may be used. One such substitute is the requirement that the candidate graduate from a program and that graduation can not occur without demonstration of the knowledge or skill in quesiton. What adaptations are made may well depend on the licensure situation and the specific circumstances.

C. *Job content domains should be defined on the basis of accurate and thorough information about the job.* The definition of a job content domain can be derived through an analysis of tasks, activities and/or responsibilities of the job incumbents. Worker specifications may include knowledge, abilities, job skills or even personal characteristics judged to be prerequisites to effective behavior on the job. For example, if licensure in a particular occupation implies that the licensee will need to establish rapport with clients, as might be the case for polygraph operators, the licensure board may decide that evidence of prior experience in maintaining such relationships be part of the licensure test.

D. *Job content domains should be defined in terms of what an employee needs to do or know without training or experience on the job.* It is important, when developing the test blueprint, to separate those skills that the licensing board would *like* the candidate to have from those that are *necessary* prior to licensure (entry level skills critical for the protection of the public).

E. *A job content domain may be restricted to critical or frequent activities or to prerequisite knowledge, skills or abilities.* The definition of the domain should include the *major* aspects of the job, and not seldom performed activities (unless such seldom performed activities are deemed critical for the protection of the public). There may be things that a licensed person *should* be able to do, but if these are not really job requirements, they should not be tested. It would be nice to assume that all candidates for licensure in pharmacy have good interpersonal skills. However, that is not part of licensure, even though the absence of these skills may doom the person to failure as a pharmacist.

F. *Sampling of a job content domain should ensure that the measure includes the major elements of the defined domain.* The test will not be long enough to include all of the skills included in the content domain. The actual test items will be a sample from the domain of possible items. A careful balance must be maintained such that the items selected are an appropriate representation of the domain.

G. *A test developed on the basis of content sampling should have appropriate measurement properties.* Wherever possible, the entire licensing procedure should be pretested. The usual statistics related to items and the test should be developed and examined.

H. *Persons used in any aspect of the development or choice of procedures to be validated on the basis of content sampling should clearly be qualified.* As note above, a responsibility of the agency is to see that all judges, and others involved in the licensure procedure are well trained.

There is no statistical index which attests to content validity. Some indices lend support to such evidence. In Principle G, above, for example, pretesting is recommended, along with the derivation of means, variances, measures of internal consistency, item statistics, etc. These are all parts of the collection of content validity evidence.

Additional content validity evidence may be collected by using expert judges to examine and rate items in terms of how the items relate to the content specifications or objectives. Hambleton (1980) describes several ways that such judgments may be obtained and he provides illustrations of forms that may be used for this purpose. He advocates asking expert judges to match items with objectives (when objectives are the basis for the test specifications), but this method could be modified easily to fit a program that uses more traditional test blueprints. He also advocates asking different judges to rate the extent to which an item reflects the objective or domain specification. This method can also be modified to fit the more traditional test blueprint format. Do not be misled by the title of Hambleton's work: "Test Score Validity And Standard-Setting Methods." These content validity rating methods relate to score validity and the illustrations of formats are found in appendices. (There is also a useful rating scale for making judgments about individual multiple-choice test items, thatmay enhance the validity and reliability of any multiple-choice test.)

Smith and Hambleton (1990) also discuss other issues related to content validity. Such issues include the extent that local conditions (within a particular state) need to be taken into account in examining content validity in professions in which a national examination is used for licensure. This issue is also discussed by Nelson (1994). Smith and Hambleton suggest additional types of evidence that might be useful in examining content validity. They also discuss some interesting methods of using criterion-related evidence in a licensure setting.

Criterion-Related Validity

It has been argued that the collection of criterion-related validity evidence is a critical part of identifying competent candidates and protecting the public from incompetent ones (Hecht, 1979). Such a task is easy to describe. One simply correlates scores from the test with some criterion measure. However, the definition of the criterion is not an easy task. In the current literature in the licensure field, there seems to be a relatively high consensus that boards should not be putting much effort in gathering evidence of criterion-related validity.

The primary issue, of course, is what constitutes a reasonable external criterion measure. The criterion measure, in this aspect of validity, typically occurs after the administration of the licensure examination. Given that the purposes of licensure testing, as noted above, are identifying candidates with requisite critical knowledge and skills and protecting the public from incompetent candidates, what would constitute a valid criterion? At the time of testing, one either has or does not have sufficient knowledge and skills needed to be at the entry level, thus the criterion is actually determined by the content of the test. It would be tautological to say that the criterion is the score on the test (it is not reasonable to make the test its own criterion).

Similarly, if the criterion is some measure of "errors" that put the public in danger (the most reasonable criterion measure for licensure), then an effective licensure test (one that has few false positives—licenses few people who should not be licensed) would successfully screen out those who might endanger the public and the criterion measure would not exist. Virtually all those who are licensed would score "zero" on the criterion measure (they would not make errors). If the licensure test did a poor job of screening, then the board would know about it quickly enough to take appropriate action without having to undergo special statistical studies of the test. In most cases, licensure boards have ways to suspend licenses for individuals who are a threat to the public.

At present we will concur with most of our colleagues that licensure boards should not be concerned with criterion-related validity. But the suggestions made by Smith and Hambleton (1990) on this topic may be of interest to some boards that feel a need for more than content validity evidence.

Instructional and Curricular Validity

Instructional and curricular validity may, or may not, be part of the validity evaluation process in licensure examinations. If the agency requires or provides training that precedes the test, evidence should exist showing that the knowledge and skills being tested appear in the curriculum. Instructional validity would be important should a challenge be lodged that candidates had no opportunity to learn what is being tested (i.e., the test was not instructionally valid). In other words, job-specific skills which can be learned only *after* licensure should not appear on the test.

The evidence from content validity evaluations should provide satisfactory evidence, within the construct validity concept, that the primary claims for licensure examinations have been met. Collecting the evidence is sometimes difficult and time-consuming, but will lead to better practices. Again, an agency may be well advised to seek professional assistance in either the design or the conduct of the evaluation study, or both.

SUMMARY

In this chapter, we have attempted to identify some of the basic, psychometric issues associated with licensure testing. In particular, we have looked at *reliability* as a general concept and the requirements pertaining to reliability that appear in various professional guidelines. Specifically, we discussed measures of *internal consistency, stability and equivalence, or equivalent forms.* We recommend the development of equivalent forms, wherever possible. Also discussed was *decision-reliability* and the methods that can be used to estimate it.

Validity was the other psychometric issued treated in this chapter. For many, if not most, licensure examinations, *content validity* is of primary concern. The *construct issues* deal with whether candidates possess sufficient knowledge and skills to qualify for licensure and whether passing the test will protect the public from incompetent candidates. We close the chapter by recommending that agencies spend the time and effort necessary to collect evidence with respect to these vital construct issues.

REFERENCES

American Educational Research Association, American Psychological Association, & National Council on Measurement in Education. (1985). *Standards for educational and psychological testing.* Washington, DC: American Psychological Association.

American Council on Education. (1936). *The construction and use of achievement examinations.* Washington, DC: Author.

Brinegar, P. (Ed.) (1990). *Occupational and professional regulation in the states: A comprehensive compilation.* Lexington, KY: National Clearinghouse on Licensure, Enforcement and Regulation.

Cohen, J. A. (1960). A coefficient of agreement for nominal scales. *Educational and Psychological Measurement, 20,* 37-46.

Cronbach, L. J. (1951). Coefficient alpha and the internal structure of tests. *Pyschometrika, 16,* 297-334.

Ebel, R. L. (1951). Estimation of the reliability of ratings. *Psychometrika, 16,* 407-424. (Reprinted in Mehrens, W. A. & and Ebel, R. L. [1967]. *Principles of Educational and Psychological Measurement A book of Selected Readings,* pp. 116-131. Chicago: Rand McNally.)

Equal Employment Opportunity Commission and others. (1978). Adoption by four agencies of uniform guidelines on employment selection procedures. *Federal Register, 43,* 38290-38315.

Feldt, L. S., & Brennan, R. L. (1989). Reliability. In R. L. Linn (Ed.), *Educational measurement,* (3rd ed.; pp. 105-146). Washington, DC: American Council on Education.

Geisinger, K. F. (1992). The metamorphosis of test validation. *Educational Psychologist, 27,* 197-222.

Hambleton, R. K. (1980). Test score validity and standard setting methods. In R. A. Berk, (Ed.), *Criterion-referenced measurement: The state of the art* (pp. 80-123). Baltimore, MD: The Johns Hopkins Press.

Hecht, K. A. (1979). Current status and methodological problems of validating professional licensing and certification exams. In M. A. Bunda & J. R. Sanders (Eds.), *Practices and problems in competency-based education* (pp. 16-27). Washington, DC: National Council on Measurement in Education.

Huynh, H. (1976). On the reliability of decisions in domain-referenced testing. *Journal of Educational Measurement, 13*(4),253-264.

Linn, R. L. (1979). Issues of reliability in measurement for competency-based programs. In M. A. Bunda & J. R. Sanders (Eds.), *Practices and problems in competency-based education* (pp. 90-107). Washington, DC: National Council on Measurement in Education.

Livingston, S. A. (1972). Criterion-referenced applications of classical test theory. *Journal of Educational Measurement, 9*(2), 13-25.

McClung, M. S. (1978). Are competency testing programs fair? Legal? *Phi Delta Kappan, 59,* 397-400.

Messick, A. (1989) Validity. In R. L. Linn (Ed.), *Educational measurement,* (3rd ed.; pp. 13-103). Washington, DC: American Council on Education.

Nelson, D. S. (1994). Job analysis for licensure and certification exams: Science or politics. *Educational Measurement: Issues and Practice, 13*(3), 29-35.

Raju, N. S. (1982). The reliability of a criterion-referenced composite with the parts of the composite having different cutting scores. *Educational and Psychological Measurement, 42,* 113-129.

Shepard, L. (1994). Evaluating test validity. In L. Darling-Hammond (Ed.) *Review of research in education 19* (pp. 405-450). Washington, DC: American Educational Research Association.

Smith, I. L., & Hambleton, R. K. (1990). Content validity studies of licensing examinations. *Educational Measurement: Issues and Practice, 9*(4), 7-10.

Subkoviak, M. (1976). Estimating reliability from a single administration of a criterion-referenced test. *Journal of Educational Measurement, 13*(4), 264-276.

Subkoviak, M. (1980). Decision consistency approaches. In R. A. Berk (Ed.), *Criterion-referenced measurement: The state of the art* (pp. 129-185). Baltimore, MD: The Johns Hopkins Press.

Society for Industrial and Organizational Psychology, Inc. (1987). *Principles for the Validation and Use of Personnel Selection Procedures (3rd Ed.).* College Park, MD: Author.

ITEM BANKING

Betty A. Bergstrom

Richard C. Gershon

Computer Adaptive Technologies, Inc.

Item banks developed by licensure agencies range from a collection of items stored on index cards to highly sophisticated electronic databases. Regardless of the storage mechanism, most banks contain items that have been organized and referenced according to procedures established by the licensure agency. This chapter outlines useful practices for building and maintaining a computerized item bank. We address storage of item text, graphics, and statistical history. We deal with the creation of paper-and-pencil and computerized tests from an item bank and the use of Item Response Theory (IRT) to calibrate and equate item banks. New directions in item banking are also discussed.

Apparently coined in England during the mid-1960s, the term "item bank" was used to describe a group of test items that were "organized, classified and catalogued like books in a library" (Choppin, 1985). Subsequently, Bruce Choppin and others interested in item banking based on Item Response Theory (Hathaway, Houser, & Kingsbury, 1985) attempted to distinguish between "item banks" (a collection of items calibrated with an IRT measurement system and equated to a common scale) and "item pools" (collections of items grouped by content but not calibrated). This distinction has not been widely embraced and often today the terms "item bank" and "item pool" are used interchangeably.

Computerized item banking employs a computer software program to store collections of test items and their associated classifications and statistics. Computerization allows easy storage and retrieval of hundreds (for some organizations the number may be thousands or even tens of thousands) of items. A well-organized, well-maintained computerized item bank can facilitate and enhance the construction of both paper-and-pencil and computerized tests. Items can be sorted and filtered to enable easy review by content experts and psychometric staff.

The basic plan for item bank construction includes writing content valid, grammatically correct items (see Chapters 5 & 6), categorizing items according to the content outline or "blueprint" that the testing agency utilizes, and entering the items into the computerized bank.

Once a valid item bank is created, the orchestrated efforts of content experts and psychometricians are required to maintain it. Content experts must review the item bank on a systematic schedule to ensure that (a) items are current and relevant to the field of practice; (b) duplicate and similar items are identified and flagged; and (c) content within the bank is representative of the test blueprint. Psychometricians must also review the bank to guarantee that (a) the range of item difficulty is appropriate; (b) misfitting items have been identified and flagged for rewrite; and (c) the pass/fail standard is current.

Licensure and certification agencies test a large range of candidates. Some agencies test less than 50 candidates per year whereas others test hundreds of thousands of candidates. Still, even agencies that test relatively few candidates usually have item banks of at least several hundred items. Although switching to computerized item banking involves the initial cost of developing or purchasing software and possible conversion costs for existing items, graphics, and statistics into the computerized bank, cost savings are realized in the long run by reducing professional and clerical time for item maintenance and test production. Another important benefit of computerization is reduction of error—the more data are manually manipulated, the greater the chance for mistakes. Thus, even very small testing agencies will benefit by computerizing their item banks.

The following sections of this chapter outline various computerized item banking components. Licensure agencies need to review their item banking needs (both current and future) to decide which components of computerized banking are applicable for them.

ITEM STORAGE

From original draft through ultimate "retirement," an item should be maintained in the computerized bank. The life cycle of an item typically includes development, review by content and bias panels, field test, rewrite, test administration, analysis, review/rewrite, and additional test administrations. Some of these steps may be repeated more than once. A computerized item bank should provide a means of storing, retrieving, and maintaining test items and related descriptive information (Schroeder, 1993). The descriptive data that licensure organizations store varies. The types of information that may be stored in an item bank are as follows:

Item Identifier

Each item must be assigned a unique identifier (ID) which may be a number, a character, or a combination of the two. Whenever changes are made to an item, a new item ID should be assigned. Many organizations add extensions to an existing number to indicate that the item has been revised (i.e., 1004 becomes 1004a). If item statistics are being maintained over time, it is essential that the item ID be updated with each change. Once a new ID has been assigned, the old item and the new item can be compared to assess the impact of the change on item performance. Remember that changes as innocent as altering the orientation or order of the choices, or simply changing the font, have been shown to affect item difficulty (Gershon & Bergstrom, 1993).

Item Type

Items types include multiple-choice questions (MCQ), short answer, matching, essay, etc. Some licensure organizations develop tests that include a specified percentage of item types on each test. Including this field allows the test developer to sort by item type for test construction.

Classification Schemes

The item bank should store all relevant classifications for each item. Many licensure organizations store multiple content classifications with an item; for example, in some medical areas an item is classified by content (anatomy, physiology, etc.) and by type of patient (pediatric or adult). The National Council of State Boards of Nursing classifies items for the NCLEX-RN examination along two dimensions of content codes, nursing processes and client needs (Haynie & Way, 1994). Another common scheme is Bloom's Taxonomy, in which the item is categorized by the cognitive processes required to answer the item (Bloom, Englehart, Furst, Hill, & Krathwohl, 1956). Additional types of classifications may include task, process performed, or instrumentation required. If items are classified by a nested content outline, the bank should be capable of storing the nested structure.

Licensure organizations develop content outlines and test blueprints according to job analyses and input by experts from the field. A test blueprint defines the scope of practice and the content areas essential for demonstrating competence. Adherence to the blueprint is crucial to confirming test validity. Care must therefore be taken to ensure that items in the bank are classified correctly. Storing items with classification data in a computerized bank allows an agency to easily sort the entire bank or a test to determine if the percentage of items by classification meets the blueprint specifications.

Computerization, however, does not assure test validity. Whether items are stored in a computerized bank or on index cards, validity requirements remain the same. Items must be reviewed by members of the profession to ensure that they are current and relevant to the field of practice and tests must be reviewed to confirm that they meet blueprint specifications.

References

The item bank should provide for storage of references. This information allows the licensure agency to cite a specific reference if the validity or accuracy of an item is questioned by a candidate or by an item review committee.

Author

Storing the name of the author of an item allows the licensure agency to contact the original source if the item needs additional references, clarification, or rewriting. A convenient item bank feature enables the production of a report to each item writer on the performance of their items after piloting has been completed. An even more helpful feature produces the text of all items that must be rewritten by a given author after failure on a test pilot or following review by a content review committee.

Item Status

All items should be coded with a status to indicate the current use of the item. For example, an untested item may be coded as "new," whereas an item that appears on a test but is not counted toward the candidate's score may be coded as "experimental." Agencies may wish to code items as "secure" or "non-secure" to indicate whether the item can be used on a practice test or as an example item. An item that has been used for testing should probably never be deleted from a bank— rather it should be coded as "retired." This ensures that archival records are kept intact and enables test developers to avoid rewriting the same poorly performing item.

Testing Dates

The item bank should store the dates that an item was used and when it is scheduled for next use.

Equivalent Items

Stored with an item should be a list of "equivalent" ("similar" or "overlapping" or "mutually exclusive") item IDs. An equivalent item contains similar content information or cues the correct answer. Once a particular item is selected for a test, equivalent items can be flagged so that they do not appear on the same test. A related list should include items that are different enough to be included on the same test, but too similar to appear on the same page. This is especially important if the test is assembled by the computer. When tests are manually assembled, content experts check for overlapping items; however, if test construction is automated, the only way to prevent overlap is by careful coding of the items in the bank. In practice, it may be impossible to do this in sufficient detail, and thus computer-generated tests should always be carefully reviewed by content experts before administration (Stocking, Swanson, & Pearlman, 1993).

Comments

A field for comments about an item is especially useful: Content experts may wish to comment on the relevancy of an item to the current field of practice; psychometricians may want to note an unusual statistic for a particular group or test administration. Reasons for retiring an item from the active bank should also be included in the comments.

Cases

A case is a graphic or a common piece of text (such as a reading passage) that is referenced by multiple items. Cases should be stored separately from the item and referenced by a case ID number. When an item is reviewed, the case should also be available for review. Conversely, when a case is reviewed, all dependent items (items that refer to the case) should be available. For some cases, all related items must be used together, and possibly in a specified sequence. For other cases related items may be separated. The item bank should be able to store information regarding any required sequence of items which share a common case.

Distractors

The correct answer, the number of "distractors" ("response alternatives" or "alternative choices"), and the weights for each distractor (if used) should be stored.

Statistical History

The item bank should store appropriate statistics for each administration of the item on each test form. Statistics for any group analyses performed should also be stored. Essential fields include:

- Test name
- Test form
- Date of administration
- Sequence number of the item on the form
- Number of candidates included in the analysis
- Number of candidates answering the item correctly
- Number of candidates omitting the item
- Group included in the analysis (males, females, first timers, all, etc.)

Optional fields might include:

- Classical statistics (e.g., discrimination and difficulty indices)
- Item Response Theory Statistics (e.g., item difficulty, standard error)
- Statistics for each distractor (e.g., weights and proportion of candidates responding to each option)
- Statistics to indicate differential item functioning (e.g., Mantel-Haenszel statistics, or IRT based DIF analyses)

Psychometric professionals can review item performance over time, and compare items individually or within categories. Storage for statistics should be user defined and have the capability for future expansion.

User-Defined Fields

Ideally an item bank should contain some user-defined fields to allow the licensure agency to store additional information unique to their specific needs.

COMPUTERIZED ITEM BANKING

In its simplest form, a computerized item bank is a word processing document containing the item text, and perhaps some simple scheme for identifying the item author and content codes. Basic statistics, manually keyed into the document, may be included. In reality, this is probably the most common type of computerized item bank in use today (Gullickson & Farland, 1990).

Agencies that store items and related information in a word processing document, but have added merge codes to enable easy creation of final text, answer keys, and content distributions, are using a slightly more advanced computerized bank. This type of bank may be adequate for many organizations, but it requires a great deal of manual processing time and fails to take advantage of the potential power that today's computer can afford the test developer. Although word processing may appear to get the job done (i.e., the test gets produced), it is still not the best tool for the job.

Relational Databases

A true computerized item bank must include a database component. A simple database affords minimal opportunities to sort items by content schemes, item difficulty, test administration date, etc. In the most basic system, a single database contains a single record for each item in the bank. Typically this record will contain an item identifier, content classification, and status (new, used, retired, etc). In many cases this record will also contain the item text itself, or a position indicator (such as a file name) where the text for the item is maintained. This is where many computerized item banks currently stop, and if each item is to be used only once, this simple item bank may be sufficient.

At a higher level of computerization, a fully relational database system can be constructed to maintain all information associated with the life of a test item. Relational databases can exponentially increase the functionality of the item bank; for example, the statistics obtained from each administration of an item can be stored in a related *History* database containing one record per test administration per item. The History database is a "child" to the main (parent) *Items* database. Thus for each item in the bank, there can be multiple history "children." This type of relationship is also sometimes referred to as a *one-to-many* type system. The History database would minimally contain the number of persons who viewed the item and how many persons answered the item correctly. A more complete database would also include classical and IRT statistics such as item difficulty and item discrimination indices.

Another example of a related database in a full-featured item bank is a test database—a list of all tests associated with the item bank, including those already administered and those currently under construction. A related database to the test database would include an administration database consisting of one record per test administration per test (another parent-child relationship where the test is the parent and the administrations of that test are the children). This database should include administration dates, number of persons taking the exam, and pass/fail rate.

The concept of the "parent-child relationship" is quite important. In a relational database system each database is connected to at least one of the other databases through one or more "key fields." In the case of the relationship between the Items and History databases, the key field is the item identifier. To "look up" the history for that item, all items from the History database with the same item identifier are selected. This idea is not limited to the key field, but can also include additional filters; for example, to look up all of the times that an item was used in the last 2 years, both the item identifier and the date would serve as the filter. For organizations with extremely large item banks, the "look up" criteria can become much more complicated. The test developer may wish to locate all items (a) within a specific content area; (b) that have been administered at least two times to over 500 people; and (c) with item statistics in an acceptable range.

Complicated filtering conditions with large databases can be accomplished through "Structured Query Language" or "SQL"—a language relatively universal to all computer systems (microcomputers and mainframes). SQL is used to combine information from multiple databases in order to retrieve specific information. This language is *not* a programming language, but can be used by end-users (including psychometricians and clerical staff) to specify or "query" information whenever they need it. Filter capabilities for selection purposes can be maximized by using SQL-type queries rather than setting an actual filter on an extremely large database.

Maximizing Computer Efficiency

Two factors of speed influence the efficiency of the computerized item bank: (a) the speed in which data can be moved from the hard disk to the program and ultimately to the screen; and (b) the speed in which data can be found. The first factor is dependent upon the quality of the computer hardware and operating system. For instance, operating on a network, or from within Microsoft Windows™ greatly slows data access compared to using a stand-alone computer operating under DOS. Increasing local random access memory (RAM), and the inclusion of a fast local hard disk will serve to greatly improve speed in this regard.

The second factor—the speed in which data can be found—is largely dependent upon the quality of the underlying software being used. For example, in the case of a moderately difficult query applied to a 5,000-item bank, a poorly constructed query system could take long minutes or even hours to find the items that are needed. The same query would take a fraction of a second if programmed correctly. Computer Adaptive Technologies, Inc. (Gershon, 1994) recently demonstrated this speed advantage to one of the major national testing organizations that was using a mainframe to load up to 30,000 person records to their system each week. The loading process was taking up to 6 hours. Improved software on a personal computer enabled them to download all records and sort them in just under one minute.

Text Editing

Another component that can make a computerized item bank more useful for the test developer is an integrated word processor. Text editing within database software is usually awkward; however, if the item bank software integrates a word processor with the relational database system, item editing and paper-and-pencil test production become infinitely easier. This type of integrated system should provide the test developer with all of the database capabilities plus state-of-the-art word processing capabilities including access to thousands of fonts, spell checking, formatting options, styles, codes, etc. When the item is actually stored as a word processing file, the stem and the distractors can be stored together, and the item is edited as one contiguous piece of "What-You-See-Is-What-You-Get" (WYSIWYG) text.

An efficient item bank will communicate directly with the word processor using features like the Windows Dynamic Data Exchange (DDE), which enables a database to start up a popular word processor such as Microsoft Word or WordPerfect just once at the beginning of the session. Later editing calls to the word processor result in a simple *transfer* of the item or test text to the word processor using DDE. Thus, the word processor does not need to be restarted for each editing procedure. This is particularly important within a Windows operating environment, where it may take up to a minute each time the program is started.

The item bank should also be capable of transferring item text back into the item bank without exiting the word processing software. Some item banks use "dedicated" word processing programs; in such instances, the word processor used was written specifically for the item bank and therefore cannot fully conform to any particular industry standard word processing program. This type of system results in increased learning time for the users, and undoubtedly means that there are significantly fewer editing features available. Given the power of today's computers, there is no reason to settle for poor performance in text editing. Minimal editing requirements should include access to spell and grammar checkers, multiple fonts, columns, subscripts and superscripts, bold and italics, equation editors, etc. Medical and legal licensing boards should also have easy access to available custom spell checkers.

The ability to edit on-line combined with the portability of computers allows an item bank to be edited at virtually any location. Some organizations already use portable computers to transport their item banks to remote sites, allowing test committees to participate in item writing sessions and draft test production.

Integrating Graphics

Whenever possible, graphics should be stored "on line" in order to facilitate easy layout and graphical editing. There are several excellent graphics editing programs available on the market today, which can be used to produce graphics from scratch as well as edit or enhance scanned images produced by other sources. A graphic should be stored in a format that can be used to produce camera-ready copy, and later to produce a screen image for use in computer-administered testing. Many images scanned from a paper image require at least some manual editing before they are suitable for screen display, but this is *not* usually the case when the printed image is originally prepared on the computer. The layout file that was previously used to produce a camera-ready paper image can usually produce a suitable screen image as well.

A well-constructed item bank will include the capacity to bank images as well as text. And when an image is used within the text of an item, object linking and embedding (OLE) can be used to edit the graphic without leaving the item bank. OLE enables graphics created by other programs to be imported directly into a test item. "Live" OLE links can also be created; for example, when spreadsheets are used to produce graphics and numbers for multiple items, a simple edit in the original spreadsheet will result in all of the items in the item bank being automatically updated as well. When editing an item on screen, the graphic can be moved and resized without leaving the item banking software. OLE further allows the image to be edited by simply clicking on the image. This results in the original program which created the graphic to appear on the screen so that the desired change can be made. When editing has been completed, the item should reappear on the screen with the modified graphic appearing in place. This type of functionality can savedozens of hours of test construction and layout time on a single test!

Multiple Language Support

Some licensure agencies administer tests in more than one language. An item bank with integrated word processing software that supports foreign languages is essential for developing test forms in alternate languages. Identical items available in more than one language can be stored under the same item ID, particularly when the item is expected to perform similarly regardless of base language. Such is likely to be the case with mathematical and short-answer items, but usually not true for items with long text passages. When a test is created in English, a comparable test in the second language can be automatically generated.

Automated Item Writing

The item development process can be facilitated by integrating an item writing diskette with the item banking program. An item writing diskette allows content experts to write items at home directly onto a diskette. Item writers enter the item identifier, item text, correct answer, comments, and references. This type of software can be configured to present the item writer with any classification scheme created by the licensure organization. The contents of the diskette are then imported directly into the item bank saving manual entry time, eliminating typographical errors, and ensuring standardized formatting. Diskettes can be exchanged among item writers and team leaders to facilitate the item writing process.

Item Bank Capacity

Item banks are theoretically capable of storing an infinite number of items. Licensure agencies need an item bank that can store all of their items and allow considerable room for expansion. This is a function of both the limits of the software as well as the hardware. A minimal configuration will include at least twice as much hard disk space as would be required to store all existing items, plus all of the items likely to be created in the next 5 years. (Note: Twice as much space will be needed to perform database maintenance functions.)

Statistical Analysis

Some item banks have the ability to analyze test results as part of the original software; others interface with a statistical module. At the very least, an item banking program must have the ability to easily import statistics from standardized formats such as ASCII or xBase.

Pool Book Production

A good item banking program will provide the licensure agency with user-defined options for pool book production. A pool book is effectively a printed copy of the contents of the item bank (for obvious reasons a pool book is not usually referred to as a *bank book*). The printed pool book may include all of the items in the bank or a user-defined subset. In addition to the identifying number, item text, and correct answer, each pool book may optionally include item classification, statistical history, item author, reference, and comments about the item. Case text and graphics should be included with each item, and the software should allow layout options such as printing each item on a separate page. Item pool books can act as an archival "hard copy" or can be used by test committees to aid them in item writing and review.

Security

Item banks for high-stakes licensure examinations should have a user-definable, multilevel security system. In most agencies, different levels of personnel will need access to the item bank. For example, some clerical personnel will only need access to item text to enter new items, whereas psychometric staff require access to test definition and test layout as well.

Similarly, many organizations maintain multiple item banks for different examinations. In many cases, some of the persons working on one item bank have no need to have access to the other banks. In larger testing organizations, security will need to be cleared on the test level, such that once a test has been created, embedded items can be modified only by project managers. Typically, limited access to various parts of the item bank will be automatically maintained by a password system that identifies the user when the item banking software is executed. The software should then be responsible for limiting access as appropriate.

Security can be improved even further through a variety of means, including limiting access with the use of regular network security, external hardware keys, and embedded encryption (the process of scrambling or "encoding" text to make it impossible to read without a proper password). A hardware key scheme prohibits access to a system unless the key (a small box connected to the printer port of a user's computer or to the network file server) is attached. Typically, the key must be present *and* a password given for access to be granted. In this way, even if the entire item bank is stolen, the software will refuse to reveal the item text unless *both* the correct password is entered *and* the hardware key is present.

USING AN ITEM BANK TO CREATE AND ARCHIVE TESTS

Once items have been entered in a computerized item bank, paper-and-pencil tests or computer-administered tests can be created. A computerized item bank can be used to automatically create camera-ready copy for paper-and-pencil tests or computerized tests, store all previously administered tests, easily create new test forms, and store overall test statistics such as dates administered, number of candidates examined, reliability, etc.

Automated Item Selection

Items for inclusion on a test can be selected manually, randomly drawn by the computer from all existing items in the bank, or drawn by the computer from prespecified parameters. There are currently a number of highly sophisticated schemes for automated test construction (Armstrong, Jones, & Wu, 1992; Boekkooi-Timminga, 1990; Stocking et al., 1993). Although some licensure agencies may wish to pursue these advanced algorithms, most test developers are satisfied to use less complicated item-selection algorithms that choose items within prespecified parameters such as content, item type, and item difficulty.

Typically, a test will be prepared to include a specified number or percentage of items from various content domains. In the case of a computerized item bank, these conditions can be defined by creating a computerized test plan ("blueprint" or "template"). Each cell in the test plan describes how many items must be included to fill a particular condition (for example, there must be five items from content area 1, and seven items from content area 2). These are *unique* conditions because they refer to rules which apply only to a single cell in the test plan. There can also be *parallel* sets of conditions, such as a condition that 50% of the items on the test must be new, and 50% must have been contained on a previous test. There are also *total* conditions which apply to all items on the test, such as a rule that all items must have been approved by a specific committee, or that all items must fall within a specified difficulty range.

Once the test plan has been created, it should be accessible whenever creating a new test. The item bank should be able to use the test plan automatically to pull items from the bank which fill the test plan conditions. A good banking program will also be able to conduct an "audit" of items manually selected for inclusion in the bank, to ascertain whether or not all of the conditions in the test plan have been met. On-screen warning messages or a written report should inform the test developer if and where insufficient items are available to meet the plan. This procedure can be accomplished in microseconds on the computer, but would otherwise take hours or even days when completed by hand.

The item bank should have the capability to reorder automatically—or allow for easy manual reordering—existing tests to create new test forms. When an item is selected for test inclusion, any graphics, tables, or cases associated with it should automatically be included.

Camera-Ready Copy for Printed Tests

Computerized item banking software should provide the capability to edit a test created from within the bank using standard word processing features such as spell check and the ability to change font type and size. An advanced bank will also be able to reorder test items so that the blank space typically left on some pages is minimized. This automation component can save days of manual layout work, while ensuring accuracy of item keys. Test administration formats, such as instructions, examples, and layout should be stored in separate electronic files for easy import into a test document. An additional essential feature is the ability to produce both paper-and-pencil and electronic answer keys.

Computerized Tests

A modern item bank will be able to produce tests for both computerized and paper-and-pencil administration. Most certification and licensure organizations have at least contemplated using computers to administer their tests. Although there are a myriad of reasons for and against this approach, the important consideration for the purpose of this chapter is that agencies would be well advised to purchase or create an item bank which has the *capability* for the creation of computer-administered tests.

Tests that contain only items with short text require almost no user intervention to be included on a computer-administered test, as long as the items are stored in an appropriate item bank. Items containing longer text passages are also simple to convert, although the choice of administration software and hardware may narrow. The differences in the two modes of administration are most apparent when it comes to graphics. As mentioned earlier, most graphics or visuals that have been prepared for paper-and-pencil test administration are not directly transferrable to computerized administration. The relatively limited resolution of any computer screen compared to a printed page may necessitate some editing of the paper-and-pencil graphic. If a bank is to be used to produce both paper-and-pencil and computer test forms simultaneously, the bank of visuals must be prepared to store both print and screen versions of each illustration.

A quality item bank will allow the production of a paper copy of the computerized exam as well as the computer-administered version. This can be used to produce parallel versions or a paper copy of the computerized test for proofreading purposes.

It is also wise to ensure that item banking software integrates well with test administration software. Banking software should be capable of easily producing output files compatible with test administration software. Test administration software should not only be compatible with the item bank, but should also be functional regardless of the test administration vendor. In the event that the licensure agency changes to a different administration vendor, compatible software ensures that a painful translation procedure, which could even result in the need to repilot computer administered test items or ultimately force renorming of the test, can be avoided.

Archiving Tests

A "test bank," consisting of all the tests that have been created within the item bank, is an important part of a complete item banking program. The text of the test should be stored with all of the historical statistics for each time the test was administered, including dates of administration, number of candidates examined, and test reliability. Group analyses and DIF analyses should be included with the test's statistical history, and a comments field should also be available to store comments relating to overall test performance.

IRT CALIBRATED ITEM BANKS

If a licensure agency tests a minimum of 100 to 200 candidates per year, calibrating and equating their item bank using an Item Response Theory (IRT) model will provide additional valuable statistical information. An IRT model compares the difficulty of the item with the ability of the candidate and estimates the probability that the candidate will correctly answer the item. The major advantage of IRT models over classical test theory is that classical item and test characteristics (or statistics) vary depending upon the group of candidates taking the test whereas IRT item and test characteristics do not. Classical indices of item difficulty, point-biserial correlation, and reliability may all change if candidates differ in ability distribution (Hathaway et al., 1985). In licensure testing this often proves to be true; for example, a spring candidate population may be more able than a winter candidate population. An IRT model, such as the Rasch model or the three parameter logistic model, allows for the calibration and equating of items onto a common scale and also allows for the identification of items that perform poorly. To calibrate items with the Rasch model, however, requires a candidate population of at least 100 to 200 candidates (Linacre, 1994), whereas the three parameter model requires 1,000 to 2,000 candidates to estimate item parameters (Green, Bock, Humphreys, Linn, & Reckase, 1984).

New items are equated to the bank scale by administering them on tests with previously calibrated items from the bank. This procedure is called common-item equating (Wright & Stone, 1979). Other methods such as common-person equating for linking IRT item parameters onto a common scale are discussed by C. David Vale (1986) as well as in Chapter 12 of this book. Before items are added to the calibrated bank, the fit of the items should be assessed to determine their suitability for inclusion.

Using an IRT model as a measurement system requires that the group of items be "unidimensional." This means that all of the items in the bank are defining one dimension (e.g., the ability to practice law). The bank of calibrated test items is a set of coordinated questions that develop, define, and quantify a common theme and provide an operational definition of the dimension (Wright & Bell, 1984). Of course, unidimensionality is an abstract idea, always violated to some extent in real life. Many licensure tests comprise items from different content areas—indeed the validity of the test is assured by the inclusion of items that are representative of these different areas as specified by the test blueprint. However, in *most* cases, the rules underlying item response theory are quite robust, and the items for a licensure examination can be calibrated with an appropriate IRT model. Still, it is highly recommended that an IRT expert be consulted when making initial decisions regarding unidimensionality and the appropriateness of using existing items when creating an IRT-based item bank.

When an IRT measurement system is used, a measure of the precision of the item calibration and ability estimate is available for each item and each candidate. This makes it possible to calculate a priori a reliability estimate for any score on a test drawn from the calibrated bank. The size of the error of measurement will depend on which items are selected, how many items are selected, and the candidate's raw score on that set of items (Hathaway et al., 1985).

There are a number of advantages to using an IRT model to calibrate and equate all items within a licensure test bank:

- Easy preparation of parallel test forms
- Comparison of individual candidate performance over time (for candidates who repeat the test)
- Comparison of group performance over time (to evaluate overall candidate proficiency or proficiency by school, program, or specific content area)
- Usage of the item bank for computerized adaptive testing

Creating an Item Bank for Computerized Adaptive Testing

Computerized adaptive testing is a form of test administration in which each candidate takes an individualized test administered on a computer. Candidate competence is continually assessed on-line, and the difficulty of each item administered is targeted to the current ability estimate of the candidate. This mode of testing typically requires an IRT calibrated item bank.

The ability to order all of the items on the same scale is essential for computerized adaptive testing. Because all items are on the same scale in an IRT calibrated item bank, the particular items that are administered to a given candidate are irrelevant. Each individualized adaptive test created from the calibrated bank is automatically equated to every other test that has been or might be drawn from the bank (Wright & Bell, 1984; Masters & Evans, 1986).

When all items in the bank are calibrated to the same scale, a pass/fail point, (criterion-referenced standard) can be established for the entire item bank. Thus, all candidates are measured against the same criterion-referenced standard regardless of the group of candidates with whom they are examined, the particular set of items they are administered, or when they take the test. This makes it possible to determine a candidate's pass/fail status with respect to the basic dimension that the items define.

To use an item bank for computerized adaptive testing, the bank must meet additional constraints. Following are some observations for maintaining item banks for computerized adaptive testing suggested by Mary Lunz, Ph.D., Director of Testing for the Board of Registry, American Society of Clinical Pathologists (Lunz & Deville, 1994).

Proportional Distribution

Items in the bank should be distributed proportionally to the test blueprint. For example, if 10% of the adaptive test will be drawn from a specific content area, then approximately 10% of the items in the bank should cover that content area. Most adaptive test algorithms allow for content balancing so that the items administered to each candidate follow content percentage specifications. Adherence to the test blueprint ensures that test validity, as defined by a job analysis and content experts, is maintained. When some content areas in the bank have fewer than the blueprint-specified percentage of items, the existing items will be over sampled.

Range of Difficulty

The range of difficulty of items in the bank should reflect the range of ability of the candidate population. Calibrated item difficulties should be adequately distributed within each content area as well as across the entire item bank. Because each candidate is being administered an individualized test in which the difficulty of the items presented varies according to the estimated ability of the candidate, the range of items available for selection by the computer must adequately cover the distribution of candidate ability. When the range of calibrated item difficulty is adequate, the bank can provide appropriately targeted examinations, thus increasing measurement precision and therefore, increasing the amount of information gained about the candidate (Bergstrom & Stahl, 1992).

Current Relevancy

Items in the bank must be carefully screened for current relevancy to the field of practice. Because any item in the bank may be selected by the computerized algorithm for administration, outdated items must be removed from the active bank.

Security

For security purposes, the more high-quality items in the bank the better. Large numbers of items limit the number of candidates who are exposed to any one item (Stahl & Lunz, 1993).

Long Term Maintenance

Item bank maintenance is especially crucial when item banks are used for adaptive testing. The estimated ability of the candidate is calculated from the bank parameter values for the items. Thus, the item bank must be continually monitored for both parameter drift and relevance of all items to the current field of practice. When a bank is used to create paper-and-pencil tests, items that appear on a particular test form are checked by content experts to ensure that they are "good" items. Because this is not the case with adaptive tests, agencies administering computerized adaptive tests must have scheduled, systematic reviews of all items in the bank.

NEW DIRECTIONS IN ITEM BANKING

Computerized testing, multimedia, and integration will be the major themes in the item bank of tomorrow. Computerized testing is just beginning to take the world by storm. There are at least three national networks owned by computer administration vendors, and dozens more that belong to individual corporate and certification organizations. In many cases, vendors and government agencies have set up multiple testing centers which blanket a given state, allowing easy and constant access for all examinees.

Fixed length and adaptive computer tests are currently administered to hundreds of thousands of individuals and the numbers are expected to grow exponentially into the 21st century. Some of these examinees are taking tests on antiquated main frame or hand-held computers with limited display or memory capacity. The future will allow all candidates to take their tests on computers with color monitors, full-size keyboards, and answering devices like mice or touch screen panels. But the real revolution will occur when tests are readily capable of displaying situations that are more real-life oriented using technology such as video clips and actual audible conversations. Advanced technology is already available to provide a computer "reader" or to automatically extend testing time limits in order to satisfy the Americans with Disabilities Act. In the future, computers will also be used to record verbal answers to questions, or even to "video record" responses to test items.

All of the above scenarios will require item banks to have new features including the ability to store sound and multi-media clips along with item text and to interface with test administration modules that include these multimedia components.

CONCLUSION

Most licensure agencies can probably streamline their test production through the use of computerized item banking. Agencies should carefully review their needs, taking into account the number of items in their bank and their procedures for item review and test production.

Options for acquiring software for computerized item banking include:

- Developing customized software. This option has the advantage of providing the agency with the precisely unique specifications they require. Unfortunately, it is also usually associated with high development costs.
- Purchasing off-the-shelf software. Sufficient for most testing organizations, off-the-shelf item banking software varies greatly in price. Purchasers should keep in mind that their item banking needs will increase as additional items are written and tests administered. Therefore, the greater the flexibility in the program and the greater the speed and capacity of the software, the longer the item bank will fulfill their requirements.
- Customizing off-the-shelf software. Some software developers are willing to customize their software. This may provide a good solution for organizations with unique requirements and result in significant savings in cost and aggravation over "from scratch" software development.

Prior to purchasing item banking software, careful consideration should be given to present and future item banking needs. Testing agencies should request working demonstration copies of the software products and compare features including storage capabilities, speed, and ease of item text editing and test production. It would be prudent to involve those personnel who will actually have to use the software—including psychometricians, content specialists and clerical staff—in the decision about which product to purchase. From item creation to test administration—use of computerized item banking can capitalize on advanced technology to streamline production procedures and construct psychometrically sound tests.

REFERENCES

Armstrong, R. D., Jones, D. H., & Wu, I. (1992). An automated test development of parallel tests from a seed test. *Psychometrika, 57,* 271-288.

Bergstrom, B. A., & Stahl, J. A. (1992, April). *Assessing existing item pool depth for computer adaptive testing*. Paper presented at the annual meeting of the National Council on Measurement in Education, San Francisco, CA.

Bloom, B. S., Englehart, M. D., Furst, E. J., Hill, W. H., & Krathwohl, D. R. (1956). *Taxonomy of educational objectives: The classification of educational goals. Handbook 1: Cognitive domain*. New York: David McKay Co.

Boekkooi-Timminga, E. (1990). A cluster-based method for test construction. *Applied Psychological Measurement, 14*, 341-354.

Choppin, B. (1985). Principles of item banking. *Evaluation in Education, 9*, 87-90.

Gershon, R. C. (1994). *CAT ITEM BANK (computer program)*. Chicago, IL: Computer Adaptive Technologies, Inc.

Gershon, R. C., & Bergstrom, B. A. (1993, January). *What's the DIF?: Scaling, equating and differential item functioning on the MEAP*. Paper presented at the annual meeting of the Michigan Educational Research Association, Novi, MI.

Green, B. F., Bock, R. D., Humphreys, L. G., Linn, R. L., & Reckase, M. D. (1984). Technical guidelines for assessing computerized adaptive tests. *Journal of Educational Measurement, 21*(4), 347-360.

Gullickson, A., & Farland, D. (1990). Using micros for test development. *Tech Trends, 35*(2), 22-26.

Hathaway, W., Houser, R., & Kingsbury, G. (1985). *A regional and local item response theory based test item bank system*. (ERIC Document Reproduction No. ED 284 883)

Haynie, K. A., & Way, W. D. (1994, April). *The effects of item pool depth on the accuracy of pass/fail decisions for the NCLEX™ using CAT*. Paper presented at the annual meeting of the National Council on Measurement in Education, New Orleans, LA.

Linacre, J. M. (1994). Sample size and item calibration stability. *Rasch Measurement Transactions, 7*(4), 328.

Lunz, M. E., & Deville, C. W. (1994, April). *Validity of item selection: A comparison of automated computerized adaptive and manual paper and pencil*. Paper presented at the annual meeting of the American Educational Research Association, San Francisco, CA.

Masters, G. N., & Evans, J. (1986). Banking non-dichotomously scored items. *Applied Psychological Measurement, 10*, 355-367.

Schroeder, L. L. (1993, Summer). Criteria for an item banking system. *CLEAR Exam Review*, pp. 16-18.

Stahl, J. A., & Lunz, M. E. (1993, April). *Assessing the extent of overlap of items among computerized adaptive tests*. Paper presented at the annual meeting of The National Council of Measurement in Education, Atlanta, GA.

Stocking, M. L., Swanson, L., & Pearlman, M. (1993). Application of an automated item selection method to real data. *Applied Psychological Measurement, 17*, 167-176.

Vale, C. D. (1986). Linking item parameters onto a common scale. *Applied Psychological Measurement, 10*, 333-344.

Wright, B. D., & Bell, S. R. (1984). Item banks: What, why, how. *Journal of Educational Measurement, 21*, 331-345.

Wright, B. D., & Stone, M. H. (1979). *Best test design*. Chicago, IL: MESA Press.

DIFFERENTIAL ITEM FUNCTIONING IN LICENSURE TESTS

Barbara S. Plake

University of Nebraska-Lincoln

When test scores are used to make important decisions, as is typically the case with licensure tests, the validity of test score interpretations is extremely critical. The validity of the decision (e.g., pass or fail the licensure examination) relies heavily on the validity of the test score that is used in making the licensure decision. So, although validity is always a critical component in test score interpretation, it has increased importance when the score is used in high-stakes decision situations such as licensure testing.

Issues in validity for licensure tests have been addressed in Chapter 4 of this volume. The focus of this chapter is on techniques that have been developed for identifying one source of test interpretation invalidity: differential item functioning (DIF) by identifiable groups. The chapter begins with a discussion of what constitutes differential item functioning and under what circumstances differential item functioning poses a source of test interpretation invalidity. Next, various methods for identifying test items that function differentially are highlighted. This section focuses principally on multiple-choice test items although a separate subsection on applications of DIF methods with constructed-response type items is presented. The chapter ends with a conclusion section that makes recommendations for future developments in the area of identification of test items that function inappropriately for different subpopulations.

This chapter concentrates on the individual items that comprise the test, not on administrative or other aspects of testing that also might influence examinee test performance. Specifically, this chapter considers ways to identify items that function differentially for identifiable subpopulations. Other reasons for score performance differences (e.g., speeded conditions, administration medium, test anxiety/wiseness) are extremely important. However, these issues are beyond the scope of this chapter.

The focus of this chapter is on discussing different approaches that have promise for identifying items that function differentially in licensure tests. It is not the intent of this chapter to present step-by-step details on calculating these various methods. The reader should reference other books that present formulas for such calculations, particularly Berk (1982), Camilli and Shepard (1994), and Holland and Wainer (1993). Further, this chapter is not designed to be a comprehensive resource for DIF methods; instead, the chapter samples from these methods those techniques that are relevant or dominant in use for DIF analysis with licensure test applications.

WHAT IS DIFFERENTIAL ITEM FUNCTIONING?

It is expected that test items will show different performance across members of the examinee population. After all, if everyone performed exactly the same on the item, it would provide no useful information in differentiating those who qualify for licensure from those examinees who do not. Therefore, an item is not identified as functioning differentially based on overall differences in performance by examinees. When an item shows differences in performance for examinees in the population, however, the basis for that performance difference should be specifically that the examinees differ on the knowledge or achievement that is assessed by the item. When the item shows different performance as a function of differing levels on the trait the item is designed to assess, the item is functioning properly. However, when differences in performance are attributable to extraneous sources of variance, such as ethnic group membership, then the item is not functioning properly. If the item was scored as an operational item in the test, performance on the item could be a basis for invalid test interpretations.

Differential item functioning is often defined as differential item performance by subpopulations of examinees who are equal in the underlying trait measured by the test (Cole & Moss, 1989). To ascertain whether a test contains items that show DIF, many analytic methods are available to compare item performance by subgroups of examinees who have been matched on overall test performance.

Although any identifiable subgroup of examinees could be compared, typically DIF analyses have focused on detecting differential item performance for gender or ethnic groups. In most applications of the methods discussed in this chapter, two distinct groups of examinees are identified: the reference group and the focus group. In the study of DIF for ethnic groups, for example, the reference group is often white examinees and the focus group consists of members of a particular ethnic group, such as African-American examinees. For many to the methods discussed in this chapter, only two groups can be considered in the DIF analysis (e.g., males and females, white examinees and Hispanic examinees; low SES and high SES). In some instances, the methods can be generalized to more than two mutually exclusive groups; however, these extensions are beyond the scope of this presentation.

It is important to note that differential item performance, per se, is not *prima facie* evidence that the test item is biased. Bias is a judgment that may be made due to the presence of items in a test that show differential item performance by identifiable subgroups of examinees in the population. However, some sources of DIF by identifiable subgroups may be appropriate and contribute to valid test score interpretations. For example, on a broad-based licensure test for a discipline with subspecialties, differential item performance may be appropriate and expected by examinees with differential training in the subdisciplines. Therefore, differential item performance by some subpopulations of examinees does not necessarily warrant conclusions about item or test bias.

METHODS FOR DETECTING DIFFERENTIAL ITEM FUNCTIONING

Even when the best item writers are employed and the test development practices are excellent, there is the potential for inappropriate items to appear in the operational version of a licensure test. Most test developers desire to identify such items and eliminate them from the test score to improve the validity of test score interpretations. The purpose of this section is to identify several methods useful for identifying items that may be contributing to differential item performance. These methods are distinguished by when they are applied in the test process. The first set of methods is applied during the test development process. The second set of methods relies on test performance data by examinees. Illustrations of applications of these methods follow in the next section. Generalizations of these methods to tests that require examinee performances, as in constructed response tests or clinical sets, follow.

DIF METHODS DURING TEST DEVELOPMENT STAGES

Probably the best way to eliminate differentially functioning items from a licensure test is to use good test development practices. Through the table of specification (or test blueprint), all critical components that contribute to valid test score interpretations should be identified. These include, in addition to test content, appropriate levels of cognitive processing, and necessary levels of prerequisite skills. Therefore, test content areas that are deemed unnecessary should not be covered by the test questions. The items are written to command an appropriate level of cognitive processing and features such as readability level, test wiseness, and item flaws should have been considered in the item development process. A readability analysis could provide useful information about the level of reading skill needed to perform adequately on the test. Here is an example of a potential contributor to test score differences that may be appropriate: If reading at a specific level is relevant to the licensure decision, then examinees who differ on their reading skill should perform differently on the test questions. On the other hand, if minimal reading skill is needed, then a test with an elevated readability level would likely advantage good readers. Under those conditions, reading level would be a source of unwarranted differential item performance. Good test writing practices aid in eliminating unwarranted sources of test score variance, and therefore, in reducing the potential for differential item functioning by subpopulations in the examinee group.

A second approach used during the item development stage is to employ a panel of experts to review the test items for inappropriate characteristics. Often the panel consists of persons knowledgeable about the targeted subpopulations being considered in the differential item functioning analysis. These panel members are usually asked to review each item and identify items that have potential for being offensive or misleading to members of the targeted groups. Items so identified are typically revised or removed from the item pool.

DIF METHODS BASED ON ANALYSIS OF TEST PERFORMANCE

In order to use data-based DIF methods, a group of examinees must have taken the test under operational test conditions. Sometimes pilot data or pretest data are used to identify items that show differential item functioning. In order for these data to generalize to the operational administration, common administration features must be maintained.

These data-based methods seek to identify test items that show differences in test performance between members of identifiable subpopulations. It is important to remember, however, that it is not simply the difference in test scores between identifiable subgroups that signals a concern for differential item functioning. These identifiable groups may, in fact, differ in their knowledge or achievement the licensure test measures. If that is the case, this difference in test performance is a meaningful and warranted source of score interpretation. Instead, what indicates the presence of differential item functioning is differences in item performance between subgroups of examinees that have been matched on the knowledge or achievement measured by the test.

One important issue in the application of these analytic methods for identifying items that function differentially for matched subgroups of the examinee population is how to form the matched subgroups. Optimally, an external measure of the latent trait (or underlying construct or performance domain) would be used; however, that is almost never available (in fact, if such a valid and reliable alternative method existed, the licensure test probably would not be needed). Instead, most methods utilize the overall licensure test score as the matching criterion. Of course, this is potentially a source of invalidity because the matching variable consists of performances on the very items that are being investigated as suspect for contributing unwarranted score variance. Some of the methods address this problem through attempts to refine the matching criterion by eliminating those items that have been shown to have differential item performance (Clausen, Mazor, & Hambleton, 1993). Although this appears, logically, to be a needed step, reducing the number of items that contribute to the matching criterion weakens its reliability (Zwick, 1990). Therefore, this is not an accepted practice. Because the analytic methods are often used in tandem with methods used in the test development stages, the items that make up the total operational test often have already been subjected to one screening for sources of differential item functioning. It is hoped this serves to strengthen the use of the total test score as the matching criterion for these analytic methods.

Two general classes of analytic methods are presented: those that rely basically on classical test theory (CTT) and those that are founded in item response theory (IRT). The reader is referred to other chapters in this volume for fundamentals of these two theories.

CTT-Based Methods

Approaches that are based on classical test theory focus on item difficulty as a fundamental indicator of item performance. The subpopulations are matched on overall test score, or in test score ranges. Then the number of examinees in the identifiable subgroups correctly answering each item is compared. Three different variations of this approach are Scheuneman's Chi-Square, Log-linear analysis, and Mantel-Haenszel method.

Scheuneman's Chi-Square

This method, suggested by Scheuneman in 1975, begins with dividing the examinees into categories based on total test score (usually three to five categories are formed). For each item, Scheuneman's Index, $C2$, is computed as a function of the number of correct answers for members of each group, summed across the test score categories. As a test statistic, $C2$ asymptotically follows a chi-square distribution with degrees of freedom equal to the number of test score categories.

Several variations of this method have been proposed, including those by Camilli (1979) and Marascuilo and Slaughter (1981). The "full chi-square" method (Camilli, 1979) includes the number of incorrect as well as correct answers in the computation. These methods tend to produce very similar results; however, the sample size requirements for the full chi-square method are somewhat higher than those for Scheuneman's Chi-Square method.

Log-Linear Analysis

In applying log-linear approaches, nominal level data are all that is required. Three variables can be formed for a log-linear approach to identifying items showing differential item functioning: group membership (0 for reference group, 1 for focus group membership); total score category (typically three to five categories); and item response (0 for correct, 1 for correct). These variables form the bases of a three-way contingency table specified for each item in the test. Based on the specification of the models of interest, goodness-of-fit measures are then calculated (e.g., likelihood ratio chi-square, G^2). Significance test for differences in G^2 support conclusions regarding DIF. A model is specified containing terms (or components) reflecting possible sources of differential performance for examinee groups. This model, with each term adding sequentially to the others, forms a hierarchial model. The first term in the model focuses on the main effect of ability. The second term added to the model addresses the potential for a main effect difference between groups. The final, third term, then is sensitive to an interaction between group and ability. The process involves a sequential series of hypothesis tests, designed to assess the unique, additional contributions of individual components of a model to conclusions regarding differential item performance by examinee groups. If it is found through the sequential hypothesis testing procedure that the group and group by ability terms do not significantly improve the fit of the data to the model, it is generally concluded that no DIF exists. If the group term significantly improves the fit of the data to the model, then the conclusion is typically that uniform differences in item performance are present. It is only when the third, interaction term, provides a significant contribution to the fit of the data to the model that the interpretation of differential item performance is justified. More information on the log-linear approach to DIF can be found in Van der Flier, Mellenbergh, Ader, and Wijn (1984).

Mantel-Haenszel Method

The Mantel-Haenszel (MH) shows similarities to both the chi-square approaches and the log-linear methods presented above. Originally developed for use in medical applications, this method was introduced by Holland and Thayer (1986) as a technique for investigating differential item functioning.

The MH method is based on the odds ratio at each of the score points for the test. Two-by-two contingency tables are formed for each of the possible score values. Chi-square statistics are calculated at each of these score points, converted to odds ratios (similar to a proportion) in order to be on the same scale, and weighed by the product of the frequency of right and wrong responses divided by the frequency of responses. A significance test reveals those items for which it is more likely for a member of one group to get the item right than for a member of the other group.

Comparison of Scheuneman's Chi-Square, Log-linear, and Mantel-Haenszel Procedures

These three methods share a common characterization of the data as categorical. The two chi-square type methods, Scheuneman's Chi-Square and Mantel-Haenszel, differ primarily in the number of matched score categories. The Scheuneman method requires dividing the examinees into three to five categories based on total test score whereas the MH method creates distinct categories at every score point. Therefore, more data are needed for the MH method than for Scheuneman's Chi-Square. One important difference between the MH approach and the other two is that the MH method is not sensitive to inconsistency in differential item performance at differing score points in the distribution of test scores (e.g., interactions cannot be detected as in the log-linear method). Consider an item that revealed a complex pattern of performance difference such that low-scoring males were more likely to get the item right than their equally able low-scoring female counterparts, but for males with high overall test scores, they were less likely to get the item right than females with the same overall test score. The MH statistic is not sensitive to such inconsistent patterns of differential item functioning. If this kind of DIF was of interest, methods such as the log-linear approach would be more appropriate. Other methods, such as those based on item response theory (see below) are also sensitive to inconsistent patterns of DIF across the ability continuum and are attractive alternatives to the MH methods in those instances.

The chi-square based methods have been criticized for the use of gross categorization of test scores to form the ability groups. Obviously, the MH method, which employs as many ability groups as there are overall test score points, provides a more fine-grained analysis of item performance by ability for group members.

All three methods can be used with moderate numbers of examinees (e.g., 100 per identifiable subpopulation) and are relatively inexpensive to compute using standard statistical software packages. The log-linear method typically involves several analytical steps, which can result in higher cost than the other approaches based on classical methods.

Item Response Theory Based Methods

Item response theory provides a mathematical model that links performance on an item to specific features of the item (difficulty, discrimination, pseudo-guessing) with characteristics of the examinees (typically ability on the unidimensional trait being measured). This mathematical function may take on a variety of forms, depending on the specific item response theory model (1-, 2-, or 3 parameter models are frequently used in practice; for multiple-choice items, the 3-parameter model has been shown to have desirable features due to the inclusion of the pseudo-guessing parameter). Regardless of the specific item response model used, this mathematical relationship between item characteristic(s) and examinee ability can be described through an item characteristic curve (ICC). This curve represents the relationship between examinee ability and the probability the examinee will correctly answer the item. The key features from item response theory that show promise for detecting items that show differential item functioning are estimates of the item parameters (principally the difficulty parameter, b) and overall shape of the item characteristic curve.

IRT methods are very demanding in sample size and cost. Minimum sample size is generally given as 1,000 for the 3-parameter logistic model. Programs to perform the item calibrations and estimation of examinee ability can be difficult to implement and costly to run. Further, IRT models are based on the assumption of unidimensionality of the underlying latent trait being measured. Many licensure programs will find these requirements prohibitive for using item response theory approaches.

Wright, Mead, and Draba (1976) provide an index for quantifying the difference in b parameter values between two populations that is based on the Rasch model. In the Rasch model, the a parameter (discrimination) values are assumed to be invariant across the items in the test and no guessing is assumed. Therefore, the only reason for differences in item performance is the item's difficulty (i.e., the b parameter) and the examinee's ability (i.e., Θ). After calibrating the test items using data from the two groups and converting them to the same scale, Wright et al. suggest the calculation of an index that is approximately distributed as a t-statistic. They suggest using a critical value of plus or minus 2 to detect items that show differential item functioning.

Lord (1977, 1980) suggested an approach that involves a simultaneous test of the differences between the a and b parameters for two groups. This methods involves several calibrations: first with the two groups combined in order to get improved estimates of the c parameter. Then these c values are held constant and the a and b parameters are re-estimated for the two groups separately. These estimates would then need to be transformed to the same scale. An asymptotical chi-square test is available to test the simultaneous equality of the a and b parameters for the two populations of interest.

Linn and Harnish (1981) proposed a method that only requires one item calibration. Using the calibrations based on the total sample size, ability estimates (Θ) for members of the focal groups are determined. Then estimated test performance and actual test performance for focal group members are compared; DIF is assessed using a standardized difference score.

Rudner, Getson, and Knight (1980) proposed a method that is based on the item characteristic curves for the two groups. The items are calibrated separately for the two groups and then put onto a common scale. The area between these two ICCs is then determined. No statistical test is available to detect DIF using this approach. However, items showing large differences can be identified for further analysis or study.

Comparison of Item and Ability Estimation Approaches

Lord's method has not been used very much in empirical studies, in part due to the large demand for item calibrations (for total group and each of the comparison groups). Some research has shown that it does not agree well with other empirical methods for assessing DIF (Shepard, Camilli, & Averill, 1981). The Linn and Harnish method is promising as it only requires one calibration (for the total group). This is particularly important as many times there are insufficient numbers of members of the focus group to provide stable item parameter estimates. The Wright et al. method has been shown to confound other sources of model misfit with the DIF results, leading to inappropriate statements of DIF for certain items (Shepard, Camilli, & Williams, 1984). Rudner's approach is not used much in application due to the lack of appropriate statistical tests.

APPLICATIONS OF ANALYTIC METHODS TO TEST DEVELOPMENT

Test developers have used evidence about test items' performance to make decisions about test development, test scoring, and future test administration. The purpose of this section is to highlight some of these applications and to provide a critical analysis of their appropriateness for creating valid and reliable licensure examinations.

Golden Rule. One noteworthy application of item performance data for developing licensure examinations is what has come to be known as the "Golden Rule Method." This method resulted from an out-of-court settlement between the Golden Rule Insurance Company and Educational Testing Service. For more information about that case and the details of the settlement, see Phillips (1993).

Actually, this method does not incorporate differential item functioning data (that is why it was not identified as one of the methods for identifying items that perform differentially for subpopulations of examinees). Instead, this approach is based on overall performance differences by identifiable subgroups of examinees.

Based on pilot or pre-testing, the proportion of examinees correctly answering each item in each of the identifiable subgroups is determined (for example, Hispanic examinees and White examinees). When selecting test items for the operational test, items are selected first that show minimal between-group performance differences. Items that show large between-group performance differences are only considered for inclusion in the test if there are not other available items to satisfy the test specifications.

This method has received strong reactions from the measurement community. (See the 1987 issue of *Educational Measurement: Issues and Practice, 6,* for commentary by Faggen, Rooney, Linn & Drasgow, Bond, Jaeger, & Weiss.) Concerns focused on using empirical decisions, rather than table of specifications, for forming the test content. In 1987, then ETS President Gregg Anrig published a statement in which he details why ETS now feels the settlement was a mistake (Anrig, 1987).

Item Pool Maintenance. Many licensure test programs have item banks that are maintained over a period of years. Chapter 8 of this volume is specifically devoted to the development and maintenance of item banks for licensure test purposes. Typically, item information denoted in the bank consists of item classification, history of item administration and performance data, and occasionally information about DIF is detailed. Evaluations from panel members regarding appropriateness could also be maintained in the item bank data base. It is strongly recommended that DIF data be routinely gathered and reported in the item bank data base in order to monitor the status of the item with regard to differential item functioning. An item may have passed initial screening for DIF and subsequently be found to perform differentially for other, or even the same, identifiable subgroups. DIF analysis should be an ongoing part of the statistical analysis program.

Operational program applications. Even in the best of circumstances, when item development practices are exemplary and control/monitoring systems routinely in place, items occasionally will show differential performance on operational licensure examinations. The licensure administrator then has to decide on the best approach to deal with test scores that may not support valid and fair interpretations. First and foremost, any item that shows differential item functioning must be scrutinized for bias. If differential performance is supported by the construct being assessed, then the differential performance is valid, and the item should be maintained in the operational test score. However, if the differential item performance is an extraneous source of score variance, and not part of the construct being measured, serious problems exist when using the total test score for licensure decisions. One obvious solution would be to remove the item from the examination and rescore the test for all examinees. Although this has the advantage of removing the offending item from the test score, it has serious consequences. First, removing the item from the test changes the overall match of the test to the table of specifications. This is particularly worrisome for categories where limited numbers of items make up that component of the test. Further, changing the number, and character, of the items in the operational test will distort the cut score or standard previously established for determining those who pass the examination and those who do not.

This is another reason why differential item functioning is particularly crucial in licensure examinations. Not only are the decisions being made from performance on the examination high-stakes, and therefore, necessitate high standards for test validity, but decision reference points often are already in place and are subject to distortion when decisions to redesign the test occur after test administration. Test developers in licensure applications, therefore, must pay serious attention to those methods which are designed to diminish the presence of items that are potentially biased. Methods such of those described in this chapter are aimed at just that kind of effort.

APPLICATIONS OF DIF METHODS WITH PERFORMANCE-TYPE ASSESSMENT

The methods presented and discussed so far in this chapter are designed for use with multiple-choice items. Licensure programs have used performance-type assessments in their licensure tests for decades. These are frequently referred to as "clinical sets" in licensure testing applications. Unfortunately, there is very little known about the applicability or generalizability of these DIF methods to performance-type assessments.

The concern for differential item performance with performance-type assessments should be very high because there is additional potential for extraneous factors to influence test performance (Dorans & Schmitt, 1991; Miller, Spray, & Wilson, 1992; Oppler, Campbell, Pulakos, & Borman, 1992; Zwick, 1992). Often performance-type assessments are scored on a subjective basis. Many times, it is obvious to the scorer not only the quality of the performance, but the status of the examinee on many of the group identifiable traits used with objectively scored tests (ethnic group membership and gender, for example). Therefore, scorer subjectivity is a source of differential performance that was not present with multiple-choice tests.

In addition to scorer subjectivity, some forms of performance-type assessments may be more prone to tap construct-irrelevant factors. For example, in instances where the examinee brings prepared materials to the testing site (as in portfolios), there is the possibility that some candidates may have unequal access to support services or high quality materials. Although some advocates of the performance assessment movement speculate that the advent of performance-type assessments will reduce group differences and improve test fairness, some evidence suggests the opposite may in fact result (Dunbar, Koretz, & Hoover, 1991). Therefore, the need for strong methods for assessing potential differential performance on performance-type assessment tasks is extremely high.

When developing performance-type assessments, tasks rather than items are the units that are scored. If the performance-type tasks yield dichotomous performance outcomes (right/wrong, for example) then the methods described above will work. It is the polychotomous nature of the score scales the leads to problems in generalizing the current methods to performance-type assessments. Some of the issues that need to be addressed when generalizing DIF methods to polychotomously scored tasks are: (a) How should the matching variable be defined? and (b) What analysis should be used to ascertain the presence of differential task functioning?

With performance-type tasks, typically fewer tasks make up the assessment. Therefore, there are fewer data points to use when forming the matched groups. This reduces the reliability of group categorization decisions. Zwick, Donoghue, and Grima (1993) report on a simulation study testing the efficacy of several strategies for forming matched groups for the purposes of differential task functioning analysis. These authors also provide some suggestions for extensions of the MH method to polychotomously scored items. These methods show promise for applications with performance-type tasks used in licensure testing.

CONCLUSIONS

The purpose of this chapter was to discuss differential item functioning in licensure tests. The high-stakes nature of licensure testing creates an environment where validity of licensure test score interpretations (particularly as they relate to licensure decisions) is extremely crucial. Factors that improve the validity of licensure test scores should be enhanced and those factors that decrease the validity of interpretations from licensure tests should be removed or reduced as much as possible. Factors that are irrelevant to the construct being measured, and the licensure decision being made, are examples of factors that should be removed from the test scores.

One way of identifying such task-irrelevant factors is through differential item functioning analyses. The purpose of these methods is to draw attention to items that show unexpected differences in performance across equally able members of identifiable subgroups of the candidate population.

The methods discussed in this chapter show promise for aiding in the removal or reduction of factors irrelevant to the construct being assessed by the licensure test. However, these methods are typically only applicable to dichotomously scored assessments. Much attention is needed in the development of DIF methods useful with performance-type assessments, such as clinical sets and portfolio assessments.

In addition to concentrated efforts needed in the area of polychotomously scored assessments, better theoretical bases are needed for explaining extraneous sources of score variance. It is one thing to find items in a test that show differential item functioning between identifiable subgroups of the candidate population. It is quite another to be able to reason whether this shown difference is part of the construct being assessed or a source of test interpretation bias. Empirical methods are only useful in singling out items that show unexpected score differences; theory is needed to understand and improve interpretations based on these empirical results. Recent work by O'Neill and McPeek (1993) and Schmitt, Holland, and Dorans (1993) show promise in contributing to the theory of differential item functioning for identifiable subpopulations. With a theory to rely upon, test developers will have a foundation to use in developing test questions that, by design, reduce unwanted sources of test score differences between subgroups. Until we reach this level of sophistication, the empirical results will drive these decisions.

Only those methods that direct attention to performance differences between matched subgroups were discussed at length in this chapter. Many earlier methods that were based simply on differences in overall group performance between identifiable subgroups of the candidate populations (such as the transformed item difficulty method, the Golden Rule procedure) were not considered as true DIF methods. Two categories of empirical methods were presented, those based on classical test theory and those from item response theory.

Licensure testing programs with large examinee populations have the luxury of more choice when considering empirical DIF methods. The CTT approaches are amenable to both small and large testing programs and those with large and small testing support budgets. Only testing programs with large examinee populations to draw from, and relatively large human, computer, and fiscal support systems will be able to use the IRT-based methods. Recent research has shown that comparable results often occur between these two methods (Hambleton & Rogers, 1989). Another issue in deciding between CTT- and IRT-based methods is the degree to which the licensure decision is based on a unidimensional construct. IRT methods, as presented in this chapter, assume an underlying unidimensional construct. Many licensure areas consist of subcategories or subdisciplines that may not be strongly unidimensional as a set. These issues must be addressed before a decision about the methods is finalized.

Licensure testing, unlike other kinds of testing, typically ends with a final decision of pass or fail. The decision rule is often set in advance and is based on an analysis of the licensure test performance that is deemed sufficient for a pass decision. The cut score decision, therefore, is also inextricably tied to the validity of interpretations based on candidate performance on the licensure test. The validity of these decisions is linked to the validity of the interpretations that are made as a function of the candidates' test scores. Task-irrelevant influences on test scores, therefore, are doubly dangerous in licensure testing: They affect the validity of the test score and they affect the validity of the cut score. It is, therefore, extremely critical that licensure tests are scrutinized for unwarranted sources of test performance. Differential item functioning methods provide an approach for identifying potential sources of test invalidity. In the environment of high-stakes licensure testing the costs of errors are extremely high; DIF provides a means to purification of the test score to match more directly those knowledges, skills, and abilities that are salient to the licensure decision.

REFERENCES

Anrig, G. R. (1987, January). "Golden Rule": Second thoughts. *APA Monitor,* p. 3.

Berk, R. A. (Ed.). (1982). *Handbook of methods for detecting test bias.* Baltimore: Johns Hopkins University Press.

Bond, L. (1987). The Golden Rule settlement: A minority perspective. *Educational Measurement: Issues and Practice, 6,* 18-20.

Camilli, G. (1979). *A critique of the chi square method for assessing item bias.* Unpublished manuscript, University of Colorado, Laboratory of Educational Research, Boulder.

Camilli, G., & Shepard, L. A. (1994). Methods for identifying biased test items. *Measurement methods for the social sciences* (vol. 4), Thousand Oaks, CA: Sage Publications.

Clausen, B., Mazor, K., & Hambleton, R. K. (1993). The effects of purification of the matching criterion on the identification of DIF using the Mantel-Haenszel procedure. *Applied Measurement in Education, 2,* 269-280.

Cole, N. S., & Moss, P. A. (1989). Bias in test use. In R.,L. Linn (Ed.), *Educational measurement* (3rd ed.; pp. 201-219). New York: Macmillan Publishing Co.

Dorans, N. J., & Schmitt, A. P. (1991). *Constructed response and differential item functioning: A pragmatic approach* (ETS Research Report 91-47). Princeton, NJ: Educational Testing Service.

Dunbar, S. B., Koretz, D. M., & Hoover, H. D. (1991). Quality control in the development and use of performance assessments. *Applied Measurement in Education, 4,* 289-303.

Faggen, J. (1987). Golden Rule revisited: Introduction. *Educational Measurement: Issues and Practice, 6,* 5-8.

Hambleton, R. K., & Rogers, H. J. (1989). Detecting potentially biased test items: Comparison of IRT area and Mantel-Haenszel methods. *Applied Measurement in Education, 4,* 313-334.

Holland, P. W., & Thayer, D. T. (1986). Differential item functioning and the Mantel-Haenszel procedure. In H. Wainer & H. I. Braun (Eds.), *Test validity* (pp. 12-145). Hillsdale, NJ: Lawrence Erlbaum and Associates, Inc.

Holland, P. W., & Wainer, H. (1993). *Differential item functioning.* Hillsdale, NJ: Lawrence Erlbaum Associates, Inc.

Jaeger, R. M. (1987). NCME opposition to proposed Golden Rule legislation. *Educational Measurement: Issues and Practice, 6,* 21-22.

Linn, R. A., & Drasgow, F. (1987). Implications of the Golden Rule settlement for test construction, *Educational Measurement: Issues and Practice, 6,* 13-17.

Linn, R. A., & Harnish, D. (1981). Interactions between item content and group membership in achievement test items. *Journal of Educational Measurement, 18,* 109-118.

Lord, F. M. (1977). A study of bias using item characteristic curve theory. In N. H. Poortinga (Ed.), *Basic problems in cross-cultural psychology* (pp. 19-29). Amsterdam: Switts & Vitlinger.

Lord, F. M. (1980). *Applications of item response theory to practical testing problems.* Hillsdale, NJ: Lawrence Erlbaum Associates, Inc.

Marascuilo, L. A., & Slaughter, R. E. (1981). Statistical procedures for analyzing item bias based on chi square statistics. *Journal of Educational Measurement, 18,* 105-118.

Miller, T., Spray, J., & Wilson, A. (1992, July). *A comparison of three methods for identifying nonuniform DIF in polytomously scored test items.* Paper presented at the annual meeting of the Psychometric Society, Ohio.

O'Neill, K. A., & McPeek, W. M. (1993). Item and test characteristics that are associated with differential item functioning. In P. W. Holland & H. Wainer (Eds.),

Differential item functioning (pp. 255-276). Hillsdale, NJ: Lawrence Erlbaum Associates, Inc..

Oppler, S. H., Campbell, J. P., Pulakos, E. D., & Borman, W. C. (1992). Three approaches to the investigation of subgroup bias in performance measurement: Review, results and conclusions. *Journal of Applied Psychology, 77,* 201-217.

Phillips, S. E. (1993). The *Golden Rule* remedy for disparate impact of standardized testing: Progress of regress? *Education Law Reporter,* pp. 383-427.

Rooney, J. P. (1987). Golden Rule on "Golden Rule." *Educational Measurement: Issues and Practice, 6,* 9-12.

Rudner, L. M., Getson, P. R., & Knight, D. L. (1980). Biased item detection techniques. *Journal of Educational Statistics, 5,* 213-233.

Scheuneman, J. S. (1975, April). *A new method of assessing bias in test items.* Paper presented at the meeting of the American Educational Research Association, Washington, DC.

Schmitt, A. P., Holland, P. W., & Dorans, N. J. (1993). Evaluation hypotheses about differential item functioning. In P. W. Holland & H. Wainer (Eds.), *Differential item functioning* (pp.255-276). Hillsdale, NJ: Lawrence Erlbaum and Associates.

Shepard, L. A., Camilli, G., & Averill, M. (1981). Comparison of procedures for detecting test-item bias with both internal and external ability criteria. *Journal of Educational Statistics, 6,* 317-375.

Shepard, L. A., Camilli, G., & Williams, D. (1984). Accounting for statistical artifacts in item bias research. *Journal of Educational Statistics, 9,* 93-128.

Van der Flier, H., Mellenbergh, G., Ader, H. J., & Wijn, M. (1984). An iterative item bias detection method. *Journal of Educational Measurement, 21,* 131-145.

Weiss, J. (1987). The Golden Rule bias reducation principle: A practical review. *Educational Measurement: Issues and Practice, 6,* 23-24.

Wright, B. D., Mead, R. J., & Draba, R. (1976). *Detecting and correcting test item bias with a logistic response model.*(Research Memorandum No. 22). Chicago: University of Chicago, Department of Education, Statistical Laboratory.

Zwick, R. (1990). When do item response function and Mantel-Haenszel definitions of differential item functioning coincide? *Journal of Educational Statistics, 15,* 185-197.

Zwick, R. (1992, April). *Differential item functioning analysis for new modes of assessment.* Paper presented at the annual meeting of the National Council on Measurement in Education, San Francisco.

Zwick, R., Donoghue, J. R., & Grima, A. (1993). Assessment of differential item functioning performance tasks. *Journal of Educational Measurement, 30,* 223-251.

10|

ESTABLISHING PASSING STANDARDS

Craig N. Mills[1]

Educational Testing Service

INTRODUCTION

When tests are used to determine eligibility for a license, a passing standard or cut score must be established that divides the test scores into two categories: eligible for license or not. Standard setting has been widely researched and there are many reviews available (see, for example, Jaeger, 1989; Mills & Melican, 1988; Berk, 1986; Hambleton, 1980; Hambleton & Eignor, 1980; and Shepard, 1980a, 1980b), yet there is limited practical advice available for conducting standard setting studies and establishing standards. The one available resource (Livingston & Zieky, 1982) is somewhat dated. The purpose of this chapter is to provide a practical discussion of the entire standard setting process[2]. The steps in a standard setting study are explained. Commonly used standard setting methods are described, examples are provided, and the methods are critiqued. Procedures for conducting a standard setting study and adjusting the resulting preliminary standard are also explained. The chapter also discusses factors other than test performance that can be considered in setting standards on licensure tests.

[1]The author wishes to express his appreciation to Jay Breyer, Jim Impara, Skip Livingston, Jerry Melican, Maria Potenza, Nancy Thomas-Ahluwahlia, and Michael Zieky who, despite their disagreement with some of my positions, provided valuable reviews of this chapter.

[2]This chapter assumes that other important steps in the test development progress (e.g., establishing test specifications, conducting a job analysis) have already been completed. These steps are discussed in other chapters.

Standard setting is a multiple-step process involving different groups. There are typically three groups involved in the process: the "test sponsor," the investigator, and expert raters (or judges). The term "test sponsor" refers to the organization (e.g., licensure board), that has ultimate responsibility for the testing program. Although the sponsor may contract for testing services (test development, administration, and statistical analysis), it bears responsibility for the soundness of the test and testing program and has policy, financial, and legal responsibility as well. The investigator is the individual (or group) responsible for conducting the standard setting study and advising the test sponsor on all aspects of it. The investigator may be an employee of the sponsor, a testing services provider, or an independent consultant. The investigator's responsibilities extend from initial discussion of the design of the study through the actual data collection and analysis, and extend (typically) to acting as a resource during the deliberations leading to the establishment of the operational standard. Expert raters are typically educators and/ or practitioners in the field who are convened on one or more occasions to provide judgments about the test, examinees, and (possibly) the appropriateness of the recommended standard.

It is important to identify clearly which parties are involved in each step and what their specific responsibilities are. For example, test sponsors will often use an external investigator to conduct the standard setting study. This is sound practice if standard setting expertise is not available within the sponsor's organization, but does not exempt the sponsor from the responsibility of establishing the final standard. Figure 1 lists the steps in establishing a standard and the parties involved in each step. Each step is explained in the remainder of the chapter.

DETERMINE THE NEED FOR A STANDARD

In most licensure settings, the decision to develop a test is based on the need to make decisions about individuals (e.g., the individual has sufficient knowledge and skills to receive a license or not). However, it is important that the development of the licensure test itself is justified. It is appropriate, for example, for a legislative body to decide that there is sufficient risk to the public from ill-prepared practitioners that a test to distinguish between individuals who can provide appropriate service and those who cannot is necessary.

Livingston and Zieky (1982) suggest that test sponsors be prepared to justify the use of a standard. Although it may be true that fairer licensure decisions will result from the program than from a case-by-case consideration of applications, it is likely that there will be resistance to the imposition of a test. Test sponsors should know the likely criticisms and be ready to respond to them and contrast the fairness of the program with current practice. Several other issues should be considered as well. The sponsor should ensure that the appropriate reliability and validity analyses will be conducted. Administrative procedures should be addressed. For example, how often will individuals be allowed to test? Will periodic license renewal be required? Will current practitioners be "grandfathered" into the program? Under what conditions (if any) should exceptions be granted? How much advance notice will be given of the requirement to pass the test? These issues

Determine the Need for a Standard
Design the Study
    Selecting a Standard Setting Method
            Normative Standards
            Absolute Standards
                Arbitrary Standards
                Absolute Methods: Evaluation of the Test
                Absolute Methods: Evaluation of Individuals
            Setting Standards on Performance Assessments
                Simple performance assessments
                Complex performance assessments
    Planning Study Procedures and Analyses
            Multiple Iterations
            Providing Feedback on the Ratings
            Discussion of Ratings
            Placing Limits on the Judgments
            Adjusting Ratings for Guessing
            Providing Feedback on Examinee Performance
            Timing of the Ratings
            Item Criticisms
    Select Expert Raters
Conduct the Study
    Introductory Session
    Defining Minimal Competence
    Training the Raters
Evaluate Results and Establish Standard
    Adjusting the Standard
            Standard Error of Measurement Adjustment
            Observed Score Distribution Adjustments
            Other Factors That May be Considered
Document the Study

Figure 1. Steps in standard setting

are more directly related to the operational aspects of the testing program than to the establishment of a standard, but can affect standards. Interested readers are referred to Livingston and Zieky (1982) for a discussion of these and other issues.

DESIGN THE STANDARD SETTING STUDY

As is true in any inquiry, the design of the standard setting study is critical. Important considerations include selecting a standard setting method, identifying the data collection methodology, specifying analyses, and ensuring that the expert judges will have appropriate information and training, and the individuals representing the sponsor (i.e., the board) are aware of their responsiblity in setting the standard.

SELECTING A STANDARD SETTING METHOD

Standard setting methods fall into two broad categories, normative and absolute. *Normative standards* limit the number of individuals eligible for licensure by specifying a *percentage or number* of individuals who will be granted a license or by specifying a point in the distribution of scores as the standard (e.g., one standard deviation below the mean or the 55th percentile of the national norm group). *Absolute standards* are set to specify a specific required *level of performance* on the test. All individuals who attain that level of performance are granted a license, regardless of the number or percentage of individuals falling above or below the standard.

Normative Standards

An advantage of normative methods is that the passing rate is known before the test is administered. This can be useful when, for example, financial awards are based on test results and only a limited number of awards are available. For example, a scholarship or fellowship program might have a fixed amount of money to award and a set amount for each award. Awards will be granted to the individuals with the highest test scores until the funds are exhausted. Consider, for example, the test scores shown in Table 1. Suppose a university scholarship program has sufficient funds to support the six "most deserving" new students based solely on test scores (not a recommended practice, but used here for illustrative purposes). In the first year, awards are made to students receiving test scores of 93 and above, however, in the second year, the cut off is 96. If the rewards available are limited, it can be appropriate to use normative methods. These methods can also be used in a two-step selection process. For example, a test might be used to select some fixed number of individuals within the examinee group who would then proceed through an extensive interview process as finalists in a multi step assessment program.

Student	Year 1	Year 2
1	99	99
2	97	98
3	96	98
4	96	97
5	94	96
6	93	96
7	92	95
8	90	93
9	87	90
10	85	86

Table 1. Scores of the Top 10 Examinees in 2 Years

In most licensure situations, however, the intent is not to select a limited number of individuals, but rather it is to verify whether or not each individual should receive the benefits accorded to those who demonstrate at least "minimal competence." There is, therefore, typically no reason to limit the number of individuals passing the test. In fact, use of a normative procedure will not guarantee that all individuals who pass the test have similar levels of skill. If a test is administered to a particularly able group of examinees, some able individuals will not pass simply because there are so many high scoring examinees. Conversely, if the examinee group is not particularly able, some with relatively low scores will pass. Suppose the test results in Table 1 were for a licensure exam. The seventh highest scoring examinee in Year 2 seems deserving of licensure if the sixth person in Year 1 is. For this reason, normative standards are typically inappropriate in licensure settings.

Absolute Standards

Absolute standards are used to make judgments about each individual's test performance without regard to other individuals who have taken the test. Returning to Table 1, for example, suppose the standard was set at 96. In Year 1, only three individuals would pass the test. In Year 2, however, six examinees would pass. Regardless of the ability of the group tested, individuals demonstrating "acceptable" performance would be licensed each year.

Absolute standard setting methods fall into three broad categories: arbitrary methods, methods based on evaluation of test content, and methods based on judgments of expected or observed examinee performance.

Arbitrary Standards

Arbitrary standards[3] are established without regard to test content and difficulty. A test sponsor might, for example, make a statement such as "70% represents passing in most courses, so 70% will be the cut off on the test." Arbitrary standards have, appropriately, fallen into disuse. The primary reason these standards are inappropriate is that they do not take into account any characteristics of the test-taking population, the test, or the interaction between the two. As a result, the standards are likely to be unfair to some or all test takers.

Absolute Methods Based on Evaluation of the Test

The most commonly discussed standard setting methods based on evaluation of test content are the Nedelsky (1954), Angoff (1971), Jaeger (1978), and Ebel (1979) methods. These methods all require subject matter experts to rate every item in the test. With the exception of the Jaeger method, the methods also require estimation of the difficulty of items (or sets of items in the Ebel method) for a hypothetical group of "minimally competent" examinees.

---

[3]The term "arbitrary standard" is used in a specific sense here. All standard setting decisions are arbitrary in some sense. This does not, however, necessarily imply capriciousness. An arbitrary decision can be based on consideration of many factors associated with the test and the conditions under which it is being used. In this section, arbitrary means that the standard is set without regard to any of these factors.

The Nedelsky Method. Raters using the Nedelsky method evaluate each answer option of a multiple-choice question to predict whether or not the "minimally competent examinee" would identify it as incorrect. Item difficulty for those examinees is then estimated by assuming that they guess randomly among the remaining options. Because the rating task requires evaluation of the attractiveness of each option, the Nedelsky method ensures consideration of each component of each item (the question, incorrect options, and correct answer).

A modification of the Nedelsky procedure allows judges to rate distractors as "uncertain" (Saunders, Ryan, & Huynh, 1981). In this case, it is assumed that the minimally competent examinee will eliminate these distractors half of the time. The probability that the minimally competent examinee will provide a correct response is calculated similarly to the more common method, but "uncertain" distractors count as half an option.

An example of the Nedelsky method as it is typically implemented[4] is depicted in Figure 2. The figure shows one rater's evaluation of 10 multiple-choice questions. The first five items are five-option items and the remainder contain four options. For Item 1, the rater eliminated options A, C, and D, predicting that the minimally competent examinee would be able to identify those options as clearly incorrect. Thus, predicted item difficulty is .50 (assuming that minimally competent examinees guess randomly between the two remaining options). Probabilities are determined similarly for all items and summed to determine the expected test score of the minimally competent examinee. The average of these scores across raters is the initial estimate of the cut score.

There are at least four drawbacks to the method. First, it can only be used with multiple-choice tests because each distractor must be rated. Second, the assumption that examinees eliminate clearly incorrect options and then guess randomly among the remaining options does not reflect typical test taking behavior (Melican, Mills, & Plake, 1987). Third, some types of items (e.g. "multiple multiple choice[5]" items) are difficult to rate (Melican & Thomas, 1984). Finally, the estimated item difficulties cannot vary along the full range of difficulty, but are limited to discrete points on a non-symmetrical scale (Brennan & Lockwood, 1980). For a four-option multiple-choice question, for example, the only possible estimates of item difficulty are .25, .33, .50, and 1.00. Despite these drawbacks, the Nedelsky method remains popular in certain professions (although its popularity appears to have declined in recent years).

The Angoff Method. Raters using the Angoff method estimate the difficulty of each item for a hypothetical group of minimally competent examinees, usually by estimating the proportion of such a group that would answer the item correctly. The estimated cut off score for a judge is calculated by summing the item difficulty estimates.

---

[4]The Nedelsky method, as first published, required consensus among the raters on each distractor.

[5]Multiple multiple choice items typically present a list of possible answers of which one or more may be correct. Examinees must first identify which answers are correct and then locate the option that contains all correct answers.

Item		Options				Remaining	Probability
1	A̶	B	C̶	D̶	E	2	.50
2	A	B̶	C	D	E	4	.25
3	A̶	B̶	C̶	D	E̶	1	1.00
4	A	B	C	D̶	E	4	.25
5	A	B̶	C̶	D	E	3	.33
6	A	B̶	C	D̶		2	.50
7	A	B	C	D		4	.25
8	A	B	C̶	D̶		2	.50
9	A̶	B	C	D		3	.33
10	A̶	B	C̶	D		2	.50
				Recommended Cut Score for This Rater:			4.41

Figure 2. An example of the Nedelsky Method for 1 Rater and 10 Items

An example of the Angoff method is shown in Figure 3. Ratings of five experts for 10 items are shown. Cut scores range from 5.20 to 7.25 and average 6.59. Thus, the estimated cut score is seven items correct.

The Angoff method is the most commonly used standard setting method (Sireci & Biskin, 1992). Ratings are easily obtained, calculation of a cut score is simple, and the method can be easily explained. However, the method also has drawbacks. Raters may judge item difficulty solely on the stem of the item. Because distractors play an important role in item difficulty, raters who do not evaluate them carefully may over- or underestimate item difficulty. Furthermore, even with extensive training, the correlation between raters' estimates of item difficulty and actual item difficulty are often low (Melican & Mills, 1987; Cross, Impara, Frary, & Jaeger, 1984). Other criticisms include the subjectivity of the ratings, concern with the reliability of the method, and the sensitivity of the method to the level of expertise of the judges (Maurer, Alexander, Callahan, Bailey, & Dambrot, 1991).

There are several variations of the Angoff method. Commonly, data collection is simplified by providing raters with a fixed number of equally spaced data points to estimate performance of the minimally competent group (Bernknopf, Curry, & Bashaw, 1979). Some variations limit the number of estimates available, but use a non symmetric scale (ETS, 1976). The non-symmetric scale is designed to limit the effect of raters' tendencies to under-estimate item difficulty, but there is debate about whether this modification is appropriate. Other modifications include the use of multiple iterations (Melican & Mills, 1987; Cross, Impara, Frary, & Jaeger, 1984) and incorporation of ratings of item relevance.

The Ebel Method. The Ebel method requires an additional type of judgment about test questions. Items are rated on both their difficulty (easy, moderate, or hard) and relevance (essential, important, acceptable, or questionable). The ratings

Item	A	B	C	D	E
1	0.90	0.85	0.65	0.50	0.80
2	0.75	0.80	0.55	0.70	0.80
3	0.80	0.85	0.60	0.85	0.70
4	0.65	0.60	0.45	0.65	0.60
5	0.55	0.75	0.45	0.65	0.55
6	0.60	0.55	0.35	0.75	0.60
7	0.75	0.60	0.40	0.80	0.55
8	0.80	0.75	0.60	0.50	0.75
9	0.65	0.65	0.50	0.45	0.45
10	0.80	0.70	0.65	0.90	0.85
Cut Score	7.25	7.10	5.20	6.75	6.65
				Average Cut Score	6.59

Figure 3. An Example of the Angoff Method for 5 Raters and 10 Items

are used to place items into a 3 X 4 matrix. Next, raters estimate the percentage of items in each cell that will be answered correctly by the minimally competent examinee. The standard is calculated by multiplying the number of items in each cell by the proportion of items the minimally competent examinee is expected to answer correctly and summing the values. Variations on the method involve modifying the values of the relevance scale (Garvue et al., 1983; Skakun & Kling, 1980) or using a different scale, for example, item importance (Cangelosi, 1984; Skakun & Kling, 1980).

An example of one rater's application of the Ebel method is shown in the four panels in Figure 4. The top panel shows the rater's placement of items into the cells in the matrix. Items 1, 8, and 15, for example, have been rated as easy and essential. The next panel contains the count of items in each cell. The rater's predictions of the proportion of items in each cell that will be answered correctly by the minimally competent examinee are shown in the third panel. The values for each cell in the last panel are calculated by multiplying the number of items in each cell (the second panel) by the predicted performance for that cell (the third panel) The products are summed to produce a cut score.

An advantage of the Ebel method is that raters explicitly evaluate each item not only on its difficulty, but also on its relevance. Rating items on both dimensions allows hard, but essential, items to receive a higher rating than hard items of more questionable relevance. This provides raters the opportunity to adjust explicitly their expectations of performance based upon their evaluation of the appropriateness of the test content. (This practice could be viewed as inappropriate because, presumably, test content is based on a job analysis or similar procedure and all content is, therefore, presumed to be relevant.) Predictions of the expected performance of minimally competent examinees are based on groups of items, not

Placement of 15 Items into Categories by One Judge			
	Essential	Very Important	Important	Not Relevant
Easy	1, 8, 13	2, 14		
Moderate	9	3, 6, 12		7, 11
Hard		15	4, 5, 10,	

Number of Items Per Category			
	Essential	Very Important	Important	Not Relevant
Easy	3	2		
Moderate	1	3		2
Hard		1	3	

Predicted Proportion Correct by Category			
	Essential	Very Important	Important	Not Relevant
Easy	0.95	0.85	0.75	0.50
Moderate	0.90	0.80	0.60	0.30
Hard	0.75	0.60	0.45	0.15

Cutoff by Category and for Total Test			
	Essential	Very Important	Important	Not Relevant
Easy	2.85	1.70	0.00	0.00
Moderate	0.90	2.40	0.00	0.60
Hard	0.00	0.60	1.35	0.00
Total Test Cut Score			10.4

Figure 4. An Example of the Ebel Method for 1 Rater and 15 Items

individual items, which may be more accurate than predicting individual item performance. No research has been conducted, however, to verify this assumption. The requirement that judges perform multiple rating tasks makes training of judges, collection of data, and analysis of the data more complex than for other methods.

The Jaeger Method. The Jaeger method differs from other methods in the class in several ways. It incorporates ancillary information about the ratings of other experts and the impact of the ratings on passing rates in an iterative data collection design[6]. The concept of the minimally competent examinee is not explicitly used. The item rating is based on a judgment about the importance of the item in relation to the decision to be made (e.g., "Should every beginning practitioner be able to

---

[6]Since the introduction of the Jaeger method, the provision of ancillary information (e.g., data on the ratings of other raters, impact of the ratings on passing rates) in iterative procedures with other standard setting methods has increased.

Should Every Beginning Practitioner Answer This Item Correctly?					
Item	Rater 1	Rater 2	Rater 3	Rater 4	Rater 5
1	Y	Y	Y	Y	Y
2	Y	Y	N	Y	N
3	Y	N	N	Y	N
4	N	N	Y	N	N
5	N	Y	Y	Y	Y
6	Y	Y	N	N	Y
7	N	Y	N	Y	Y
8	Y	Y	Y	Y	N
9	Y	N	Y	Y	N
10	N	N	N	N	Y
Total	6	6	5	7	5
Cut Score					5.8

Figure 5. An Example of the Jaeger Method for 5 Judges and 10 Items

answer this item correctly?"). Selection of raters is not limited to individuals with subject matter expertise.

Initial standards are established by counting the number of items for which raters provide an affirmative response. Following the initial ratings, judges may revise their ratings after reviewing their cut scores, those of other judges, and the resulting passing rates.

Figure 5 contains an example of the initial ratings provided by five raters using the Jaeger method on a 10 item test. All raters agree that Item 1 should be answered correctly by beginning practitioners and all except Rater 5 agree that Item 10 need not be. Individual standards range from five to seven items correct with an average cut score of six items answered correctly.

Because the Jaeger method focuses more on an evaluation of test content than the interaction of the minimally competent examinee with test content, the standard setting process can include individuals who have an interest in the test results and content expertise, but who lack the familiarity with the examinee group necessary to focus on the minimally competent examinees only. Raters should, however, have sufficient experience with entry-level practitioners to be able to evaluate the test content relative to realistic expectations of the performance of those individuals. A potential drawback is that the rating task implies that passing status could be denied on the basis of an answer to a single item even though this is not how the method is implemented. Also, there is no clear rationale for how feedback about the expected pass rate or the test scores recommended by other raters should lead to revisions to individual item ratings.

Summary. Methods based on the evaluation of test content are popular. Among the advantages of the methods are (a) cut scores can be estimated prior to the administration of tests, (b) familiarity with groups of examinees (not specific individuals) is the basis upon which judgments are made, and (c) the rating tasks tend to be straightforward. However, the methods also have drawbacks. Estimating performance on individual items is difficult. Most raters are not able to estimate item level performance with great accuracy (Lorge & Kruglov, 1953; Thorndike, 1982; and Bejar, 1983). Another drawback of the methods is that they do not provide data on expected pass rates or misclassification errors. There is no way to evaluate the results of the individual judgments to determine their "accuracy."

Absolute Methods Based on the Evaluation of Individuals

Standard setting methods in this class rely on judgments of the expected passing status of individuals. Cut scores are established to maximize the agreement (typically) between the examinees' expected passing status and the observed test scores. The best known methods in this category are the contrasting groups and borderline group methods (Livingston & Zieky, 1982).

Contrasting groups. The contrasting groups method requires score distributions for two groups of examinees: those expected to pass (competent) and those expected not to pass (not competent). Judgments of who is expected to pass and who is not expected to pass are typically made by the instructors who have trained the examinees. The method allows assessment of the number of classification errors (qualified individuals who fail and unqualified individuals who pass). Several assumptions are made about the method. First, the group of examinees at hand are representative of examinees who will be licensed using the same test. Second, the test will be used to make a decision about the group of examinees on hand and who have been classified as either competent or incompetent by their instructor and for future examinees who will not be classified by instructors or others independent from the test. Third, the more competent examinees will obtain higher scores on the test and the less competent examinees will obtain lower scores, but some examinees classified as competent will obtain low scores and some examinees classified as incompetent will obtain high scores.

To illustrate the contrasting groups method a data set was generated for a hypothetical sample of 342 examinees. Based on assumption one above, these examinees are assumed to be a representative sample of all examinees who will be licensed or not based on their score on the licensure examination. These data are shown in Table 2 (a graphical representation is shown in Figure 6). In this data set, 224 candidates were classified as competent (expected to pass) and 118 were classified as not competent (not expected to pass).

In the contrasting group method the candidates are classified prior to testing (or, if after testing, without knowledge of the test score). After the test has been administered and scored, the distribution of examinee scores are partitioned at each score point into those examinees who were previously classified as competent and those who were classified as incompetent. The cut score is established by identifying the score that best represents the importance of the decision. That is,

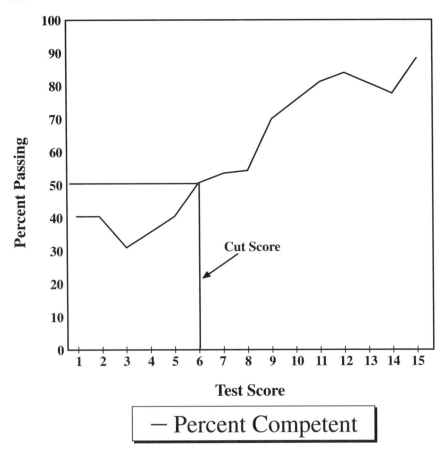

Figure 6. Example of the Contrasting Groups Method

if it is equally unacceptable to pass someone who should have failed as it is to fail someone who should have passed, the standard will be set at the score point where 50% of the examinees were classified as competent and 50% were classified as incompetent. In Table 2 this point corresponds to a score of 6. If passing an incompetent candidate was a more serious error (e.g., suppose it was considered twice as bad to license an unqualified candidate as to deny a license to a qualified candidate), then one might select the cut score such that the number of qualified who pass is twice that of the number of unqualified who pass. In Table 2 there is no passing score that corresponds exactly to that criterion, but the score of 9 comes closest (where 71% of those who scored a 9 were classified as competent, i.e., were expected to pass).

When using actual data, it may be the case that the distributions of scores for those expected to pass and those not expected to pass do not fit the assumptions above. Specifically, the scores of the examinees classified as competent do not

Score	Competent	Not Competent	% Passing
1	2	3	40
2	4	6	40
3	3	8	27
4	5	10	33
5	8	12	40
6	14	14	50
7	16	14	53
8	15	12	56
9	25	10	71
10	30	9	77
11	35	7	83
12	30	5	86
13	18	4	82
14	11	3	79
15	8	1	89
Total	224	118	

Table 2. Hypothetical Score Distributions for the Contrasting Groups Method

increase smoothly and the number of examinees classified as incompetent do not increase progressively at each lower score point. For this reason, Livingston and Zeiky (1982) have proposed techniques for smoothing the data (statistically adjusting the distributions) to accommodate the unevenness that might occur when dealing with real data, especially when the number of examinees is relatively small.

Borderline Group. The borderline group method bases the cut score on the test performance of individuals who have been independently designated as neither competent nor incompetent[7]. The cut score is typically placed at the median of the scores of the borderline examinees. If, however, the consequences of the decision are such that the costs of passing individuals who are not qualified is unequal to the costs of failing those who are, a different placement of the cut-off score may be considered.

Figure 7 depicts the performance of 108 examinees classified as borderline on a 15-item test. The median of the group (i.e., the cut score) is at a score of 9.

A weakness of the method is that the number of examinees rated as borderline is often small. Thus, a cut score may be established using a small and possibly unstable distribution of scores. Furthermore, the distribution of scores for the borderline group overlaps with those of competent and not competent groups. As a result, a cut score that fails half the borderline group students is likely to be

---

[7]Some experts object to the borderline group as being the wrong group upon which to base a cut score. Their argument is that the cut score should identify the minimally competent, not those who are neither competent nor incompetent. See Kane (1994) for a discussion of this issue.

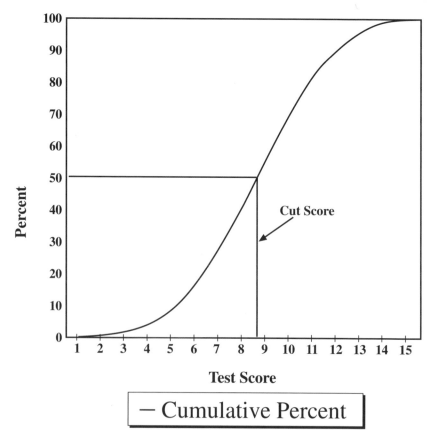

Figure 7. Example of the Borderline Group Method

different from one that best separates competent and not competent groups. In most situations, if it is possible to collect borderline group ratings, it will also be possible to collect data to implement the contrasting groups method. If so, contrasting groups is preferable because the data are directly related to the decision to be made (establishing a standard that separates competent from incompetent examinees).

Setting Standards on Performance Assessments

A recent trend in assessment is the inclusion of performance tasks in tests. Some of these tasks are relatively simple (e.g., writing an essay), but complex performance assessments are also gaining popularity. Complex performance assessments require examinees to perform tasks that have many components, each of which is important to job success. Such assessments are viewed as more relevant than the traditional multiple-choice tests that dominate most licensure tests.

Despite increasing use of performance assessments, there are many psycho-metric issues to be addressed. Issues such as topic selection, generalizability of the results, and scoring methods are being actively researched. Similarly, little guidance is available for establishing cut scores on complex performance assessments although this area is also being actively researched. This section describes some of the methods under investigation.

Simple Performance Assessments

In some cases a complex assessment may generate a simple result. For example, a diagnostician might be given a series of laboratory results and be required to write a report summarizing those results. A single score may be generated to summarize the adequacy of the report. In such cases, an independent group of raters (i.e., not the individuals who score the assessment) might read the reports and classify them as acceptable, unacceptable, or borderline. The contrasting groups or borderline group method can then be used to determine the cut score. In these cases, many of the limitations of these methods are reduced because the judgments are made on a work product, not on the individual. Thus, in the case of a performance assessment that yields a single, summative score, the standard setting task is relatively straightforward.

Complex Performance Assessments

In contrast to the simple example above, consider a laboratory assessment in which the examinee is required to draw a sample, conduct tests using the sample, and write a report. Several such tasks might be included in a single examination so that different types of samples must be drawn using different equipment, different analyses will be conducted, and several different types of reports may be required (e.g., an internal report, a report for a third party, or a report to the patient). As a result, there may be many tasks and each task may assess multiple (but not necessarily all) dimensions of performance. Thus, there can be several types of scores (in this example, scores within task, task scores, and a test score). Thus, the assessment is multi dimensional and the standard setting process will need to take this into account. An example of a complex performance assessment is shown in Figure 8. The test consists of three tasks (A, B, and C). Five skills are assessed, but not every skill is assessed for every task. Skills 1 through 4 are assessed on two of the tasks, but Skill 5 is only assessed in Task B. Scores are generated on, for example, a scale of 1 to 4 on each skill.

Skill	Tasks		
	A	B	C
1	X		X
2		X	X
3	X		X
4	X		
5		X	

Figure 8. A Design for a Complex Performance Assessment

FIRST STAGE

TASK A			Skills		
Score	1	2	3	4	5
1					
2			X		
3	X				
4				X	

Judgement   _____ Poor
     _____ Mediocre
     _____ Satisfactory
     _____ Noteworthy
     _____ Excellent

SECOND STAGE

		Tasks	
Rating	A	B	C
Poor			
Mediocre			X
Satisfactory			
Noteworthy	X		
Excellent		X	

Judgement   _____ Novice
     _____ Competent
     _____ Accomplished
     _____ Highly Accomplished

Figure 9. Data Collection Forms for a Two Stage Single Dominant Profile Analysis

Three methods have been proposed for setting standards on assessments such as the one described above. These are two-stage judgmental policy capturing (Jaeger, 1994), extended Angoff (Hambleton & Plake, 1994), and multi-stage dominant profile analysis (Putnam, Pence, & Jaeger, 1994). The methods have not been used operationally and it is unclear how (or if) they will be implemented. That notwithstanding, they represent the current state-of-the-art and should be considered by test sponsors using complex assessments.

Two-stage Judgmental Policy Capturing. Judgmental policy capturing relies on regression analysis of raters' judgments about profiles of scores to determine the standard. In the first stage, raters are shown profiles of scores on skills measured by each task. The raters judge the profile (e.g., Poor, Mediocre, Satisfactory, Noteworthy, Excellent[8]). For the second stage, profiles are generated based on evaluations of the individual task ratings in the first stage. These profiles are then rated according to the decision to be made on the basis of the test results (e.g., Novice, Competent, Accomplished, and Highly Accomplished). Figure 9 contains

___
[8]These labels were used by Jaeger (1994) to collect judgments designed to identify superior performance. Different labels might be used in different settings.

two examples of profiles. The first is a profile of skill scores on Task A and the second contains a profile for the three tasks.

Extended Angoff. Hambleton and Plake's (1994) extended Angoff method is an extension of the Angoff method described earlier in this chapter. That is, raters provide their expectations of the score of a minimally competent examinee on each dimension for which scores are generated. The Angoff method is extended by allowing raters to weight the skills according to their perceptions of the relative importance of each skill. Cut scores are established by multiplying the ratings by the weights and summing the resultant values.

Multi-Stage Dominant Profile. The multi-stage dominant profile method (Putnam, Pence, & Jaeger, 1994) was implemented as part of the same study in which the two-stage policy capture analysis and the extended Angoff methods were introduced. It was developed in response to raters' dissatisfaction with the other methods, especially the extended Angoff method. The method incorporates more direct data collection about raters' policies regarding acceptable performance through a three-stage process: policy creation, feedback, and implicit policy generation.

Policy Creation. In this stage, raters generate profiles depicting their perceptions of acceptable performance. The profiles show scores on each skill within each task that, taken together, would be considered acceptable. Multiple profiles are generated to depict the variation in performance that can be considered acceptable. A written statement is generated summarizing the policies underlying the profiles.

Feedback. Raters review their profiles and the profiles of other experts. Additional profiles are generated and evaluated by the experts.

Implicit Policy Generation. A series of "challenge profiles" (profiles that reflect the policy statements in most, but not all ways) are generated and submitted to raters for a final evaluation. Raters judge these profiles with a simple Yes/No response to the question of whether or not the performance was acceptable. Final standards are generated through a logistic regression.

Issues in Setting Standards on Complex Performance Assessments. As noted above, the use of complex performance assessments is not yet widespread and there are many issues to be resolved before standards for professional practice emerge. However, as such assessments gain popularity, they will undoubtedly be used as part of the licensure process.

To date there are no established methods for setting standards on complex performance assessments. The methods that have been proposed are complex (conceptually, operationally, and analytically). Furthermore, the methods require raters to consider issues (such as the weighing of scores) that have not traditionally been part of the rating portion of a standard setting study. At this point, it is unclear whether the methods will be refined in ways that allow their routine use in licensure settings or whether other methods will have to be developed.

WHICH METHOD IS BEST?

None of the methods described above can be designated as the "best" because there is no way to verify their validity. However, Berk (1986) has listed criteria for evaluating standard setting methods. Using prior research, the *Standards for Educational and Psychological Testing* (American Educational Research Association, American Psychological Association, & National Council on Measurement in Education Joint Committee, 1985) and court decisions, Berk developed technical and practicability criteria that can be applied to all methods. Drawing from Fitzpatrick (1984), he also listed additional criteria that apply specifically to methods based on evaluation of test content. Berk's criteria are summarized below:

Technical Criteria

1. The method should classify test takers into mutually exclusive groups.
2. The method should be sensitive to the difficulty of the test.
3. The method should incorporate evaluation of the opportunities examinees have had to learn the material presented (unless that information is gathered elsewhere)[9].
4. The method should yield appropriate statistical information.
5. The method should take into account differences between the "true" standard (on the true-score scale) and the observed standard.
6. The method should allow for evaluation of classification errors.

Practicability Criteria

7. The method should be easy to implement.
8. The results should be easy to compute.
9. The explanation of the method should be understandable by people who are not experts in measurement.
10. The method should be credible.

Additional Criteria

11. The effect of "social comparisons" (raters comparing themselves to other, more influential raters) should be minimized and informational influences maximized.
12. Exposure to the opinions of others can result in raters changing their views to conform to the opinions of others and should be avoided.
13. Group discussion among the raters is desirable, but is likely to be biased in favor of the majority opinion of the group unless structured procedures are implemented to ensure that all positions are stated.
14. The effect of normative judgments about ratings can be limited by providing objective information about test performance.
15. If opportunities are provided for revision to judgments, public statements of initial positions should be avoided.

No method satisfies all of the criteria. Depending on the situation, however, any of the methods described in this chapter can yield an acceptable and defensible cut score. However, consideration of these criteria in conjunction with other information (e.g. the importance of the decision, political considerations in the process, etc.) can help guide the selection of the most appropriate method for a given situation.

---

[9]An argument can be made that this criterion should not apply to licensure tests. If the content of a question covers a critical component of the professional that is required to protect the public, opportunity to learn may be relatively unimportant to the licensure decision.

Planning Study Procedures and Analyses

Data collection procedures in standard setting studies can be complex. Among the decisions that will affect procedures are whether (a) multiple iterations will occur; (b) feedback will be provided about the ratings of others; (c) raters will discuss their ratings and, if so, at what point; (d) limits will be placed on judgments of item difficulty (e.g., use of discrete categories with the Angoff method); (e) corrections for guessing will be applied to the ratings or the resulting standard; and (f) actual test or item performance information will be provided during the ratings and, if so, at what points. Another decision that will affect procedures is the timing of the study (before or after the test has been administered). Procedures should also address how item criticisms will be handled. Each issue is summarized briefly below.

MULTIPLE ITERATIONS

Some standard setting studies involve multiple iterations. Following an initial rating, additional information is provided. This information can consist of summaries of the ratings of individual judgments, data on item performance, information on the effect of the initial ratings on passing rates, and so on. The exact information provided depends on the design of the study and the data available. In some cases, there are two iterations and in others, three iterations occur.

The Jaeger method incorporates iterative judgments into the process. Following the introduction of the Jaeger method, iterative procedures became more popular with other methods as well (Mills & Melican, 1990; Melican & Mills, 1987; Cross, Impara, Frary, & Jaeger, 1984). Given the increased interest in providing feedback to raters, iterative procedures are gaining acceptance. However, use of an iterative procedure assumes the capability to summarize ratings in a standardized manner as the study progresses (i.e., on a "real-time" basis). If this cannot be done, the value of an iterative procedure is lessened although group discussion (based, for example, on a show of hands about item ratings) is a useful method for providing a basis for revising initial ratings.

PROVIDING FEEDBACK ON THE RATINGS

A common feature in iterative procedures is the provision of information to the raters on the ratings provided by others. Research indicates that providing information on the ratings of other experts often results in revisions to initial ratings (Friedman & Ho, 1990; Busch & Jaeger, 1990; Melican & Mills, 1987). Typically the number and magnitude of revisions is small. However, the studies suggest that the revisions usually result in reduced variation across judges and increased accuracy with regard to actual item difficulty.

DISCUSSION OF RATINGS

Allowing judges to discuss their ratings, identify items for which there is significant variation among the ratings, and determine items that one or more raters may have misinterpreted is common. Most iterative procedures provide for group discussion of ratings. The timing and extent of the discussion vary. Some investigators allowing discussion during the initial rating, some during the second iteration (e.g., Busch & Jaeger, 1990), and some following the second iteration (Melican & Mills, 1990). Given the advice of Fitzpatrick (1984) that group discussion can have negative influences, discussion during the first rating is probably undesirable. Even when discussion occurs following the initial rating, the investigator should ensure that the discussion is structured in such a way that a single individual cannot dominate and that all raters have opportunities to provide input to the discussion.

PLACING LIMITS ON THE JUDGMENTS

Some investigators place lower limits (i.e., chance) on the ratings provided. However, some items are quite difficult and particular distractors may be appealing to individuals with partial knowledge, so it is not uncommon for examinees to score below chance on those items. Therefore, this practice is not recommended. Reid (1985) investigated the effect of placing upper limits on ratings. Raters first estimated item difficulty for the total group and then estimated difficulty in the minimally competent group. This procedure resulted in lower ratings than a control group, which rated item difficulty for the minimally competent group twice. Reid concluded, however, that the results were inconclusive as to whether the procedure resulted in more "realistic" estimates. Neither placement of lower or upper bounds on ratings has been widely used.

ADJUSTING RATINGS FOR GUESSING

Some investigators apply corrections for guessing to estimates of item difficulty. If a test is scored using a penalty for incorrect answers, each rater's cut score may be adjusted downward to correct for this penalty (Livingston & Zieky, 1982). Cross et al. (1984) point out that the wording of the task assigned to the raters can alleviate the need for corrections for guessing. Asking the judges to estimate what examinees would *do* incorporates guessing behavior in the estimates. Asking what the minimally competent examinee would *know* does not incorporate guessing and provides a statistically appropriate basis for making a correction for guessing[10]. Melican and Plake (1984) point out, however, that this adjustment, which raises the standard, may be overly harsh if examinees omit questions.

PROVIDING FEEDBACK ON EXAMINEE PERFORMANCE

When standards are to be set on existing tests for which performance data (item difficulty and score distributions) are available, the data can be provided during the standard setting study. This can serve to set an upper limit on ratings, but unlike the Reid (1985) procedure, the data are from examinees, not from raters' previous estimates of performance. Norcini, Shea, and Kanya (1988) and Melican and Mills (1986) recommend this procedure as one that can improve the accuracy and consistency of ratings. Some investigators have also attempted to use performance data to calibrate ratings as a means of equating (Rogosa, 1982; Thorndike, 1982).

---

[10]If the test is scored on the basis of the number of questions answered correctly, corrections for guessing may still apply. If raters estimate what an examinee would know, the estimates do not include the number of questions that would be answered correctly due to guessing.

TIMING OF THE RATINGS

Typically, item ratings are collected in a special study using an intact test form. An expert group is convened and trained. The experts then provide estimates in one meeting. One study (Norcini, Lipner, Langdon, & Strecker, 1987) suggests that it may be possible to conduct the ratings by mail. This study is limited, however, in that the same raters provided three sets of ratings (before, during, and after the meeting) and the raters were the same individuals who wrote the test questions.

Ratings can be provided when the questions are written, when they are reviewed, when pretest data have been collected, or immediately following the first administration of the test. If a study incorporates feedback to raters on examinee performance, ratings need to occur following either pretesting or the first administration. Using pretest data is appealing because the data can be used to establish a cut score before the test is administered (examinees then know the "rules of the game before they play"). Care should be taken, however, to ensure that the pretest data are reliable. If examinees are aware that the pretest does not count, there is a risk that they will not take the test seriously and pretest statistics will indicate that the questions are more difficult than they really are.

ITEM CRITICISMS

It is not unusual for experts to object to the wording or key of a question during the rating session, especially if test development committees (who typically provide item reviews as part of their work) provide the judgments. It is important to recognize that, although items may need additional reviews and revisions, they are presented to judges under the assumption that they are of sufficient quality to be administered to examinees in their current form. Thus, ratings should be provided on the items as presented. A mechanism should be available, however, to allow experts to register their concerns and suggest item revisions. This will allow raters to identify items for further review (or discussion following the rating) without distracting them from the task at hand. Ratings can be gathered on the original and revised version of the item and, following a decision about which version will appear in the test, the appropriate ratings can be used to derive the standard.

Initial study results are often modified (see the section "Adjusting the Standard" below), so decisions are required at this stage concerning which method will be used to modify the study results and, if the method relies on expert ratings, forms will be required to collect those data.

Select Expert Reviewers

Virtually all standard setting methods require input from experts. Not all members of a profession will be qualified to be raters and different methods may require experts with different experience. Experts will need specific knowledge, skills, and experiences for the tasks they are to perform. The selection process should ensure, to the extent possible, that experts represent the full diversity of the profession and the various constituencies affected by the test. A more complete discussion of the qualifications of expert raters can be found in Jaeger (1991).

A typical question that arises is how many judges are required. The usual answer is "as many as can be obtained," but this provides little practical guidance.

Norcini, Shea, and Grosso (1991) argue that acceptable results can be achieved with as few as five raters. Jaeger (1991), however, recommends calculating the number of raters based on the standard error of the mean of the ratings and the standard error of measurement of the test. Jaeger's work suggests that the number of raters should be substantially greater than Norcini et al. recommend. The exact number depends on the precision desired. In one example, Jaeger's procedures would require 13 raters to obtain a standard error in the ratings that is one quarter the standard error of measurement of the test.

CONDUCT THE STUDY

If the study design and planning have been comprehensive, there will be sufficient staff, materials, and equipment on-site for the study. Thus, the mechanics of data collection, form design, etc. are not discussed here. However, an important component of the study is the initial training of the raters. The training session, held prior to the actual rating of test items, frequently consists of four components: explaining the process, setting the context of the task, developing a common definition of the minimally competent examinee, and training judges to rate items.

Although the standard setting literature indicates that training is important (Mills & Melican, 1988; Fitzpatrick, 1984; Livingston & Zieky, 1982) little documentation is available regarding specific approaches to training. Much of the available literature addresses training in the context of applying the relevant procedure, not training related to defining minimal competence (Mills & Melican, 1986; Francis & Holmes, 1983).

An approach to developing a definition of minimal competence was proposed by Mills, Melican, and Ahluwalia (1991). The approach relies on group discussion to establish the definition of minimal competency and requires a substantial time commitment.

Introductory Session

Most raters will not have previously participated in a standard setting study and are unlikely to be familiar with standard setting techniques. An introductory session that provides an overview of the process, their roles, the data collection forms and use of the data can minimize confusion later. Raters will vary in their knowledge of test content, the purpose of the test, and the overall licensure process. They are also likely to vary in their support for the use of the test in the licensure process. The initial session should address these issues to reduce the probability that the ratings will be affected.

An understanding of the decision to be made on the basis of the test results is important. If, for example, the test is an assessment of academic knowledge, raters need to understand that predicting on-the-job performance is not of concern. Raters should understand that the test will not assess every aspect of the job and that their task is not to critique the test or its content, but rather it is to estimate performance on the instrument as it exists. Knowledge necessary to protect the public is an appropriate focus. Raters frequently have concerns about test content, the adequacy of content coverage, and test format. These are important concerns, however, they have usually been addressed separately as part of the test development process.

Typically, for licensure examinations, a job analysis will have been conducted and the test content specifications will be the basis for the content specifications.

A brief discussion of the development of the content specifications and test items can address these concerns and reduce their effect on the ratings. As a result, raters should understand what work has occurred prior to the study and their role in the overall process.

Defining Minimal Competence

An explicit definition of minimal competence is required for most standard setting procedures. Simply, minimal competence is the "minimal level of knowledge and skills required for licensure." Unfortunately, this simple definition is not an operational definition of minimal competence and, therefore, is inadequate given the variety of skills being tested, the different ways they can be acquired, and the possible compensatory effects that strengths in one area might have for weaknesses in another area.

A discussion of minimal competence may begin by delineating the skills routinely required in practice. Refinements can then address typical and minimally acceptable proficiency (such as common, but acceptable errors). Using the test specifications can limit the discussion to those skills assessed by the test. Each major area of the specifications should be discussed.

The initial discussion about the range of skills in the general population of practitioners can be refined to focus on the level of those skills required for licensure. For example, inefficient procedures may not represent good practice, but they may be acceptable when the focus is the granting of a license. Statements of typical proficiency should be refined further to apply directly to the granting or renewal of a license.

The purpose of the discussion is to develop a concise definition of minimal competence. When completed, it may address the following statements:

A minimally competent examinee must know AT LEAST ...

A minimally competent examinee would not be expected to ...

The purposes of the training are to (a) set the context within which the ratings can occur; (b) define the tasks to be performed (and those not to be performed) by the raters; (c) eliminate, to the extent possible, the effect of irrelevant variables from the rating session; and (d) develop a common definition of minimal competence. The goal is not to have agreement on all ratings, but to ensure that differences are not due to irrelevant factors.

Training the Raters

Following the establishment of a definition of minimal competence, but prior to the actual ratings, a training session should be held to ensure that raters understand the rating task and have some understanding of the difficulty of the questions to be rated. The need for training is evident when the literature on accuracy of item ratings is reviewed. Numerous studies have documented the tendency of judges to under-estimate item difficulty and to achieve only modest correlations between actual and estimated difficulties (Lorge & Kruglov, 1953; Halpin & Halpin, 1983; Bejar, 1983; Thorndike, 1982; Schaeffer & Collins, 1984).

However, as noted previously, provision of information on item difficulty can improve ratings. Therefore, training which allows raters to compare their estimates with actual data is appropriate (Mills & Melican, 1986). The training should also include practice on all types of items included in the test because research has also shown that certain characteristics of questions can make them more difficult to rate accurately (Melican & Thomas, 1984; Smith & Smith, 1988).

There is no generally established guideline for how extensive the training should be. However, Reid (1991) has proposed three criteria for determining whether raters are well trained. According to Reid, ratings should be stable over time, consistent with the relative difficulties of items, and realistic relative to actual performance. Saunders and Mappus (1984) suggest that final results may be more consistent, accurate, and homogeneous if the results from raters who do not meet training criteria are eliminated from the analysis. Care should be taken in doing so, however, because the representativeness of the group may be threatened (Reid, 1991) and it is not necessarily the goal of a standard setting study to reduce variations in the ratings. Furthermore, unless the criteria for exclusion are established prior to the study, criticsms may be raised about the appropriateness of the procedure.

EVALUATE RESULTS AND ESTABLISH STANDARDS

The results of the study should be carefully reviewed to ensure that the experts understood the task, were diligent in their application of study procedures, and that the procedures established were adequate. A careful review of the results can identify flaws in the study that may possibly be corrected. In some cases, this pre analysis will lead to the conclusion that the study must be repeated. Although it is unpalatable to repeat a study, there are occasions when this is the only feasible solution. For example, in some cases, it will become clear that most raters did not understand their assigned tasks. In this case, there is no way to use the study results appropriately and new panels must be convened.

Many factors can (and should) be considered in the establishment of the final standard. The standard setting data are of great importance and value; however, it should be remembered that this information was provided in a very specific setting, focusing (usually) on only the content of the test or the test and the examinees taking it. It is not unusual for test sponsors to carefully plan a standard setting study, but to ignore the need to consider the results of that study in the context in which it will be applied. For example, a standard that is too stringent could result in serious shortages of licensed professionals, whereas one that is too lenient could put the public at risk. In either case, the entire testing program could be called into question. Therefore, planning should include consideration of how the cut score derived from the study will be evaluated and, if necessary, adjusted, and by whom.

Adjusting the Standard

The test sponsor's governing board or council typically has the ultimate responsibility for establishing the standard. If the board adequately represents all interested constituents, it may receive the study results directly and establish the standard. However, sponsors often wish to include others in the evaluation of the study results before establishing the standard. For example, a review group composed of representatives from employer organizations may be convened to review the study results and recommend the final standard. Ultimately, however, the final decision rests with the test sponsor or legal authority charged with establishing the standard. Both the advisory panel and the decision makers will need to consider whether or not the study results require adjustment. Several methods of adjusting the standard are available.

Standard Error of Measurement Adjustment

The standard error of measurement is an estimate of the dispersion of individuals' observed scores around their true scores (see Chapter 7, Impara & Stoker for a more extensive discussion). Errors of measurement can result in two types of classification errors. Individuals whose true score is just above the cut score may fail because errors of measurement result in an observed score that is lower than both the true score and the cut score. Lowering the cut score by a multiple of the standard error of measurement decreases the likelihood of this type of error. However, it increases the likelihood that individuals whose true score is slightly below the cut score will pass. The method is implemented by considering (a) the relative seriousness of each type of classification error and (b) the effect of measurement error on scores near the cut score. For example, if it is worse to fail a qualified individual than to pass an unqualified one, one standard error of measurement might be subtracted from the study value. Adjusting for errors of measurement is a common and defensible method for establishing cut scores[11].

There are, however, disadvantages to the standard error of measurement adjustment. It assumes that the cut score derived from the study is "correct" and that the only adjustments required are those necessary to account for measurement errors. Furthermore, discussions about the relative costs of the two types of error are sometimes in contradiction to the test results. It is not unusual for test sponsors to state initially that passing someone who should fail is worse than failing someone who should pass. Using the standard error of measurement adjustment, this would lead to a decision to raise the cut score. However, in practice, raters' expectations of performance often exceed actual performance and result in a need to lower the cut score (not due to errors of measurement, but due to overly optimistic ratings). Although the standard error of measurement adjustment should be a philosophical one that does not rely on test data, decision makers are often reluctant to make the decision without information about the impact of the adjustment. Although pass rates are useful in assessing the reasonableness of a cut score, the standard error of measurement adjustment can be criticized if it appears to have been used solely to adjust the pass rate without regard for the philosophical basis for the adjustment. However, methods for directly incorporating ratings of expected passing rates have been proposed and are described in the next section.

---

[11]It has also been suggested that cut scores might be adjusted using the standard error of the judges. This treats the raters as a random sample of potential panelists and the cut score is adjusted to compensate for possible sampling error. The method suffers from many of the same drawbacks as the standard error of measurement adjustment.

Observed Score Distribution Adjustments

The knowledge that experts have about the examinee population and their expectations about the percentage of the population that will pass the test can be used in conjunction with other information to establish final standards. The methods proposed by Beuk (1984), De Gruijter (1985), and Hofstee (1983) incorporate judgments about the expected performance of examinees. These methods assume that experts can provide estimates of the passing rate. All of the methods require observed score distributions, therefore, they cannot be implemented prior to the administration of the test (although the data can be collected prior to the test administration and applied before scores are reported). One of the strengths of these methods is that because the data used to calculate the adjustment are collected without knowledge of score distributions, they are less susceptible to criticisms that the standard was arbitrarily adjusted to yield an acceptable pass rate.

The Beuk Method

The Beuk (1984) method requires an estimated cut score and passing rate from each rater. The adjustment is a function of the variability of the experts' estimates of the cut score and passing rate. To implement the method, a line with slope equal to the ratio of the standard deviations of the experts' estimates of the cut score and passing rate is drawn through a point defined by the average absolute cut score and average passing rate. The intersection of this line and the cumulative frequency distribution becomes the recommended cut score. An example of the method is shown in Figure 10.

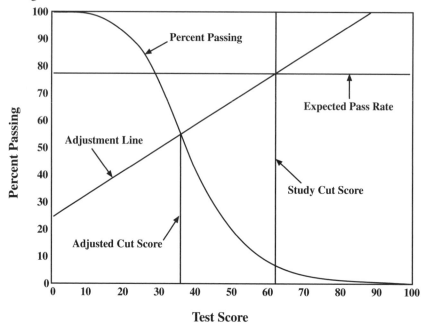

Figure 10. An Example of the Beuk Method

The Beuk method is straightforward. The only data required are a frequency distribution of test scores, the estimated cut scores and the expected passing rates. The computations are simple and the adjustment is logical; the more the judges agree on their estimates on one dimension (i.e., cut score or passing rate) the smaller the adjustment on that dimension. In practice, however, some experts have difficulty specifying expected passing rates if they have not had experience with large numbers of newly licensed practitioners.

The Hofstee Method

The Hofstee method requires estimates of the highest and lowest acceptable cut scores and passing rates. Two points are plotted using these four numbers. One point is defined by the minimum acceptable cut score and the maximum acceptable fail rate. The maximum acceptable cutoff score and minimum acceptable fail rate define the second point. Any point falling on the line segment defined by these two points is considered an acceptable combination of cut score and failing rate. The intersection of the line segment with the cumulative frequency distribution of scores defines the cutoff score. An example of the Hofstee method is shown in Figure 11.

The method is not complex. However, in practice the method is not always effective. The line segment depicting acceptable cut scores for any judge may not intersect the cumulative frequency distribution (Mills & Melican, 1987). In this case, the method cannot be used to adjust the standard because there is no acceptable combination of cut score and pass rate. (See the line for Judge 1 in

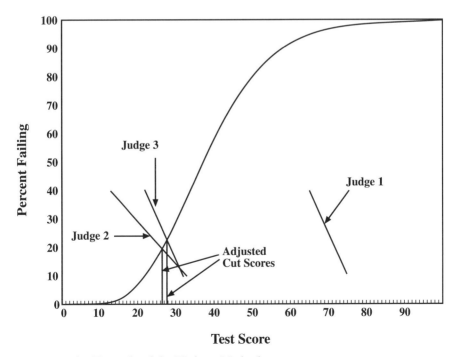

Figure 11. An Example of the Hofstee Method

Figure 11.) There are also questions about the global judgments of cut scores. If, for example, an Angoff method has been used, and separate estimates of minimum and maximum acceptable cut scores are collected, the calculated Angoff cut will not necessarily lie within the specified range of acceptable cuts.

The De Gruijter Method

The De Gruijter (1985) method is similar to the Beuk method. However, the De Gruijter method bases the adjustment on individuals' uncertainty about the accuracy of their own ratings. After the raters have provided estimates of the cut score and expected passing rate, they also provide estimates of their uncertainty of the accuracy of their estimates. The adjustment is a function of the ratio of these uncertainty estimates.

The uncertainty ratings are the strength of the method. It is the only method that incorporates raters' confidence in their ratings. The method is, however, computationally complex and difficult to explain. Further, experts frequently have difficulty specifying their uncertainty (Mills & Melican, 1987). Figure 12 shows an example of the DeGruijter method.

OTHER FACTORS THAT MAY BE CONSIDERED

In addition to consideration of test reliability, estimates of test difficulty, and expected passing rates, there are other factors that may result in adjustments to the

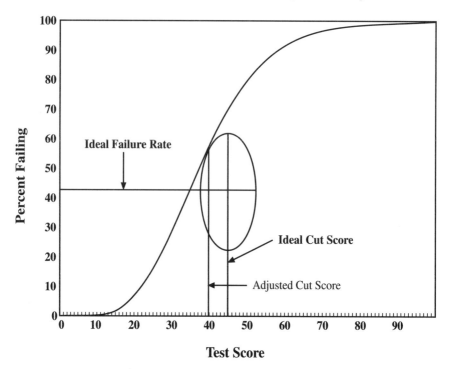

Figure 12. An Example of the DeGruijter Method

standard. Geisinger (1991) has listed several types of supplemental information that may be considered. The supplemental information that may be considered includes:

Organizational or Societal Needs[12]

If the number of individuals needed can be predicted accurately, the cut score can reflect this. It may be unreasonable to designate individuals as passing a test if they have little opportunity to be hired (Equal Employment Opportunity Commission, Civil Service Commission, Department of Labor, & Department of Justice, 1978).

Adverse or Disparate Impact Data

Consideration of passing rates for gender, race, and ethnic subgroups should be considered. This topic is covered in depth in Chapter 2.

Anomalies in the Rating Process

In the course of the study (or evaluation of the results) it may become apparent that there were problems with the evaluations provided by the judges. These problems could result in elimination of one or more rater's judgments or a new study. In other cases, the problems may require less severe remedies. Possible problems include (a) individuals who are designated as experts may prove not to have sufficient expertise for the task, (b) one or more raters may have misunderstood the task, (c) personal stakes in the outcome of the test may affect a rater's estimates, (d) some raters may be unduly influenced by others, (e) the group of raters may be insufficiently representative of the field, and (f) a rater has provided clearly inappropriate ratings (e.g., all items receiving the same rating). As noted previously, decisions to eliminate ratings should be based on previously enunciated criteria to avoid the appearance of arbitrary manipulation of the results.

Opportunities to Retest

If tests are not offered frequently, failing the test may result in significant delays in the opportunity for entry to practice (upon taking and passing a subsequent test). Thus, it is especially important that individuals who fail the test are truly below the cut score. Within the bounds of other constraints (protection of the public, for example), a more lenient standard might be established if the opportunities for retesting are limited.

MULTIPLE STANDARD SETTING TECHNIQUES YIELD DIFFERENT RESULTS

On some occasions, a test sponsor may implement multiple standard setting methods or conduct multiple studies using a single method. Norcini and Shea (1992) and Mills and Melican (1990) have shown that consistent standards can be obtained across groups and occasions using the same method. However, it is equally clear that different methods yield different results (see Jaeger, 1989). If multiple methods are used, a rationale will be required for choosing the method implemented or for the manner in which the results from the different methods are combined to arrive at a final standard.

---

[12]This issue is not relevant to licensure tests, but is included for completeness.

DOCUMENT THE STUDY

Establishing a cut score defines an arbitrary division of a continuous variable into a dichotomy. It does not represent "truth," but rather it is a representation of the collected wisdom (values) of professionals concerning the minimum skills necessary to enter the profession. Furthermore, because tests measure only a portion of what is important for success and because strengths in one area can often compensate for weaknesses in another, there will always be people who are qualifed, but are denied licensure and some who are not qualified, but receive a license. This is not to say, however, that standards are indefensible. If a standard is developed based on the reasoned judgment of experts using a professionally accepted methodology, it can be defended. Comprehensive documentation of the study planning, procedures, and outcomes will play an important role in the event of a legal challenge.

All aspects of the process should be documented. Memos covering the planning process, the selection of experts, the actual study and the deliberations leading to the final standard should be included in the documentation. Samples of data collection forms should be retained as should the results of the analyses.

CONCLUSION

Establishing a passing standard is an integral part of most licensure programs. Despite years of research, there is still no one best method of setting a cut score that can be aplied in all circumstances. However, there is a substantial body of research and practice that can guide the design and conduct of a standard setting study and the final establishment of the standard. This chapter has explained the steps in establishing a standard, reviewed methods available, and identified issues to be addressed during the process.

REFERENCES

American Educational Research Association, American Psychological Association, & National Council on Measurement in Education. (1985). *Standards for educational and psychological testing.* Washington, DC: American Psychological Association.

Angoff, W. H. (1971). Scales, norms, and equivalent scores. In R. L. Thorndike (Ed.), *Educational measurement* (2nd ed., pp. 508-600). Washington, DC: American Council on Education.

Bejar, I. I. (1983). Subject matter experts' assessment of item statistics. *Applied Psychological Measurement, 7,* 303-310.

Berk, R. A. (1986). A consumer's guide to setting performance standards on criterion-referenced tests. *Review of Educational Research, 56,* 137-172.

Bernknopf, S., Curry, A., & Bashaw, W. L. (1979, April). *A defensible model for determining a minimal cutoff score for criterion referenced tests.* Paper presented at the annual meeting of the National Council on Measurement in Education, San Francisco.

Beuk, C. H. (1984). A method for reaching a compromise between absolute and relative standards in examinations. *Journal of Educational Measurement, 21,* 147-152.

Brennan, R. L., & Lockwood, R. E. (1980). A comparison of the Nedelsky and Angoff cutting score procedures using generalizability theory. *Applied Psychological Measurement, 4*, 219-240.

Busch, J. C., & Jaeger, R. M. (1990). Influence of type of judge, normative information, and discussion on standards recommended for the National Teacher Examinations. *Journal of Educational Measurement, 27*(2), 145-163.

Cangelosi, J. S. (1984). Another answer to the cut-off score question. *Educational Measurement: Issues and Practice, 3*(4), 23-25.

Cross, L. H., Impara, J. C., Frary, R. B., & Jaeger, R. M. (1984). A comparison of three methods for establishing minimal standards on the National Teacher Examinations. *Journal of Educational Measurement, 21*, 113-129.

De Gruijter, D. N. M. (1985). Compromise models for establishing examination standards. *Journal of Educational Measurement, 22*, 263-269.

Ebel, R. L. (1979). *Essentials of educational measurement* (3rd ed.). Englewood Cliffs, NJ: Prentice-Hall.

Educational Testing Service. (1976). *Report on a study of the use of the National Teachers' Examination by the State of South Carolina.* Princeton, NJ: Author.

Equal Employment Opportunity Commission, Civil Service Commission, Department of Labor, & Department of Justice. (1978). Uniform guidelines on employee selection procedures. *Federal Register, 43*(166), 38290-38315.

Fitzpatrick, A. R. (1984, April). *Social influences in standard-setting: The effect of group interaction on individuals' judgments.* Paper presented at the annual meeting of the American Educational Research Association, New Orleans.

Francis, A. S., & Holmes, S. E. (1983, August). *Criterion-referenced standard-setting in certification and licensure: Defining the minimally competent candidate.* Paper presented at the annual meeting of the American Psychological Association, Anaheim.

Friedman, C. B., & Ho, K. T. (1990, April). *Interjudge consensus and intrajudge consistency: Is it possible to have both in standard setting.* Paper presented at the annual meeting of the National Council on Measurement in Education, Boston.

Garvue, R., Falkowski, C., Hoffman, L., McGuire, M., Mills, C., Rachal, J., Ransen, D., & Teddlie, C. (1983). *The 1983 National Teacher Examinations Core Battery Louisiana validation study: Final report.* Baton Rouge, LA: Louisiana State Department of Education.

Geisinger, K. F. (1991). Using standard-setting data to establish cutoff scores. *Educational Measurement: Issues and Practice, 10*(2), 17-22.

Halpin, G., & Halpin, G. (1983, August). *Reliability and validity of 10 different standard setting procedures.* Paper presented at the annual meeting of the American Psychological Association, Anaheim.

Hambleton, R. K. (1980). Test score validity and standard-setting methods. In R. A. Berk (Ed.), *Criterion-referenced measurement: The state of the art* (pp. 80-123). Baltimore, MD: Johns Hopkins Press.

Hambleton, R. K., & Eignor, D. R. (1980). Competency test development and standard setting. In R. M. Jaeger & C. K. Tittle (Eds.), *Minimum competency achievement testing: Motives, models, measures, and consequences* (pp. 367-396). Berkeley, CA: McCutchan.

Hambleton, R. K., & Plake, B. S. (1994, April). *Using an extended Angoff procedure for setting standards on complex performance assessments.* Paper presented at the annual meetings of the American Educational Research Association and National Council on Measurement in Education, New Orleans.

Hofstee, W. K. B. (1983). The case for compromise in educational selection and grading. In S. B. Anderson & J. S. Helmick (Eds.), *On educational testing.* San Francisco: Jossey Bass.

Jaeger, R. M. (1978). *A proposal for setting a standard on the North Carolina High School Competency Test.* A paper presented at the spring meeting of the North Carolina Association for Research in Education, Chapel Hill, NC.

Jaeger, R. M. (1989). Certification of student competence. In R. L. Linn (Ed.), *Educational measurement* (3rd. ed.; pp. 485-514). Washington, DC: American Council on Education and National Council on Measurement in Education.

Jaeger, R. M. (1991). Selection of judges for standard setting. *Educational Measurement: Issues and Practice, 10*(2), 3-14.

Jaeger, R. M. (1994, April). *Setting performance standards through two-stage judgmental policy capturing.* Paper presented at the annual meetings of the American Educational Research Association and National Council on Measurement in Education, New Orleans.

Kane, M. (1994). Validating the performance standards associated with passing scores. *Review of Educational Research, 64*(3), 425-462.

Livingston, S. A., & Zieky, M. J. (1982). *Passing scores: A manual for setting standards of performance on educational and occupational tests.* Princeton, NJ: Educational Testing Service.

Lorge, I., & Kruglov, L. K. (1953). The improvement of the estimates of tests difficulty. *Educational and Psychological Measurement, 13*, 34-46.

Maurer, T. J., Alexander, R. A., Callahan, C. M., Bailey, J. J., & Dambrot, F. H. (1991). Methodological and psychometric issues in setting cutoff scores using the Angoff method. *Personnel Psychology, 44*, 235-262.

Melican, G. J., & Mills, C. N. (1986, April). *The effect of knowledge of item difficulty for selected items on subsequent ratings of other items using the Angoff method.* Paper presented at the annual meeting of the American Educational Research Association, San Francisco, CA.

Melican, G. J., & Mills, C. N. (1987, April). *The effect of knowledge of other judges' ratings of item difficulty in an iterative process using the Angoff and Nedelsky methods.* Paper presented at the annual meeting of the American Educational Research Association, Washington, DC.

Melican, G. J., Mills, C. N., & Plake, B. S. (1987, April). *Accuracy of item performance predictions based upon the Nedelsky standard setting method.* Paper presented at the annual meeting of the National Council on Measurement in Education, Washington, DC.

Melican, G. J., & Plake, B. S. (1984, April). *Are corrections for guessing and Nedelsky's standard setting method comparable?* Paper presented at the annual meeting of the National Council on Measurement in Education, New Orleans.

Melican, G. J., & Thomas, N. (1984, April). *Identification of items that are hard to rate accurately using Angoff's standard setting method.* Paper presented at the annual meeting of the American Educational Research Association, New Orleans.

Mills, C. N., & Melican, G. J. (1986, April). *Training judges using previously rated items: The effect on subsequent ratings.* Paper presented at the annual meeting of the American Educational Research Association, San Francisco, CA.

Mills, C. N., & Melican, G. J. (1987, April). *An investigation of three methods for adjusting cut-off scores.* Paper presented at the annual meeting of the American Educational Research Association, Washington, DC.

Mills, C. N., & Melican, G. J. (1988). Estimating and adjusting cutoff scores: Features of selected methods. *Applied Measurement in Education, 1,* 261-275.

Mills, C. N., & Melican, G. J. (1990, April). *Equivalence of cut-scores derived from randomly equivalent panels.* Paper presented at the annual meeting of the National Council on Measurement in Education, Boston.

Mills, C. N., Melican, G. J., & Ahluwalia, N. T. (1991). Defining minimal competence. *Educational Measurement: Issues and Practice, 10*(2), 7-10.

Nedelsky, L. (1954). Absolute grading standards for objective tests. *Educational and Psychological Measurement, 14,* 3-19.

Norcini, J. J., Lipner, R. S., Langdon, L. O., & Strecker, C. A. (1987). A comparison of three variations on a standard setting method. *Journal of Educational Measurement, 24,* 56-64.

Norcini, J. J., & Shea, J. (1992). The reproducibility of standards over groups and occasions. *Applied Measurement in Education, 5*(1), 63-72.

Norcini, J. J., Shea, J., & Grosso, L. (1991). The effect of numbers of experts and common items on cutting score equivalents based on expert judgment. *Applied Psychological Measurement, 15*(3), 241-46.

Norcini, J. J., Shea, J. A., & Kanya, D. T. (1988). The effect of various factors on standard setting. *Journal of Educational Measurement, 25*(1), 57-65.

Putnam, S. E., Pence, P., & Jaeger, R. M. (1994, April). *A multi-stage dominant profile for setting standards on complex performance assessments.* Paper presented at the annual meetings of the American Educational Research Association and National Council on Measurement in Education, New Orleans.

Reid, J. B. (1985, April). *Establishing upper limits for item ratings using the Angoff method: Are the resulting standards more "realistic"?* Paper presented at the annual meeting of the National Council on Measurement in Education, Chicago, IL.

Reid, J. B. (1991). Training judges to generate standard-setting data. *Educational Measurement: Issues and Practice, 10*(2), 11-14.

Rogosa, D. (1982). Discussion of "item and score conversion by pooled judgment." In P. Holland & D. Rubin (Eds.), *Test equating* (pp. 319-326). New York: Academic Press.

Saunders, J. C., & Mappus, L. L. (1984, April). *Accuracy and consistency of expert judges in setting passing scores on criterion-referenced tests.* Paper presented at the annual meeting of the American Educational Research Association, New Orleans.

Saunders, J. C., Ryan, J. P., & Huynh, H. (1981). A comparison of two approaches to setting passing scores based on the Nedelsky procedure. *Applied Psychological Measurement, 5*(2), 209-217.

Schaeffer, G. A., & Collins, J. L. (1984, April). *Setting performance standards for high-stakes tests.* Paper presented at the annual meeting of the National Council on Measurement in Education, New Orleans.

Shepard, L. A. (1980a). Technical issues in minimum competency testing. In D. C. Berliner (Ed.), *Review of research in education: 8* (pp. 30-82). Itasca, IL: F. E. Peacock.

Shepard, L. A. (1980b). Standard setting issues and methods. *Applied Psychological Measurement, 4,* 447-467.

Sireci, S. G., & Biskin, B. H. (1992). Measurement practices in national licensing examination programs: A survey. *CLEAR Exam Review, 3*(1), 21-25.

Skakun, E. N., & Kling, S. (1980). Comparability of methods for setting standards. *Journal of Educational Measurement, 17,* 229-235.

Smith, R. L., & Smith, J. K. (1988). Differential use of item information by judges using Angoff and Nedelsky procedures. *Journal of Educational Measurement., 25,* 259-285.

Thorndike, R. L. (1982). Item and score conversion by pooled judgment. In P. Holland & D. Rubin (Eds.), *Test equating* (pp. 309-318). New York: Academic Press.

EQUATING

Judy A. Shea

University of Pennsylvania

John J. Norcini

American Board of Internal Medicine

INTRODUCTION

Testing programs nearly always need examinations that measure the same thing, but are composed of different questions (i.e., alternate forms of the same test). When different questions are used, however, there is no assurance that scores on the forms are equivalent; different sets of items might be easier or harder and, therefore, produce higher or lower scores. Equating is used to overcome this problem. Simply stated, it is the design and statistical procedure that permits scores on one form of a test to be comparable to scores on an alternate form.

A hypothetical example will help explain why equating is needed. Suppose Fred takes a certifying examination for aspiring baseball umpires. The examination has 100 questions sampled from the domain of questions about baseball rules and regulations. Fred gets 50 questions right and receives a score of 50. Ethel also takes an examination about baseball rules and regulations, but her test is composed of 100 different items. Ethel gets 70 questions right. Does Ethel know more about baseball than Fred? Or, might it be that Fred's test was much more difficult than Ethel's test, and contrary to appearances, Fred knows more about baseball than Ethel? The answers to these questions lie in equating, the process of ensuring that scores from multiple forms of the same test are comparable.

Equating is a technical topic and it generally requires a considerable background in statistics. The goal of this chapter is to provide a helpful and readable introduction to the issues and concepts, while highlighting useful references that will provide technical details. The chapter begins with some general background and then presents common equating designs and an overview of methods and statistical techniques. For the most often used design, the common-item design, discussion will be expanded and examples will be provided. This will be followed by a consideration of factors that affect the precision of equating and an outline of some basic research questions. Finally, examples of currently available software will be inventoried.

BACKGROUND

At the outset it should be noted that the term "equating" implies that scores from different forms of a test will be rendered interchangeable. In fact, few data sets ever meet all of the strict assumptions that lead to interchangeable or equated scores. A more technically correct term would be scaled or comparable scores (American Educational Research Association, American Psychological Association, & National Council on Measurement in Education, 1985). In keeping with this notion, an attempt has been made to use the terms "scaled" or "comparable" scores throughout the chapter.

Reasons for Multiple Forms

There are at least three reasons to have multiple forms of a test. The first is security. Many testing programs administer high-stakes examinations in which performance has an important impact upon the examinee and the public: conferring a license or certificate to practice a profession, permitting admittance to a college or other training program, or granting credit for an educational experience. For a test score to have validity in any of these circumstances, it is crucial that it reflect the uncontaminated knowledge and ability of the examinees. Therefore, security is a concern and it is often desirable to give different forms to examinees seated beside each other, those who take the examination on different days, or those who take the examination on more than one occasion (Petersen, Kolen, & Hoover, 1989).

A second and related reason for different test forms is the current movement to open testing. Many programs find it necessary or desirable to release test items to the public (Holland & Rubin, 1982a). When this occurs, it is not possible to use the released items on future forms of a test without providing examinees an unfair advantage.

A third reason for different forms is that test content, and therefore test questions, by necessity changes gradually over time. Knowledge in virtually all occupations and professions evolves and it is crucial for the test to reflect the current state of practice. For example, it is obvious that today's medical licensure and certification examinations should include questions on HIV and AIDS, whereas these topics were not relevant several years ago. Even when the knowledge does not so obviously change, the context within which test items are presented is at risk of becoming dated. One could imagine a clinical scenario in medicine where descriptions of a patient's condition should be rewritten to include current drugs; in law one might want to include references to timely cases and rulings, especially if they lead to different interpretations of the law. It sometimes happens also that the correct answer to previously used questions simply changes. When this occurs it is necessary to rewrite or replace the item. [As will be discussed later, equating assumes that the test scores are based on parallel forms of the test. Thus, if the changes in content are too severe, it is not appropriate to equate.]

Reasons to Equate

Given that different forms of an examination are necessary, it is important to ensure that the scores on one form of the test have the same meaning as the scores on another form. This issue of equivalence is important in most educational endeavors, but it is crucial in licensure and certification. Differences in pass/fail decisions across forms will undermine the meaning of a license or certificate. For example, through the 1970s, medicine was very popular and, according to some observers, it attracted the best and the brightest students. As medicine in general became less attractive in the 1980s, the quality of students entering, and therefore finishing, medical school may have declined. Without a method for ensuring the equivalence of pass/fail decisions on the licensing examination over time, students who passed in 1975 might have been more able than those who passed in 1990. This could have created "vintages" of licensed physicians. The license would not reflect the same standard over time and to know what it meant, it would be necessary to determine when a physician was granted the license. Consider as well, how unfair that would have been to the physicians seeking licensure. Some of those who were not good enough in 1975 would be by 1990 and vice versa.

Thus, the primary reasons for requiring equivalence are maintenance of the meaning of licenses/certificates and fairness to examinees. As stated in Lord (1977) (and later paraphrased in *Standards for Educational and Psychological Testing* [AERA, APA, & NCME, 1985]), "Transformed scores y* and raw scores x can be called 'equated' if and only if it is a matter of indifference to each examinee whether he is to take test X or test Y" (p. 128). If this condition is met, it is then possible to make comparisons that are of interest to testing programs: among performances of different examinees who took alternative test forms, and among items and overall test scores that are given to various groups. A caveat is that in most cases, particularly those common to licensure and certification settings, equating is meant to adjust for unintended differences in form difficulty. As such, the real burden of creating parallel forms falls to test development. Thus, it is imperative that test developers and psychometricians collaborate to achieve the goal of producing interchangeable scores (Brennan & Kolen, 1987).

Conditions for Equating

In its simplest form, the process of equating has two components: selection of a data collection design and transformation of scores using a specific set of statistical techniques and methodologies. As will be discussed later in the chapter, there are several sound alternatives to choose among for both of these components. However, it is important to be acquainted with the four basic requirements or conditions for equating: (1) the different forms of the test should measure the same attribute, (2) the resulting conversion should be independent of the data used in deriving it, (3) scores on the tests, after equating, should be interchangeable in use, and (4) the equating should be symmetric (Angoff, 1971/1984). Cook and Eignor (1991), Dorans (1990), and Petersen et al. (1989) provide very clear and extensive discussions of these requirements.

COMMON EQUATING DESIGNS

The first step in equating two forms of an examination is selection of a design. This involves two joint considerations: specifying which forms will be given on which occasions, and specifying which examinees will take which examination forms. Optimally, equating and the issues related to it will be a prospectively considered and integrated part of any testing program that must compare the performances of examinees and examinations over time. When equating details are not prospectively built into a testing program, it may sometimes be possible to change standard operating procedures to create a strong equating design. More often than not, however, the design that is actually used follows from the administrative procedures of the testing program already in place before the topic of equating becomes relevant (e.g., periodic administration to different groups of examinees, simultaneous administrations of several different test forms). Fortunately, adherence to already existing procedures is not a problem because several suitable equating designs exist.

Specification of a Design

Designs for equating vary along a continuum from straightforward to complex. Four basic designs serve as the building blocks of nearly all other commonly used strategies: (a) a single-group design—one group of examinees takes two (or more) forms of a test, (b) an independent groups and examination design—each examinee group takes a different form of the exam, (c) a counterbalanced design—each examinee group takes both (or all) forms of the exam, and (d) a common-item design—each examinee group takes a different form of the examination plus an anchor test composed of the same items. Each of these designs will be further explained below. In addition, more complex variations on these basic designs will be briefly presented. [Other authors conceptualize designs in somewhat different ways and they also use different terminology. See, for example, Petersen et al., 1989; Crocker & Algina, 1986]. Nevertheless, there is general consensus on which are the most basic designs.

Single group design. The simplest of the designs, though least practical by itself, is to give both (or all) forms of a test to a single group of examinees. The design could be portrayed as the following:

Group A
Form X +
Form Y

With this design, observed differences between test scores on the forms are due to differences in difficulty between the forms. In practice, this design is rarely used because it is difficult to convince examinees to take more than one form of an exam and it is expensive to carry out as well. Even if examinees can be persuaded, scores on the second form may be contaminated by factors such as fatigue or practice. [There are ways to control for such unwanted effects; see the discussion below regarding counterbalanced designs.] Most importantly for licensure and certification settings, this design does not capture what actually happens in practice. That is, interest is most often in comparing scores for groups of examinees who take forms on different occasions or who take different forms, rather than looking at examination performance for two forms given at the same time.

Independent-groups design. A much more common situation is the one in which Examinee Group A takes Test X and Examinee Group B takes Test Y. For example, a licensing board might give an examination (Test X) in the fall of one year to one group of examinees (Group A) who just completed the required training for a profession. The next year a similar examination (Test Y) would be given to the new group of examinees (Group B) who recently completed their required training. The alternate forms are designed to be as similar as possible. In order to compare the performances of the two cohorts of examinees, psychometricians at the licensing board wish to transform the scores of one group (e.g., Group B) so that they are on the same scale as the other group (Group A). Schematically, the design would look like this:

Group A	<—	*Group B*
Test X		Test Y

This design would also apply when alternate forms are assigned to various examinees who take the examination simultaneously. For example, the design pertains when forms are assigned to examinees so that those sitting beside each other receive different tests.

When choosing an equating design, it is important to realize that no one direction of score transformation is inherently better than another. For example, with simultaneous administration of several forms, it is just as good to transform Test X scores so that they are on the Test Y score scale, as to transform Test Y scores so that they can be reported on the Test X score scale. However, in most licensure and certification settings, administrations occur over time. Thus, it makes most sense to report the more current scores on past scales; there is rarely a compelling reason to go back and change the scale on which earlier scores were reported.

Counterbalanced-groups design. The counterbalanced groups design is slightly more elaborate than the independent groups design. Both groups of examinees take both (all) forms of an examination. The presentation of forms would be counterbalanced (half of both examinee groups would receive Test X followed by Test Y and the other half would receive Test Y followed by Test X) to avoid factors such as practice and fatigue (Skaggs & Lissitz, 1986b). Schematically, the design would look like this:

Group A	—>	*Group B*
Test X +		Test Y +
Test Y		Test X

A design such as this is appealing because the comparability of forms can be directly evaluated; they are taken by the same group of examinees. For the same reason, examinees in various groups can be compared. However, like the single group design, this is rarely used in practice for obvious reasons: It is seldom practical to give examinees more than one complete test form because of limitations on examinees' and examiners' time and resources.

Common-item design. In contrast to designs that rely solely on the total test, an alternative is to adjust scores for examinees based on their performance on a set of common items that is administered to both groups. For example, Group A would take Exam X and Common Item Set U; Group B would take Exam Y and also take Common Item Set U. The schematic of this basic equating design could be more precisely specified as follows:

Group A	--->	Group B
Test X +		Test Y +
Common Set U		Common Set U

The common-item test, also called an anchor test, can be either external or internal to the focal test. Items that comprise the external anchor are usually not included in the examinees' reported test scores (Kolen, 1988). They are often presented as a separate section of the test, perhaps as a final test booklet. In contrast, with an internal anchor the common items are dispersed throughout the examination and are typically included as scored items that count towards the reported test score. The flexibility of the common-item design makes it useful in many different settings.

More complex designs. As mentioned in the introduction to this section, equating designs can be quite complex and often involve more than two examinations and two groups of examinees. Let us assume that a testing program that has been in existence for many years decides to begin equating examination scores. They have one administration per year and only one form of the examination is created for each administration Both of these procedures need to remain in place. In addition, it will be necessary to adhere to the longstanding policy that the same items never appear in two consecutive examinations. What might an equating plan look like for this organization?

For convenience, let us say that the base year will be 1987; examination scores in future years will be transformed to be on the same scale as this initial administration. In 1987 we will give Test S to Group A. In 1989, Group C takes Test U, which needs to be rescaled to Test S. Two years later, in 1991, Group E is administered Test W which is equated to Test S, through Test U. This pathway is shown in the top of the diagram.

Recall that items cannot be reused in consecutive years. The 1988 Test T will, of course, be given to Group B but it cannot be linked to the base year. However, in 1990 the Group D test takers can take Test V, which has items in common with both Test S and the 1988 form (which is being ignored in this diagram). Two years later, in 1992, Group F is administered Test X, which is equated to Test S, through Test V. This pathway for the even-numbered years is shown in the bottom of the diagram. Finally, the 1993 examination will be "double-linked" to previous forms through the items it has in common with 1990 and 1991. A design such as this may be depicted as follows:

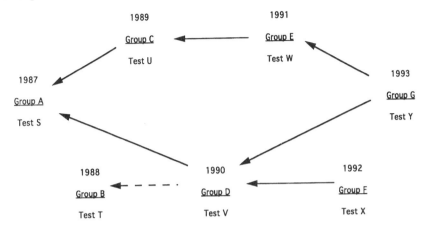

Designs such as these are referred to as chained or braided designs. One problem in the implementation of equating over time is that errors can accumulate. Such problems can be overcome by interlacing the groups/examinations at prespecified intervals. For example, in the diagram above, the 1993 form was linked to both 1990 and 1991. The reason for doing this is to insure that separate "strains" of the examination do not develop, such as an "even year" strain and an "odd year" strain. Note also, that the 1988 form and the 1992 form were not used in the current chain. However, both would be brought into future equatings via shared items with 1994, which might also share with 1991. Drawing schematics can help visualize how checks can be built into the system, as well as define what is practical for any particular organization. Literature evaluating these complex chaining or braiding designs is very useful for highlighting issues and problems that can occur over time and threaten the integrity of the equating (Petersen, Cook, & Stocking, 1983), as well as bringing out problems that cannot be detected in short-term designs and evaluations.

For the design above, one could add a common-item test to each administration. Moreover, the common-item set could change over time. That is, the common-item set used to link Test X and Test Y need not be the same as the common-item set used to link Test Y and Test Z. The implication of this is that the content of the common-item link is allowed to change over time to better reflect the goals of the testing program and to maintain security of the examination forms.

Another design that deserves mention is a preequating design. Originally discussed by Educational Testing Service (Holland & Rubin, 1982b), preequating refers to inclusion of different groups of items in multiple examination forms. The preequated items are not included in the examinees' test scores but the necessary data are collected to allow calculation of equating transformations. The preequating can be done in either an item (Kolen & Harris, 1990) or section format (Holland

& Thayer, 1985). Preequated items are then subsequently assembled into a form(s) and administered at a later date. Preequating permits rapid scoring when the time between administration of the forms and deadlines for reporting results is short. Also, implementation of a preequating design builds in some protection against administering a seriously flawed exam. A possible design for one administration might look like the following:

Group A	Group B	Group C
Test X +	Test X +	Test X +
PE Form A	PE Form B	PE Form C

Eventually, preequated (PE) Forms A, B, and C would be put together to form Test Y. The transformations would be calculated prior to administration and when Test Y is administered, it could immediately be reported on the Test X scale. The preequated forms would not contribute to examinees' test scores at the initial administration. Naturally, however, one would want the PE forms to look like other parts of the test so that examinees would apply equal effort. [The same holds true for any section of experimental or pretested questions that is not included in examinees' scores.]

The number of other designs that could be developed is large, as are the statistical techniques for performing the equatings. Fox example, preliminary methods have been developed for multidimensional equating (Hirsch, 1989) and equating with confirmatory factor analysis (Rock, 1982). At this point, these technically demanding procedures have not gained widespread use.

In sum, the specific design and direction of equating that one chooses will be closely intertwined with the more general structure, policies, and procedures of the testing program. The most important points in the discussion of design are: (a) design simply refers to how data are collected from various examinees and, (b) there are four simple designs that serve as building blocks for more complex structures. The remainder of the chapter will utilize the Independent-Groups and Common-Item Designs, the most typical equating situations (Cook & Eignor, 1991).

Selection of Examinees

In the process of defining an equating design it is necessary to specify the sample of examinees who will take the forms on which the equating transformations will be based. The most important consideration in designating equating subsamples is whether they are random or nonrandom selections of examinees (some authors refer to equivalent and nonequivalent groups, see Dorans [1990] or Petersen et al. [1989]). Several designs call for the selection of random samples of examinees to receive various test forms (see Angoff, 1971/1984) because it is reasonable to assume that they are of equivalent ability. However, in practice it is usually not feasible to do this and, more often than not, the structure of the testing environment and practical considerations dictate that the samples will be nonrandom.

A second issue, independent of the random-nonrandom decision, is specifying exactly which examinees will be included in the equating subsamples. Examinees involved in equating need not necessarily be all those who take a particular form at a particular administration (Harris, 1987). It is best to select fairly large groups of examinees, who exhibit some variability in performance but whose skills and training are relatively homogeneous. That is, even though groups cannot be precisely equivalent, efforts are made to create groups that are as comparable as possible.

Emphasizing homogeneity may mean omitting some test takers. For example, many testing programs allow examinees to take multiple administrations of the exam, either because they are trying to better earlier performance (e.g., MCAT scores, GREs), or because they failed to meet established pass-fail or cutoff points. In these instances, it is better to limit the equating transformations to first-time takers of the examination, because they tend to have known training and educational experiences. Similarly, one might not want to include examinees who are admitted to the examination following unusual training or educational experiences, or those who elect to take the examinations at various times of the year. Several investigators have found sizable performance differences between examinees taking spring and fall administrations of an examination (Cook & Petersen, 1987; Petersen et al., 1983; Schmitt, Cook, Dorans, & Eignor, 1990). Seasonal shifts have also been reported for a medical licensing examination (Nungester, Dillon, Swanson, Orr, & Powell, 1991). Whatever the final decisions regarding selection of examinees, the samples used in equating should be well justified and explained to all interested parties (AERA, APA, & NCME, 1985).

A third consideration in selecting or describing samples of examinees relates to deciding whether they differ only slightly in ability, or whether they differ considerably. The former is referred to as horizontal equating, and is applicable in most testing programs where the abilities of the examinees remain fairly constant from one administration to another (e.g., examinees sitting for licensure and certification examinations). The latter is referred to as vertical equating and is quite common in programs such as educational achievement and aptitude testing programs where there is a desire to compare scores for examinees at different grades or training levels. In horizontal equating, the tests are designed to be similar and differ for only unintended reasons. In vertical equating, the tests are intentionally designed to differ in difficulty (Cook & Eignor, 1983).

Technically, many of the procedures for horizontal and vertical equating are the same. The practical difference is that the accuracy and precision of equating are typically much greater in the case of horizontal equating (Skaggs & Lissitz, 1986b). However, even in large, ongoing testing programs in which horizontal equating should suffice, there may be subtle but consistent changes in the examinees' abilities over several administrations. For example, examinees sitting for certification in internal medicine showed consistent declines in performance over a period of several years (Norcini, Maihoff, Day, & Benson, 1989). Admittedly, the distinction between horizontal and vertical equating designs is not always clear. Nevertheless, asking the question focuses attention on expected examinees' abilities and helps to elucidate the equating procedure and anticipated equating results.

In sum, selection of designs and examinees was considered separately because it is important that the issues relevant to each be considered. In practice, many discussions of equating describe various designs by jointly specifying how the samples of examinees and the selection of items or forms occurred. One of the most widely known typologies was provided by Angoff (1971/1984). Among the designs he describes are Design I: Random groups—one test administered to each group; Design II: Random groups—both tests administered to each group, counterbalanced; Design III: Random groups—one test administered to each group, common-equating test administered to each group; and Design IV: Nonrandom groups—one test to each group, common-equating test administered to both groups. Familiarity with this work provides a very thorough background and is helpful when reading current literature.

EQUATING METHODS AND PROCEDURES

Having chosen a design and the examinees, it is necessary to select a method for transforming the scores from the various forms to be on the same scale. Specific transformation or equating procedures fall within two psychometric theories: conventional (traditional) test theory and item response theory. Within traditional test theory there are several equating methods. The most common and well studied are the equipercentile method and linear equating methods. In contrast, methods falling under the rubric of item response theory (IRT) have only been widely discussed for the past 10 to 15 years, but they are proliferating rapidly. At this point, the IRT models that have received the most attention in the published literature are the one-parameter (Rasch) and three-parameter models, based on logistic estimation procedures (Baker, 1985; Hambleton & Swaminathan, 1985; Hambleton, Swaminathan, & Rogers, 1991; Lord, 1980; Wright & Stone, 1979). However, marginal maximum likelihood estimation procedures (Bock & Aitkin, 1981) are becoming quite popular.

The focus of this section of the chapter will be on general assumptions and equating methods that can be associated with estimation procedures from either conventional or item response theory. The interested reader is referred to the references listed above for more extensive discussions. In addition, this discussion assumes that test scores are sums of dichotomously scored items (right/wrong). Methods for other types of data are just becoming widely available (Baker, 1992; Thissen, 1991). As such, existing equating methodologies are, for the most part, not yet useful for clinical data or data derived from item formats that produce other than 0/1 responses.

Traditional Test Theory

Equipercentile equating. Equipercentile equating is a method of transforming scores so that, when the equating is complete, two scores are said to be comparable if they have the same percentile or rank within their respective examinee group. This method makes no statistical assumptions about the tests to be equated. However, the result is that the distributions underlying each form are identical in all moments (i.e., they have the same distribution). The procedure stretches or compresses the two distributions so that this outcome is achieved.

Equipercentile equating is typically done by computer, though it is relatively easily done by hand. The general procedure has several steps and application to an independent-groups design is sketched below. For a thorough and detailed example, the reader is referred to Angoff (1971/1984). Procedures are slightly more complicated for common-item designs; see Angoff (1971/1984), Dorans (1990), and Thorndike (1982) for descriptions of alternative procedures.

1. A distribution of test scores is developed in a tabular format, and percentile ranks or relative cumulative frequency distributions are prepared. This is done separately for each form of the examination taken by a different group of examinees.

2. The cumulative distributions for each form are plotted on a graph and each graph is smoothed. Smoothing, as the term suggests, is the process of transforming the sometimes jagged curve that is produced by plotting actual distributions to a "smooth" curve. In the past, smoothing was done by hand. It can also be done analytically, for example by the rolling weighted average method (Angoff, 1971/1984), or any of several very sophisticated methods detailed by Fairbank (1987), Hanson (1991), and Kolen (1991).

3. Once the distributions are plotted and smoothed, a table is made showing the raw scores from each form that correspond to several different percentiles. For example, the table would show what score from Form X and what score from Form Y correspond to a percentile rank of 85. This is repeated for many (usually about 30) other percentile ranks. Rather than selecting every possible percentile, the investigator may select many smaller increments in the part(s) of the distribution where he or she is most interested in precision. Also, numerous closely spaced points will have to be taken at both ends of the distributions where scores are rare.

4. A second graph is made showing the relationship between pairs of scores entered into the table above. If necessary, this graph is also smoothed.

5. From the final graph, a table is made showing the appropriate conversions between the two test score distributions. For example, it might show that a score of 5 on Exam X is equivalent to a score of 4 on Exam Y.

The major advantage of the equipercentile technique is that it is quite suitable for describing curvilinear relationships between scores on different tests. But, a fairly significant disadvantage that causes many investigators to choose other models is that the process of smoothing is quite subjective. Moreover, this method forces distributions of two scores to be the same, even when there may be legitimate reason for having very different distributions (i.e., the purpose of the examination changes and it becomes more or less difficult). As Cook and Petersen (1987) discuss, this method is entirely data dependent. If other observed distributions of test scores were equated, a different conversion table would emerge. This is likely to be particularly true at the tails of the distribution where there are few data points. Clearly, large samples are needed for precise equating. On the other hand, with large samples that sometimes occur in licensure and certification programs, scores will be observed over the entire range including the area that contains the cutting score. Overall, the equipercentile method has been widely used and continues to be the preferred method for some testing programs (e.g., American College Testing). In some sense, it remains the standard against which other methods are compared.

Linear equating. The second common equating procedure is linear. The general formula that applies is a linear transformation of the form $Y = AX + B$, where A and B are parameters that use standard score terms to express the ideas of equating $[(x - m_x)/s_x = (y - m_y)/s_y]$, X refers to scores on Test X, and Y refers to scores on Test Y (Petersen et al., 1983). This general linear formula is applicable in many different designs, among them being Angoff Designs I through IV described above (Angoff, 1971/1984). However, the designs differ in the way in which the transformation constants, A and B, are calculated.

The computational formulas appropriate for a common-item design with nonrandom groups (Designs IVa in Angoff parlance) are shown below to illustrate how straightforward the linear equating process is. This example was selected because it represents the most common scenario in licensure and certification testing: Different forms of an examination are administered on different testing occasions. The derivation of the formulas, attributed to Tucker (Gulliksen, 1950), is presented in Angoff (1971/1984). The goal is to calculate the coefficients that fulfill the equation $Y = AX + B$ where $A = s_{y_t} / s_{x_t}$ and $B = M_{y_t} - AM_{x_t}$. The four equations to be solved are:

$$M_{x_t} = M_{x_a} + b_{xu_a}(M_{u_t} - M_{u_a})$$
$$M_{y_t} = M_{y_b} + b_{yu_a}(M_{u_t} - M_{u_b})$$
$$s_{x_t}^2 = s_{x_a}^2 + b_{xu_a}^2(s_{u_t}^2 - s_{u_a}^2)$$
$$s_{y_t}^2 = s_{y_b}^2 + b_{yu_b}^2(s_{u_t}^2 - s_{u_b}^2)$$

Where:

M_{u_t} = the observed mean of Groups A and B on the Common Set U

M_{u_a} = the observed mean of Group A on Common Set U

M_{u_b} = the observed mean of Group B on Common Set U

M_{x_a} = the observed mean of Group A on Exam X

M_{y_b} = the observed mean of Group B on Exam Y

b_{xu_a} = the regression coefficient from regressing Exam X scores for Group A on Common Set U scores

b_{yu_b} = the regression coefficient from regressing Exam Y scores for Group B on Common Set U scores

$s_{u_t}^2$ = the observed variance of Groups A and B on Common Set U scores

$s_{u_a}^2$ = the observed variance of Group A on Common Set U scores

$s_{u_b}^2$ = the observed variance of Group B on Common Set U scores

$s_{x_a}^2$ = the observed variance of Group A on Exam X scores

$s_{y_b}^2$ = the observed variance of Group B on Exam Y scores

The list of all of the components for the equations is long, but calculation of the appropriate terms and the ultimate transformation of scores can quite easily be done with standard software packages such as SPSS (Norusis, 1992), SAS (SAS Institute, Inc., 1989), SYSTAT (Wilkinson, 1992), and BMDP (Dixon, 1990). The two examples below are based on applications to typical testing situations and they illustrate how easy the computations can be.

Returning to the example of hypothetical scores on the baseball rules and regulations test, it is possible to illustrate what is involved in equating, and in fact, why equating is necessary. Recall that Fred (as a part of Group A) received a score of 50 on the Form X 100-item baseball test. Ethel (as a part of Group B) received a score of 70 on the Form Y 100-item baseball test. The question to answer is how these scores compare to one another. Ultimately, a direct comparison can be made after the scores for Group A Test X are transformed to be on the same scale as the Group B Test Y scores. For the moment, we will forget about the performance of individuals and focus on group statistics.

Scenario #1—tests of different difficulty. Assume that in addition to their respective 100-item Forms, Groups A and B also took the same 30-item set of common items, referred to as Test U. Performance on the form-specific items (often called "unique" items in the literature) and the common items might look as follows:

	X Mean	X *SD*	U Mean	U *SD*
Group A	60	7	15	3
	Y Mean	Y *SD*	U Mean	U *SD*
Group B	65	8	11	5

Before the equating is done, some observations can be made from these data that foreshadow the results after equating. Notice that Group B did not score nearly so well on the common items as Group A, even though their scores on the form-specific items (Test Y) were somewhat higher. This suggests that Group A Test X scores will in all likelihood be "raised" when they are transformed to the Group B Test Y scale.

Proceeding with the equating will clarify the relationship. Other computations (not shown here) indicate that the combined performance of Groups A and B on the Common Item Set U has a mean of 13 and a standard deviation of 4. The result of regressing Group A Test X scores on Group A Common Set U scores is .90. The result of regressing Group B Test Y scores on Group B Common Set U scores is .80. These are all of the data that are needed to complete the equating transformation. Into the formulas given previously we substitute the following:

$$M_{x_t} = M_{x_a} + b_{xu_a}(M_{u_t} - M_{u_a})$$
$$= 60 + .90(13 - 15) = 58.20$$
$$M_{y_t} = M_{y_b} + b_{yu_a}(M_{u_t} - M_{u_b})$$
$$= 65 + .80(13 - 11) = 66.60$$

$$s_{x_t}^2 = s_{x_a}^2 + b_{xu_a}^2 (s_{u_t}^2 - s_{u_a}^2)$$
$$= 7^2 + .90^2(4^2 - 3^2) = 54.67$$
$$s_{y_t}^2 = s_{y_b}^2 + b_{yu_b}^2 (s_{u_t}^2 - s_{u_b}^2)$$
$$= 8^2 + .80^2(4^2 - 5^2) = 58.24$$

Further substitution results in the equating coefficients:

$$A = s_{y_t} / s_{x_t}$$
$$= 58.24^{1/2}/54.67^{1/2} = 1.03$$

$$B = M_{y_t} - AM_{x_t}$$
$$= 66.6 - 1.03(58.2) = 6.65$$

Thus, $Y = AX + B$ becomes $Y = 1.03X + 6.65$.

Glancing at the formula tells us that roughly 6 or 7 points need to be added to all Group A Test X scores before they can be compared to Group B Test Y scores. More precisely, Fred's score of 50 is transformed to 58.15 ($Y = 1.03(50) + 6.65$). Thus, his score is lower than Ethel's score but not as much as it originally appeared. This result should be reassuring to all Group A test takers. Test developers might want to ask why Form X is more difficult than Form Y.

Scenario #2—Examinee groups with different ability. This time let us assume that Group B had the better performance on the common items. The scores are:

	X Mean	X SD	U Mean	U SD
Group A	60	7	11	5
	Y Mean	Y SD	U Mean	U SD
Group B	65	8	15	3

What will happen to Fred's score in this case? Intuitively, one might guess that the Group A scores will be lowered. Not only do they score lower on a similar test, they do much worse (about a standard deviation worse) on the common items.

As before, the regression coefficient regressing Group A Test X scores on Group A Common Set U scores is .90. The regression coefficient regressing Group B Test Y scores on Group B Common Set U scores is .80. When these data are appropriately substituted into the equations the resulting linear equation is: $Y = 1.28X - 15.70$. That is, Fred's score of 50 becomes a 48.30. The intuitions were correct and all Exam X scores will be lowered. In this scenario, test developers and administrators would do well to ask why the apparent ability of the two groups was different. Did they set out anticipating group differences (i.e., vertical equating) or is some selection or training factor creating the differences? Perhaps the licensure or certification examination is becoming more or less attractive to certain groups of examinees.

Creating scenarios such as the two presented is a very helpful learning tool. Those involved with equating may find it useful to create other scenarios that represent their own testing situation. For example, if the equating groups have equal mean performances, but their variances are very different, there will be an obvious and predictable impact on equating (i.e., the score distribution will expand or contract depending on which is chosen as the base form). Similarly, the equating transformation is influenced by the degree of correlation between the anchor test and the whole test forms (Budescu, 1985). As a postscript it should be noted that the examples provided above were hypothetical, and numbers were chosen for ease of calculation. In actual testing situations, the process may be a bit less straightforward.

A clear advantage of linear equating methods is their ease of implementation. Also, linear methods do not have subjective components such as the equipercentile method does with smoothing. On the other hand, they are fairly simplistic and assume that a simple linear equation is sufficient to describe the relationship between score distributions.

Common-item equating also depends on making a number of statistical assumptions. They are spelled out in Braun and Holland (1982), Kolen and Brennan (1987), and Petersen et al. (1989). The two assumptions that receive the most attention and are the most readily testable are: (a) linearity of the regression of the whole test form score on the anchor test score, and (b) homogeneity of the residual variation about the regression (Braun & Holland, 1982). Other requirements depend on the specific mathematical transformation being utilized. For example, Thorndike (1982) says that equating must involve equally precise (i.e., reliable) tests, and that both (all) tests should have the same correlation with a third measure. In contrast, Angoff (1971/1984) presents formulas for tests of unequal reliability. It is advisable that users of test equating procedures become familiar with the specific assumptions of the techniques under consideration (or in use). Petersen et al. (1983) present a very helpful table comparing the widely used Tucker and Levine methods. It is important to repeatedly perform checks to assess how well the test data continue to meet the assumptions of the model.

Item Response Theory

Item response theory (sometimes called latent trait theory) has been increasingly studied over the past 10 to 20 years (Wright & Stone, 1979; Lord, 1980; Hambleton & Swaminathan, 1985). The goal of the theory is to model performance on a trait using observed test scores. There are numerous item response theory models, developed from competing mathematical frameworks (Birnbaum, 1968; Bock & Aitkin, 1981; Swaminathan & Gifford, 1982, 1983). The most basic IRT model, often referred to as one-parameter model, says that performance on a particular item is a function of the examinee's ability and the difficulty of the item. More complex models add item discrimination to the prediction model (two-parameter model) and a chance or guessing factor (three-parameter model). Before a discussion of equating within IRT can occur, it is helpful to (a) review some basic concepts from item response theory and (b) contrast IRT with traditional test theory. More extensive discussion of the models is beyond the scope of this chapter. For more detail the reader is referred to Hambleton and Swaminathan (1985), Hambleton et al. (1991), Lord (1980), and Baker (1985).

General concepts. The usual outputs of IRT calibrations are sets of item parameters and estimated person (i.e., examinee) abilities. Item parameters are conceptually analogous to item statistics in that they describe features of an item: the b-parameter refers to the difficulty of an item, the a-parameter refers to discrimination, and the c-parameter is a pseudo-guessing factor. However, it is important to note that IRT parameters are not numerically or statistically equivalent to traditional item statistics. Similarly, person (examinee) abilities, expressed as thetas with standard errors, quantify how well each person performed, though they do not appear as, nor are they equivalent to, raw scores.

Estimation of item and person parameters is generally an iterative process, occurring is successive stages until an acceptable amount of precision is reached (the termination values are determined by various software programs and can be adjusted by the user). In the end, one obtains a matrix of item parameters (with standard errors attached to each parameter) and a vector of estimated person abilities (with standard errors for each estimate). Because item and person parameters are jointly estimated, they are placed on the same [arbitrary] scale within a calibration run. In one popular program (BILOG, Mislevy & Bock, 1989), the estimates of person ability have a range of -3 to +3 and are centered on 0 with a standard deviation of 1. Item difficulties are centered above or below this mean, depending on if the items are generally difficult for the average test taker (above) or easy (below) for the average test taker. Item discrimination varies between 0 and infinity, though the upper range is usually set at around +2. The pseudo-guessing factor varies between approximately 0 and the reciprocal of the total number of item choices (e.g., .20 for an item with five answer choices).

Information from the estimated item parameters and ability estimates is portrayed in item characteristic curves (ICC), the building blocks for all IRT models. This focus on individual items is a significant departure from conventional test theory where the focus is on total test scores. An ICC is a plot describing how the characteristics of an item interact with a person's ability. Stated another way, it is a graph showing the probability of a correct response to a particular item over the entire ability range. Usually it is an S-shaped curve with the examinee ability scale along the abscissa and the probability of a correct response on the ordinate. A sample is shown below.

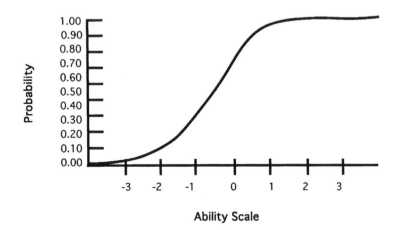

Curves located to the right of the midpoint of the ability distribution represent difficult items whereas curves located to the left of the midpoint represent easy items. Steep curves indicate highly discriminating items. Lower asymptotes above 0 suggest that guessing is influencing estimates for the lowest ability examinees.

ICCs are summed over all items to create test characteristics curves that describe the function of all items over all test takers. Finally, with IRT one is able to calculate information functions. This is a measure of the precision of estimation for each item over the entire ability range. Information functions can be summed over all items to create test information functions (TIF). TIFs identify at what point(s) in the ability distribution of examinees, information is maximized for a set of items. Roughly, information is inversely related to the standard error of estimate for person ability. If most test items match the ability of the examinees *and* the items are highly discriminating, the test characteristic curve will be a steeply peaked curve, the peak representing the point on the ability scale where the test provides the most information. If the majority of the items do not match the average ability of examinees, the curve will be very flat, suggesting the test provides minimal information along the ability distribution.

Comparison to traditional test theory. Traditional test theory is based on what Hambleton and Swaminathan (1985) describe as a set of weak assumptions. Because the assumptions are weak, the theory is applicable in most typical testing situations. On the other hand, tests based on traditional test theory have some shortcomings: (a) the item statistics (p-values and r-biserials) apply only to the specific group who took the examination on which the scores are calculated; (b) comparisons of scores are limited to situations where examinees take parallel examinations; and (c) it is presumed that scores are equally precise over the entire range of ability.

In contrast to traditional test theory, item response theory is based on a set of very strong assumptions. First, it is assumed that the test data are unidimensional, meaning that they measure only one trait or ability (multidimensional models have been developed but they are not widely used at this time) (Hambleton & Swaminathan, 1985). Second, the data must exhibit local independence (Lord, 1980). Simply stated, this is the requirement that for examinees of the same ability, responses to particular items are uncorrelated. Third, it is assumed that the test is not speeded. The one-parameter model also requires that all items in an examination be equal in discrimination and that "guessing" by examinees does not influence responses to any items. Clearly, this is quite a stringent set of assumptions.

Additional reading in item response theory will show that many early studies focused on assessing data-model fit for particular data sets (Hambleton & Murray, 1983; Shea, Norcini, & Webster, 1988), comparing techniques for investigating fit of the models to the data (Hambleton & Rovinelli, 1986), or investigating how robust the models were to violations of the assumptions (Dorans & Kingston, 1985). As with methods resulting from conventional test theory, there is rarely a clear answer to the question of "how much misfit is too much?" However, sizable departures from unidimensionality and equal item-total discrimination are relatively easy to spot. When violations do occur, the user should select a more complete model, or use conventional equating methodologies.

For all models, when the observed test data appropriately fit the model, item response theories theoretically offer several advantages over conventional test theory. The advantages that are most relevant to equating are that estimates of examinees' abilities are independent of the particular sets of items on which the ability estimates are based, and similarly, estimates of item parameters (i.e., difficulty and discrimination) are independent of the particular set of examinees on whom the item parameter estimates are based. For example, proponents of the theory would suggest that if all test items were divided into odd-even numbered subsets, or easy-hard subsets, the same ability estimates would be obtained for an examinee regardless of which subtest he/she took. Similarly, estimated item parameters are theoretically the same for subsamples of examinees such as highest and lowest ranked class members, or first-time test takers and repeaters (though they will have to be rescaled by a constant because scaling within a single IRT run is arbitrary).

Other advantages are also present with IRT, such as more accuracy in transformation at the extremes of the scale. Also, because IRT statistical manipulations are conducted at the item level, rather than the total test score level, IRT offers the possibility of item preequating (e.g., deriving equating transformation data before an operational form is actually administered) (Cook & Eignor, 1983; 1991). At this point it is appropriate to reiterate a previously stated caution. The advantages of IRT described above are achieved if, and only if, the model of interest fits the actual test data. In reality, this rarely occurs. Moreover, high quality calibration of item and person parameters requires larger sample sizes than linear equating methods, especially when the common joint maximum likelihood estimation procedures are used.

Equating procedures. For purposes of this discussion, assume the data to be equated adequately fit the model(s) of interest. How then, does one equate? As discussed by Cook and Eignor (1991) IRT equating is a three-step process: (a) select a design, (b) place parameter estimates from different samples on a common scale, and (c) equate test scores. The issue most relevant for equating becomes selecting the appropriate methodology for placing item parameters on the same scale.

In general, there are three methods for transforming item parameters generated from different samples of examinees to be on the same scale. The most straightforward is concurrent calibration. Data for multiple examination forms and examinees are simultaneously calibrated and scaled within one computer run, thus the item and ability estimates are automatically on the same scale (i.e., Steps 2 and 3 are completed simultaneously). This method would probably be the ideal but limitations on computer resources make this procedure impractical on occasion. Moreover, if items are calibrated following one test administration and performance is reported to examinees, it does not usually make much sense when the next administration occurs to recalibrate the items taken by the original sample.

The alternative equating methods use a common-item design. The first of these alternatives is called the fixed-b design. In this method, all items for one examination form are calibrated (i.e., the as, bs, and cs are estimated as are the person abilities). Then, the item parameter estimates for the common items, in particular item difficulties, are entered as fixed values into the subsequent run for the second form. All other (non-common) items (Step 2) and all ability estimates (Step 3) will be scaled around these preset values.

A second alternative is to employ a rescaling technique based on the relationships between item parameters estimated for common-item links. The simplest rescaling procedure, applicable only when the data meet the assumptions of the Rasch model, calculates the mean item difficulties for the two sets of common items, estimated independently (Wright & Stone, 1979). The difference in the means is computed and this value is added to the difficulty estimates (Step 2) *and* ability estimates (Step 3) for the test form to be transformed (Baker, 1985; Wright & Stone, 1979).

Another common-item alternative, appropriate regardless of the IRT model, is referred to as the mean and sigma method (Hambleton & Swaminathan, 1985). Ability and item estimates are transformed using the equation $y = Ax + B$, where $A = s_y/s_x$ and $B = y - Ax$. The As and Bs are used to transform estimated item difficulties ($b_i^* = Ab_i + B$), item discriminations ($a_i^* = a_i/A$), and ability estimates $\Theta_a^* = A\Theta_a + B$.

Variations on the mean and sigma method include the robust mean and sigma methods proposed by Linn, Levine, Hastings, and Wardrop (1981) and Stocking and Lord (1983). These variations take into account the accuracy of estimation and give less weight to outliers among the common items. Similarly, a second method proposed by Stocking and Lord (1983), referred to as the characteristic curve method, improves on the basic linear procedure by making use of the discrimination parameter and the entire ability distribution in addition to the difficulty parameter in calculating the transformation coefficients. Thus, theoretically it could be expected to result in a more exact transformation.

It is beyond the scope of this chapter to report and evaluate these alternative transformation techniques (see McKinley [1988] for a comparison of several methods). However, there is an abundant literature that makes comparisons among the various IRT procedures as well as between IRT and conventional equating methods (e.g., Baker & Al-Karni, 1991; Skaggs & Lissitz, 1986a).

Finally, a note should be made about Step 3. The procedures for placing parameter estimates on a common scale are also used to transform ability estimates. If it is tenable to report rescaled ability estimates on a theta scale (typically ranging from -3 to +3), then the equating procedure is complete. In most cases, however, it is necessary to translate the theta estimates for both forms to a scale that makes more sense to examinees (i.e., corresponding estimated true scores). For example, examinees and other interested parties may be accustomed to seeing scores reported on a scale with a mean of 500 and a standard deviation of 100. If it is important to maintain this scale, the procedures and an example for doing this final transformation are provided in Cook and Eignor (1991).

In sum, there are many potential benefits of item response theory that support test equating. The need to meet the strict assumptions of these models has already been mentioned and should not be dismissed.   More practically, the largest disadvantage is the unfamiliarity of both testing professionals and consumers with the theory. Equally important is the lack of research clearly supporting the utility of a particular IRT methodology. Although each theory has its supporters, as does each method of parameter transformation (usually linked directly to a particular software program), it is not at all clear when the potential benefits accrued from using IRT outweigh the uncertainties. For the time being, conventional methods are a better choice and there is unlikely to be an appreciable loss of precision in licensure and certification examinations due to their use. Cook and Eignor (1983) offer a very clear discussion of the basic issues.

Comparison of Equating Procedures

During the 1980s and early 1990s there have been numerous studies comparing the outcomes of various equating techniques in horizontal and vertical equating settings. A complete review cannot be provided here; the reader is referred to Petersen et al. (1983) and Skaggs and Lissitz (1986b) as examples of excellent reviews and methodologies.

Overall, several authors have concluded that when the tests to be equated are similar in content and difficulty, and the design describes a horizontal equating situation, IRT methods are neither consistently better nor worse than conventional methods. Both conventional and IRT methods work well, particularly the three-parameter logistic model (Lord, 1980; Marco, Petersen, & Stewart, 1983; Petersen et al., 1983). When the tests do differ in content and length, or the anchor test differs from the remainder of the test(s), some authors have found that methods based on the three-parameter item response model perform better (e.g., Petersen et al., 1983) whereas others support use of conventional methods (e.g., Skaggs & Lissitz, 1986a). In part, the differences among studies are due to how the tests were designed, whether the data were real or simulated, and the choice of criterion. Current research results do not consistently support, at least from a psychometric perspective, the superiority of any one method. In fact, as noted by Skaggs and Lissitz (1986b) "it is unreasonable to expect a single equating method to provide the best results for equating all types of tests" (p. 495).

Conclusions regarding vertical equating are more straightforward. Most, though not all, researchers have concluded that vertical equating is problematic for both conventional and IRT methods, particularly the one-parameter Rasch model (Harris & Hoover, 1987; Loyd & Hoover, 1980; Gustafsson, 1979). See Harris (1991) and Skaggs and Lissitz (1988) for exceptions.

How should a researcher then choose a procedure, given the breadth of research results? Theoretically, IRT has some appeal *if* the data meet the assumptions of the model(s). The assumptions must be tested thoroughly; they cannot be assumed to be met. Further, it is doubtful that typical data produced by certifying and licensure examinations would provide adequate fit with the one-parameter IRT model. IRT methods require expertise in actually using the techniques, as well as in explaining them to interested users and consumers. At this point, few licensure and certifying bodies have ready access to individuals with the training to use IRT methods appropriately, although if an agency is just embarking on equating, it is probably as easy to learn IRT methods as conventional methods.

In summary, there are few differences among methods when examinations are parallel and examinees are of nearly equal ability. Conventional methods have the advantages of being easier to apply, understand, and explain to consumers. Consequently, without compelling reasons to the contrary, conventional methods are preferable. What should actually happen is that testing organizations should compare the two classes of methods to determine which fits their situation the best.

FACTORS AFFECTING THE PRECISION OF EQUATING

Numerous factors affect the precision of equating. Consistent results over many studies suggest general guidelines that might be followed in initiating and maintaining an equating program. Topics pertinent to a common-item design are listed below. Few authors study all facets simultaneously.

Anchor Test Length

A rule of thumb for many years has been that the common-items link should be roughly 20% the length of the total test or 20 items, whichever is longer (Angoff, 1971/1984). For conventional equating, lengths over 20 items seem not to have an advantage if the examinee groups are similar in ability (Klein & Kolen, 1985; Norcini, 1990). For IRT, some researchers have reported that much shorter anchor tests (as few as two or five well-chosen items) work well (Raju, Bode, Larsen, & Steinhaus, 1986; Vale, 1986). However, other researchers working within IRT suggest 15 to 20 items are more appropriate (Hills, Subhiyah, & Hirsch, 1988; Wingersky, Cook, & Eignor, 1986). Unless there is a persuasive need for a very short anchor, in light of the equivocal results regarding length, the 20% guideline still seems sensible.

Content Representation

One of the most widely cited studies with the anchor test design is by Klein and Jarjoura (1985). They investigated differences between content-representative anchors and longer, but nonrepresentative anchors; all anchors were matched to the total test in terms of difficulty. They included two different equating methods and results were evaluated with several different statistics. Overall, they found that content representation was very important for accurate equating results, especially when the groups of examinees were nonrandom. These results were supported by Petersen, Marco, and Stewart (1982) who concluded from their comparison of numerous linear equating models that even moderate differences in content between an anchor and the total test led to substantial error.

Difficulty of Anchor Test

Another characteristic of anchors that is often studied is difficulty. That is, researchers ask about the effects on equating when the anchor test is, and is not, similar in difficulty to the scored test. Petersen et al. (1982) found that differences in difficulty between an anchor and the total test were related to substantial error. Similarly, in a companion piece comparing error of equating for conventional and

IRT equating methods, they found that differences in difficulty between the anchor test and the form-specific items resulted in substantial error for the linear methods investigated, especially when the samples of examinees differed in ability (Marco et al., 1983). However, it might be noted that the differences did not affect error for the IRT-based methods, nor in situations when the examinee samples were random.

Ability of Examinee Groups

Studies looking at the results of vertical equating are not particularly encouraging. Though vertical equating will typically not be a problem for licensure and certification agencies where approximately equivalent groups take examinations over time, there is ample research to suggest that even when the differences in ability between the groups involved in the equatings are small, the impact upon equating may be sizable (Angoff & Cowell, 1986; Petersen et al., 1982). It should be noted, however, that some authors have found that all commonly used models are fairly robust to differences in examinee ability (Harris & Kolen, 1986).

Examinee Sample Size

Almost as often as researchers have asked how many common items are needed, they have also asked how many examinees are needed. In one article, a minimum sample size of 400 was recommended (Brennan & Kolen, 1987) for conventional equating techniques. However, another study found that errors of equating were not appreciably bigger with samples of 250 than of 500 (Norcini, 1990). Similar results using linear equating were found for samples of 200, 300, and 400, even when the samples were disparate in ability (Shea, Dawson-Saunders, & Norcini, 1992). More strikingly, a recent study that combined sample sizes of 25, 50, 100, and 200 with various smoothing techniques applied to the equipercentile method suggested that very small samples could be appropriate in some situations. These results are not definitive but they should be encouraging to examiners who consistently deal with small groups of test takers (Livingston, 1993).

In contrast to conventional methods, it is generally accepted that large samples are necessary for some item response theory software packages. Cook and Eignor (1991) suggest that as many as 2,000 examinees are needed for stable initial item calibration with joint maximum likelihood calibration. Smaller samples (i.e., a few hundred examinees) are sufficient for other IRT estimation procedures, such as marginal maximum likelihood and Bayesian (Drasgow, 1989; Harwell & Janosky, 1991; Stone, 1992).

In sum, several studies have concluded that equating works best when the characteristics of the common items represent those of the total test. Though few authors have studied variations in content, difficulty, length, and ability groups simultaneously, it is generally recommended that the common-item set should mirror the total test in content and statistical properties (Cook & Eignor, 1991). In essence, the higher the correlation between the anchor and the test, the more effective the equating (Thorndike, 1982). This is certainly the most conservative approach, especially when outcomes of equating have a significant and immediate impact on examinees' professional lives.

From the foregoing discussion, it is fair to conclude that many of the potentially troublesome issues surrounding equating can be averted by sound test construction processes. Potthoff (1982) presents many test construction ideas, and raises issues that deserve thoughtful consideration. Brennan and Kolen (1987) similarly list test development guidelines.

ISSUES THAT NEED MORE RESEARCH

Throughout this chapter, several topics have been mentioned that warrant additional attention. Many of the topics were outlined by Brennan and Kolen (1987). A partial list would include the following topics.

Scale Drift

Several investigators have shown that drift occurs over time with linked/chained equatings (Cook & Eignor, 1983; Petersen et al., 1983). More research is needed to identify (a) the conditions under which scale drift does and does not occur and (b) the effectiveness of methods to prevent it.

Security Breaches

Security breaches are always a threat to the validity of examination scores; they are particularly relevant to equating when they involve items in a common-item link. Most certifying examinations are administered under relatively secure conditions. Nevertheless, examination books do turn up missing from time to time, or test takers become acquainted with specific items. Simulations that consider issues such as the number of items affected and the length of time until discovery (e.g., several administrations) would prepare test agencies for possible future needs.

Changes to the Common-Item Link

Inevitably, changes will occur in a common-item link. Perhaps it will be discovered that an item was miskeyed, or perhaps new discoveries in a particular field will require that the answer to an item changes. When this occurs, decisions need to be made about alterations to the common-item link and the impact that such alterations have on examinee scores. Dorans (1986) provides a detailed and thorough account of the impact of several possible decisions, depending on the characteristics of the item.

Location Effects for Anchor Items

Many authors have discussed the effect of location or context of items upon examinee performance (e.g., Cook & Petersen, 1987; Harris, 1991; Kingston & Dorans, 1984; Kolen & Harris, 1990). Most of the studies have not focused on internal common-items links, though Thorndike (1982) did note that anchor items should be presented to examinees taking different forms at the same points so that practice and fatigue could be avoided. Because the performance on anchor items is especially important in determining examinees' scores, the impact of location should be further investigated.

Rounding

The numerous texts and empirical papers on the topic of equating provide an abundance of formulas and examples. However, there appears to be little uniformity regarding how many decimal places are used throughout the statistical manipulations, and there is no mention at what stages rounding occurs. The implicit consensus is that it is best to work with maximum precision throughout the equating process, but this is not explicitly stated (for exceptions see Potthoff, 1982 and Brennan & Kolen, 1987). Hand calculations using the scenarios presented earlier show that level of precision can make a difference to examinees, particularly those who score near the cutting score.

Equating Based on Standard-Setting Judgments

To this point, the discussions of equating have assumed that the goal is to transform scores on a test form so that they are comparable to scores on an alternate examination form. In a licensure or certification situation, however, actual test scores are sometimes less important than pass-fail decisions. Nevertheless, the scores of all examinees are transformed as usual and the cutting score or pass-fail point is among the scores that are altered. The rescaled cutting score is then used to make the pass/fail decisions. This ensures that the same licensure or certification decisions are being made regardless of which form of a test is taken.

For some kinds of licensure and certification situations, however, score equating may not work very well. For example, when the number of examinees is small or the pass-fail point is located far from the mean, score equating does not work well (Brennan & Kolen, 1987). Conventional equating might also not be optimal when nontraditional testing formats are used (e.g., essays, performance tests), or testing time is limited so that long anchor tests are impractical.

Several recent studies by Norcini and colleagues (Norcini, 1990; Norcini & Shea, 1992; Norcini, Shea, & Grosso, 1991; Norcini, Shea, & Lipner, 1994) have sought to address this issue by applying a common-item design and a linear statistical technique to the data gathered when experts set standards. In other words, rather than inputting data from examinees' scores (mean, standard deviations, etc.) into the formulas listed above for the common-item design, the data that are used in the calculations are generated via application of a standard-setting technique to each item in an examination. Specifically, for many licensure and certification examinations, the pass/fail point is chosen using a variation on Angoff's standard-setting method (Angoff, 1971/1984). As part of this process, a group of experts meets and each makes judgments about the proportion of borderline examinees who would respond correctly to each item. The result of this procedure is that each judge has "scores" on the whole test and the anchor test. Statistics summarizing these scores over all judges can readily be put into the equating formulas. Cutting score equivalents produced by this method can be compared to the results obtained by traditional score equating and to a criterion.

The series of studies concluded the following:

1. Rescaling based on experts' judgments (approximately 8 to 10 judges per group) was more accurate than equating based on examinee samples of 100, 250, and 500, and performed about the same as equatings based on samples of 1,000 and 2,000 examinees.
2. Results were stable for 25 or more common items and 5 or more judges. The amount of error was approximately 1 item on a 100-item test. Increasing the number of common items or judges resulted in little improvement in precision.
3. Transformed Angoff values were stable when compared to original estimates and bias in the estimates was small. This implies that rescaled Angoff values could be included in an item bank, and equivalent pass-fail decisions would result regardless of which items were chosen for a particular form of the test.
4. Use of judges' estimates in a common-item design was robust to unusual, or at least mismatched, common-item links that were fabricated of items either high or low in difficulty, and high or low in discrimination.

In sum, this area of research is still in its infancy but the issue it raises, equating at the cutting score, has relevance for certifying and licensing organizations. Results of early studies are encouraging but need to be extended to other types of examinations and judges.

Criteria to Evaluate Equating

Criteria used to evaluate the outcomes of equating procedures vary from one investigation to another. In empirical studies, such evaluation is often done by equating a test to itself and looking at how much variation (drift) has occurred over the numerous equatings. Another strategy is to define a "gold standard" criterion based on logically and/or theoretically acceptable arguments. In either case, researchers are apt to evaluate how well equated scores meet their criteria by reporting mean differences, mean absolute differences, or root mean square errors. Although these results are often convincing and informative, they frequently do not address the needs in practice for evaluating equating results in ongoing testing programs. Skaggs and Lissitz (1986b) provide a very thoughtful discussion of the issue. Additionally, Kolen (1990) points out the wisdom of using a "no equating" condition as a criterion.

Standard Errors of Equating

Closely related to the topic of appropriate criteria is the issue of standard error. For several of the conventional, linear methods, standard errors of equating have been developed. See, for example, the discussion presented by Petersen et al. (1989). Similarly, Jarjoura and Kolen (1985) present a method for estimating standard errors of equipercentile equating. In their discussion they point out that use of an inappropriate method (i.e., a linear method for a curvilinear relationship) can be particularly troublesome at the extremes of the distribution, where cutting scores are often located.

Misfitting Items

If IRT methods are used with the common-item design, the psychometrician needs to expend considerable effort ensuring that the items in the link (as well as the total tests) meet the assumptions of the particular model under investigation. Though models may be robust with a few misfitting items (Cook, Eignor, & Wingersky, 1987), research has not defined the limits outside of which misfit will adversely affect the results.

Biased Items

Another aspect of equating that has only recently received attention is bias or differential item functioning (Candell & Drasgow, 1988; Linn et al., 1981). This is a question of whether the items perform differently than expected with certain subpopulations of examinees, for example, white and African American examinees, or men and women. If so, then such items should not routinely be included as common items (and should not even be in the test form). Cook et al. (1987) discuss the importance of making sure that none of the items in the anchor test are biased for any examinee subgroup.

Alternative Item Formats

There is a need to investigate optimal equating designs and statistical techniques for item types other than multiple-choice questions (MCQs). Certainly, MCQs remain representative of most testing programs. However, in many fields there is a desire to move away from MCQs towards new formats such as performance tests and simulations. Investigations are quickly needed to explore how equating can be performed with alternative formats such as standardized patients, essays, and portfolios that involve new issues such as multiple correct answers and longer testing times per "item," thus limiting the number of test items available.

Multidimensional Tests

Many examinations used in professional licensure and certification settings comprise multiple dimensions. Clearly this is a problem for the widely used IRT models. Exploratory IRT work has begun to address multidimensional equating (Hirsch, 1989), as well as determine how bias results from multidimensionality (Oshima & Miller, 1992), but the methods are not widely used. On the other hand, multidimensionality does not specifically pose a problem for equatings within conventional theory, if the tests to be equated are similarly multidimensional (Cook & Petersen, 1987).

Adaptive Testing

Throughout the testing field there is an increased emphasis on adaptive testing. (See Wainer, 1990, for a comprehensive overview.) Generally speaking, this is the procedure of administering different sets of items to each examinee, targeted to his or her ability level. Consequently, each examinee may take different subsets of items, and raw scores will not be directly comparable. A somewhat different issue, but still presenting the same problem, is that of tailored testing. In tailored testing, examinees are allowed to select examination modules based on training and practice characteristics and interests.

It is not immediately clear how equating could be applied to adaptive testing using conventional equating techniques. An item bank in which all of the items have been placed on the same scale using IRT procedures presents one solution to these problems. However, issues of order and context effect could be potentially troublesome because the location of item presentation will undoubtedly be different for the calibration sample than for future examinees for whom the item is selected during an administration (Petersen et al., 1989).

Matching Examinee Samples on Ability

Angoff and Cowell (1986) have shown that even slight heterogeneity in the two equating groups can seriously impact on the equating transformations. A solution to this problem may lie in matching, that is, artificially improving the correspondence between the two examinee groups involved in the equating by matching on some examination score or external criterion (Dorans, 1990). A set of empirical studies in a special issue of *Applied Measurement in Education* (Wise, Plake, & Mitchell, 1990), using both real and simulated data (Eignor, Stocking, & Cook, 1990; Lawrence & Dorans, 1990; Livingston, Dorans, & Wright, 1990; Schmitt et al., 1990), explored matching under several different conditions and with different methods. Though theoretically a sound idea, the results suggest that, at best, matching is risky (Kolen, 1990; Skaggs, 1990).

Other Issues

As one thinks about the test development and administration procedures for a specific testing program, in all likelihood issues that have not been discussed, and for which there is little research, will arise. For example, it many be necessary to give test forms in different languages. Or, examinees with special needs may require altered test administration procedures. A third example is the need to decide what to do when test administration procedures are nonstandard for some examinees (the electricity goes out, there is distracting noise around the testing site). At this point, research cannot suggest how to handle each of these unique events, except to reiterate that the purpose of equating is to construct test scores that are equivalent, thus insuring fairness to examinees. Adaptation of the best studied methods described in this chapter should provide helpful responses.

SOFTWARE OPTIONS

Performing the statistical transformations required for equating can be done by hand (or hand-calculator) if examinee samples are small and the less complex conventional linear procedures are used. However, for ongoing testing programs some type of software will almost always be needed.

With an examination scoring system already in use, and a desire to employ conventional linear methods, it is not too demanding to write programs for equating procedures using a standard statistical software package such as SPSS (Norusis,

1992), SAS (SAS Institute, Inc., 1989), SYSTAT (Wilkinson, 1992), or BMDP (Dixon, 1990), or, if the expertise is available, using a language such as Fortran or C. Alternatively, a relatively new program for the widely used common-item design is LEQUATE. The program can handle either internal or external anchors, and it implements two widely used linear procedures (Tucker and Levine) (Waldron, 1988). It runs on IBM/PC and compatible DOS-based PCs. Documentation and the program are available free of charge from William J. Waldron, Tampa Electric Company, P.O. Box 111, Tampa, FL 33601.

Within item response theory (IRT) there are many choices; the three most widely used to date are BICAL, LOGIST, and BILOG. Published reviews and comparisons of various software programs are often helpful in making a selection decision (e.g., Harwell & Janosky, 1991; Mislevy & Stocking, 1989; Stone, 1992).

BICAL was developed for the one-parameter (Rasch) item calibration and equating (Wright & Stone, 1979); as such it has relatively limited uses. It provides estimated item parameters (the b or difficulty parameter only) and person ability estimates. It uses maximum likelihood estimation procedures and is available for DOS-based PCs. In the past 20 years, the program has evolved from BICAL to newer versions called BIGSTEPS, MSCALE, and MSTEPS. BIGSTEPS is the currently recommended PC version; it can reportedly handle responses for 20,000 examinees and 3,000 items. Information and prices on the program can be obtained from MESA Press, 5835 S. Kimbark Avenue, Chicago, IL 60637; (312) 702-1596 or (312) 288-5650 (phones); (312) 702-0248 (FAX).

LOGIST is a very comprehensive and flexible program, developed by Educational Testing Services. It uses maximum likelihood estimation procedures and the user can select the one-, two-, or three-parameter IRT models. A strength of this program is that it has been in use for many years so there is ample literature to read for educational and comparative purposes. It does require relatively large sample sizes for calibration. At this point it is only available for use on a mainframe but a personal computer version is forthcoming. Copies are available from Educational Testing Service, Rosedale Road, Princeton, NJ 08541.

BILOG has become a popular IRT alternative in recent years. It uses marginal maximum likelihood item parameter estimation procedures, and is capable of handling one-, two-, or three-parameter IRT models. Scale scores can be estimated with maximum likelihood, Bayes, or Bayes modal procedures. The program is available for DOS and OS-2 based systems. Recent versions for UNIX operating systems are also available and a Windows version is nearly ready for release. The user's manual is clear and helpful. Information regarding the software may be obtained from Scientific Software International, 1525 East 53rd Street—Suite 530, Chicago, IL 60615-4530, (800) 247-6113 (phone); (312) 684-4979 (FAX). SSI also offers several other IRT-based software programs appropriate for item formats other than dichotomously scored (right/wrong) items: BIMAIN, MULTILOG, PARSCALE, and TESTFACT.

With LOGIST and BILOG, equating can be achieved with concurrent calibration or the fixed bs method. However, if one is using a common-item design and does not wish to recalibrate at each administration, then another method will have to be used to calculate the transformation constants and then rescale the estimated-item parameters and person abilities. One possibility that works reasonably well is to use a standard statistical software package, such as SPSS (Norusis, 1992), SAS (SAS Institute, Inc., 1989), SYSTAT (Wilkinson, 1992), or BMDP (Dixon, 1990), and do your own programming. An alternative is to get access to routines used by other investigators that were specifically designed for this purpose. Examples are EQUATE and EQUATE 2.0, programs written in FORTRAN for use on DOS-based PCs. EQUATE was developed for dichotomously scored items and uses the test characteristic curve method of equating. EQUATE-2 extends EQUATE capabilities to include graded or nominal scoring procedures. They were designed by Frank Baker and colleagues at the University of Wisconsin (Baker, Al-Karni, & Al-Dosary, 1991; Baker, 1993) and are available upon request from Frank Baker, Department of Educational Psychology, Educational Sciences Building, 1025 W. Johnson Street, University of Wisconsin, Madison, WI 53706.

Final examples that one might find useful are RASCAL and ASCAL, marketed by Assessment Systems Corporation. RASCAL computes item parameter estimates and person ability estimates within the one-parameter (Rasch) IRT model. ASCAL performs the same tasks for the two- and three-parameter models. RASCAL estimates are based on an unconditional maximum likelihood estimation procedure and ASCAL used Bayesian modal estimation. With RASCAL, the user can "fix" item difficulties to predetermined values. With ASCAL, the user can link (i.e., equate) items from different administrations onto a single scale during one run. Both programs run on DOS-based personal computers. They reportedly can handle up to 250 test items and several thousand examinees (30,000 for RASCAL and 15,000 for ASCAL).

A potential benefit of RASCAL and ASCAL for some users is that they can be integrated into a broader testing system called MicroCAT. MicroCAT is a relatively complete test-design and administration system. Within the multifunction system, it is possible to develop items (with graphics), print test forms, do item and test analysis, and create result report forms. If IRT is chosen for item analysis, items can be calibrated with RASCAL or ASCAL. Conventional item analysis (and thus, score equating) is also available. MicroCAT is available from Assessment System Corporation (2233 University Avenue, Suite 440, St. Paul, MN 55114). It is also available from SAGE Publications, Inc. (P.O. Box 5084, Thousand Oaks, CA 91359-9924). It might also be noted that the user can work with personnel at Assessment System Corporation to develop customized packages to meet one's particular needs.

REFERENCES

American Educational Research Association, American Psychological Association, & National Council on Measurement in Education. (1985). *Standards for educational and psychological testing*. Washington, DC: American Psychological Association, Inc.

Angoff, W. H. (1984). *Scales, norms, and equivalent scores*. Princeton, NJ: Educational Testing Services. Originally published in R. L. Thorndike (Ed.),

(1971). *Educational measurement* (2nd ed.). Washington, DC: American Council on Education.

Angoff, W. H., & Cowell, W. R. (1986). An examination of the assumption that the equating of parallel forms is population-independent. *Journal of Educational Measurement, 23*, 327-345.

Baker, F. B. (1985). *The basics of item response theory.* Portsmouth, NH: Heinemann.

Baker, F. B. (1992). Equating tests under the graded response model. *Applied Psychological Measurement, 16*, 87-96.

Baker, F. B. (1993). EQUATE 2.0: A computer program for the test characteristic curve method of IRT equating. *Applied Psychological Measurement, 17*, 20.

Baker, F. B., & Al-Karni, A. (1991). A comparison of two procedures for computing IRT equating procedures. *Journal of Educational Measurement, 28*, 147-162.

Baker, F. B., Al-Karni, A., & Al-Dosary, I. M. (1991). EQUATE: A computer program for the test characteristic curve method of IRT equating. *Applied Psychological Measurement, 15*, 78.

Birnbaum, A. (1968). Some latent trait models and their use in inferring an examinee's ability. In F. M. Lord & M. R. Novick, *Statistical theories of mental test scores* (pp. 392-479). Reading, MA: Addison-Wesley.

Bock, R. D., & Aitkin, M. (1981). Marginal maximum likelihood estimation of item parameters: An application of the EM algorithm. *Psychometrika, 46*, 443-445.

Braun, H. I., & Holland, P. W. (1982). Observed-score test equating: A mathematical analysis of some ETS equating procedures. In P. W. Holland & D. B. Rubin (Eds.), *Test equating* (pp. 9-49). New York: Academic Press.

Brennan, R. L., & Kolen, M. J. (1987). Some practical issues in equating. *Applied Psychological Measurement, 11*, 279-290.

Budescu, D. (1985). Efficiency of linear equating as a function of the length of the anchor test. *Journal of Educational Measurement, 22*, 13-20.

Candell, G. L., & Drasgow, F. (1988). An iterative procedure for linking metrics and assessing item bias in item response theory. *Applied Psychological Measurement, 12*, 253-260.

Cook, L. L., & Eignor, D. R. (1983). Practical considerations regarding the use of item response theory to equate tests. In R. K. Hambleton (Ed.), *Applications of item response theory* (pp. 175-195). Vancouver, BC: Educational Research Institute of British Columbia.

Cook, L. L., & Eignor, D. R. (1991). An NCME instructional module on IRT equating methods. *Educational Measurement: Issues and Practice, 10*(3), 37-45.

Cook, L. L., Eignor, D. R., & Wingersky, M. S. (1987, April). *The effect on IRT equating of using linking items with problematic item response functions.* Paper presented at the annual meeting of the American Educational Research Association, Washington, DC.

Cook, L. L., & Petersen, N. S. (1987). Problems related to the use of conventional and item response theory equating methods in less than optimal circumstances. *Applied Psychological Measurement, 11*, 225-244.

Crocker, L., & Algina, J. (1986). *Introduction to classical and modern test theory*. New York: Holt, Rinehart, and Winston.

Dixon, W. J. (Ed.). (1990). *BMDP statistical software*. Berkeley, CA: University of California Press.

Dorans, N. J. (1986). The impact of item deletion on equating conversions and reported score distributions. *Journal of Educational Measurement, 23*, 245-264.

Dorans, N. J. (1990). Equating methods and sampling designs. *Applied Measurement in Education, 3*, 3-17.

Dorans, N. J., & Kingston, N. M. (1985). The effects of violations of unidimensionality on the estimation of item and ability parameters and on item response theory equating of the GRE verbal scale. *Journal of Educational Measurement, 22*, 249-262.

Drasgow, F. (1989). An evaluation of marginal maximum likelihood estimation for the two-parameter logistic model. *Applied Psychological Measurement, 13*, 77-90.

Eignor, D. R., Stocking, M. L., & Cook, L. L. (1990). Simulation results of effects on linear and curvilinear observed- and true-score equating procedures of matching with a fallible criterion. *Applied Measurement in Education, 3*, 37-52.

Fairbank, B. A., Jr. (1987). The use of presmoothing and postsmoothing to increase the precision of equipercentile equating. *Applied Psychological Measurement, 11*, 245-262.

Gulliksen, H. (1950). *Theory of mental tests*. New York: Wiley.

Gustafsson, J. E. (1979). The Rasch model in vertical equating of tests: A critique of Slinde and Linn. *Journal of Educational Measurement, 16*, 153-158.

Hambleton, R. K., & Murray, L. M. (1983). Some goodness of fit investigations for item response models. In R.K. Hambleton (Ed.), *Applications of item response theory* (pp. 71-94). Vancouver, BC: Educational Research Institute of British Columbia.

Hambleton, R. K., & Rovinelli, R. J. (1986). Assessing the dimensionality of a set of test items. *Applied Psychological Measurement, 10*, 287-302.

Hambleton, R. K., & Swaminathan, H. (1985). *Item response theory: principles and applications*. Boston: Kluwer-Nijhoff Publishing.

Hambleton, R. K., Swaminathan, H., & Rogers, H. J. (1991). *Fundamentals of item response theory*. Newbury Park, CA: Sage Publications.

Hanson, B. A. (1991). A comparison of bivariate smoothing methods in common-item equipercentile equating. *Applied Psychological Measurement, 15*, 391-408.

Harris, D. J. (1991). A comparison of Angoff's design I and design II for vertical equating using traditional and IRT methodology. *Journal of Educational Measurement, 28*, 221-235.

Harris, D. J. (1987, May). *Effect of comparability of examinee groups*. ACT Research Report Series 87-5. Iowa City, IA: American College Testing.

Harris, D. J. (1991). Effects of passage and item scrambling on equating relationships. *Applied Psychological Measurement, 15*, 247-256.

Harris, D. J., & Hoover, H. D. (1987). An application of the three-parameter IRT model to vertical equating. *Applied Psychological Measurement*, *11*, 151-159.

Harris, D. J., & Kolen, M. J. (1986). Effect of examinee group on equating relationships. *Applied Psychological Measurement*, *10*, 35-43.

Harwell, M. R., & Janosky, J. E. (1991). An empirical study of the effects of small datasets and varying prior variances on item parameter estimation in BILOG. *Applied Psychological Measurement*, *15*, 279-291.

Hills, J. R., Subhiyah, R. G., & Hirsch, T. M. (1988). Equating minimum-competency tests: Comparisons of methods. *Journal of Educational Measurement*, *25*, 221-231.

Hirsch, T. M. (1989). Multidimensional equating. *Journal of Educational Measurement*, *26*, 337-349.

Holland, P. W., & Rubin, D. B. (1982a). Introduction: Research on test equating sponsored by Educational Testing Service, 1978-1980. In P. W. Holland & D. B. Rubin (Eds.), *Test equating* (pp. 1-6). New York: Academic Press.

Holland, P. W., & Rubin, D. B. (Eds.) (1982b). *Test equating*. New York: Academic Press.

Holland, P. W., & Thayer, D. T. (1985). Section pre-equating in the presence of practice effects. *Journal of Educational Statistics*, *10*, 109-120.

Jarjoura, D., & Kolen, M. J. (1985). Standard errors of equipercentile equating for the common item nonequivalent populations design. *Journal of Educational Statistics*, *10*, 143-160.

Kingston, N. M., & Dorans, N. J. (1984). Item location effects and their implications for IRT equating and adaptive testing. *Applied Psychological Measurement*, *8*, 147-154.

Klein, L. W., & Jarjoura, D. (1985). The importance of content representation for common-item equating with nonrandom groups. *Journal of Educational Measurement*, *22*, 197-206.

Klein, L. W., & Kolen, M. J. (1985, April). *Effect of number of common items in common-item equating with nonrandom groups*. Paper presented at the annual meeting of the American Educational Research Association, Chicago.

Kolen, M. J. (1988). An NCME instructional module on traditional equating methodology. *Educational Measurement: Issues and Practice*, *7*(4), 29-36.

Kolen, M. J. (1990). Does matching in equating work? A discussion. *Applied Measurement in Education*, *3*, 97-104.

Kolen, M. J. (1991). Smoothing methods for estimating test score distributions. *Journal of Educational Measurement*, *28*, 257-282.

Kolen, M. J., & Brennan, R. L. (1987). Linear equating models for the common-item nonequivalent-populations design. *Applied Psychological Measurement*, *11*, 263-277.

Kolen, M. J., & Harris, D. J. (1990). Comparison of item preequating and random groups equating using IRT and equipercentile methods. *Journal of Educational Measurement*, *27*, 27-39.

Lawrence, I. M., & Dorans, N. J. (1990). Effect on equating results of matching samples on an anchor test. *Applied Measurement in Education*, *3*, 19-36.

Linn, R. L., Levine, M. V., Hastings, C. N., & Wardrop, J. L. (1981). Item bias in a test of reading comprehension. *Applied Psychological Measurement, 5,* 159-173.

Livingston, S. A. (1993). Small-sample equating with log-linear smoothing. *Journal of Educational Measurement, 30,* 23-39.

Livingston, S. A., Dorans, N. J., & Wright, N. K. (1990). What combination of sampling and equating methods works best? *Applied Measurement in Education, 3,* 73-95.

Lord, F. M. (1977). Practical applications of item characteristic curve theory. *Journal of Educational Measurement, 14,* 117-138.

Lord, F. M. (1980). *Applications of item response theory to practical testing problems.* Hillsdale, NJ: Lawrence Erlbaum Associates.

Loyd, B. H., & Hoover, H. D. (1980). Vertical equating using the Rasch model. *Journal of Educational Measurement, 17,* 179-193.

Marco, G. L., Petersen, N. S., & Stewart, E. E. (1993). A test of the adequacy of curvilinear score equating models. In D. Weiss (Ed.), *New horizons in testing* (pp. 147-177). New York: Academic Press.

McKinley, R. L. (1988). A comparison of six-methods for combining multiple IRT item parameter estimates. *Journal of Educational Measurement, 25,* 233-246.

Mislevy, R. J., & Bock, R. D. (1989). *PC-BILOG 3: Item analysis and test scoring with binary logistic models.* Mooresville, IN: Scientific Software.

Mislevy, R. J., & Stocking, M. L. (1989). A consumer's guide to LOGIST and BILOG. *Applied Psychological Measurement, 13,* 57-75.

Norcini, J. J. (1990). Equivalent pass/fail decisions. *Journal of Educational Measurement, 27,* 59-66.

Norcini, J. J., Maihoff, N. A., Day, S. C., & Benson, J. A., Jr. (1989). Trends in medical knowledge as assessed by the certifying examination in internal medicine. *Journal of the American Medical Association, 262,* 2402-2404.

Norcini, J. J., & Shea, J. A. (1992). Equivalent estimates of borderline group performance in standard setting. *Journal of Educational Measurement, 29,* 19-24.

Norcini, J., Shea, J., & Grosso, L. (1991). The effect of numbers of experts and common items on cutting score equivalents based on expert judgment. *Applied Psychological Measurement, 15,* 241-246.

Norcini, J. J., Shea, J. A., & Lipner, R. S. (1994). The effect of anchor item characteristics on equivalent cutting scores. *Applied Measurement in Education, 7,* 187-194.

Norusis, M. J., & SPSS, Inc. (1992). *SPSS for Windows. Base system user's guide.* Release 5.0. Chicago: SPSS, Inc.

Nungester, R. J., Dillon, G. F., Swanson, D. B., Orr, N. A., & Powell, R. D. (1991). Standard-setting plans for the NBME comprehensive part I and part II. *Academic Medicine, 66,* 429-433.

Oshima, T. C., & Miller, M. D. (1992). Multidimensionality and item bias in item response theory. *Applied Psychological Measurement, 16,* 237-248.

Petersen, N. S., Cook, L. L., & Stocking, M. L. (1983). IRT versus conventional equating methods: A comparative study of scale stability. *Journal of Educational Statistics, 8*, 137-156.

Petersen, N. S., Kolen, M. J., & Hoover, H. D. (1989). Scaling, norming, and equating. In R. L. Linn (Ed.), *Educational measurement* (3rd ed.; pp. 221-262). New York: American Council on Education-Macmillan Publishing Company.

Petersen, N. S., Marco, G. L., & Stewart, E. E. (1982). A test of the adequacy of linear score equating models. In P. W. Holland & D. B. Rubin (Eds.), *Test equating* (pp. 71-135). New York: Academic Press.

Potthoff, R. F. (1982). Some issues in test equating. In P. W. Holland & D. B. Rubin (Eds.), *Test equating* (pp. 201-242). New York: Academic Press.

Raju, N. S., Bode, R. K., Larsen, V. S., & Steinhaus, S. (1986, April). *Anchor-test size and horizontal equating with the Rasch and three-parameter models.* Paper presented at the annual meeting of the National Council on Measurement in Education, San Francisco.

Rock, D. A. (1982). Equating using the confirmatory factor analysis model. In P. W. Holland, & D. B. Rubin (Eds.), *Test equating* (pp. 247-257). New York: Academic Press.

SAS Institute, Inc. (1989). *SAS/STAT user's guide* (version 6, fourth ed.). Cary, NC: SAS Institute, Inc.

Schmitt, A. P., Cook, L. L., Dorans, N. J., & Eignor, D. R. (1990). Sensitivity of equating results to different sampling strategies. *Applied Measurement in Education, 3*, 53-71.

Shea, J. A., Dawson-Saunders, B., & Norcini, J. J. (1992, April). *The effects of equating when examinee groups vary in size and ability.* Paper presented at the annual meeting of the American Educational Research Association, San Francisco.

Shea, J. A., Norcini, J. J., & Webster, G. D. (1988). An application of item response theory to certifying examinations in internal medicine. *Evaluation and the Health Professions, 11*, 283-305.

Skaggs, G. (1990). To match or not to match samples on ability for equating: A discussion of five articles. *Applied Measurement in Education, 3*, 105-113.

Skaggs, G., & Lissitz, R. W. (1986a). An exploration of the robustness of four test equating models. *Applied Psychological Measurement, 10*, 303-317.

Skaggs, G., & Lissitz, R. W. (1986b). IRT test equating: Relevant issues and a review of recent literature. *Review of Educational Research, 56*, 495-529.

Skaggs, G., & Lissitz, R. W. (1988). Effect of examinee ability on test equating invariance. *Applied Psychological Measurement, 12*, 69-82.

Stocking, M. L., & Lord, F. M. (1983). Developing a common metric in item response theory. *Applied Psychological Measurement, 7*, 201-210.

Stone, C. A. (1992). Recovery of marginal maximum likelihood estimates in the two-parameter logistic response model: An evaluation of MULTILOG. *Applied Psychological Measurement, 16*, 1-16.

Swaminathan, H., & Gifford, J. A. (1982). Bayesian estimation in the Rasch model. *Journal of Educational Statistics, 7*, 175-191.

Swaminathan, H., & Gifford, J. A. (1983). Estimation of parameters in the three-parameter model. In D. Weiss (Ed.), *New horizons in testing* (pp. 13-30). New York: Academic Press.

Thissen, D. (1991). *MULTILOG user's guide, version 6.0.* Mooresville, IN: Scientific Software.

Thorndike, R. L. (1982). *Applied psychometrics.* Boston: Houghton Mifflin, 1982.

Vale, C. D. (1986). Linking item parameters onto a common scale. *Applied Psychological Measurement, 10*, 333-344.

Wainer, H. (1990). *Computerized adaptive testing: A primer.* Hillsdale, NJ: Lawrence Erlbaum.

Waldron, W. J. (1988). LEQUATE: Linear equating for the common-item nonequivalent-populations design. *Applied Psychological Measurement, 12*, 323.

Wilkinson, L. (1992). *SYSTAT: Statistics (Version 5.2).* Evanston IL; SYSTAT, Inc..

Wingersky, M. S., Cook, L. L., & Eignor, D. R. (1986, April). *Specifying the characteristics of linking items used for item response theory item calibration.* Paper presented at the annual meeting of the American Educational Research Association, San Francisco.

Wise, S. L., Plake, B. S., & Mitchell, J. V., Jr. (Eds.) (1990). *Applied Measurement in Education, 3*(1).

Wright, B. D., & Stone, M. H. (1979). *Best test design: Rasch measurement.* Chicago: Mesa Press.

Section Three
Emerging Practices

COMPUTERIZED TESTING IN LICENSURE

C. David Vale

Insurance Testing Corporation

Computerized testing has come out of the laboratory and into the field. By rough estimates, over a million licensure and certification examinations are currently given by computer each year, and the number is rising. Computerized testing is not appropriate for every application, however. Computerized tests always result in significantly greater direct costs than paper-and-pencil tests. To justify their use, a computerized test must result in a net dollar saving. This means that something in the process of computerization must offer a cost reduction that more than offsets the direct cost of computerization. The purpose of this chapter is to identify the areas in which computerization can result in dollar savings and to help the reader determine if, and in what form, computerized testing is appropriate for a specific application.

It may be possible to make the case that a computerized test is useful because it can implement new question types or questioning strategies and thus measure something that cannot be measured by other means. Such an application has yet to be demonstrated in licensing. This chapter will thus ignore this possibility, dealing exclusively with the use of computerization of traditional test questions as a means of saving costs.

SCHEDULING EFFICIENCY—AN OBVIOUS ADVANTAGE

The success of computerized testing in licensure today is due in large part to the scheduling improvements it has offered. Consider a typical paper-and-pencil license testing program: Tests are given every 2 weeks and must be scheduled 2 weeks in advance. Say a candidate decides on October 1 to take a licensure test. The scheduling deadline for the October 14 test has just passed and the first test available is October 28. The candidate takes and fails that test, learns of the failure on November 10, and must reschedule for November 25. A typical computerized testing program is different: Tests are given daily and candidates need to register only one day in advance. Thus, the candidate could fail the first test on October 2, study hard that night, and take the retest on October 3. Assuming the candidate passed the second time in either scenario, the result of computerization would be a time saving of almost 2 months. If passing a test stands between a candidate and a career, a 2-month time saving can be significant.

Why does a computerized testing program offer such scheduling improvements? The direct costs in a testing program can be divided into five categories: (1) registering a candidate to take a test, (2) providing a place for the candidate to take the test, (3) providing a medium on which to present the test, (4) providing someone to proctor the examination, and (5) scoring and reporting the results. An optimal administration design must balance all five of these categories. If the criterion for design is minimal cost, the least expensive combination of elements must be found.

Paper-and-pencil administration offers significant freedom to choose a low-cost design. The minimal expense in administration is achieved by requiring the candidate to mail an application and a check (avoiding telephone and credit-card charges), administering the test in idle space that is normally used for other purposes (e.g., Saturday in a high-school cafeteria), presenting the questions on an inexpensive medium (e.g., paper), using part-time personnel earning supplemental (lower wage) income to administer the test, and limiting expensive equipment to a single site (e.g., scoring and reporting results from a central office). The optimal economic design results in the often seen massed administration of paper-and-pencil tests and 2- to 4-week advance registration requirements.

A computerized testing program has less freedom in design. The media for test presentation are not readily portable; this suggests implementation in a permanent site. The media, as well as the space to store them, are relatively expensive; this suggests that relatively few be used. When the costs of equipment and space are balanced against the cost of proctoring, small, frequent sessions usually result. In its optimal configuration, computerized administration is significantly more expensive than paper-and-pencil administration. Historically, this naturally gave rise to the offering to candidates of improved services such as rapid scheduling and score reporting.

Computerized administration is not essential to achieve the scheduling advantages typically obtained through computerized testing. However, when the design appropriate for computerization (and yielding the scheduling advantages) is applied to paper-and-pencil testing (e.g., small, frequent sessions; rapid scheduling; onsite score reporting), its costs are nearly as great as full computerization. The direct cost of a computer system adequate for implementing multiple-choice licensure tests is only about $300 per testing station per year, which translates to about one dollar per test in a center that gives one test per station per day. Thus, if daily testing is implemented, the additional costs of computerization are small.

Scheduling improvements, from a scientific perspective, are not very interesting. Psychometric journals rarely publish articles documenting the time saved through efficient handling of candidates. As a point of comparison with psychometric savings discussed below, however, remember that the time savings achieved through scheduling improvements are on the order of 1 to 2 months.

Note, however, that these time savings translate into dollar savings only when the time has value. Time typically has great value when a candidate must pass a test to get a license to practice a profession. When the translation is achieved by comparing the earning power of an unemployed individual with that of a licensed individual, the figures are large enough to defy belief. Anecdotal experience suggests that these savings are meaningful to licensure candidates. Time has less value if the candidate can practice the profession on a provisional license while attempting to pass the test. Similarly, time has less value to certification candidates than to license candidates because the connection between having the certification and earning money is less direct. If the decision to computerize a test is based on the improvements possible in scheduling efficiency, it is wise to first verify that the time saved is truly valuable.

SOME PRACTICAL ISSUES IN COMPUTERIZATION

Although the time savings through changes in the approach to scheduling may appear to strongly recommend the computerized approach, there are some practical issues that should at least be considered before embarking on the path of computerization.

Computer Anxiety and the Unique Nature of the Medium

Two concerns have been expressed since computerized tests were first proposed: First, are the results of a computerized test comparable to those of a paper-and-pencil test? Second, will the computer create undue anxiety in the examinees that will affect their performances on the tests?

The answer to the first question is relevant only if a test is administered in both computerized and paper-and-pencil modes. In that case, fairness is an issue. However, if a test is only administered in computerized mode, the fairness issue does not exist. The paper-and-pencil mode is in no sense a standard to which the computerized mode will be compared.

Nevertheless, studies comparing the two modes have found differences to be rare. Kiely, Zara, & Weiss (1986) found no differences between modes for unspeeded Armed Services Vocational Aptitude Battery (ASVAB) subtests, when the entire item fit on a single computer screen. Even items containing graphics showed no difference. The differences they found were for reading-comprehension items that required the candidate to scroll the screen to see the passage. White, Clements, and Fowler (1985) found comparable scores on the Minnesota Multiphasic Personality Inventory (MMPI) administered in both modes, although they noted that the availability of a "cannot say" response on the computer resulted in significantly more omits. Lukin, Dowd, Plake, and Kraft (1985) found no differences between scores on measures of anxiety, depression, or psychological reactance across modes. Moreno, Wetzel, McBride, & Weiss (1984) found arithmetic, vocabulary, and reading comprehension tests of the ASVAB similar across modes. Greaud & Green (1986) did, however, find a substantial difference between modes for a speeded test. Thus, to summarize, if the computer simply presents text (or high-quality graphics), the candidate is not rushed (i.e., the test is not speeded), and no complicated manipulations (e.g., scrolling a long screen) are required, the results from the two modes are psychometrically equivalent.

Regarding the question of computer anxiety, although it undoubtedly exists in isolated cases, it is not prevalent. Burke, Normand, and Raju (1987) found no difference in anxiety for the two modes. They also found that examinees preferred taking the test on the computer. White, Clements, and Fowler (1985) found that examinees preferred the computerized mode. Lukin et al. (1985) found that 85% of examinees preferred the computerized mode. Wise, Barnes, Harvey, and Plake (1989) found that neither the degree of anxiety toward computers nor the amount of experience with computers had any effect on test scores. In summary, examinees tend to prefer the computerized mode of administration and do not appear to suffer anxiety toward it.

Availability and Economics of Computerized Testing Centers

Recall that the significant advantages obtained through computerized testing result from the rapid, convenient scheduling and the immediate availability of results. It is easy, with commercially available software, to set up a computer to administer a test, even an adaptive one. It is quite feasible to set up a local area network and collect results from multiple testing stations in a database. But it is a major endeavor requiring significant testing volume to set up a cost-effective wide-area testing network complete with the management and support personnel necessary to operate it.

How does such a network operate? Consider as an example ITC's (Insurance Testing Corporation) network of insurance testing centers. All exam registration (money collection) and scheduling is done centrally in St. Paul, Minnesota. Candidates can register for their exams by mail or by phone (paying with a credit card). Candidates who register by phone can schedule their exams in the same call; those who register by mail must call to schedule. All scheduling is done interactively; candidates do not express preferences for dates and times with their mail registrations. Candidates can take their tests at any of the 58 centers in the network at any time a seat in the chosen center is available.

The testing centers consist of testing computers connected to redundant network servers through a local area network. The server computers contain the tests. All test material is encrypted using the National Bureau of Standards' Data Encryption Standard (DES). The servers are also stored in a thick steel safe that is bolted to the floor of the testing center.

Each night, when the registration phone center in St. Paul closes, testing schedules are assembled for each of the testing sites. These schedules are sent electronically to each of the sites using fast modems and standard phone lines. (Except for periodic modem communication, such as this, the sites operate autonomously.) Typically, the test item banks are stored at the sites and only test assembly information is sent with the schedule. If a candidate chooses to take a test at an out-of-state location (e.g., a Pennsylvania test at an Oregon center), the complete test will be sent; only those tests administered frequently are stored at a site.

The next morning at each center, 30 to 45 minutes before the first scheduled test of the day, a test proctor logs into the testing center's computer system by entering a password. As part of the log-in process, electronic mail sent from St. Paul is displayed for the proctor to read. The system is then ready to administer tests. At that point, the testing system initiates a call to St. Paul to communicate that it is up and running. (If sites do not report in 30 minutes prior to the first scheduled test, alarms go off in St. Paul.)

As candidates arrive, their identifications are checked, the system is explained to them, and they are seated at testing stations to take their tests. The testing stations are standard personal computers with slightly modified keyboards; the relevant keys are color coded and a few of the key descriptions have been changed. Although the proctors generally explain everything a candidate will need to know to take a test, each candidate receives an on-line tutorial that provides the detail essential to taking the test.

When a candidate finishes a test, his or her results are presented on the computer screen. A paper copy of the score report is printed at that time and is usually ready by the time the candidate emerges from the testing room. In some states, these score reports are considered official. In most, however, the communication of results to the states is electronic.

When a site closes for the day, test results for all candidates who tested are electronically communicated to St. Paul. There they are stored in a database and assembled for reporting to the states. This reporting generally takes place the next morning, less than 24 hours after the test was taken.

Figure 1 shows the direct cost of operation of 45 testing centers, for which cost data were available as of this writing, as a function of center size. This figure was based on data through the first 9 months of 1993. The abscissa represents the number of testing hours per year. The ordinate is the cost per hour of testing. (Actual dollar values are not included as they are considered confidential information.) As may be intuitively obvious, the cost per hour drops as the testing volume

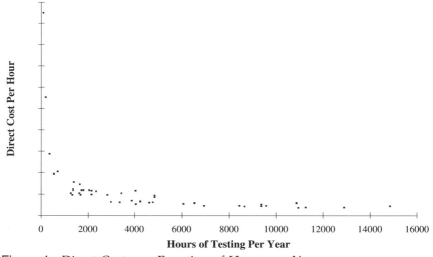

Figure 1. Direct Cost as a Function of Hours per Year

at a site increases. This is because certain fixed costs of establishing a center need to be paid, whether tests are given or not (e.g., rent). Although some aspects of the fixed costs can be tailored to the anticipated volume of the site (e.g., the amount of office space), others cannot. In ITC's centers, fixed costs that do not vary according to the volume of the center include costs of the redundant network servers, a steel safe in which to put the network servers, and a telephone line. Also, the time to open a center (45 minutes before the first candidate arrives) is the same regardless of whether 2 or 60 tests are given that day.

The costs shown in Figure 1 are for centers that have been optimized for cost to the greatest degree ITC's center concept would allow. Even so, costs rise dramatically as the annual testing hours fall below about 1,000. Political, rather than economic, concerns require ITC to have a few such centers. For insurance tests, ITC has found that an average of between three and four centers per state is needed. A national testing program giving 2-hour tests would have to administer almost 90,000 exams per year to get to the 1,000-hour point, where the cost curve flattens out. This is an optimistic figure, however, because it is unlikely that any program will be able to evenly distribute its examinations across centers.

As of this writing, there are two testing networks available to administer tests that are national in scope. One is operated by Sylvan-Kee Systems. The other is operated by Drake Training and Technologies. The ITC network is also available in specific regions, but does not approach national scope. This means that the choice of testing networks for the implementation of computerized tests is some-what limited. Although the costs of using such a network vary by application and vendor, the number of vendors and available testing stations has not grown large enough yet that national computerized testing services are a commodity.

The availability of testing networks is a key issue in the implementation of a computerized test. Although the economics of time suggest that candidates will support rather hefty fees for the convenience of computerization, it remains to be seen in practice how high a fee candidates will endure without complaint. Fees as high as $30 per hour are occasionally mentioned for national service of small programs; but because the actual fees are negotiated and usually private, exact numbers are difficult to pin down. In the case of insurance and real-estate candidates, a mandatory per-test increment of $30 ($10 to $15 per hour) for computerization does not seem to cause problems. Whether candidates would readily accept a per-test surcharge of $75 to $100 is an empirical question.

Legal Defensibility of Computerized Tests

Perhaps the most comprehensive review of the potential legal challenges to a computerized test is contained in a compendium entitled "Collected Works on the Legal Aspects of Computerized Adaptive Testing" (NCSBN, 1991), a collection of works commissioned by the National Council of State Boards of Nursing in anticipation of its effort to implement computerized adaptive forms of the exami-nations it publishes for the licensure of Registered and Licensed Practical nurses. After pointedly noting that there was no case law directly on point (because no one had yet been sued over a computerized test), the contained works consider the possible mechanisms of legal attack on computerized or adaptive tests. This discussion is largely drawn from that document and a paper by Mehrens and Popham (1992); readers interested in further details are directed to those sources.

In considering the possibility of legal challenge, it is worth noting that the successful suit will not be based simply on a candidate's distaste for computers or tests, but must have some basis in law. There are relatively few laws on which a challenge can be based. The first possibilities are the 5th and 14th amendments to the United States Constitution. The Constitution prohibits the federal and state governments from denying life, liberty, or property without due process of law and requires these governmental units to provide all citizens with equal protection under the law. A license is considered property.

As discussed by O'Brien (1991), constitutional cases are difficult to make. First, the due process principles require only that the requirements for allowing an individual to practice a profession bear a rational relationship to his or her fitness to do so; historically this has only required that the examination ask questions related to the domain of knowledge required by the profession. Second, claims alleging violation of the equal protection requirements must prove intent; if a process appears neutral, it need bear only a "fair and substantial relationship" to the competence required by the license. Thus, a challenge to a computerized test on constitutional grounds is likely to be successful only if it can be shown that it was intentionally used to discriminate unfairly or to deny a license.

Beyond Constitutional grounds are statutory ones. Title VII of the Civil Rights Act of 1964 significantly extends the equal-protection concept for minorities and other protected classes. Title VII allows a case to be made if discrimination occurs, even if it is not intentional. Furthermore, its application is not limited to governmental units. Finally, the Rehabilitation Act of 1973 and the Americans with Disabilities Act (ADA) of 1990 prohibit discrimination against people with disabilities and require reasonable accommodation of such individuals.

In general, the research literature has not shown that computers discriminate against minorities. The challenges to computerization appear far more likely to be based on ADA. Accommodations for physical disabilities have long been made by most organizations offering licensure tests in any mode. The ADA brings mental disabilities more to the forefront, however. As O'Brien (1991) points out, the ADA may require the accommodation of computer-phobes, a subgroup of test-phobes. Practical experience suggests that learning disabilities are a frequent source of requests for alternate testing modes. Legally, if a licensed professional supports a candidate's request for an alternate testing mode, there appear to be two defenses for denying it. First, the accommodation must be "reasonable." This implies that the accommodation should not compromise the integrity of the test and that it should not be outrageously expensive; of course, what compromises the test or constitutes outrageous expense may be the subject of litigation. Second, the individual should be otherwise "qualified." Although case law with respect to the Rehabilitation Act of 1973 seems clear that this means an individual must meet all of the requirements for a license in spite of a handicap, not except for it (O'Brien, 1991), case law has not developed with respect to ADA. Current belief is that an individual should not be barred from taking a test simply because he or she will be unable to meet other requirements for licensure (Warren, 1992).

Does this present special problems for a computerized test beyond those that exist in a paper-and-pencil test? Potentially, it does. Although candidates are equally free to request alternate forms of any test based on their disabilities (e.g., oral, rather than paper and pencil), requesting a paper-and-pencil form rather than a computerized one is a relatively frequent request. If the test is pre-formed, this is only a logistic inconvenience. If the computerized test is tailored based on examinee responses, it may not be feasible to administer a comparable test via paper and pencil.

GREATER EFFICIENCY THROUGH MODERN PSYCHOMETRIC METHODS

Computerization allows tests to be made psychometrically more efficient by tailoring them to the candidates who take them. There are two ways to tailor a test. First, the difficulty of the test items may be adjusted to the ability of the candidate. A test is more efficient if it does not waste time giving items that are clearly too difficult or too easy for the candidate. Second, the length of the test may be tailored to the candidate. There is no point in continuing a test when the measurement is sufficiently accurate to achieve the purpose for which the test was intended. Tailoring the difficulty of a test has typically been called computerized adaptive testing (CAT; Wainer, 1990; Weiss, 1983). Tailoring the length of a test has been referred to by a variety of names including sequential testing (Linn, Rock, & Cleary, 1972; Reckase, 1983; Weitzman, 1982), adaptive mastery testing (AMT; Kingsbury & Weiss, 1983; Weiss & Kingsbury, 1984), and computerized mastery testing (CMT; Lewis & Sheehan, 1990). To properly explore the potential utility of these techniques, however, an appropriate statistical framework is necessary. Item Response Theory (IRT; Hambleton & Swaminathan, 1985; Lord, 1980) offers such a framework.

At this point the reader should be aware of two things: (a) the remainder of this section makes heavily mathematical arguments regarding the utility of adaptive and sequential testing for licensure and certification programs, and (b) the conclusions of these arguments are of interest primarily to those programs that administer several thousand examinations each year. Readers representing smaller programs who would not even consider using adaptive or sequential testing methods can skip the rest of this section without a loss of useful information.

Item Response Theory

Item Response Theory refers to a family of mathematical models that express the probability of an item response as a function of numerical item characteristics and the underlying ability of the examinee. IRT is of use to computerized testing because it both allows the computation of comparable scores when different items are administered to candidates and suggests which items will be most appropriate for assessing the ability of a given candidate.

IRT models differ in the number of abilities they encompass, the number of item parameters they include, the form of the function that relates the item response to the underlying ability, and the type of item responses they accept. The most general form of IRT model to be widely accepted in practical ability or achievement testing applications is the three-parameter logistic model. It requires a dichotomous (e.g., right/wrong) item response and describes the probability of a correct response as a logistic ogive (an s-shaped function) in three item parameters and one ability parameter. Mathematically, the model is specified in Equation 1.

$$P(u_g = 1|\theta) = c_g + (1 - c_g)\Psi(z_g) \quad [1a]$$

or

$$P(u_g = 1|\theta) = \Psi(z_g) + (1 - \Psi(z_g))c_g \quad [1b]$$

where

$$\Psi(z) = 1/(1+\exp(-z))$$

and

$$z_g = 1.7a_g(\theta - b_g).$$

In Equation 1, u_g is the scored response to item g: 0 for incorrect, 1 for correct. The ability parameter is represented by the Greek letter theta (θ). The item parameters are a_g, b_g, and c_g. The constant 1.7 is a historical artifact that causes the logistic model to closely resemble its cousin, the normal model. It remains as a convenience to those psychometricians who think of a parameter magnitudes in that scale.

Equations 1a and 1b are mathematically equivalent. Equation 1a is the form typically seen, because it is computationally simpler. Equation 1b is useful for illustration, however, because it is more amenable to a conceptual treatment. To wit, consider that Ψ represents the probability that the examinee knows the correct answer to the item. This model, in concept, implies that there is a bell-shaped probability (density) distribution relating the relative likelihood that examinees at points along the theta dimension will know the correct answer. This distribution is centered on the difficulty (b parameter) of the item and its dispersion is related to the a parameter (the standard deviation of the distribution is $.588a$). The probability that an examinee will know the correct answer is equal to that proportion of the distribution that is below the examinee's ability level (θ). Equation 1b then gives the probability that an examinee with ability equal to a value of θ will answer the item correctly. This probability is computed as the sum of the probability that the examinee knows the correct answer (Ψ) plus the joint probability that the examinee does not know the answer ($1-\Psi$) and successfully guesses (c_g).

Figure 2 gives a graphical depiction of several three-parameter test items. The horizontal axis indicates the underlying ability, typically expressed on a standard scale ranging, practically, from about -3 to +3. The a parameter indicates how well the item discriminates among levels of ability and relates to the slope of the curve. High a parameters result in steep slopes near the middle of the curve and shallow slopes at the tails. The b parameter refers to the difficulty of the item and is equal to the point on the horizontal axis that corresponds to the vertical midpoint of the curve (i.e., $[1+c]/2$). Difficult items have curves that plot toward the right side of the horizontal axis. The *c* parameter is the pseudo-guessing parameter, conceptually equivalent to the probability a candidate of very low ability would have of answering the item correctly. Although it is reasonable to expect this to be the reciprocal of the number of alternatives, in practice there is some variability around this value depending on other characteristics of the item.

The *a*, *b*, and *c* parameters that gave rise to Item 1 were (.4, .0, .25); this represents an item of modest discriminating power, middle difficulty, and probably four alternatives. Item 2 is a more discriminating version with the same difficulty (.8, .0, .25). Finally, Item 3 is like Item 2, but more difficult (.8, .5, .25).

Two reduced versions of the three-parameter model are also popular. If the *c* parameters are all assumed to be zero, the two-parameter model results. This model is appropriate if it is not possible to answer the items correctly by guessing. If, in addition to holding the *c* parameters at zero, all *a* parameters are held to a constant value, the one-parameter logistic or Rasch model results.

In concept, the Rasch model does not seem appropriate for use with multiple-choice licensure items; correct guessing is obviously possible and items probably differ substantially with regard to how well they discriminate (correlate with) ability. There is an ongoing debate among psychometricians, however, regarding which model is practically appropriate(Traub, 1973; Hambleton & Swaminathan, 1985). Although the Rasch model makes some conceptually unappealing assumptions regarding two of the parameters, available statistical techniques do not allow these parameters to be estimated accurately when the three-parameter model is used. It has long been known that the individual parameters are difficult to

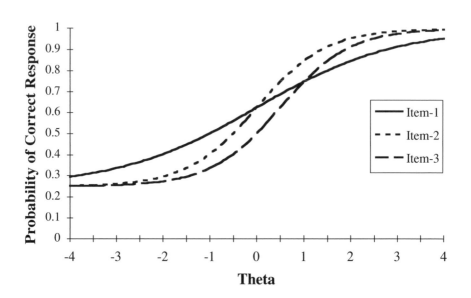

Figure 2. Three Item Characteristic Curves

estimate, in part because errors in the estimation of one parameter can be compensated by errors in another and several sets of item parameters can yield models that fit the data about equally well (Thissen & Wainer, 1982). Proponents of the Rasch model would say this suggests using a simpler model. Advocates of the three-parameter model would counter that declaring the parameters by fiat at values known to be incorrect (e.g., zero for the c parameter) is probably more harmful than poorly estimating the parameters using the best techniques available. For analyses presented in this chapter, the three-parameter model has been used exclusively. The analyses are intended to set bounds on the maximum improvement that can be expected through psychometric means; thus, the model that (if its assumptions are met and its parameters are accurately estimated) will give the best results was used.

Regardless of the model, a major appeal of IRT is the method of scoring it allows. The curves shown in Figure 2 are referred to as item characteristic curves (ICCs), item response functions (IRFs), or response likelihood functions. They express the probability of a correct response as a function of ability (or whatever psychological dimension theta may represent). Inversely, they express the likelihood of a level of ability given a correct response. Each item has complementary response functions for correct and incorrect responses. Figure 3 shows the IRF for both correct and incorrect responses to the same item. The increasing function is for the correct response, indicating that the probability of a correct response goes up as ability increases. The corresponding IRF to the incorrect response indicates decreasing probability of an incorrect response as ability rises.

The individual IRF does not allow much of an estimate of ability, based on the item response. If the response is correct, any higher level of ability is more likely. But the utility of IRT is in how it combines IRFs from responses to multiple items. If the assumptions of IRT hold, the likelihood of a pattern of item responses (e.g.,

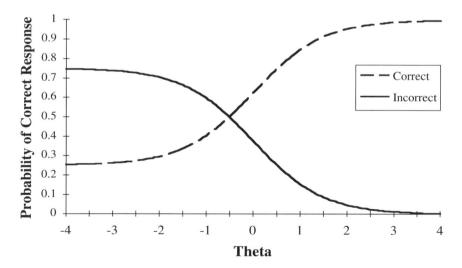

Figure 3. Complementary Item Response Functions

those obtained by a given examinee) can be obtained by simply multiplying the individual response functions together. The assumption necessary to allow this is local independence, a character resulting from unidimensionality. In essence, what this means is that if all of the items in a test measure a single trait (in a factor analytic sense), the responses to items given to someone whose ability level is constant (typical, during the course of a test, for most examinees) will be statistically independent. It is a basic tenet of probability that the joint probability of independent events is the product of their individual probabilities.

Figure 4 shows the IRFs for responses to the three items used for Figure 2, two answered correctly and one (the difficult one) answered incorrectly. It also shows the resulting likelihood function. A good estimate of the candidate's ability is that level of ability corresponding to the maximum of the likelihood function. This is called the maximum-likelihood ability estimate. In this example, the maximum-likelihood estimate of theta is .23. Note that an estimate can be obtained from any set of test items and expressed on this same ability scale; scores thus computed will be comparable, even if they are obtained from different sets of items.

The likelihood function can, without compromising its character as a likelihood function, be scaled to any size that is convenient. One common scaling is to make the area under the curve equal to one. This done, the likelihood can be considered a Bayesian posterior probability density function, indicating the distribution of abilities that would result if all possible candidates with the same set of responses to the same items were plotted. (If the scaling is accomplished without changing the shape of the distribution, an uninformative or uniform Bayesian prior has been applied.) The standard deviation of that posterior distribution is akin to the standard error of measurement (*SEM*). (It differs in that the classical *SEM* refers to a distribution of observed scores around a true score and this is a Bayesian

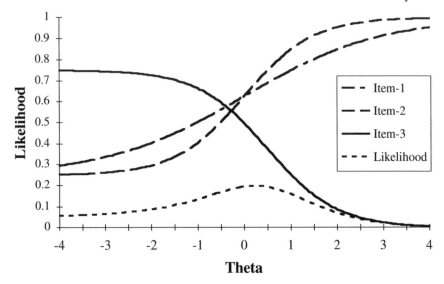

Figure 4. Likelihood as the Product of Item Response Functions

distribution of true scores around an observed score. They are equivalent, however, if an uninformative prior is applied.) A laudable measurement objective is to minimize the variance of this distribution. This can be accomplished by administering more items, better items, or items more appropriately matched to the examinee.

A useful index provided by IRT is the item information function. Mathematically the information function is the ratio of the squared slope of the IRF to the conditional variance of the item response at a level of theta. The formula for information in the three-parameter logistic model is given by Equation 2 (after Birnbaum, 1968, Eqs. 20.2.3 and 20.4.16).

$$I(\theta, g) = \frac{[P_g^{'}(\theta)]^2}{P_g(\theta)[1 - P_g(\theta)]} \qquad [2a]$$

or

$$I(\theta, g) = \frac{2.89(1 - c_g) a_g^2 \psi^2[z_g]}{\psi[z_g] + c_g \Psi^2[-z_g]} \qquad [2b]$$

where

$$P_g^{'}(\theta) = 1.7(1 - c_g) a_g \psi[z_g]$$

and

$$\psi[z] = \exp(-z) / (1 + \exp(-z))^2$$

Equations 2a and 2b are equivalent. Equation 2a presents a conceptual formulation of information; 2b presents a computational one. The numerator of Equation 2a is the squared derivative of the item response function. As the IRF becomes steeper, the information increases. The denominator is the conditional variance of the dichotomously scored item. Note that the variance of such an item at a point on the theta scale (i.e., the conditional variance) is solely determined by the probability of a correct response at that point.

Practically, information indicates how effectively a given item will reduce the variance of the posterior distribution (and thus the *SEM*) as a function of the item characteristics and the point on the theta dimension. Figure 5 shows graphs of the information functions for two items. The flatter of the curves (Item 1) is for a middle-difficulty item (.4, .0, .25) with a modest *a* parameter. The more peaked of the curves is for a more difficult item (Item 3) with a higher *a* parameter (.8, .5, .25). Several things are important to note from the figure. First, items with high *a* parameters generally have higher information peaks, indicating that they can do a better job of shrinking the *SEM*. Second, note that the point along the theta dimension at which the curve peaks varies with the difficulty of the item. Third note that the higher the information peak, the more rapid the drop-off; items with high *a* parameters provide their advantage over a relatively small range of ability.

Figure 5. Information Functions

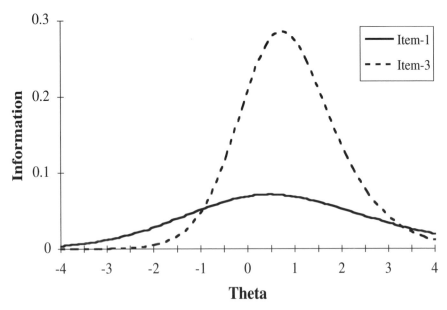

It may be obvious at this point that the efficiency of a test can be improved by the judicious choice of items. Information could be maximized (and *SEM* minimized) by selecting those items that provide the highest level of information at the candidate's level of ability. The fact that the test must be administered to determine what this level is has given rise to the adaptive test, a test that attempts to administer items most appropriate to its estimate of the examinee's ability at any point in the test. A simple adaptive strategy begins by assuming an initial estimate of ability near the population mean and choosing items and updating ability sequentially throughout the course of the test. At each stage, the next item is chosen based on the current estimate of ability. After each item is administered, the estimate of ability is updated.

Recall that IRT scoring results in a posterior distribution. The mean or mode of this distribution can be taken as an estimate of ability. Its standard deviation can be taken as an estimate of the *SEM*. In a pure measurement application, the interest is in obtaining a posterior distribution with as small a variance as possible. In classification (e.g., licensure) testing, there is a passing point to be considered. Then the interest is in classifying the candidate on the proper side of the passing score with as little chance of error as possible. Figure 6 illustrates the situation with a cut score. The curve represents the posterior probability density of a 120-item test composed of items with $a = .5$, $c = .25$, and difficulties peaked at the candidate's ability of $\theta = .3$. The probability of misclassification is the proportion of the posterior distribution that falls on the wrong side of the passing point, set here at .0 and indicated by the arrow. Both the mean and the variance of the posterior distribution are important in determining the probability of

Figure 6. Probability of Misclassification

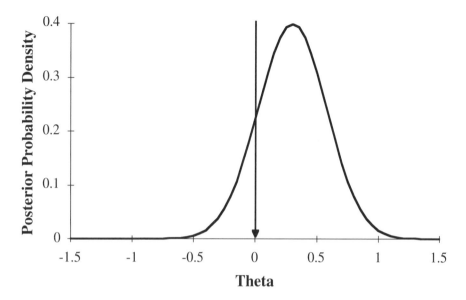

misclassification. If an acceptable probability of misclassification can be specified, the test can be terminated when the portion of the distribution that overlaps
the cut score reaches this level. This is essentially the AMT procedure (Weiss &
Kingsbury, 1984).

Applicability of Psychometric Improvements to Licensure

Few in the psychometric community would argue against the utility of adaptive
testing or tailored termination (sequential testing), in the proper applications. But the
application is critical to determining the utility. For example, the average discriminating power of the item pool (average *a* parameter) is critical to establishing how much
advantage an adaptive test will have over a conventional one. Similarly, an adaptive
test excels at providing high information over a wide range of ability, which is more
appropriate for a measurement than a classification application. Furthermore, the
position of the passing point in the distribution of ability is significant to determining
the utility of tailored termination. Rather than attempting to summarize published
research results descriptive of specific situations, this section provides a mathematical
model that allows the utility of the methods to a specific environment to be ascertained,
subject to a few simplifying assumptions.

Consider the concept of an ideal test. The ideal test makes assumptions known
in reality to be unduly optimistic. In the results shown below, four such assumptions
were made: (a) The items fit the IRT model perfectly; (b) the item parameters are
estimated without error; (c) the item pool is very large, in fact infinite in size; and (d)
in the case of an adaptive test, the test is adapted perfectly, with no allowance made
for the fact that an examinee's level of ability must be known a priori to do this.

Note that these are significant assumptions, but they are directional. No real test could perform any better than a test evaluated under these assumptions. Obviously, there is no advantage to be gained by using items that do not fit the model, by using parameters other than the true ones, by using a smaller item pool, or by adapting a test other than perfectly. Thus, the ideal test provides a bound of how well a test can perform. The bound is useful because, if the ideal test does not provide sufficient benefit to suggest the more complicated adaptive procedure, neither will the real test. Note also that these assumptions favor an adaptive test more than a conventional one; a conventional test cannot take advantage of perfect adaptation. Thus, these assumptions also place a bound on the relative advantage of the adaptive test.

As a meaningful application of the concept, consider the following reasonable application environment: For many licensure and certification examinations, the range and distribution of item difficulty can be tailored as desired. Assume that items are available at any level of difficulty desired by the testing algorithm. Experience with insurance licensure item banks and anecdotal data informally collected from other researchers suggest that a reasonable a parameter value would be .5. Similarly, experience suggests that although there is some variability among items, the average c parameter for four-alternative items is about .25. Thus, assume a parameters fixed at .5 and c parameters fixed at .25. Finally, for the first evaluation, assume the passing point is set at $\theta = .0$, a value that would (assuming a standard normal distribution of ability) result in a 50% passing rate.

A few characteristics of IRT will assist in the analyses of the ideal test (and allow exact analytic solutions rather than simulated ones). The characteristics, detailed by Birnbaum (1968), are that:

1. The item information functions (Equation 2) can be added together to obtain the test information.
2. Maximum-likelihood ability estimates tend to be normally distributed around a mean equal to the true value of the parameter they estimate (θ).
3. The variance of the distribution of maximum-likelihood estimates is given by the reciprocal of the test information function evaluated at the value of the parameter (θ).

These characteristics imply, for a mastery decision, that the probability of misclassification for any particular level of ability can be obtained from that portion of the distribution of ability estimates that fall on the wrong side of the passing point. Thus,

$$P(Misclass|\theta) = \Phi(-|\theta - \theta_c|/SEM) \qquad [3]$$

where

$$\Phi[x] = \frac{1}{\sqrt{2\pi}} \int_{-\infty}^{x} \exp(-t^2/2)dt$$

and

$$SEM = \frac{1}{\sqrt{\sum_g I(\theta, g)}}$$

An ideal conventional test would be constructed of items that provided the most information at the passing point. An ideal adaptive test would be constructed by selecting items that provided maximum information at the ability level (theta) of each candidate tested. The peak of the information function occurs at $b_g = \theta$ for items in which guessing is not possible. For items where guessing is possible, the ideal difficulty (Birnbaum, 1968, Eq. 20.4.22) is

$$b_g = \theta - \frac{1}{1.7a_g} \ln\left(\frac{1+\sqrt{1+8c_g}}{2}\right) \qquad [4]$$

Note that, as Equation 4 implies, the ideal difficulty of an item when guessing is possible is somewhat easier than when guessing is not possible.

Thus, a comparison of the classification accuracy of conventional and adaptive tests is quite straightforward using a bank of items that differ only in difficulty. An ideal conventional test is composed of items with difficulty fixed to provide maximum information at the passing point. An ideal adaptive test, composed of items peaked at each candidate's true ability level, provides a level of information at all ability levels that is equivalent to the maximum level provided only at the passing point by a conventional test.

The comparison of fixed versus variable test length is a bit more complicated, however. Consider the situation in which a fixed-length test is terminated early when the ability estimates and standard errors leave an acceptably small probability of misclassification. This will result in shorter tests for those individuals with ability levels distant from the passing point. The overall probability of misclassification will rise, however, if tests are only shortened. The result that a shorter test leads to higher misclassification probability does not yield a meaningful comparison of fixed versus variable test length. To properly compare fixed-length and variable-length tests, with respect to misclassification probability, either the misclassification probability or the average test length must be held constant. To achieve a truly fair comparison, the items saved by early test termination for candidates with ability levels distant from the passing point must be reallocated and given to candidates closer to the passing point. How should test lengths be optimally distributed?

As a tool for redistribution, consider the derivative of the misclassification probability with respect to test length. This derivative, a function of the test characteristics and the point on the underlying ability (θ) continuum, indicates how much reduction in misclassification probability can be achieved for each item delivered. The derivative, assuming here for simplicity that items differ only in difficulty, is given by Equation 5. (Note that without this assumption of item equivalence, the evaluation of relative test length is not meaningful.)

$$\frac{dP(Misclass|\theta)}{dL(\theta)} = \phi\left[|\theta - \theta_c|\sqrt{L(\theta)I(\theta,g)}\right]\frac{|\theta - \theta_c|\sqrt{I(\theta,g)}}{2\sqrt{L(\theta)}} \qquad [5]$$

where $I(\theta,g)$ is the information provided by any of the equivalent items at ability θ and $L(\theta)$ is the test length in items. (Note that for a fixed level of theta, the information value for the items will be constant; a conventional test will have all items peaked to provide maximum information at the passing point and an adaptive test will have all items peaked to provide maximum information at the candidate's ability level.) This derivative indicates where to get the "most bang for the buck" in terms of items administered. In concept, optimal allocation can be achieved by taking test length from where it will do the least good (low derivative) and putting where it will do the most good (high derivative). Note that, for a specific level of theta, the derivative decreases as test length increases. Therefore, a point will retain the highest derivative only until test length reaches the point where the derivative is higher at another point along theta. Although the concept of moving items around until an optimal allocation is achieved is appealing in concept, practically it is difficult and computationally time-consuming. The ultimate objective of such reallocation, however, is to achieve a distribution of test lengths that causes the derivative to be constant.

For a specified constant, Equation 5 can be solved (numerically) for the optimal test length $L(\theta)$ at any value of theta. The overall test length for theta distributed standard normal is thus:

$$L = \int_{-\infty}^{+\infty} L(\theta)\phi(\theta)d\theta \qquad [6]$$

For a specified average length L, Equation 6 can be solved (again numerically) for optimal conditional lengths (those that result in a constant derivative and average length L). The overall probability of misclassification can then be computed, based on the conditional lengths, as

$$P(Misclass) = \int_{-\infty}^{+\infty} P(Misclass|\theta)\phi(\theta)d\theta \qquad [7]$$

Figure 7 shows the misclassification probabilities as a function of test length for all types of ideal test. Both adaptive tests provide minor improvements over their non-adaptive counterparts. Larger differences obtain between fixed and variable-length versions.

Figure 8 shows the transpose of Figure 7, the test lengths required to obtain a given overall probability of misclassification. The distances between the curves indicate items saved by the various testing strategies. Note that a fixed-length adaptive test shows a relatively constant saving of about four items. Figure 9 shows the proportionate reduction in test length of three testing strategies compared to the fixed-length conventional strategy. The variable-length tests show the larger savings, especially when a low misclassification probability is desired.

Thus, in theory, significantly greater savings are possible through tailored termination than through tailored item difficulty. It is informative, however, to look at the optimal distribution of test lengths. Figure 10 shows optimal adaptive test lengths to achieve an average test length of 120. Two somewhat troublesome issues are apparent from Figure 10. First, optimal test lengths near the passing point (θ=0) exceed 300 items. Although this number of items may be manageable on the part of the examinee, it is sufficiently different from the average or the reasonable low point (at θ=1, a bound outside which roughly one third of the candidates will fall) to cause scheduling difficulty. Perhaps of greater concern, however, is the drop in test length very near the passing point. The optimal length function suggests a sort of triage: Terminate when you are confident a candidate

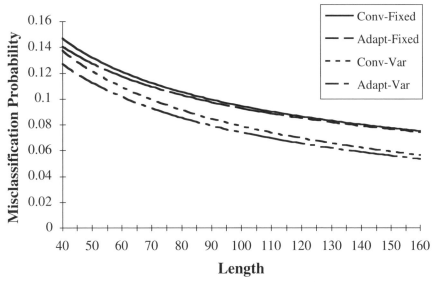

Figure 7. Misclassification Probability as a Function of Average Test Length

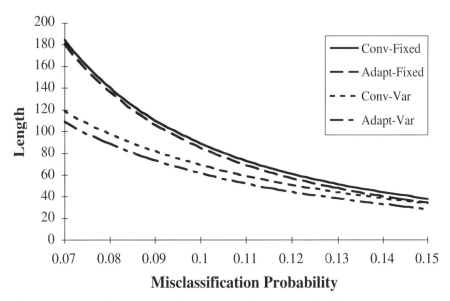

Figure 8. Length Required for Misclassification Probability

has passed or failed, give a long test if you are not sure, and quickly write off candidates that are too close to call. Flipping a coin to decide the fate of marginal candidates, although mathematically optimal, may be politically unwise. (Note that this problem would not occur in a real test, however, because a number of items would have to be administered to determine that the candidate was too close to call.)

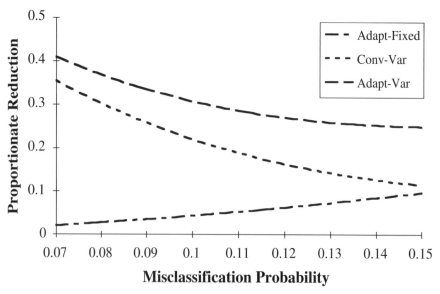

Figure 9. Length Reduction Compared to Fixed-Length Conventional

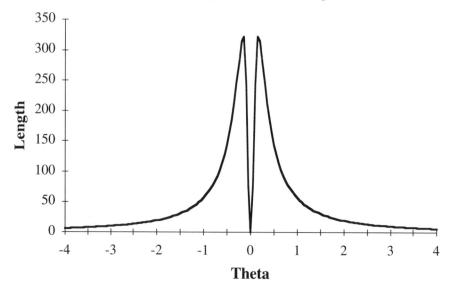

Figure 10. Optimal Lengths for 120-item Average Length Adaptive Test

The optimization strategy can be altered to fill in the void around the passing point. If the optimization algorithm is so altered, the test lengths required become as shown in Figure 11. (Note that only the variable-length tests are affected by this modification.) The savings resulting from variable termination are uniformly reduced by about 10 items.

The resulting proportionate reductions in test length (with the void filled), compared to a fixed-length conventional test, are shown in Figure 12. As a practical point of comparison, consider a 120-item fixed-length conventional test. This would yield a misclassification probability of .086. At this level of error, a fixed-length adaptive test will reduce test length by about 3%, a variable-length conventional test will reduce it by about 22%, and a variable-length adaptive test will reduce it by about 30%.

Consider practically what this means. If a fixed-length adaptive test is used rather than a 120-item conventional test, it need only be 116 items long. Assuming that the conventional test is a 2-hour test, the candidate will be able to go home 4 minutes early. The real savings are with the variable-length adaptive test. A candidate should come planning to spend 5 hours testing. Typically, the candidate will go home about 3 1/2 hours early. Sometimes the candidate will go home after just a few minutes. Are there any savings? To save, on average, about half an hour, a candidate has had to block out 5 hours rather than 2. Although a testing center of moderate size (10 or more stations) will be able to take advantage of the average for scheduling, it is likely that a variable-length test will still require a longer time block to ensure that everyone can test; this will translate into higher exam fees. Is this a saving? Perhaps a less significant one than the 1 to 2 months saved by simple computerization.

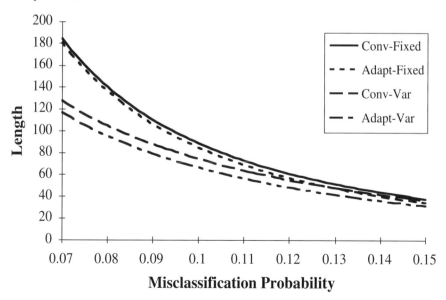

Figure 11. Length Required When the Void is Filled

It can be argued, with some justification, that the above analysis is too harsh on the tailored tests. Specifically, the mastery problem is most difficult when the passing point is set right in the middle of the ability distribution. With the cut set at θ = .0, as above, 50% of the candidates would pass. Consider a somewhat simpler classification problem with the cut set at θ = .5. In this case, about 31% of the candidates would pass. Figures 13 and 14 correspond to Figures 7 and 8 above (those with the void not filled). Note that all test forms achieve comparable error rates with fewer items, but that proportionate reductions in test length (compared to a fixed-length conventional test) are remarkably similar in relative and absolute magnitude. Even with the cutting score shifted substantially from the center of the ability distribution, the fixed-length adaptive test offers only modest improvement over its conventional counterpart.

Although the ideal test concept has been applied to only two variations of one testing application here, the application seems a reasonable depiction of the typical licensure testing environment. In this environment, there seems to be relatively little advantage available from adaptive testing. Furthermore, to take advantage of the item savings available through tailored termination seems to result in unpredictable variation in testing times to a degree that is unacceptable from an operational perspective. Note that the more simplistic approach of terminating an otherwise fixed-length test when a candidate has clearly passed it will result in less variability. Its disadvantage, however, is only that a few candidates will get to go home unexpectedly early and the net psychometric result will be an increased error rate.

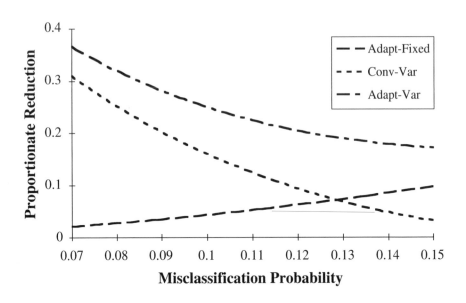

Figure 12. Length Reduction When the Void is Filled

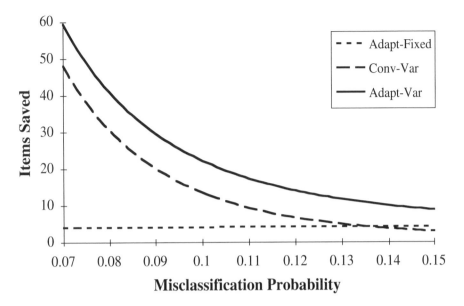

Figure 13. Item Savings With Passing Point at 0.5

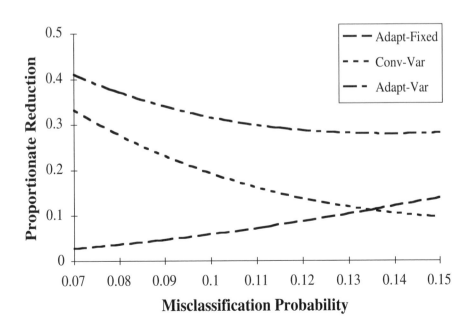

Figure 14. Length Reduction with Passing Point at 0.5

ISSUES IN TEST DESIGN

Although the above analyses may suggest that tailored item difficulty or test length may not yield great practical advantage in licensure or certification applications where a pass/fail decision must be made, there will be applications where they do not cost much and are useful. For those cases, there are a few additional details of test design worth discussing.

Content Stratification of a Tailored Test

Although most licensure tests make a pass-fail decision based on a single score, many of these tests also report subtest score results. Furthermore, many of these tests stratify their content to a great degree, sometimes associating the content of each item to a point in a job analysis. IRT and the adaptive testing methods discussed above assume a unidimensional test. Stratification implies multidimensionality. What are the implications of such stratification on practical test design?

IRT and tests based on IRT assume that all items in the test measure the same dimension. According to the IRT model, the only selection that should occur is to maximize the precision of measurement—that is, select items with high a parameters, low c parameters, and b parameters near the theta level of the candidate. When a test consists of subtests that clearly measure different characteristics (e.g., arithmetic, vocabulary, and reading comprehension), Thomas and Green (1989) have shown that it is better to measure each characteristic separately and then average the scores on them rather than to treat them all as a single unidimensional test.

Licensure tests generally consist of subtests that measure characteristics that are less distinct. A test of life insurance knowledge, for example, may be divided into subtests on policy forms, policy options, and policy riders. For purposes of conventional test construction, each section may be further subdivided. Yet, factor analysis and all other analyses may fail to confirm any psychometric distinction between even the subtests, much less their subdivisions.

The issues regarding how to analyze these data are quite complex. First, the psychometric perspective would argue for analyzing the test as a whole; psychometrically it hangs together and better item calibration can be obtained by treating it this way. Politically, it would make more sense to calibrate the item bank by subtests; if the subtests are all calibrated along a (single) common dimension, any differences among subtest scores provided in a diagnostic score report are indicative only of measurement error and not actual competence differences. Operationally, it would be best to treat each category of stratification as a single dimension because the simple (nonstratified) adaptive testing strategies could be used within each.

Kingsbury and Zara (1989) have suggested one way of stratifying an adaptive test. Their model is appropriate when the items are calibrated along a single dimension and behave, psychometrically, as if they measure the same thing; the need for stratification is political rather than psychometric. Specifically, what they suggest is that the item pool be stratified according to content and that the percentage of items to be drawn from each stratum be specified. The adaptive procedure then, at each stage, selects the psychometrically best item from the stratum for which the actual percentage is most deficient when compared to the specified percentage.

Another technique for accomplishing stratification has been suggested by Swanson and Stocking (1993). Their technique, more mathematical and less algorithmic, applies a compensatory optimization approach. Items are described by their characteristics (e.g., being an arithmetic item) and a target test profile, in terms of the characteristics, is specified. The characteristics may be differentially weighted. The item selection process then sums the weighted deviations of actual characteristics from the target ones and selects the item that minimizes the summed deviations. Unlike the Kingsbury and Zara approach, the Swanson and Stocking approach does not guarantee stratification precisely as prescribed.

Consider one final stratification strategy, suggested here an unresearched but imminently practical solution to the stratification problem. Consider first the algorithm for the fixed-length case. Begin by grouping all items into content strata and assigning an item quota to each stratum. Begin item selection with an unrestricted search for the best item. Then, as each stratum quota is reached, mark all items in that stratum as unavailable. As the final item is selected, there will be only one stratum that has not reached quota. If the stratum quotas are integers, the exact number of specified items will be drawn. This technique has computational simplicity and exact stratification as advantages over the Swanson and Stocking method. Over the Kingsbury and Zara method it offers the advantage of extending the choices for the psychometric best item while still assuring proper content stratification.

As a modification of this method for variable length, start by assigning quotas based on the shortest test that will be administered. Select items only from strata having at least half an item remaining in their quotas. As the test grows beyond the minimum length, adjust the quotas. Note that stratification can never overfill a stratum by more than half an item so if the test reaches a length where all quotas are integers, the stratification will be exact.

Finally, as a reminder, note that stratification is an issue only if items within a scoring dimension (i.e., an IRT dimension) are considered dissimilar. If political considerations are consistent with psychometric ones, no within-dimension stratification will be necessary; both will agree that the items all measure the same thing and differ only in their psychometric characteristics.

Randomization

Computerized testing, to achieve the scheduling advantages discussed earlier, must be offered on a relatively continuous (e.g., daily) basis. This means that individuals who do not pass the test on the first attempt may be exposed to the test several more times before passing. It is important that each test they take be sufficiently different from the previous ones that their passage is indicative of mastering the domain and not just a specific test. Furthermore, test coaching for a specific test often takes the form of training for the test rather than for the substance of the test. A test for which the exact item content cannot be predicted is effective in reducing the utility of such coaching.

Adaptive tests will, to a degree, be unique on each presentation. In a pure adaptive test, a candidate will receive the same items on a second administration only by answering the items in the same way each time. If the first attempt to pass was not successful, the second attempt using this strategy is not likely to be either. The issue of coaching is still relevant, however, and certain specific patterns of responses to a pure adaptive test will lead to a passing score every time.

Randomization may be introduced into any of the test types discussed above. The precise mechanism depends on the type of test. Consider first an adaptive strategy. A pure adaptive test selects what it considers the most appropriate item for administration at each stage. Randomization may be added by selecting the two, three, or more most appropriate items at each stage and then randomly choosing among them. (See Kingsbury and Zara, 1989, for a description of Randomesque item selection, as proposed for use in a nurse licensure examination.) Scoring, via IRT, is done the same way, regardless of whether randomization is introduced.

Consider next a conventional test, one in which a fixed set of items is administered regardless of the response the examinee makes. In concept the simplest solution is to construct a collection of sets of parallel items. If such a collection were available, in which all items in a set were psychometrically equivalent, parallel random forms could be constructed by randomly selecting one item from each of the sets in the collection to form a test. In practice, it is virtually impossible to assemble truly parallel item sets. Tests drawn as described would have varying psychometric characteristics. If the tests are to be scored using IRT, this is not a problem. If, however, the scoring is to be done by traditional proportion correct, additional psychometric balancing is required.

One approach to psychometric balancing that has been applied in work at the Insurance Testing Corporation (ITC) involves paired random sampling and balancing according to a similarity criterion. Specifically, items are drawn in pairs, resulting in twice as many items as are required for the test. (If the bank is stratified and three items are required from a stratum, six items are drawn from that stratum.) Then the item from each pair that, in concert with the items thus far selected, maximizes a similarity function is selected. The process may iterate to convergence for better balance.

The similarity function for this procedure should reflect the overall parallelism of the tests. One simple function is the difference between the average difficulty of the test and that of the item bank as a whole. More comprehensive functions compare the similarity of the test characteristic curve or the information function of the test to that of the item bank as a whole. Details and performance of the methods are beyond the scope of this chapter, however.

Finally, consider a test with variable termination. It is possible to order the items selected for the conventional test such that, at any stage in the test, similarity with the target is maximal. Unless the items were all equivalent, however, IRT scoring would be required to determine when to terminate the test. If IRT is used for scoring, no psychometric balancing would be necessary.

Passing Points for Tailored Tests

In concept, a passing point for any of the types of computerized tests is no different than a passing point for a conventional test. If a conventional test is administered on a computer and scored, like a paper-and-pencil test, via the number of items answered correctly, the issues in setting and using a passing point are identical to those faced when using a paper-and-pencil test. Tailored tests raise several issues that cloud the concept, however. First, how can a passing point be set on the theta continuum? Second, how can a passing point be set on a reference test in the more familiar number-correct scale? Finally, can and should a passing point from a paper-and-pencil test be transferred to a computerized test?

There are several ways to set a passing point relative to the theta continuum. If a reference test exists, it will have a test characteristic curve. The test characteristic curve for a fixed test is simply the sum of the item characteristic curves, or

$$T(\theta) = \sum_g P\big(u_g = 1 | \theta\big) \qquad [8]$$

If the passing point has already been set in terms of the number correct, the passing point in theta can be determined by solving Equation 8 for theta. Graphically this can be accomplished by identifying the theta value that corresponds to the number correct at which the passing point is set.

There are two somewhat more elegant ways to set the passing point using raw judgmental data, both derived from techniques of maximum-likelihood scoring. First, if the Angoff (1971) procedure is altered and judges are asked to evaluate whether the minimally competent candidate would most likely answer the question correctly or incorrectly, the standard likelihood equation shown as Equation 9 (after Hambleton & Swaminathan, 1985, p. 84) could be used to estimate theta from the dichotomous judgments.

$$\sum_g \frac{a_g\big(u_{gj} - P_g(\theta)\big)\big(P_g(\theta) - c_g\big)}{P_g(\theta)\big(1 - c_g\big)} = 0. \qquad [9]$$

If data are available from a passing-point study done using the classic Angoff method, the passing point can be obtained by solving Equation 10 for theta. Note that Equations 9 and 10 are identical, except R_{gj} (judge j's probabilistic rating) has been substituted in Equation 10 for the scored item response. This rating, as is typically true of the Angoff technique, is for the proportion that will answer correctly, not the proportion who would know the correct answer. The passing point would be set at the average theta of the judges, whether set using Equation 9 or 10.

$$\sum_g \frac{a_g\big(R_{gj} - P_g(\theta)\big)\big(P_g(\theta) - c_g\big)}{P_g(\theta)\big(1 - c_g\big)} = 0. \qquad [10]$$

The method of Equation 10 is similar to that proposed by Kane (1987), except for one significant difference. Kane had suggested averaging the item judgments across judges and then applying a formula comparable to Equation 10. Kane's approach assumes that all judges agree on a common theta and differences are due to errors in judging the proportion. It seems more reasonable to believe that the judges would have different opinions regarding the ability level of the minimally competent candidate and differences in ratings would result both from errors in judgment and differences of opinion. The average opinion (different from the opinion level underlying the average rating) seems a more reasonable value to select for a passing point. In addition to greater consistency with the conceptual model of IRT, it also allows the use of different sets of items across judges.

A passing point set on the theta scale can easily be transferred back to the number-correct scale of any reference test for which item parameters, relative to the theta scale, have been estimated. The passing point on the reference test is simply the test characteristic curve (Equation 8) evaluated at the passing point on theta. Regarding a choice of reference test, this can be a conventional test previously used, a theoretical reference test based on hypothetical item parameters, or a test composed of all the items in the item bank; IRT affords great flexibility in how the score may be expressed.

SUMMARY

Computerized testing offers significant advantages over paper-and-pencil testing. Although the psychometric advantages for licensure and certification testing appear to be small, the scheduling advantages that typically occur with computerization are great, especially when the time saved has value. Furthermore, issues of anxiety, comparability, and defensibility of the computerized mode do not appear to be significant. The difficulty in computerizing a test appears in finding a service network that can deliver the tests in a timely manner and in geographically appropriate locations. The small number of testing networks currently available renders the feasibility of implementing any small program questionable at this time. This difficulty will pass as more networks become available and more computerized tests make the operation of these networks more efficient and affordable.

REFERENCES

Angoff, W. H. (1971). Scales, norms, and equivalent scores. In R. L. Thorndike (Ed.), *Educational Measurement* (2nd ed.) (pp. 508-600). Washington, DC: American Council on Education.

Birnbaum, A. (1968). Some latent trait models and their use in inferring an examinee's ability. In F. M. Lord & M. R. Novick, *Statistical theories of mental test scores* (pp. 397-479). Reading, MA: Addison-Wesley.

Burke, M. J., Normand, J., & Raju, N. S. (1987). Examinee attitudes toward computer-administered ability testing. *Computers in Human Behavior, 3,* 95-107.

Greaud, V. A., & Green, B. F. (1986). Equivalence of conventional and computer presentation of speed tests. *Applied Psychological Measurement, 10,* 23-34.

Hambleton, R. K., & Swaminathan, H. (1985) I*tem response theory: Principles and applications.* Boston: Kluwer-Nijhoff.

Kane, M. T. (1987). On the use of IRT models with judgmental standard setting procedures. *Journal of Educational Measurement, 24,* 333-345.

Kiely, G. L., Zara, A. R., & Weiss, D. J. (1986). Equivalence of computer and paper-and-pencil Armed Services Vocational Aptitude Battery tests (AFHRL-TP-86-13). San Antonio: Air Force Human Resources Laboratory.

Kingsbury, G. G., & Weiss, D. J. (1983). A comparison of IRT-based adaptive mastery testing and a sequential mastery testing procedure. In D. J. Weiss (Ed.), *New horizons in testing* (pp. 257-283). New York: Academic Press.

Kingsbury, G. G., & Zara, A. R. (1989). Procedures for selecting items for computerized adaptive tests. *Applied Measurement in Education, 2*, 359-375.

Lewis, C. L., & Sheehan, K. (1990). Using Bayesian decision theory to design a computerized mastery test. *Applied Psychological Measurement, 4*, 367-386.

Linn, R. L., Rock, D. A., & Cleary, T. A. (1972). Sequential testing for dichotomous decisions. *Educational and Psychological Measurement, 32*, 85-95.

Lord, F. M. (1980). *Applications of item response theory to practical testing problems*. Hillsdale, NJ: Erlbaum.

Lukin, M. E., Dowd, T. E., Plake, B. S., & Kraft, R. G. (1985). Comparing computerized versus traditional psychological assessment. *Computers in Human Behavior, 1*, 49-58.

Mehrens, W. A., & Popham, W. J. (1992). How to evaluate the legal defensibility of high-stakes tests. *Applied Measurement in Education, 5*, 265-283.

Moreno, K. E., Wetzel, C. D., McBride, J. R., & Weiss, D. J. (1984). Relationship between corresponding Armed Services Vocational Aptitude Battery (ASVAB) and computerized adaptive testing (CAT) subtests. *Applied Psychological Measurement, 8*, 155-163.

National Council of State Boards of Nursing (NCSBN). (1991). *Collected works on the legal aspects of computerized adaptive testing*. Chicago: Author.

O'Brien, T. L. (1991). Legal issues raised by the computerized nature of the exam. In *Collected works on the legal aspects of computerized adaptive testing*. Chicago: National Council of State Boards of Nursing.

Reckase, M. D. (1983). A procedure for decision making using tailored testing. In D. J. Weiss (Ed.), *New horizons in testing* (pp. 237-255). New York: Academic Press.

Swanson, L., & Stocking, M. L. (1993). A method and heuristic for solving very large item selection problems. *Applied Psychological Measurement, 17*, 151-166.

Thissen, D., & Wainer, H. (1982). Some standard errors in item response theory. *Psychometrika, 47*, 397-412.

Thomas, T. J., & Green, B. F. (1989) Item presentation controls for computerized adaptive testing: Content balancing vs. mini-CAT (Report 89-1). Baltimore: Johns Hopkins University, Psychometric Laboratory.

Traub, R. E. (1983). A priori considerations in choosing an item response model. In R. K. Hambleton (Ed.), *Applications of item response theory* (pp. 57-70). Vancouver, BC: Education Research Institute of British Columbia.

Wainer, H. (1990). *Computerized adaptive testing: A primer*. Hillsdale, NJ: Erlbaum.

Warren, S. L. (1992, September). Americans with Disabilities Act: Impact on every day operations. Paper presented at the 1992 CLEAR conference, Detroit, Michigan.

Weiss, D. J. (1983). *New horizons in testing.* New York: Academic Press.

Weiss, D. J., & Kingsbury, G. G. (1984). Application of computerized adaptive testing to educational problems. *Journal of Educational Measurement, 21,* 361-375.

Weitzman, R. A. (1982) Sequential testing for selection. *Applied Psychological Measurement, 6,* 337-351.

White, D. M., Clements, C. B., & Fowler, R. D. (1985). A comparison of computer administration with standard administration of the MMPI. *Computers in Human Behavior, 1,* 153-162.

Wise, S. L., Barnes, L. B., Harvey, A. L., & Plake, B. S. (1989). Effects of computer anxiety and computer experience on the computer-based achievement test performance of college students. *Applied Measurement in Education, 2,* 235-241.

FUTURE PSYCHOMETRIC PRACTICES IN LICENSURE TESTING

Steven S. Nettles

Applied Measurement Professionals, Inc.

New technologies continue to emerge each year, and influence testing practices. In particular, in the last 10 years the personal computer has evolved from a curious and minimally useful tool to an indispensable partner in many certification and licensure testing programs. It is involved in every aspect—including candidate scheduling, test assembly, test administration, test scoring and analysis, and score reporting. Initially, it is used to determine the content to be included in the job analysis instrument, and later, to analyze the returned surveys. After the job analysis is completed and test specifications prepared, it can be used to bank test items written to the specifications. Assembly of test forms, and typesetting of final copy prior to printing can be expertly accomplished. When paired to an optical mark reader scanner, it can be used to score and analyze tests. As an alternative to paper-and-pencil test delivery, items can be loaded onto a computer and administered in a variety of alternate forms and can provide instantaneous feedback to candidates. Likewise, score reports can be prepared and mailed to candidates using information stored in the candidate database.

As the personal computer has gained in power, it has had significant impact on the psychometric practices of testing. Statistical packages written for the "PC" platform are now as powerful as their mainframe counterparts. This has increased the accessibility of resource hungry technologies such as Item Response Theory (IRT), making them available to many more individuals than those at universities and large testing companies. In turn, this availability has stimulated the research on new technologies, and encouraged their transition from "ivory tower" applications to real world, applied testing environments. Although the transition has not been totally painless, the initial trepidation has been overcome, and many organizations are beyond "testing the waters." They are in the operational mode of running IRT and classical psychometric test analyses concurrently. In this chapter, I will discuss what I consider to be the most significant of these technologies, as they relate to the major areas of testing, and attempt to forecast their impact on several areas of licensure testing practices throughout the 1990s.

JOB ANALYSIS AND TEST SPECIFICATIONS

Job analysis is the initial step in any well-designed licensure testing program. The purpose of job analysis is to identify the content to be included on the examination, commonly referred to as test specifications, thereby establishing content validity. A typical procedure includes the development of a sufficient number of task and/or knowledge/skill/ability (KSA) statements that totally describe the important job activities. These statement are then subjected to evaluation by a group of job experts in which the most important activities are identified through a rating process. The rating results are used to develop test specifications—the content areas to be covered on the examination and their relative emphasis. A common procedure involves a committee of job experts making rational decisions about the structure and relative weighting of the content. For example, the structure may be defined as three major content areas, and the relative weighting may be 20% for Content Area I, 35% for Area II, and 45% for Area III.

Several methods exist for making these determinations statistically. However, not all have a sound empirical basis. Specifications are sometimes determined by initially combining several rating scales together for each activity statement to determine a "criticality value." For example, in a job analysis study of law enforcement special agents, Sistrunk and Smith (1982) calculated a "Task Importance Value" by multiplying the difficulty and criticality ratings together and then adding the time spent rating to this product. Test section weights are sometimes calculated by summing individual criticality values for all task/KSA statements determined to be in that section. Although this procedure may have intuitive appeal, it has no more statistical basis than the rational approach described earlier. Although both rational and empirical procedures may yield the same results, it has been my experience that a carefully conducted rational judgement procedure produces very usable test specifications.

Rosenfeld and Thornton (1978) were among the first to use a more sophisticated statistical approach in job analysis in an occupational testing setting. To develop an interim task list, existing job descriptions were reviewed, and interview and observation techniques were used. The resulting task list was reviewed and revised in several states by advisory committees. This version was pilot tested prior to preparation of the final instrument. The task list was mailed to a large number of incumbents in all participating states for evaluation using several rating scales. Principal component factor analysis was used to verify the rational groupings of tasks into a smaller number of dimensions. Similarly, hierarchical cluster analysis was used to group incumbents who reported similar patterns of time usage. The

results indicated that the factor analysis groupings confirmed the rational groupings. The authors attributed this to the extensive review and revision that was
undertaken in the development phase. The cluster analysis revealed nine clusters of
incumbents, some of whom were performing more specialized duties. The major
job dimensions were linked to cognitive abilities by both measurement experts in
a group session, and job incumbents and their supervisors through the mail with
extensive directions. The authors concluded that the most preferable way to
accomplish this linking was in a group session with measurement experts directing
job experts in the process.

Shaefer, Raymond, and White (1993) evaluated the efficacy of two different
statistical strategies, cluster analysis and multidimensional scaling (MDS), and two
different rating scales, frequency and similarity, for establishing test specifications.
Task frequency ratings and task similarity ratings were collected on a sample of 125
tasks for emergency nurses. Cluster analysis was used as the primary procedure,
with MDS used for interpretation for both scales. The authors determined that the
results based on similarity ratings, as opposed to frequency ratings, were more
useful and interpretable. However, they do not recommend discarding frequency
ratings, as they may be useful in helping to organize traditional multiple-choice
examinations, and provide insight into another dimension of content description. A
further caution is offered in that the results are based on the study of an occupation
that may be more homogenous in terms of work activities than other occupations.
Despite these caveats, this study provides a promising direction for future studies
to pursue when empirical data are desired to supplement domain specifications
based on expert committee judgement.

A common procedure in establishing test specifications is the use of a taxonomy
or typology for item classification within content area as an additional level of
specificity. The rationale is that because differing cognitive demands are required for
the successful performance of the required job activities, test specifications should
reflect the cognitive demands of the target job. For example, medical laboratory
technologists are required to collect tissue samples and evaluate them for various
abnormal conditions. Because collecting requires a different cognitive level than
evaluating, items written to assess the former should be written at a different cognitive
level than the latter. In Bloom's taxonomy (Bloom, Englehart, Furst, Hill, & Krathwohl,
1956) nomenclature, "collecting" items would be written at the application level and
"evaluating" items would be written at the analysis/evaluation level. This classification
appears intuitive. However, after assisting numerous expert examination committees
in the performance of item review and revision, obtaining unanimous agreement
among them on the particular classification of a particular item is often difficult.
Although some believe that such an acceptable classification system does not exist
(see Haladyna, 1992a), test specifications using a cognitive level system can result in
an examination with additional evidence in support of content validity.

Job analysis is an area in which existing statistical techniques will represent the
"new technologies" that will be applied to job analysis data. Expert judgement will
continue to be used, but will be supplemented with empirical techniques such as
multivariate analyses. As a result, the commonly reported descriptive data may

have additional empirical evidence to support expert committee judgement. As the above studies indicate, the application of multivariate techniques to supplement the interpretation of descriptive statistics at the unit level promises a new direction in job analysis research.

ITEM FORMATS

After job analysis has been completed, a multiple-choice examination is frequently developed to assess the important content domains. The development of high quality test items and their format is the next step. Research in item format has been cyclical, but lately is an area that has drawn increased attention. Downing (1992) investigated true-false and alternate-choice multiple-choice question (MCQ) formats. The alternate-choice format is essentially a two option MCQ. When compared to the traditional simple MCQ, the advantages of these formats include greater ease of writing, and the presentation of more items to the examinee in a similar period of time. The disadvantages are that both formats are likely to result in inaccurate candidate scores because of guessing, and that true-false items may be subject to ambiguity, as many items may not be completely true or false. Downing concludes that the alternate-choice format may be appropriate in some situations for credentialing (and by extension, licensure) examinations.

Haladyna (1992b) studied various multiple choice question formats, including alternate-choice (AC), true-false (TF), complex multiple-choice (CMC) of which K-type is a subset, multiple true-false (MTF), and context-dependent item set (CDIS). In the CMC format, several potentially correct statements are presented, followed by various combinations of those statements. The MTF format is similar to the CMC, except that candidates are allowed to respond to each of the statements with either a true or false. He concludes that the CMC format should be discontinued, and that the MTF be used in its place. He feels that both the MTF and the CDIS format can be used to objectively score complex cognitive behavior efficiently.

In Haladyna (1992a), context-dependent item formats were examined exclusively. One caution on context-dependent items is that the items should be independent, so that the candidate is not penalized more than once for a wrong answer. An exception to this is in patient management problems (PMP). In PMPs candidates are presented a series of scenarios in which they are asked to gather information, process it, and select a course of action (Hixon, 1985). Provisions are made for those candidates who select an inappropriate course of action, by redirecting them to the proper path.

That CMCs not be used is congruent with Albanese (1993) in which several studies on CMCs in general, and Type K items in particular, were reviewed. Type K items present four primary statements, whereas the options are a fixed set of five combinations of the primary statements (Hubbard, 1978). Type K items were observed to have more clueing that leads to increased scores, decreased reliability, and are more likely to be deleted at key verification. However, he concluded that few studies have been done on the more general format of the CMC, and it may address some of the problems presented for the Type K format.

In other studies, it was concluded that although reliability was similar for the CMC and simple multiple-choice formats, candidates respond to fewer CMC format items in the same time period (Dryden & Frisbie, 1975), and that candidate scores on a CMC test represented a mixture of knowledge, test wiseness, and blind guessing (Kolstad, Bryant, & Kolstad, 1983). Studies by Case and Downing (1989), and Dawson-Saunders, Nungester, and Downing (1989) provide additional evidence in support of their discontinuance.

However, the results of these studies are contradicted by Nettles (1987), in which the psychometric characteristics of simple multiple-choice (SMC) and CMC items were compared. Data were collected from 3,500 individuals who had taken a self-assessment examination for a large allied health profession. In comparison to simple multiple-choice items, CMC items were found to fit the three-parameter IRT model equally well. Also, in evaluating the amount of information in the wrong options, both were identified in proportions comparable to their actual representation on the test. Additional unpublished studies using IRT three-parameter (3-PL) methodology conducted on a certification test for one allied health profession indicate that both item types are comparable in discriminating power and amount of information, as well as difficulty and guessing indices (see Table 1). Support was found for the other studies' observations that, in general, CMC items tend to be more difficult than SMC items. The one exception is that SMC items involving calculations (math items) were observed to have the lowest mean p-value.

However, another unpublished study conducted for a different allied health licensing test presented conflicting results. This study indicated support for the earlier conclusion by others that CMC items tend to be more difficult (again, excluding math items) and do not discriminate as well as SMC items. The other interesting finding was that negatively worded items were equal to positive items in discrimination and difficulty (see Table 2). This result is in conflict with other studies (see below), which have recommended against the use of negatively worded items due to their poor psychometric properties.

Table 1. Mean Item Statistics by Item Type for Group A.

Type	P-value	Point-biserial	a	b	c
SMC positive ($n=103$)	.75	.26	.46	-2.0	.14
SMC negative ($n=6$)	.73	.19	.31	-1.6	.15
SMC calculation ($n=3$)	.53	.26	.43	.3	.10
SMC data table ($n=10$)	.67	.25	.46	-1.0	.13
CMC positive ($n=18$)	.71	.29	.47	-1.2	.14

Table 2. Mean Item Statistics by Item Type for Group B.

Type	P-value	Point-biserial	a	b	c
SMC positive (n=152)	.80	.25	.52	-1.6	.24
SMC negative (n=60)	.77	.28	.52	-1.4	.23
SMC calculation (n=20)	.74	.30	.58	-1.0	.21
SMC situational set (n=22)	.75	.28	.58	-1.0	.24
CMC data table (n=3)	.67	.26	.49	-0.5	.23
CMC positive (n=39)	.71	.22	.46	-0.8	.25

The data tend to support the recommendation against the use of the specialized CMC format, the K-type item. However, the jury is still out regarding the more general format. Perhaps additional studies will show the more general CMC format to be a valuable item type. One area in which the general CMC format has great utility is in the rewriting of negatively worded items, eliminating the "except" or "not."

In general, evidence does exist for strong support in recommending against the use of negatively worded items. Negatively worded items include words in the stem such as "except," "not," "least," or "false." Harasym, Price, Brandt, Violato, and Lorscheider (1992) found that although negatively worded items are easier to write, candidates tend to find them more difficult to read and interpret correctly. These findings are somewhat supported in unpublished studies conducted by Nettles on tests constructed for purposes of licensing and certification. As Table 1 indicates, negatively worded items were found to be the least discriminatory in one study, but equal to positively worded items in another study (see Table 2) in which negatively worded items appear to be equal to positively worded items in average discrimination using both classical and IRT statistics. Anecdotally, in numerous item review meetings conducted with expert committees, some committee members invariably miss the "not" or "except" when reading this type of item, and provide inappropriate suggestions for revision. My prediction for negative items is that additional studies will support the recommendation against their use.

Research continues on the optimal number of options. Lord (1980, p. 112) indicated that three-option multiple-choice items were more appropriate for high ability candidates, whereas five-option items more suitable for lower ability candidates. Others have concluded that three-option items are easier to prepare, and more concepts can be tested due to decreased response time per question (Costin, 1970; Owen & Froman, 1987, cited in Landrum, Cashin, & Theis, 1993). Landrum, et al. (1993) composed alternate forms of an examination for an undergraduate psychology course, one with three-options and one with four-options. They found that the students scored higher on three-option as opposed to four-option items. In addition, evidence was found that three-option tests may be more difficult, after correcting for guessing. Despite these somewhat encouraging results in support of the three-option multiple-choice item, until data are collected from certification and licensing examinee populations, a migration from four-option multiple-choice items will not occur quickly.

Currently, much interest has been directed toward "authentic assessment," commonly termed performance testing, or, more generically, assessment using constructed-response items. Wainer and Thissen (1993) characterize constructed-response items as "more difficult to score reliably and objectively, but [providing] a task that may have more systematic validity" (p.103). Oral examinations can be considered a form of constructed-response assessment, and have been frequently used in licensure and certification examinations. They often present substantial potential problems to the examining body, in the form of candidate scheduling, examiner equivalency, fatigue, and bias. However, they remain a popular format, especially in medical assessment. For example, Schweibert, Davis, and Jacocks (1992) evaluated data from oral examinations given for physician certification in board specialties. They found positive correlations with medical school grade-point average (GPA) and oral examinations for several medical specialties. Oral examinations will continue to be used, but because of their inherent problems with standardization from one examinee to another and high administrative costs, with decreasing frequency.

Additional studies will be done to examine alternative ways to score constructed-response tests. Bridgeman (1992) compared quantitative GRE items using a multiple-choice, paper-and-pencil open-ended format, and a computer-based open-end format. A specially designed answer sheet was used for the open-ended paper-and-pencil format, such that candidates could grid in their answers on a machine-readable sheet. Candidates used the keyboard to enter their answers for the computer version of the open-ended questions. Although differences were observed at the item level among the alternative formats, total test scores were found to be comparable. Further, all formats rank ordered the candidates similarly, and gender and ethnic differences were trivial or nonexistent. Correlational studies with other college grades and other tests revealed significant but not meaningful differences among the formats. Bridgeman concluded that although both the open-ended and multiple-choice formats will probably produce the same results, the open-ended format is more representative of the problems the candidates will face in real life situations. He suggests that both psychometric and nonpsychometric considerations be equally weighed in the decision to use the open-ended format in testing.

Another consideration in authentic assessment is the issue of which behaviors to include in the assessment exercise. In a typical performance assessment, from all important behaviors identified by the job analysis, only a few can be selected for inclusion because of time constraints. Thus, the assessment instrument samples only a small proportion of all possible behaviors. Shavelson, Baxter, and Gao (1993) used generalizability theory to examine this issue. They describe a performance assessment as consisting of a particular combination of all possible tasks, occasions, raters, and measurement methods. Data taken from studies on California elementary students in math and science were analyzed using generalizability theory. The results from one part of their study indicated a large source of measurement error was due to the person x task interaction, indicating that the particular task sampled played a major role in students' performance scores. They concluded that this finding was consistent with other studies in that to obtain a measure of achievement that is generalizable, a large number of tasks is necessary. Based on their results, they speculated that, assuming 15 minutes per task, a total of 2.5 hours testing time would be necessary to obtain a generalizable measure of student achievement. Generalizabilty theory appears to be well suited for this type of research.

Authentic assessment measures are frequently combined with multiple-choice tests. Wainer and Thissen (1993) examined the most efficient way to combine scores from two different formats of measurement instruments. They examined possible scenarios of combining mixed-format tests using two graphic procedures. One procedure, the "ReliaMin," allows one to determine the amount of testing time needed to achieve equal reliabilities for each format. In their example, in order for a constructed response test to achieve the same reliability as a 75-minute multiple-choice chemistry test, 3 hours of testing time would be needed. More time would be necessary for an examination in a "softer science" such as arts and humanities.

They also developed a similar procedure, termed "ReliaBuck," that examines the resource expenditure (scoring costs) for equally reliable but different test formats. Again comparing a multiple-choice to a constructed-response format for a chemistry examination, they estimated that the costs for the constructed-response portion was 3,000 times more expensive than the multiple-choice format of the examination. As above, the costs associated with an arts or humanities test would be approximately three times more expensive again. They conclude that it does not appear to be economically practical to equalize the reliabilities of different components of mixed-format tests.

Perhaps the most desirable authentic assessment will be used in computer-based testing (CBT). CBT has already been applied to patient management problems (PMPs), and has demonstrated several desirable characteristics in comparison with the standard paper-and-pencil (PAP) format using latent image technology. Latent image test booklets use a special developer ink to expose the desired response text associated with the stimulus scenario. In latent image test booklets, the response text remains invisible until a special developer pen is applied. Thus, the candidate can be considered to be "constructing a response" by exposing the selected answer. The major drawback to the PAP approach is candidate advancement through the problem in an alternative manner to the specified path. Other problems include the lack of opportunity for the candidate to change his or her mind after exposing a response, and the appearance of "random" marks in the latent image area. This forces the scorer to determine if the candidate was attempting to gain an unfair advantage by discretely exposing a portion of the latent image, or if the mark was truly an accidental occurrence. Using CBT, the first problem is eliminated, in that the candidate progresses through the problem as presented by the computer. Although CBT will not allow the candidate to change his or her mind about selecting a response, the candidate will have little support in indicating a response was exposed by accident, especially if the candidate is prompted to affirm his or her choices.

As computer technology advances, and as prices drop, CD-ROMs can be used to provide still or motion pictures to supplement the scenario text. However, the storage of many images as compared to a single image can be costly in terms of storage resources. It is encouraging that a study by Shea, Norcini, Baranowski, Langdon, and Popp (1992) found both formats sufficiently similar to justify the use of still pictures for credentialing examinations. In this study, the psychometric characteristics of still pictures versus motion pictures were examined. The results indicated that still pictures were both more reliable and more difficult than motion pictures, but that both formats were highly correlated with themselves and other types of performance measures.

In summary, research will continue to identify the "perfect" item types and modes of presentation. The multiple-choice item will continue to play a major role in licensure and certification testing, and possibly, with fewer than the four- and five-option format that is popular at present. Similarly, authentic assessment will play an ever increasing role in occupational assessment. However, it is apparent that inclusion of constructed-response items can be costly both psychometrically and practically. Perhaps one way to integrate this format into existing test programs in a practical way is to combine both formats using CBT. For example, the written stem of the item could be replaced with a video application, and the candidate could respond to video options presented in the multiple-choice format. Regardless, new and better ways will be found to use authentic assessment techniques that will overcome some of the psychometric and practical shortcomings presently observed, and make the behaviors required to answer test items more similar to the behaviors required to make decisions in real life.

STANDARD SETTING

Once a test is developed, and preferably before it is administered for the first time, a passing point must be determined. Although initially many licensing tests relied on norm referencing, the current generally accepted procedure is one in which the passing point is determined through an absolute standard procedure such as those described in Livingston and Zieky (1982), specifically, the Angoff (1971), Ebel (1972), and Nedelsky (1954) techniques.

Livingston and Zieky (1982) identified the following five steps that most absolute standard methods have in common:

1. Selecting the judges to render the ratings.
2. Defining the borderline or minimally competent practitioner.
3. Training the judges to use the selected procedure.
4. Collecting the judgments.
5. Summarizing the individual judgments to arrive at a passing score.

Selection of the judges is a crucial part of the standard setting process. In general they should be experienced job experts, representative of the candidate population, so that a diversity of opinion and knowledge are represented. Jaeger (1991) identified several characteristics of an expert, including that they excel in their areas of expertise, they are able to perform domain-relevant tasks rapidly and correctly, they seem to be more aware of errors they might make, and that they are more accurate than novices in ascertaining the difficulty of a problem.

Knowing what characteristics constitute expertise, the next task for the measurement expert is to assemble a group of these individuals for a passing point study. The question is always asked, "How many judges are needed for the study?" The answer can be partially determined by evaluating the amount of error that is tolerable in the selected standard. Jaeger (1991) suggests that the number of judges can be determined by estimating a reasonable standard deviation (RSD) of recommended standards and the desired standard error of the mean (DSE), substituting these values in the equation for the standard error of the mean, and solving for n, where $n = (RSD/DSE)^2$. In his example, 4.65 was selected for the RSD, and 1.3 for the DSE, resulting in a recommendation of 13 judges. It is encouraging that this value falls within the range of general rule of thumb of 10 to 20 judges.

Training of the judges is another crucial part of the standard setting process. This training includes direction in establishing the definition of the minimally competent practitioner (MCP), as well as the actual rating process. In defining minimal competence, Mills, Melican, and Ahluwalia (1991) suggest using the test specifications as a basis for identifying entry level skills and minimally acceptable levels for the entry-level practitioner. Concerning the actual rating process, Reid (1991) suggests beginning with a practice set of items that have item statistics available. Discussion is encouraged among raters, especially for those items with diverse ratings, with the hope that judges will reconsider their initial ratings in light of the group discussion. Additional training should be provided for specific item formats that tend to be more difficult for candidates, for example, negatively worded items and those involving calculations. Reid concludes his discussion by suggesting three criteria for evaluating the training of judges, namely that standard setting ratings should (a) be stable over time, (b) be consistent with relative difficulties of the items, and (c) reflect realistic expectations.

Many studies have been done comparing the various techniques (e.g., Andrew & Hecht, 1976; Poggio, Glasnapp, & Eros, 1981; Skakun & Kling, 1980). In most of these studies, differing results were obtained for the various methods, although different groups of judges were used for each method. In general, the Ebel and Angoff procedures tend to establish higher passing points than the Nedelsky. However, Mills (1983) found agreement among three different methods. He compared the Angoff, the contrasting groups method, and the borderline group method. He attributed the congruence of results to the fact that the same group of judges were used for all three methods.

Over the past few years, the original Angoff procedure, or a modification thereof, appears to be the most commonly used of the three. The reliability of this procedure was studied by Norcini and Shea (1992). They examined the reproducibility of a set of standards in two different scenarios. In one study, they found that standards set by independent groups of experts using the same methodology (Angoff) and test content were similar. In another study, they found that similar standards were set by a subset of experts for the same test materials over 2 years elapsed time. These results are reassuring in that they indicate that the Angoff procedure appears to be quite reliable.

Once the data forming a passing score are collected, the results from each judge must be combined to produce a useful result. The most common procedure for establishing a passing score is to sum the average of the individual ratings across all items on the examination—equally weighting each item. Plake and Kane (1991) investigated two alternative approaches to combining the ratings by examining different types of error in setting a passing score. One alternative established the passing score based on the sampling variance of the average ratings. The other alternative established a passing score by selecting the best match between the judges' ratings and the actual proportion of minimally competent practitioners answering each item correctly. Using simulated data, they also varied the number of judges involved in the study (5 vs. 10) and the number of items in the examination (25 vs. 50). They observed that all three methods provided similar levels of accuracy, and that using more raters resulted in more precision. Slightly higher accuracy was found based for the 50-item test. They concluded that the traditional and simpler method of using the sum of the average judges' ratings should be the method of choice. This result is encouraging in that most Angoff studies arrive at a passing score in this manner. Also, the results indicate that the use of as many judges as practically possible is supported, and that the occasional necessity of discarding an item from the test form from which the study was conducted will probably have little practical significance on the resulting passing point.

Occasionally, the entire results of a standard setting procedure are unacceptable, because they result in a passing score that is either too high or too low. Breyer (1993) investigated this problem using the results of three hypothetical studies in which the Beuk (1984) adjustment was made. In the Beuk procedure, a compromise between an absolute method (Angoff), and a relative (norm-referenced) procedure is allowed. For example, the judges participate in an Angoff procedure, and are then asked to estimate pass rate of a group of first-time candidates for that examination. Breyer's results indicated that the Beuk procedure adjusts the cut score in favor of the judgments that have the most agreement (i.e., those judgments with the lowest standard deviation). It appears that the Beuk procedure may be useful in some situations occasionally encountered by the licensing test measurement professional. However, on a cautionary note, Geisinger (1991) suggests that the modification "procedures proposed Beuk and Hofstee [(1983)] are valiant first steps" (p. 21), but need to be better developed before they are fully endorsed.

The determination of a passing point remains a crucial part of the licensing examination process. I suspect the Angoff procedure will remain the most popular technique, and at least one study indicates support for employing the traditional procedure of summing the judges' ratings across items to determine the passing score. It is hoped future studies will occur that will provide additional empirical support for the standards set by the Angoff and other absolute standards techniques, as well as provide additional information on existing procedures for modification of the results.

TEST AND ITEM ANALYSIS

Wainer (1990) provides both an enlightening and humorous history of "mental testing," tracing testing from several hundred years B.C., where a performance test was used to determine national affiliation, and in China where proficiency tests sampling a candidate's performance were used for candidates for political office. This testing system was continually refined until, in the 19th century, the British used it as their model for establishing the Indian civil service. The British system was used as the foundation for the U.S. Civil Service System in the late 1800s. The early days of psychometrics around the turn of the century allowed the transition from individualized to mass test administration. Military testing programs were the first to use mental tests on a large scale, mainly to support the war efforts of World Wars I and II. College admissions tests began in 1901 and closely paralleled the military testing programs though the 1950s. Both of these groups are responsible for the popularity of classical test theory that is so widely used by testing groups in the fields of licensing and certification. Classical test theory continues to provide much useful information for the vast majority of tests in use today.

Although classical test theory is a very powerful model on which to base test development and analysis, some of its shortcomings are significant. According to Hambleton and Swaminathan (1985), one of the major problems is that all statistics are relative to the group of examinees who took the test. That is, the item statistics will vary from test administration to test administration, especially if subsequent test administrations are conducted on groups of dissimilar examinees. Additionally, the discrimination index is affected by the spread in variability of examinees and the p-value of the item. Further, reliability is dependent on the standard deviation of the test, the p-values, and the item discriminations. Thus, item statistics are meaningful only if they are derived from highly similar tests given to highly similar populations of examinees.

Another shortcoming is that classical test theory provides no basis for determining how an examinee might perform when confronted with a test item. For example, we may know that a particular candidate is very able, and that a particular test item is moderately difficult. We can "guesstimate" that this particular candidate will probably answer the item correctly. However, if Item Response Theory (IRT) has been used, it is possible to make a precise estimate (in terms of probability) of how a particular candidate will perform to a particular item.

Finally, classical item statistics do not inform test developers about the location of maximum discriminating power of items on the total score continuum. This precludes constructing the test to examine very efficiently for a given range (e.g., around the cut score).

A comparison between IRT and Classical Test Theory (CTT) can be made. IRT statistics are provided and their nearest counterpart in classical test theory is provided below in Table 3.

Table 3. Classical Test and Item Response Theory Comparisons.

Classical Test Theory	Item Response Theory
p -value: can range from .00 to 1.00 (high*p*-values indicate easy items)	"b" parameter: typically range from -3.0 to +3.0 (high b values indicate hard items)
item discrimination: (e.g., point biserial correlation) typically range from -.30 to +.50	"a" parameter: typically range from 0 to 2.0 (high values indicate better discrimination)
nothing similar in classical, although 1/number of options is sometimes used as an estimate of the probability of guessing the right answer	"c" parameter, also known as the guessing parameter: typically varies from 0 to .25
total test score: a measure of achievement on the particular group of items on the test	theta (Θ): the scale used to describe an examinee's ability in IRT
reliability of test: an indication of the similarity of the content domain of the test. Although no definite standard exists, a target of .90 can be considered desirable.	test information curve (TIC): sum of individual item characteristic curves (ICCs). Items can be selected to provide maximum information at various points of the TIC (e.g., around the cut score)

The work of Birnbaum (1968), Lord and Novick (1968), Rasch (1960), and Wright (1968) stimulated the measurement community during the 1970s and 1980s to provide the necessary research that enabled Item Response Theory (IRT) to become as popular as it is today.

Item Response Theory (IRT) is a more powerful (and more complicated) model of test theory. It is also known as latent trait theory—test performance can be predicted in terms of underlying traits. For example, if an underlying trait for a clerical examination is good written communication, one of the knowledges assessed in the test may be punctuation. An IRT model specifies a relationship between the observable examinee test performance and the unobservable traits or abilities assumed to underlie test performance. A successful model provides a means of estimating scores for examinees on the underlying traits. The traits must be estimated from observable examinee performance on a set of items. This is known as calibrating the item pool.

IRT proposes that a single trait underlies examinee ability, and that the probability of an examinee's performance on a test item can be determined if the difficulty of the item and ability of the candidate is known. If the assumptions of IRT can be met for a particular set of items, the performance of two examinees can be compared even if they do not take the same set of items, and item statistics are comparable even if different groups of examinees are used in their calculation. These two properties are termed item-free ability estimates and sample-free parameter estimates (Hambleton, 1989). To have invariant item parameters is very desirable when building tests using a database of test items.

IRT has an item level orientation. IRT makes a definite statement about the probability of answering an item correctly and a test taker's ability. This relationship must be estimated through item calibration—item analysis is used to determine the item statistical parameter estimate. The major result of using IRT is that both candidates and items are placed on the same scale of measurement. This feature allows use of the test to make definite predictions about examinee performance regardless of the test items presented to different examinees.

IRT provides a graphical interpretation of how well an item performs—the item characteristic curve (ICC) indicates the probability of an examinee's response based on his or her ability. The ICC is a plot of performance of an item against some measure of ability. This is usually a smooth nonlinear curve that is fitted to the data. Each item's ICC can be added to determine the Test Information Curve (TIC), a concept similar to reliability in classical test theory.

According to Hambleton and Swaminathan (1985), the characteristics of a properly fitting IRT model consist of the following:

1. Examinee performance on a test can be predicted in terms of one or more characteristics referred to as traits.
2. An IRT model specifies a relationship between observable examinee item performance and the traits or abilities assumed to underlie performance on the test.
3. Examinee scores on the underlying traits can be estimated.
4. The traits must be estimated from observable examinee performance on a set of test items.

Thus, a test properly calibrated using IRT has several useful features. Number one is that the item parameter estimates are independent of the group of examinees used from the population of examinees for whom the test was designed. Further, examinee ability estimates are independent of the particular choice of test items used from the population of items which were calibrated. That is, a different group of items (e.g., an alternate test form) can be used for different examinees, but their scores are directly comparable. Further, a model is provided that allows the matching of test items and candidate ability. Also, the precision of ability estimates are known for each examinee. Finally, test models do not require strictly parallel tests to determine reliability (Hambleton, 1989).

Because of these features, the characteristics of a test assembled using an item pool calibrated with IRT statistics are known before the test is given—the test information curve (TIC) can be used to determine the effect of each item and its impact on the total test. Additionally, the use of IRT allows pre-equating—the passing score of the test can be empirically determined prior to the administration of the test. This can be useful in situations where immediate feedback on candidate performance is desirable, for example, in computer-based test administration.

One of the areas in which IRT can play a significant part is in test construction, particularly item selection. Because the amount of information is available for each item at a specified difficulty level in a calibrated pool, items can be selected that best contribute to the total information described for the test. In three-parameter terminology, these items are typically ones that possess high discrimination (a) values and low guessing (c) values at the appropriate difficulty (b) value for the test. According to Lord (1980), the following steps are involved in test construction using IRT methodology. First, the desired test information curve is determined.

Then, items are selected to fill the area under the target information curve, filling the hard to fill areas first. As items are selected, the test information curve is calculated, with new items selected until the calculated test information curve closely approximates the target information curve. For licensing tests, the target information curve should be highly peaked near the passing score.

IRT should not be considered as a total replacement for classical test theory. Even when IRT has been determined appropriate for use, classical item statistics should continue to be used in conjunction with IRT. Classical statistics provide useful, easily understood information regarding test items, particularly information about the performance of each of the options. However, the additional use of IRT in examination development and scoring allows for significantly increased information being available regarding items and candidates in particular, and the test in general. Thus, the overall precision of measurement of the candidate population is increased, a most desirable characteristic of any testing program.

Practically speaking, it is important to remember that classical test theory is more easily understood by the testing consumer than is IRT. The typical examination committee is composed of job experts with little knowledge of testing. With a moderate amount of training, they can understand p-values and item discrimination indices, and their derivation. IRT statistics are not as intuitive, and it is considerably more difficult to explain their origin to lay persons. Popham (1993) recommends that we not expect the testing consumer to unthinkingly accept information from the IRT specialists. Part of our job as measurement experts is to present the necessary information about IRT in a comprehensible manner to the uninitiated. After having attempted to explain IRT to several examination committees, I can truly say that is easier said than done. Discussing comparisons between p-values and bs, item discrimination and as, and guessing and cs is relatively straightforward. Explaining the math behind these item statistics is considerably more difficult. Nevertheless, IRT is an important technology that will continue to play an increasing role in licensure testing.

Although IRT does allow for multidimensional, linear, and polychotomous models, most licensing and certification programs at present use the undimensional, nonlinear, dichotomously scored response models. For example, both the National Council of State Boards of Nursing (NCSBN) and the Board of Registry (BOR) used one-parameter logistic (1-PL) IRT to calibrate their item pools as a necessary prerequisite to offering their examinations using computer-adaptive testing (CAT) technology. The NCSBN have implemented their CAT program, after several years of beta testing. The BOR has also begun using CAT in their certification program.

Many testing programs may not have the sample sizes of the above two groups, but still want to use IRT in their testing program. Sample sizes of 1,000 and tests of at least 50 items are generally recommended for the two- and three-parameter logistic IRT models, but samples of only 200 and 20 items are sufficient for the one parameter model (Barnes & Wise, 1991). However, it is generally agreed that the one-parameter model is not robust to violations of the assumption of zero lower asymptote, that is, guessing introduces significant error in the estimation of the item ability estimates. Unfortunately, guessing is common in multiple-choice tests given by most licensing programs. Barnes and Wise (1991) examined the characteristics of the one-parameter model with a fixed non-zero lower asymptote. They compared the three-parameter model, and two forms of a modified one-parameter model. In MOD-1 the lower asymptote was fixed at the reciprocal of the number of response options (1/A). In MOD-2 the lower asymptote was fixed at 1/A - .05. Using simulated data, they varied the sample size (50, 100, and 200 candidates) and test length (25 and 50 items). The quality of each model was evaluated by examining the correlation between the true ability parameters and their estimates, the root mean squared errors (RMSEs) and bias of ability estimates, correlations between difficulty parameters and their estimates, RMSEs and bias of difficulty values, and RMSEs of recovered item characteristic curves. The results indicated that for all models the accuracy of item estimates improved with the longer test length. Further, the modified one-parameter models were observed to have lower RMSEs than the unmodified one-parameter model (and the three-parameter model), but the correlations between true parameters and ability estimates were comparable for both modified and unmodified one-parameter models. Although the results slightly favored MOD-2, the authors concluded that both modified models could be used effectively for multiple-choice tests with sample sizes of 200 and test lengths of 50 items, and both were an improvement over the one- and three-parameter models when only small sample sizes are available.

Because of IRT's advantages, I suspect that it will continue to play an ever increasing role in the larger licensure examination programs in the areas of test development and CAT. And for those testing programs with moderate to small sample sizes, modified one-parameter models appear to provide an avenue for experiencing the benefits of IRT.

COMPUTERIZED TEST ADMINISTRATION

During the 1980s licensing tests began to be administered with computer assistance. The first variant of computer-based testing (CBT) to be introduced involved the presentation of a paper-and-pencil test on a video screen. Technical support can be provided from either a LAN or minicomputer with dumb terminals. Candidates respond by either using the keyboard or touching the screen. An alternative form of presentation involves the use of a hand-held computer with a touch screen, thereby negating the need for a keyboard. Other options may exist, but all involve the presentation of a standard paper-and-pencil test on the computer, termed the "electronic page turner" by Friedman (1993). He identified several potential advantages to computerized testing, for both candidates and the provider of the tests. Probably the most significant advantage of this form of presentation to both groups is test security. No hard copy of the examination is provided to the candidate, and several forms of an examination can be made available simultaneously at one or more testing sites. Secondarily, instantaneous scoring and reporting of examination results are available if all scorable items have been used before. Pretest items can be included for analysis, but are not scored. Finally, test content can be more easily updated.

An alternative form of computerized testing is computer-adaptive testing (CAT). Under this model, each candidate can receive a unique form of the examination, tailored to his or her level of expertise. A typical scenario follows. An item of medium level difficulty is presented to the candidate. If the candidate answers it correctly, a slightly more difficult item is presented. If the candidate answers an item incorrectly, a slightly less difficult item is presented. The examination continues in this fashion, with items presented near the current ability estimate, until the specified content is covered, and a suitable estimate of the candidate's ability is determined. Because every candidate theoretically can be administered a unique test form of variable length, determining when to stop the examination presents a potential problem. The most common stopping rules include (a) the presentation of examinations of fixed length, or (b) the determination of a candidate's ability within a specified precision estimate, usually after a minimum number of items have been presented in all required content areas. Although at first CAT was applied to educational populations, at least one certification and one licensing examination program have begun to administer computer-adaptive examinations. However, before implementation, several issues had to be examined.

One of the first considerations is that of the size of the item bank. In an effort to provide some guidance in this area, Stahl and Lunz (1993) studied the amount of overlap in examinations using CAT for various sizes of item pools. Data were examined from five different certification examinations, with item banks ranging from 183 to 823 items. One of their results confirmed an intuitive conclusion, indicating that larger item banks tend to have a lower percentage of overlap among candidates, regardless of candidate ability. However, examinees close in ability tend to have a higher percentage of overlapping items. Considering both the amount of overlap and candidate ability, they concluded that a minimum desirable item bank size would be approximately 400–500 items, and that banks with 600–800 items are desirable.

In a national pilot study, Bergstrom and Lunz (1992b) examined the psychometric, psychological, and social attributes of CAT using a national sample of 645 medical technology students. Over 700 items were calibrated using the Rasch model (1-PL), and used as the item database for the CAT examination. They examined several issues relating to using CAT for certification examinations. Certification examinations are commonly built using spiral omnibus procedures, with easier items presented at the beginning, and more difficult items presented later in the examination. Therefore, one of their studies involved the starting difficulty (difficult, medium, or easy) of the first item presented to candidates. They found no difference in the starting difficulty of the first item, thus, no advantage appears to exist for starting the test with an easy item. They also observed that no significant differences existed in examinee performance for CATs with 50%, 60%, or 70% probability of correct response. This is of practical significance in that many item pools developed for occupational testing are targeted in the 70% range, and no major modification will be necessary for their use in CAT programs to challenge the more able examinee with items in the traditional 50% probability range of correct response.

Two final results included the observation that examinees who were allowed to manipulate their test (skip, review, and defer items) performed significantly better than those who had no control over their CAT, and those candidates who were administered the written test first did better on the CAT, suggesting a practice effect. The authors concluded that CAT is a feasible method of certification testing, and that it will likely become an accepted method of test administration.

A study by Legg and Buhr (1992) evaluated examinee attitudes toward CAT from another perspective. They analyzed data collected on college students on three adaptive tests: reading, mathematics, and writing. The data were examined to determine if examinees with different demographic characteristics (age, gender, ethnicity, ability, and experience with computers) displayed different response patterns to a questionnaire about testing conditions. It is encouraging that few differences were observed among the examinee groups that could not be addressed by expanding the pre-exam practice time.

In the standard method of CAT, examinees are not allowed to review previously answered items. The rationale is that if an examinee alters a response to an earlier item, an inaccurate estimate of his or her ability may result. However, for many licensure and certification examination programs, candidates consider this review to be one of their "basic rights." Thus, non-review of items may be a major political obstacle to the use of CAT for an occupational testing program. Lunz, Bergstrom, and Wright (1992) examined the effect of reviewing previously administered items on the estimation of students' abilities. The sample consisted of a geographically diverse group of 712 medical technology students. They were administered items from a database designed to be consistent with the test specifications of a national certification program in medical technology. Items were calibrated using the Rasch model (1-PL). Students were randomly assigned to a review group ($n=220$) or a non-review group ($n=492$). Their results indicated that the ability estimates for the students in the review group were correlated .98 before and after review. This conclusion is important because many candidate populations in this arena might feel uncomfortable without the opportunity to review and possibly change previously answered items.

Numerous studies have shown that computerized adaptive tests (CAT) can reduce test length without loss of precision in estimating a candidate's ability. Bergstrom and Lunz (1992a) examined the effect of test length on pass/fail decisions when using both CAT and paper-and-pencil examinations. The sample consisted of 645 medical technology students from 238 educational programs across the country, who were eligible for the next administration of a national certification examination. Each student took a CAT from a large bank of items, calibrated using the Rasch model (1-PL). Two versions of a written test, one short (109 items) and one long (189 items), were built from the same bank of items and were administered to the sample in a paper-and-pencil version, approximately 2 months after the CAT versions. Both written tests were analyzed using a Rasch calibration program. Their results indicated that while no significant differences existed among the CAT and paper-and-pencil tests, more pass/fail decisions could be made with 90% confidence for shorter CAT (mean length of 67 items) than with longer (189 items) paper-and-pencil tests. The authors concluded that the implementation of CAT can reduce test length and improve confidence in the accuracy of pass/fail decisions.

A caution to some of these conclusions is provided by Vale (1993). He is in agreement that IRT can result in better balanced individual tests, a basic requirement for providing computerized testing on a daily basis. However, it has been his experience that the discrimination indices typically found in most licensing and certification tests are not sufficiently high to justify the use of CAT. Additionally, he suggests that CAT is more appropriate for wide range measurement, typically found in scholastic assessment, and not for the dichotomous pass/fail decisions required in a licensing environment. Fortunately, the current decade should provide much empirical data on the use of CAT in licensing and certification examinations.

EMPIRICAL ITEM BIAS REVIEW

Item bias, in particular differential item functioning (DIF), is another issue that has a solid foothold in testing practices. The Mantel-Haenzel (Holland & Thayer, 1988) and IRT procedures are two popular techniques for investigating item bias. Although studies for licensing tests appear to be unpublished, Skaggs and Lissitz (1992) conducted an investigation of the consistency of item bias using different procedures across two forms of an eighth grade math test. They found the Mantel-Haenzel and the IRT methods to be the most consistent, but the degree of reliability was modest. A major conclusion was that more consistency existed for larger sample sizes ($n=2,000$), as opposed to smaller samples ($n=600$). Additionally, their study provided supportive evidence that when bias has been found, it is modest and tends to favor the minority group.

Swaminathan and Rogers (1990) investigated differential item functioning (DIF) using logistic regression procedures and Mantel-Haenzel. Using simulated data, they found that the logistic regression procedure was more powerful than Mantel-Haenzel for the detection of nonuniform DIF (when an interaction exists between ability level and group membership), and equally as powerful for detecting uniform DIF (when no interaction exists between ability level and group membership). Their study also supported the use of larger samples for DIF studies. They found a 75% detection rate for sample sizes of 250, and 100% detection for a sample size of 500. Perhaps the dearth of published item bias studies for licensing examinations is due to the lack of sufficient sample sizes. Only a handful of licensing programs test candidates in sufficient numbers that may provide focal groups samples of several hundred candidates (for example, the National Council of State Boards of Nursing). Although authentic assessment is designed to increase the job-relatedness of an examination, increased content validity does not preclude the presence of bias in the assessment instrument. A study by Zwick, Donoghue, and Grima (1993) addressed the topics of the application of DIF procedures to performance tests. As part of their study they applied two Mantel-Haenzel procedures to the assessment of male-female DIF in constructed response reading and writing items, collected from 2,000 eleventh grade examinees as part of the 1990

NAEP (National Assessment of Educational Progress) program. They concluded that dichotomous DIF procedures were feasible for polychotomous (constructed-response) items, but cautioned that DIF procedures are only one component of examining the validity and fairness of performance assessment.

The major stumbling block for empirical item bias procedures to many licensing and certification testing programs is that of sample size. As the studies above indicate, large sample sizes are needed to provide consistent results with accurate detection for either IRT or Mantel-Haenzel procedures. However, some IRT procedures have been examined that may allow for smaller sample sizes for one of the target groups. For example, Linn and Harnisch (1981) suggested an IRT approximation that examined the difference between expected probability of correct response and observed proportion correct for the focal group. DIF analyses using the Mantel-Haenzel procedure may prove to be the most usable for many testing programs because of its more modest sample size requirements and its relative ease of use when compared to IRT procedures.

BIAS PANEL REVIEW

Frequently the large samples necessary to conduct DIF studies are not available. An alternative to empirical bias studies is the use of "sensitivity review" panels. Mehrens and Popham (1992) suggest that every high-stakes test (one that is used for high-stakes decisions such as employment) be evaluated for content relevance and potential bias by a sensitivity review panel. This type of panel can be used when the focal group is not sufficiently large for meaningful DIF analysis (50 or more individuals). They suggest that the bias review committee have representatives of the major protected groups who will be taking the test, and all participants be thoroughly trained in the process.

A procedure for accomplishing this review may include the establishment of a bias review committee, preferably separate from the standard examination committee. This will eliminate the possibility that the reviewers may have been too actively involved in writing, modifying, and editing items to give them a truly "nonpartisan" review. The main responsibility of this committee is to review each examination item for possible bias with respect to gender and/or ethnic background. Each individual would receive thorough training on the review procedure, and respond individually to the following questions (adapted from W. J. Popham, personal communication, April 19, 1993) for each item using a rating sheet. The first three questions develop evidence in support of content validity, and the last two relate specifically to potential bias.

1. Is the content of this item necessary for successful performance as an entry level practitioner?
2. Is the task, knowledge, or skill appropriately measured by this item?
3. Of all knowledge or skills that entry level practitioners need, what percentage is represented by this test? (This question is answered after review of the complete test.)
4. Is this item biased against people due to gender, ethnic background, and/or socioeconomic status?

5. Might this item offend or unfairly penalize anyone due to gender, ethnic background, and socioeconomic status?

The rating sheets are summarized for each test item, and in those instances where less than 80% of the participants approve of an item, the item is revised before future use or deleted from the item bank (Mehrens & Popham, 1992).

The above item review procedures are recommended for every test used for licensure and certification. They should be used at initial review of the first test form to identify items that may not be appropriate for the desired purpose of the test, or have the potential to discriminate unfairly against protected classes. Later, if the sample sizes are sufficient for calculation of DIF statistics, additional items may be flagged as problematic. These items should not be automatically removed from future test use merely because of statistical evidence, but subjected to the same thorough review by a representative group of content experts. If this review fails to identify an obvious reason for the bias, Popham and Mehrens (1992) recommend that they remain in the item bank for future use.

CONCLUSIONS

Every aspect of licensure testing will continue to evolve with new directions or advances in educational and psychological measurement. Refinements to existing job analysis procedures will be made as different univariate and multivariate statistical techniques are employed to summarize the data and develop test specifications. The computer will play an ever increasing role in test construction and administration, allowing the refinement of existing item formats and the use of a variety of new item formats. It is hoped the desirable characteristics of the multiple-choice and constructed-response formats will be combined into a new format that retains the best psychometric characteristics of multiple-choice, but allows the benefits of authentic assessment to be realized in a cost-effective manner. Research will continue in the area of standard setting. Future studies will be conducted that will provide a rationale for techniques that adhere to the necessary technical requirements but are cognizant of the political realities of determining passing points for licensure examinations. Item response theory will strengthen its foothold and become the standard procedure for licensure test development and analysis for many programs. Computer-based testing, either in standard or adaptive format, will increase in popularity, eventually replacing paper-and-pencil presentations for the larger examination programs. Increasing numbers of programs will employ bias review panels prior to test administration to minimize undesirable discrimination for protected classes. Where technically feasible, empirical item bias procedures will be employed after the examination is given to ensure increased fairness to all examinees. These technological refinements and advances will help licensure testing become more precise such that both agencies and candidates will benefit.

REFERENCES

Albanese, M. A. (1993). Type K and other complex multiple-choice items: An analysis of research and item properties. *Educational Measurement: Issues and Practice*, *12*(1), 28-32.

Andrew, B. J., & Hecht, J. T. (1976). A preliminary investigation of two procedures for setting examination standards. *Educational and Psychological Measurement*, *36*, 45-50.

Angoff, W. H. (1971). Scales, norms, and   equivalent scores. In R. L. Thorndike (Ed.), *Educational measurement* (2nd ed., pp. 508-600). Washington, DC: American Council on Education.

Barnes, L. L., & Wise, S. L. (1991). The utility of a modified one-parameter IRT model with small samples. *Applied Measurement in Education*, *4*(2), 143-157.

Bergstrom, B. A., & Lunz, M. E. (1992a). Confidence in pass/fail decisions for computer adaptive and paper-and-pencil examinations. *Evaluation and the Health Professions*, *15*(4), 453-464.

Bergstrom, B. A., & Lunz, M. E. (1992b, April). Computer adaptive testing: A national pilot study. Paper presented at the annual meeting of the American Educational Research Association, San Francisco, CA.

Birnbaum, A. (1968). Some latent trait models and their use in inferring an examinee's ability. In F. M. Lord & M. R. Novick, *Statistical theories of mental test scores* (part 5, pp. 397-479). Reading, MA: Addison-Wesley.

Bloom, B., Englehart, M., Furst, E., Hill, W., & Krathwohl, D. (Eds.) (1956). *Taxonomy of educational objectives, Handbook 1: The cognitive domain*. New York: David Makay Company, Inc.

Breyer, F. J. (1993). The Beuk compromise adjustment: Possible Rx for troubled cut-score study results? *CLEAR Exam Review*, *4*(2), 23-27. Lexington, KY: CLEAR.

Bridgeman, B. (1992). A comparison of quantitative questions in open-ended and multiple-choice formats. *Journal of Educational Measurement*, *29*(3), 253-271.

Beuk, C. H. (1984). A method for reaching a compromise between absolute and relative standards in examinations. *Journal of Educational Measurement*, *21*, 147-152.

Case, S. M., & Downing, S. M. (1989). *Performance of various multiple-choice item types on medical specialty examinations: Types A, B, C, K, and X*. Philadelphia: National Board of Medical Examiners.

Costin, F. (1970). The optimal number of alternatives in multiple-choice achievement tests: Some empirical evidence for a mathematical proof. *Educational and Psychological Measurement*, *30*, 353-358.

Dawson-Saunders, B., Nungester, R. J., & Downing, S. M. (1989). *A comparison of single best answer multiple-choice items (A-type) and complex multiple-choice (K-type)*. Philadelphia: National Board of Medical Examiners.

Downing, S. M. (1992). True-false, alternate-choice, and multiple-choice items. *Educational Measurement: Issues and Practice*, *11*(3), 27-30.

Dryden, R. E., & Frisbie, D. A. (1975, April). *Comparative reliabilities and validities of multiple-choice and complex multiple nursing education tests*. A paper presented at the annual meeting of the National Council on Measurement in Education, Washington, D.C.

Ebel, R. (1972). *Essentials of psychological measurement*, pp. 492-494. Englewood Cliffs, NJ: Prentice-Hall.

Friedman, C. (1993, September). On your mark, get set, go! Are you ready to put away your pencils and computerize your testing program? In C. Friedman

(Chair), *Computer-Based Testing*. Symposium conducted at the annual meeting of the Council for Enforcement, Regulation, and Licensure, San Diego, CA.

Geisinger, K. F. (1991). Training judges to generate standard-setting data. *Educational Measurement: Issues and Practice, 10*(2), 17-22.

Haladyna, T. (1992a). Context-dependent item sets. *Educational Measurement: Issues and Practice, 11*(1), 21-25.

Haladyna, T. (1992b). The effectiveness of several multiple-choice formats. *Applied Measurement in Education, 5*, 73-88.

Hambleton, R. K. (1989). Principles and selected applications of item response theory. In R. L. Linn (Ed.), *Educational measurement*, (pp. 147-200). New York: Macmillan.

Hambleton, R. K., & Swaminathan, H. (1985). *Item response theory: Principles and applications*. Boston: Kluwer-Nijoff.

Harasym, P. H., Price, P. G., Brandt, R., Violato, C., & Lorscheider, F. L. (1992). Evaluation of negation in stems of multiple-choice items. *Evaluation & the Health Professions, 15*, 198-220.

Hixon, S. J. (1985). *An investigation of the psychometric properties of a clinical simulation examination for respiratory care practitioners*. (Unpublished doctoral dissertation, Ohio State University, Columbus)

Holland, P. W., & Thayer, D. T. (1988). Differential item performance and the Mantel-Haenzel procedure. In H. Wainer & H. I. Braun (Eds.), *Test validity* (pp. 129-145). Hillsdale, NJ: Earlbaum.

Hubbard, J. P. (1978). *Measuring medical education: The tests and experience of the national board of medical examiners* (2nd ed.) Philadelphia: Lea and Febinger.

Jaeger, R. M. (1991). Selection of judges for standard-setting. *Educational Measurement: Issues and Practice, 10*(2), 3-6, 10, 14.

Kolstad, R. K., Bryant, B. B., & Kolstad, R. A. (1983). Complex multiple-choice items fail to measure achievement. *Journal of Research and Development in Education, 17*, 7-11.

Landrum, R. E., Cashin, J. R., & Theis, K. S. (1993). More evidence in favor of three-option multiple-choice tests. *Educational and Psychological Measurement, 53*, 771-778.

Legg, S. M., & Buhr, D. C. (1992). Computerized adaptive testing with different groups. *Educational Measurement: Issues and Practice, 11*(2), 23-27.

Linn, R. L., & Harnisch, D. L. (1981). Interactions between item content and group membership on achievement test items. *Journal of Educational Measurement, 18*, 109-118.

Livingston, S. A., & Zieky, M. J. (1982). *Passing scores*. Princeton, NJ: Educational Testing Service.

Lord, F. M. (1980). *Applications of item response theory to practical testing problems*. Hillsdale, NJ: Lawrence Earlbaum Associates.

Lord, F. M., & Novick, M. R. (1968). *Theories of mental test scores*. Reading, MA: Addison-Wesley.

Lunz, M. E., Bergstrom, B. A., & Wright, B. D. (1992). The effect of review on student ability and test efficiency for computerized adaptive tests. *Applied Psychological Measurement, 16*(1), 33-40.

Mehrens, W. A., & Popham, W. J. (1992). How to evaluate the legal defensibility of high-stake tests. *Applied Measurement in Education, 5*(3), 265-283.

Mills, C. N. (1983). A comparison of three methods of establishing cut-off scores on criterion-referenced tests. *Journal of Educational Measurement, 20,* 283-292.

Mills, C. N., Melican, G. J., & Ahluwalia, N. T. (1991). Defining minimal competence. *Educational Measurement: Issues and Practice, 10*(2), 7-10.

Nedelsky, L. (1954). Absolute grading standards for objective tests. *Educational and Psychological Measurement, 14,* 3-19.

Nettles, S. S. (1987). *Psychometric characteristics of complex multiple-choice items.* (Unpublished doctoral dissertation, Rutgers University, New Brunswick.)

Norcini, J., & Shea, J. (1992). The reproducibilty of standards over groups and occasions. *Applied Measurement in Education, 5,* 63-72.

Owen, S. V., & Froman, R. D. (1987). What's wrong with the three-option multiple-choice items? *Educational and Psychological Measurement, 47,* 513-522.

Plake, B. S., & Kane, M. T. (1991). Comparison of methods for combining the minimum passing levels for individual items into a passing score for a test. *Journal of Educational Measurement, 28*(3), 249-256.

Poggio, J. P., Glasnapp, D. R., & Eros, D. S. (1981, April). *An empirical investigation of the Angoff, Ebel, and Nedelsky standard setting methods.* Paper presented at the annual meeting of the American Educational Research Association, Los Angeles.

Popham, W. J. (1993). Educational testing in America: What's right, what's wrong? *Educational Measurement: Issues and Practice, 12*(1), 11-14.

Rasch, G. (1960). *Probabalistic models for some intelligence and attainment scores.* Copenhagen, Denmark: Nielson & Lydiche.

Reid, J. B. (1991). Training judges to generate standard-setting data. *Educational Measurement: Issues and Practice, 10*(2), 11-14.

Rosenfeld, M., & Thornton, R. F. (1976). *A case study in job analysis methodology.* Princeton, NJ: Educational Testing Service.

Schweibert, L. P., Davis, A. B., & Jacocks, M. A. (1992). Reproducibility of oral exam grades and correlations with other measures of performance on three required third-year clerkships. *Evaluation & the Health Professions, 15,* 221-230.

Shaefer, L., Raymond, M. , & White, A. S. (1993). A comparison of two methods for structuring performance domains. *Applied Measurement in Education, 5,* 321-335.

Shavelson, R. J., Baxter, G. P., & Gao, X. (1993). Sampling variability of performance assessments. *Journal of Educational Measurement, 30,* 215-232.

Shea, J., Norcini, J., Baranowski, R. A., Langdon, L. O., & Popp, R. L. (1992). A comparison of video and print formats in the assessment of skill in interpreting cardiovascular motion studies. *Evaluation & the Health Professions, 15,* 325-340.

Sistrunk, F., & Smith, P. L. (1982). Multimethodological job analysis for criminal justice organizations. In J. V. Ghorpade, *Job analysis: A handbook for the human resource director,* (pp. 130-134). Englewood Cliffs, NJ: Prentice Hall.

Skaggs, G., & Lissitz, R. W. (1992). The consistency of detecting item bias across different test administrations: Implications of another failure. *Journal of Educational Measurement, 29,* 227-242.

Skakun, E. N., & Kling, S. (1980). Comparability of methods for setting standards. *Journal of Educational Measurement, 17*, 229-235.

Stahl, J. A., & Lunz, M. E. (1993, April). *Assessing the amount of overlap among computerized adaptive tests.* Paper presented at the annual meeting of the National Council of Measurement in Education, Atlanta, GA.

Swaminathan, H., & Rogers, H. J. (1990). Detecting differential item functioning using logistic regression procedures. *Journal of Educational Measurement, 27*, 361-370.

Vale, C. D. (1993, September). Should computer-adaptive testing be used in a licensing program? In C. Friedman (Chair), *Computer-Based Testing.* Syposium conducted at the annual meeting of the Council for Enforcement, Regulation, and Licensure, San Diego, CA.

Wainer, H. (Ed.). (1990). *Computer adaptive testing: A primer.* Hillsdale, NJ: Lawrence Earlbaum Associates.

Wainer, H., & Thissen, D. (1993). Combining multiple-choice and constructed-response test scores: Toward a Marxist theory of test construction. *Applied Measurement in Education, 6*(2), 103-118.

Wright, B. D. (1968). Sample-free test calibration and person measurement (pp.85-101). In *Proceedings of the 1967 ETS Invitational Conference on Testing Problems.* Princeton, NJ: Educational Testing Service.

Zwick, R., Donoghue, J. R., & Grima, A. (1993). Assessment of DIF for performance tasks. *Journal of Educational Measurement, 30*, 3, 233-251.

Author Index

E

Ebel, R.: 329, 342
Ebel, R. L.: 80, 86, 120, 121, 122, 139, 153, 164, 178, 179, 185, 223, 225, 226, 249
Educational Testing Service: 225, 249
Eignor, D. R.: 219, 249, 256, 260, 261, 270, 271, 272, 273, 274, 275, 278, 279, 282, 283, 286, 287
Eisdorfer, S.: 41, 44, 48, 56
Embretson, S. E.: 121, 139
Engel, J. D.: 119, 140
Englehart, M.: 323, 342
Englehart, M. D.: 189, 203
Equal Employment Opportunity Commission: 37, 43, 56, 63, 85, 168, 170, 185, 247, 249
Eros, D. S.: 330, 344
ETS Committee for Testing Handicapped People: 59, 85
Evans, J.: 200, 203

F

Faber, D.: 98, 114
Faggen, J.: 213, 217
Fairbank, B. A., Jr.: 263, 283
Falkowski, C.: 249
Fangman, E. J.: 98, 114
Farland, D.: 192, 203
Farmer, M.: 67, 85
Farnum, M.: 74, 86
Farrell, W. T.: 110, 114
Feldt, L. S.: 154, 164, 174, 175, 179, 185
Finberg, L.: 154, 164
Fine, S.: 97, 114
Fine, S. A.: 118, 139
Fitzpatrick, A. R.: 236, 238, 240, 249
Flanagan, J. C.: 98, 114
Fortune, J. C.: 149, 157, 163, 164
Fowler, F. J.: 111, 114
Fowler, R. D.: 293, 294, 320
Fowles, M. E.: 74, 86
Francis, A. S.: 240, 249
Frary, R. B.: 225, 237, 249
Freeman, L. D.: 36, 37, 56
Friedman, C.: 336, 342
Friedman, C. B.: 154, 164, 237, 249
Friedman, L.: 109, 114

Friedman, M.: 8, 10, 31
Frisbie, D. A.: 120, 121, 124, 125, 139, 140, 325, 342
Froman, R. D.: 326, 344
Furst, E.: 323, 342
Furst, E. J.: 189, 203

G

Gao, X.: 327, 344
Gardner, J. W.: 19, 20, 31
Garvue, R.: 226, 249
Geisinger, K. F.: 180, 185, 247, 249, 331, 343
Gershon, R. C.: 187, 189, 193, 203
Getson, P. R.: 212, 218
Gifford, J. A.: 267, 286, 287
Glasnapp, D. R.: 330, 344
Gleser, G. C.: 72, 84
Goodfellow, R. A. H.: 111, 114
Greaud, V. A.: 293, 318
Green, B. F.: 77, 85, 199, 203, 293, 314, 318, 319
Greene, J.: 161, 165
Grima, A.: 215, 218, 339, 345
Gross, L. J.: 152, 153, 156, 158, 164
Gross, S. J.: 6, 31
Grosso, L.: 240, 251, 276, 285
Grosso, L. J.: 125, 138, 139
Guerin, R. O.: 154, 164
Gullickson, A.: 192, 203
Gulliksen, H.: 264, 283
Guralnik, D. B.: 3, 31
Gustafsson, J. E.: 272, 283

H

Haladyna, T.: 323, 324, 343
Haladyna, T. M.: 122, 127, 130, 139, 140, 141
Halpin, G.: 241, 249
Hambleton, R. K.: 36, 58, 94, 96, 106, 107, 114, 116, 133, 140, 183, 184, 185, 186, 208, 216, 217, 219, 234, 235, 249, 250, 262, 267, 269, 271, 283, 298, 300, 317, 318, 332, 333, 334, 343
Hanson, B. A.: 263, 283
Harasym, P. H.: 326, 343
Harnisch, D. L.: 340, 343
Harnish, D.: 212, 217

Subject Index

A

a parameter: 299-300, 303, 305-306, 314
absolute standard procedure: 329
absolute standards: 222-223
accuracy of the inference: 150
Adaptive Mastery Testing (AMT): 298, 305
advisory committee: 100-101, 103-105, 111-112
AERA/APA/NCME Standards: 33, 37-43, 53, 55, 66, 68, 72, 84, 94, 114, 118, 122, 137-138, 168, 170-171, 179, 185, 236, 248, 254-255, 261, 281
all-in-one requirement: 155
alternate-choice: 120
alternate-choice multiple choice: 324
Americans with Disabilities Act of 1990 (ADA): 22-23, 43, 54-55, 60-61, 63, 65, 68-70, 297
amplified objective: 129, 147
amplified objective method: 129
analysis of variance (ANOVA): 153
anchor items: 137
Angoff: 223-225, 237, 246
Angoff method: 162, 317
archive: 196
assessment of a product: 151
authentic assessment: 327-329, 339, 341
automated item selection: 197
automated item writing: 195

B

b parameter: 299, 314
Bayesian posterior: 302
Bayesian prior: 302
Beuk: 244-246, 331
bias: 207, 213
  item: 207
  test: 207, 215
bias review committee: 340
Board members: 26
board members: 5, 26, 27
borderline: 176-177
borderline group: 229, 231, 233

C

c parameter: 300-301, 314
calibration: 153-154
camera-ready copy: 194, 196-197
case cluster: 127, 145
cases: 191-192, 196, 197, 199, 201
categorical data: 210
CD-ROM: 329
certification: 6, 18-19, 26, 291, 293, 298, 306, 314, 318
certification examinations: 120-122
chaining of errors: 159
civil rights: 151
Civil Rights Act of 1964: 34-37, 45, 47, 52-55, 297
Classical Test Theory (CTT): 208-209, 216, 332, 334-335